LAWRENCE OF ARABIA

THE 30TH ANNIVERSARY
PICTORIAL HISTORY

L. ROBERT MORRIS AND LAWRENCE RASKIN

FOREWORD BY MARTIN SCORSESE

ANCHOR BOOKS
DOUBLEDAY
NEW YORK LONDON TORONTO SYDNEY AUCKLAND

To Lynne, Jamie, and Josh Raskin

To Joanne, Andrew, Jamie, and David Morris

AN ANCHOR BOOK
PUBLISHED BY DOUBLEDAY
a division of Bantam Doubleday Dell Publishing Group, Inc.
666 Fifth Avenue, New York, New York 10103

ANCHOR BOOKS, DOUBLEDAY, and the portrayal of an anchor
are trademarks of Doubleday, a division of Bantam Doubleday
Dell Publishing Group, Inc.

A book from Puck Productions

Designed by Michaelis/Carpelis Design Associates

Library of Congress Cataloging-in-Publication Data

Morris. L. Robert,
Lawrence of Arabia : the 30th anniversary pictorial
history / by L. Robert Morris and Lawrence Raskin : foreword by
Martin Scorsese. – 1st ed.
p.   cm.
Includes bibliographical references (p. 237).
1. Lawrence of Arabia (Motion picture)   I. Raskin, Lawrence.
II. Title.
PN1997.L353MB 1992
791.43'72–dc20
                                 92-27800
                                      CIP

ISBN 0-385-42478-7
     0-385-42479-5 (pbk)

Copyright ©1992 by L. Robert Morris and Lawrence Raskin
Foreword copyright ©1992 by Martin Scorsese

PRINTED IN THE UNITED STATES OF AMERICA

November 1992

10 9 8 7 6 5 4 3 2 1

First Edition

CREDITS

Unless otherwise noted, all stills from *Lawrence of Arabia* contained in this book are ©
Copyright 1962, Renewed 1990 Horizon Pictures (GB) Ltd. All Rights Reserved. All other
materials relating to *Lawrence of Arabia* supplied by Sony Pictures Entertainment. ©1992
Columbia Pictures Industries, Inc. All Rights Reserved. Materials relating to *Lawrence of Ara-
bia* used by permission of Columbia Pictures Industries, Inc., 10202 West Washington Blvd.,
Culver City, CA 90232.

*We would like to express our gratitude to Ken Danvers, unit stills photographer, who took most
of the Horizon/Columbia production stills.*

Abbreviations: AG, Guinness; AQ, Quinn; BC, Cole; DL, Lean; DT, Tringham; EF, Fowlie;
FY, Young; JB, Box; JF, Ferrer; JH, Hawkins; KH, Hussein; LH, Liddell Hart; MW, Wetherell;
OS, Sharif; O'T, O'Toole; SS, Spiegel; ZM, Mohyeddin.

PHOTO SOURCES: *Academy of Motion Picture Arts and Sciences (AMPAS), Margaret Herrick
Library:* pp. 64 (sign), 65 (DL, SS, KH), 68 (O'T, camel), 69 (Philips, O'T), 72 (EF), 78
(SS, DL), 79 (Radio), 80 (BC), 84 (middle), 85 (snack), 86 (camera), 88 (track), 89 (hairdress),
90 (sew), 91 (O'T, SS, DL; camera; inset), 92 (camera), 94 (EF), 96 (trek), 98 (O'T, AG;
AG; "name"), 100 (chess), 101 (Parker, AQ; Oasis), 106 (council), 107 (JF, O'T), 109 (O'T;
Hospital), 110 (Oasis), 111, 113, 117 (DL), 119 (ladies wc), 120 (B&W), 121 (vista, horse),
124 (upper right), 126 (O'T), 127 (B&W), 129 (B&W), 133 (vista), 135 (Aqaba; JB), 137
(Tafas; camera), 187, 216 (SS). *BBC:* p. 2. *Bodleian Library, Oxford:* pp. 2 (TEL), 3 (bros.),
12 (TEL;'25, '29), 16 (TEL), 44 (Rumm), 106 (TEL), 231 (TEL). *British Academy of Film
& Television Arts:* pp. 99, 102, 105-106, 109, 110, 135 [all John Box sketches]; 139. *British
Film Institute: Posters, Stills, and Designs:* pp. 8, 11, 13 (bottom) and 18 (bottom) ©London
Film Productions Ltd., 14 (Hudd), 19, 23, 25 (top) ©1959 Comet/MGM, 26 (left) ©1962
ABP/Cavalcade, 26 (right) ©1959 Comet/MGM, 27, 30-31, 33 (bottom left) ©1958 Twen-
tieth Century-Fox, 35, 37, 38 (bottom) ©1953 Columbia Pictures, 40 ©1960 Summit
Films/MGM, 43 (TEL, O'T), 56-57, 63 (SS, Palmer), 64 (Hobbs; admin; tent), 66 (SS),
67, 68 (O'T; O'T, KH), 69 (O'T), 70 (OS), 72 (truck), 73, 77 (buckets), 78 (bullhorn), 79
(bar), 80 (BC, FY, DL), 81 (O'T, DL; JT), 83 (top), 84 (top), 85 (desert [3]), 89 (O'T, DL;
OS), 91 (sound), 93 (sand; pit; BC), 95 (FY, DL; OS), 97, 98 (Emir Feisal; AG, DL; AG,
O'T), 99 (plane, camera), 100 (OS; Dimech), 101 (AQ; AQ, KH), 102 (vista), 105 (JH, O'T;
pool), 110 (camels; DL; O'T gun), 116 (B&W), 137 (O'T), 148, 157, 160 (color), 195, 199,
226 (OS, O'T), 228, 230 (DL, film), 234. *British Museum:* p. 3 (Carch.). *Malcolm
Brown:* pp. 2 (study), 16 (cottage). *Peter Carter-Ruck:* p. 25 (Rattigan). *CBC:* p. 200 ©1972 CBC
Television Network. *Cinemathèque:* p. 38 (top) ©1960 Woodfall Productions. *CTV:* p. 224
©1990 CTV Television Network/SMW Advertising. *Daily Mail:* p. 103 (O'T family) ©1961
Daily Mail. *Phyllis Dalton:* pp. xviii, 3 (TEL), 6 (house; TEL, 1917), 46, 49-54, 58, 60, 62,
70 (Ali), 81 (ZM, O'T), 90 (PD; costumes), 92 (O'T), 98 (Feisal portrait), 99 (Newcombe;
Quayle; panorama), 101 (Arabs; O'T), 102 (1917), 106 (O'T; JH; AG; Allenby, Feisal), 109
(Old Hospital), 122 (1917), 135 (O'T), 160 (ticket). *Eddie Fowlie:* pp. 175, 178.
Steven Shapiro/Gamma Liaison: pp. 218, 219 (DL, cans). *Robert A. Harris:* pp. 47, 48 (Finney,
O'T color), 80 (EF), 96 (Johar, O'T), 107 (JF), 110 (Gasim), 112 (35mm), 121 (DL points),

210-213, 226 (DL, OS, O'T). *Hulton Picture Library:* p. 61 (soldiers). *Imperial War Museum:*
pp. 6, (TEL, 1916), 7 (Hejaz), 61 (Arabs). *Mark Kauffman:* pp. 76, 124 (center right) ©1961
Mark Kauffman. *David Lancashire:* p. 46 (bottom) ©1965 David Lancashire, 87 (bottom
left) and 124 (all on left) ©1961 David Lancashire. *Sir David Lean (Lady Sandra Lean):* pp.
41-42, 44 (patrol), 45, 46, 48 (O'T test), 63 (DL, SS, KH), 66 (DL, SS), 71, 79 (O'T, DL),
86 (O'T), 87 (O'T, ZM; O'T), 88 (O'T), 89 (DL, O'T, OS), 94 (DL), 95 (well; O'T), 107
(DL), 192, 231 (top) © Cornel Lucas. *Liddell Hart Archives for Military Research:* pp. 10, 14
(TEL, LH), 18 (funeral, grave), 44 (camels), 65 (HQ), 69 (TEL), 70, 90 (1918), 101 (TEL),
135 (tracks; TEL), 137 (TEL); 155. *Mad Magazine:* pp. 105, 173 ©1964 E.C. Publications.
M Inc.: p. 173, Nov. 1990. *Robert Morris:* p. 173 (M Inc.), 217 (bottom, both) ©1983
RCA/Columbia Pictures Home Video. *National Portrait Gallery:* p. 9 (Thomas), 15. NEA:
p. 96 © NEA Inc. *Ronald Paquet:* pp. 43 (bottom) ©1970 MGM, 77 (truck), 78 (doc), 93
(filming), 96 (Cam-El), 99 (camp), 100 (soldiers), 101 (O'T), 105 (JH), 159, 164-169, 171
(top, left and center) ©1963 Colpix Records, 172, 173 (top right) ©1963 Dell Publishing
Co. Inc. (NY), 215, 221-222, 222 (bottom left) ©1989 *Première* (France), 222 (bottom right)
©1989 The Criterion Collection. *Reading Unversity:* p. 143. *Rolls-Royce Ltd:* p. 7 (Rolls). *Royal
Commission on the Historical Monuments of England:* p. 156 (Int. Odeon). *Lee Salem:* pp. 229
(all) and 230 (bottom) ©1990 Lee Salem. *J.R. Sims:* p. 17 (TEL). *David Tringham:* pp. 69
(DT), 77 (storm), 83 (O'T), 84 (DT), 100 (FY, DT), 125 (B&W), 128 (DT), 135 (horses),
136. *Lawrence Raskin:* p. 36 (bottom) ©1960 Angus McBean, 118 (factory), 123 (bottom),
125 (gas stn.), 128 (EF), 161-163, 167 (French), 171 (top right) ©Universal Record Manufac-
turing Canada, 171 (center left) ©London Records, 171 (center right) ©1963 Pye Records
Limited (England), 171 (bottom left) ©Sutton Records, 171 (bottom center) ©1963 Audio
Fidelity Inc., 171 (bottom right) ©1971 Quality Records Ltd., 173 (French) ©1965 Editeur
IN.GRA.B.E. S.p.A. (Italy), 174, 174 (bottom) ©1962 WFCC, 202, 204, 216 (DL Oscar),
217 (top) ©1962 Horizon Pictures (G.B.) Ltd. and ©1988 CPT Holdings Inc. *Video Review:*
p. 217, (Classic) April 1983. *Vogue:* January 1963, p. 170 (top) ©Dupont 1963, (bottom)
©Elizabeth Arden 1963. *Fay Wray:* p. 22 (Saunders). *Freddie Young:* p. 12 (MW; MW, FY),
77 (plane), 78 (FY), 86 (ZM, FY), 88 (FY), 92 (FY), 95 (FY, DL, JB), 110 (flood), 156 (Ext.
Odeon), 186.

DOCUMENT SOURCES: *Robert Bolt:* pp. 149-153. *The Cue Sheet:* pp. 144-145 ©1962
Maurice Jarre. *Daily Telegraph:* pp. 103 (bottom right) ©1961 *Daily Telegraph,* 233 ©1991
Daily Telegraph. *Phyllis Dalton:* pp. 59, 61, 62, 102 (map), *Robert A. Harris:* pp. 137 (BC),
139, 142, 146, 195. *Sir David Lean:* pp. 227, 232 (DL). *Liddell Hart Archives for Military
Research:* pp. 16, 19, 20, 33. *News of the World:* p. 103 (bottom left) ©1961 News of the World.
The New York Times: p. 82, "Desert Caravan on the trail of *Lawrence,*" by John R. Woolfen-
den, June 25, ©1961. *Philip O'Brien:* p. 21 (bottom) ©1935 Doubleday Doran, 232 (TEL).
Ronald Paquet: p. 137 (call sheet). *Première:* p. 209 ©1988 *Première.* *Lawrence Raskin:* p. 21
(top) ©1937 Book-of-the-Month Club. *Reading University:* p. 17.

*"Oscar" and "Academy Awards" are registered trademarks and service marks of AMPAS. "Os-
car" statuette © AMPAS®.*

We regret any oversights or omissions, which will be corrected in future editions.

ACKNOWLEDGMENTS

"WHAT [WE] OWE YOU IS BEYOND EVALUATION."

—FEISAL TO LAWRENCE, IN DAMASCUS

When we first discussed our book idea with archivist Robert A. Harris, his response was immediate: "I envy you guys this project because of all the great people you're going to meet."

He was right.

We first approached Harris in early 1990. He had recently rescued *Lawrence of Arabia* from oblivion, and surely, we thought, he could answer some of our questions: "Why hadn't the 1962 *Lawrence* Souvenir program been reprinted? Do you know of anyone doing a book about *Lawrence*? Would you help us do a book about *Lawrence*?"

"Don't know," "No," and "Yes," were his answers. This would be the start of an interesting relationship. He was to become our mentor, and our tormentor. Bob graciously opened crucial doors so that we could approach the many people whose permission and co-operation would be needed for such an ambitious project.

Harris first introduced us to Columbia Pictures Vice-President Hollace Davids, who was positive about the project from the start. Other Columbia folk who showed early enthusiasm for our enterprise were Ivy Orta, Terry Saevig, Helen La Varre, and Chana Gandal. Lester Bordon, Su Lesser, Tracy Fabrick, Susan Christison, Lynn Fischoff, Boyd Peterson, and Marquis Davis—also at Columbia—gave much appreciated help in later phases of the project.

With David Lean heavily occupied in preparation for *Nostromo* in 1990-91, Bob Harris co-ordinated the flow of information which eventually led to Sir David's "blessing" for our project.

We were fortunate to befriend Lady Sandra Lean in mid-project. She graciously offered her home, her hospitality, her insight, and complete access to Sir David's document and photo collection. Her generous support has been invaluable to the realization of our project.

The support of Lean's assistant, Sara Foster, is gratefully acknowledged.

Editor Anne V. Coates was the first *Lawrence* person we had the pleasure to meet, on our initial research expedition to California. In England, we were welcomed on numerous occasions by Freddie Young, and his gracious wife Joan. Harris had cautioned us that Freddie, in addition to being the world's greatest cinematographer, was also one of this planet's finest persons. Once again, he was right. Playwright Robert Bolt, and Sarah Miles, opened up their home to us for some precious hours at very short notice. Bolt provided us with a unique insight into the poetry which is *Lawrence*'s screenplay.

Although we had spoken frequently with costume designer Phyllis Dalton, our first meeting followed the David Lean Memorial Service at St. Paul's, in October 1991. Phyllis was unsparing with her time, and in granting access to her precious archives of unique *Lawrence*, and T. E. Lawrence, material. The look of this volume owes much to her collection.

Following the Lean service, we spent a memorable evening with Omar Sharif. His eloquence, his love for this film, and his admiration for David Lean cannot adequately be conveyed in our allotted space.

If legends exist in the cinema industry, then Eddie Fowlie is one. *Lawrence*'s property master, and David Lean's closest friend, Fowlie related numerous stories of the adventures that occurred during the filming, and generously provided a unique tour of the Spanish filming locations.

The Rt. Hon. Sir Anthony Nutting—Cabinet Minister, T. E. Lawrence biographer, and Spiegel's *Lawrence* advisor—provided us with yet another viewpoint about the film's creation.

Second assistant director David Tringham spun his inimitable tales of on-location hi-jinks, while Winston Ryder described the intricacies of sound creation for the film. Maggie Unsworth was instrumental in making contact with many of the *Lawrence* artists.

Other creative artists who—mainly due to scheduling conflicts—could only provide the briefest of information about their experience on the film were: Maurice Jarre, John Box, Barbara Beale (Cole), Ernest Day, Roy Stevens, and—of course—Peter O'Toole.

Ronald Paquet, with possibly the world's largest collection of David Lean memorabilia, provided most of the rare items which are featured in the color section of this book.

Prof. Michael Anderegg, University of North Dakota, inspired us with his essay, "Lawrence of Arabia: the Man, the Myth, the Movie," one of the best film critiques ever written.

Prof. Steve Tabachnick, University of Oklahoma, created an essay "Leonardo of Arabia," on Lawrence as a *polymath*, while Prof. Peter Herman, University of Toronto, wrote on "The Stature of Lawrence of Arabia." Regrettably, both of these articles were lost due to space considerations.

Prof. Fred Crawford, Michigan University, introduced us to the Liddell Hart Centre for Military Archives, Kings College, University of London, the source of much interesting material about early attempts at Lawrence films. Pat Methven, Kate O'Brien, and Amanda Engineer, at the Archives provided invaluable help in accessing the information. Prof. Patrick Hill, Carleton University, and Peter Taylor,

Worthing, England, were able research assistants and invaluable informants in the U.K.

Susan Wilson, of the British Film Institute – Stills, Posters and Designs – was instrumental in co-ordinating access to the BFI collection during our visits. Dr. Linda Mehr, Robert Cushman, Howard Prouty, Lisa Jackson, David Marsh, and Janet Lorenz, at the Academy of Motion Picture Arts and Sciences, Margaret Herrick Library, co-ordinated our search for photos in L.A.; Joanne Lawson, Robert Harris's assistant at The Film Preserve, provided valuable assistance and encouragement.

Roy Frumkes, filmmaker, features editor of *The Perfect Vision,* and writer, graciously allowed us to adapt his April/May 1989 *Films in Review* (New York) articles on the *Lawrence* restoration into our present Chapter 9. The permission of Robin Little, editor of *Films in Review,* is also acknowledged.

GiannaMaria Babando, with her cinema expertise and infectious enthusiasm transcribed most of our interview tapes. Other tape transcription was done by Barb Wackid, Andrew Morris, and Noreen Fields.

Josh Raskin assisted in document photography in Phyllis Dalton's garden, and was a travel companion on research expeditions to England and Spain.

Valuable research material was provided by Dr. Philip O'Brien, Whittier College, L.A.; Edwards Metcalfe, Huntington Library, San Marino, CA; Michael Bott, Reading University, UK; Malcolm Brown, Imperial War Museum, London; Mark Kauffman, Pismo Beach, CA; William M. Gaines, *Mad Magazine,* NYC; Calvin Grondahl, Standard-Examiner, Ogden, Utah; Sir Dirk Bogarde, London; Fay Wray, L.A.; St. John Armitage, UK; Peter F. Carter-Ruck, London; Lee Salem, L.A.; David Lancashire, *The Globe and Mail,* Toronto; Peter Worthington, *Toronto Sun;* Callista Kelly and Doris Cole, InterLibrary Loans, Carleton University; Doreen Dean, British Academy of Film and Television Arts, London; Chris Matheson, San Francisco; Liz Churchman, Royal Commission on the Historical Monuments of England; Robert Towne, Pacific Palisades, CA; Dr. Karol Kulik, Michael Darlow, Martin Gilbert, UK; Kate Bannister and John Maggs, Maggs Bros. Ltd., London; Denis McDonnell and Janet A. Reisman, T.E. Notes, Honesdale, PA; Robin Gibson, National Portrait Gallery, London; Michael Anderson and Eva Goldin, Cinémathèque Ontario; Ruth Deborah Morris, L.A.; Gamma Liaison Photo Agency, New York; Al Press, Columbia Postproduction, Inwood, NY; Daniel Lau, CBS Home Video, Toronto; Michael Brooker, Eliza Fernandes, Columbia TriStar, Canada; Dr. Robert Brandeis, E.J. Pratt Library, Toronto; Roger Ebert, *Chicago Sun-Times;* Joanne Swadron, Whitby, Ontario; Metropolitan Toronto Reference Library, Picture Collection; Mike Orlando, Hollywood Canteen, Toronto; Elwy Yost, TVOntario; Henry Wolf, NYC; Jeremy Wilson, UK; Suzanne Morris, Toronto; V.M. Thompson, Melvyn Bragg, Jean Hobbs, and Phil Hobbs, Jr., UK.

Research was facilitated by Darlene MacMillan, Carleton University; Stephen Silverman, NYC; Kevin Brownlow, UK; Jane Carmichael, Imperial War Museum, London; Rafael Donato and Margaret Bodde, Scorsese Productions, NYC; Steve Kenis and Ushi Whelan, William Morris Agency, UK; Dr. Lindy Grant, Courtauld Institute, London; Samuel T. Suratt, CBS News, NYC; Prof. Ronald Nettler, Oxford University; George Turner, American Cinematographer; Jamie Raskin, Toronto; the Jordanian Desert Patrol; and Auda, our Howeitat guide, who invited us to dine with him at Wadi Rumm.

Research advice was received from Mrs. Hetty Minney, Alex and Nick de Grunwald, Monty Berman, John Gudenian, Lord Mark Bonham Carter, UK; Peter Beale, L.A.; Risa Shuman, TVOntario; Jacob Rosen, Jerusalem; Gary Crowdus, Joel Hodson, NYC; Ajai Sehgal, Ottawa.

For generously offering their homes and their hospitality, we thank Lynne Raskin, Joanne Morris, George Morris, Alf and Hilda Seegar, Colin

Harding, Joan Young, Barbara Harris, David Harris, Jamie Morris, Carlos (Hotel El Dorado, Carboneras, Spain), Anne O'Neill (Amman, Jordan), Annette Tringham, and Winston Ryder's daughter.

Good advice, and more, was provided by Rick Wilks, Bernice Eisenstein, Barry Weinstock, William Stillman, Gerald Pratley, Ron Base, David Haslam, Andy Deskin, Gavin Mitchell, Paul Axelrod and Susan Friedman, Cindy Raskin and Howard Slapcoff, David J. Morris. Lorne Vineberg, Lawrence Lee, Richard H. Stern, Cliff Lax, Wendy Dennis, Judy Bekerman, John McQuarrie.

We are also grateful for support from the Information and Entertainment Media: Noel Taylor, *Ottawa Citizen;* David Garrick, Syme Jago, Daniel McPhee, and Retta Schick, SkyDome, Toronto; Brian Bailey, Krys Jawlosewicz, and André Picard, Cinesphere, Toronto; Jeremy Brown, Jane Haughton, Brian Linehan, and Andy Barrie, CFRB Radio; Rob Davidson, and Bonnie Laufer, Global TV; Lorraine Clark and James Burgess, CITY TV; Richard Ouzounian, Karen Levine, and Jeff Brown, CBC; Bev Slopen, *Toronto Star;* Jon and Julie Williams, Table Rock Productions, L.A.; Arlene Weiskopfe, *CBS Nightwatch,* NYC; Millie Sherman, Castle Hill Productions NYC.

For quiet encouragement, we thank Albert and Shirley Raskin, Charles and Lise Wackid, Morris and Ruthe Axelrod; David Coll, Malcolm Bibby, Robin Farquhar, Irwin Gillespie, David Bernhardt, Jim Mackie, Harvey Savage; Gordon Grice, Norman Elder (Explorers Club, Toronto), David John Clark, Geoffrey Clarfield, Shin Sugino, Paul Ferris, Garfield Ingram. Michael Chas. Benjamin, Michael Murphy, Fred Silny, Effie Lazegas; Mrs. Johnson, Pat Coombs; John Pierce, Doubleday, Canada.

For professional expertise: George Hidalgo, Northwest Digital, John Przybytek, Ottawa. In Toronto: Charles Chiu, Colourgenics Photo Labs; Sandra Pover, Light Labs; Bob Mobbs and Annette MacMaster, Print-In; Gordon Mills, Mills Custom Photo Labs; Benjamin Film Laboratories; Shelley Wallach, Consolidated Theatre Services; Danuta, Black's Photography; Cathy Rideout and Brenda Cheung, DEL Property Management; Steve Raskin, Medallion/PFA Film and Video; Marilyn and Victor Shalma, Aziza Wasfi, "C" Travel.

Paul Norman, of Voyager Criterion, provided us with indispensable access to all 311,859 frames in the film, by providing us a CAV *Lawrence* laserdisc set.

And last, but definitely not least, we would like to thank the team who accepted, coddled, designed, endured, and produced this book:

At the *Mitchell Rose Literary Agency,* our extraordinary agent Mitchell Rose. Our book particularly owes thanks to him for countless suggestion of great value and diversity, and for the elimination of almost all the exclamation points. Thanks to Justin Evans and Carol Fitzgerald.

At *Doubleday,* our editor Charles Conrad, who recognized the merits of our proposal and who bravely shepherded our book through difficult times. We also thank his assistant, Jon Furay, together with Martha Levin, Harold Grabau, Kim Cacho, and Marysarah Quinn.

At *Michaelis/Carpelis Design Associates, Inc.,* Sylvain Michaelis, Irene Carpelis, and Joe Bartos, who climbed out from under the mountain of photographs and documents that we sent, and created this unique book.

At *The Type Set,* Lynn Goeller and Sue Kemmerer, who somehow managed to string together our 80,000 words in the right order.

Estelle Laurence of Arizona, for proofreading all these words. And her supermarket across the road for providing fax facilities.

We'd also like to express our appreciation for the efforts of Frederick W. Smith, Chester Carlson, and the elusive inventor of the fax machine, without whom this international effort would not have been possible.

And a special thanks to Terry Matthews, Newbridge Networks, Kanata, Ontario.

CONTENTS

FOREWORD
Martin Scorsese
xiv

INTRODUCTION
xvi

CHAPTER · 1
THE LEGEND OF LAWRENCE
1

CHAPTER · 2
THE EPICS THAT NEVER WERE
11

CHAPTER · 3
SPIEGEL AND LEAN
31

CHAPTER · 4
PREPRODUCTION
55

CHAPTER · 5
ON LOCATION
75

CHAPTER · 6
POSTPRODUCTION
139

CHAPTER · 7
PREMIERES, REVIEWS AND
OSCARS: 1962 AND 1963
155

CHAPTER · 8·
THE LOST PICTURE SHOW
189

CHAPTER · 9
RECONSTRUCTION AND
RESTORATION
201

CHAPTER · 10
PREMIERES, REVIEWS AND
VIDEO: 1989
209

CHAPTER · 11
ACCOLADES AND
CELEBRATION
227

CHAPTER · 12
LAWRENCE OF ARABIA:
AN ICON
235

CAST AND CREDITS
236

FOREWORD

I first saw *Lawrence of Arabia,* when I was twenty, at the Criterion Theater in New York on its initial release in 1962. From the opening sequence, which includes exhilarating 70mm camera shots from the point of view of a motorcycle, I realized that I was about to experience something new in cinema. As the picture unfolded, I was mesmerized by the precision of the images, the staging of the scenes, the camera movement, the acting, the costumes, the music, and the editing. It was the same excitement I felt upon hearing, for the first time, a great symphony or reading an epic work of literature.

I had seen a few David Lean pictures up to that time. I was too young to comprehend the power and mysticism of *Breaking the Sound Barrier* (1952), yet the film still haunted me. A few years later I saw *Summertime* (1955), the type of love story which normally would not have interested me at the age of thirteen. Yet I found myself enjoying it immensely and, more importantly, absorbing a special kind of clarity; a bright beauty in the imagery and the editing. Finally, I saw *The Bridge on the River Kwai* on its first run at the Palace Theater in New York. Lean's canvas was larger. It was filled with strong images, adventure, and some fascinating characters—elements he would mold into something new in his next film, *Lawrence of Arabia.*

Lawrence was the first grand-scale film constructed around a character who was not a traditional hero. As envisioned in Robert Bolt's script, Lawrence is a tormented man, full of pride and self-hatred from the outset—a doomed figure whose character was drawn from two previously disparate sources: the Epic Film, with its emphasis on the large canvas and spectacle which often overwhelmed story and character; and Film Noir, developed from 1945 on, with its emphasis on the darker side of the human condition. Lawrence is as flawed and doomed as any of the characters in the great film noirs, such as Edgar G. Ulmer's *Detour* or Jacques Tourneur's *Out of the Past.* The fusing of these two genres together into *Lawrence* created something quite new.

In *Lawrence,* the moral ambiguity that was already visible in *Kwai* crystallized and transformed. The combination of spectacle and film noir broke the form of the traditional epic picture and gave it new life. The end of the film took me by surprise. Familiar with other epic films, I expected a gigantic climactic sequence—most likely a battle scene. Instead, this ending is darkly subdued—Lawrence in the jeep on his way back to England, glancing sadly at some Bedouin and camels passing by—a man unresolved for the rest of his life. It is said now that with this film, Lean created the intelligent epic. That's true. But, for me, it's something more. It's the first interior epic, the first film of epic scale whose true canvas is the private passion of a man in anguish.

When I was thirteen, I had seen another great picture at the Criterion: John Ford's *The Searchers.* In a sense, it was a precursor of *Lawrence of Arabia.* Ford charted the history of America on film, from colonial times *(Drums Along the Mohawk)* to the pre-Civil War *(Young Mr. Lincoln).* He chronicled the coming of the railroad and the unification of the East and West *(The Iron Horse)* through the taming of the frontier *(My Darling Clementine).* He moved from the rowdy idealism of World War I *(What*

Price Glory?) to the fatalism of World War II *(They Were Expendable)* and disillusionment that followed *(The Wings of Eagles)*. Best known as the director who put the myth of the American West on screen, Ford shaped the archetypal American hero who forges into unknown territories and tames them in the name of civilization. However, with *The Searchers,* Ford appeared suddenly to revise the cinema myth he had helped create. Like Lawrence, John Wayne's Ethan Edwards was a flawed character full of psychological shading and honest weaknesses—for me, a tragic figure. This revision reflected a change in the national mood during the 1950s and was part of a climate in which a film like *Lawrence of Arabia* could eventually become possible.

Both Ford and Lean succeeded in personalizing the epic through character. They both had the courage to create monumental images to support heroes full of human flaws. Over the years, I think back on my formative moviegoing experiences from 1944 to 1965, and how the films of the 1950s and the 1960s—especially *The Searchers* and *Lawrence of Arabia*—gave me the encouragement to make films that revolved around antiheroes, such as *Mean Streets* and *Raging Bull.*

Seeing *Lawrence of Arabia* after its 1989 restoration, in its original wide-screen glory, was like seeing it for the first time all over again. Like brush strokes added to an incomplete fresco, the differences were subtle, but they changed the entire composition. In reading this book I hope you'll understand the complexities involved in the production of this film. There were so many complexities, in fact, that it seems Lean never quite had the time to complete this picture. In this restoration he got as close as possible; in fact, he never stopped tinkering with it. He would delete a few feet of film here and there even as restored scenes and soundtrack were being added. Understanding this process and seeing the final result, I had the sensation that in some very real way a film is a living thing that can never be fully completed. Even the resonance of the images can change with time.

Max Ophuls once said, "The camera exists to show things on the screen that cannot exist anywhere else, on stage or in life. Aside from that, I have no use for it. I'm not interested in photography." As the *Lawrence* restoration neared completion, I spoke about it with increasing excitement to my friend Jay Cocks, and we both recalled this statement of Ophuls's, realizing it might apply to David Lean as well. His images stay with us forever. But what makes them memorable isn't necessarily their beauty. That's just good photography. Lean's images are indelible because they contain an entire dramatic experience. They are visual repositories of some of our greatest movie memories.

It's the emotion behind those images that had endured over the years, and that continues to grow and resonate. It's the way he put feeling on film—the way he shows a whole landscape of the spirit—that is the true geography of David Lean country. And that's why, as Jay put it, in a David Lean movie there's no such thing as an empty landscape.

—*Martin Scorsese*
June, 1992

INTRODUCTION

"TRULY, FOR SOME MEN...
NOTHING IS WRITTEN UNLESS THEY WRITE IT."

—Ali to Lawrence, after rescue of Gasim

First love between a person and a film can be as intoxicating as first love between two people. It can mean just as much crazy behavior, just as many sleepless nights. As a young adolescent I became so obsessed with a certain film that I saw it over and over, spent years studying the life of its hero, regarded him as a kind of role model and even dragged my family on a long, dusty pilgrimage to a place where he had lived. If one measure of a film's greatness is its power to affect the lives of those who see it, then "Lawrence of Arabia" must be the best film I know.

Janet Maslin of *The New York Times* wrote those words in 1989 and, well, we couldn't say it any better.

In 1963, during university days, two momentous events occurred which were to have a significant effect on our later lives: we met each other, while working on a campus humor newspaper, and—we saw the film *Lawrence of Arabia.*

This first viewing (and countless subsequent ones) was profoundly influential in transforming us into passionate T. E. Lawrence enthusiasts.

Studies, marriages, travels, and careers drew us apart over the years, but from time to time our paths would cross. And inevitably, the conversation would drift back into yet another discussion of Lawrence—the man and the film.

It is difficult to recall exactly when we realized that we hadn't seen a decent version of the film on TV or in the cinema for years. The arrival of a home video version in the early '80s was exciting, but it somehow failed to evoke the heady emotions of those early viewings long

ago. "Will we ever see *Lawrence* again up on the silver screen?" we lamented.

Then—one golden day in the summer of 1988—came the first glimmer of hope. Barry Weinstock, an old friend and fellow enthusiast, casually mentioned that he'd "heard something on the radio about *Lawrence of Arabia* being restored." Scarcely even knowing what that meant, we tried to unearth more details, but with no success.

Until, in September 1988, a small announcement in *Premiere* magazine confirmed that our favorite film was about to see the light of day, so to speak, once again. Over the next few months, the phone lines to Columbia were in danger of melting from our persistent efforts to learn when the new and improved masterpiece would open soon in a theater near us.

The wait was worthwhile. The miracle had been accomplished. Scenes we'd never seen before clarified the story line. The color, the sharpness, and the sound were all better then they'd been when the film opened twenty-seven years earlier. But most important, its effect on *us* was as stunning and overwhelming as we'd recalled.

Roger Ebert, American film critic, observed: "I've noticed that when people remember *Lawrence of Arabia,* they don't talk about the details of the plot. They get a certain look in their eyes, as if they are remembering the whole experience, and have never quite been able to put it into words... It is spectacle and experience, and its ideas are about things you can see or feel, not things you can say."

Neither of us can now pinpoint the day it happened. A trip to the bookshop revealed an amazing fact: while we could choose from hundreds of books about virtually every film ever made, not one book about *Lawrence* – the film – was in print.

And there the adventure began.

Our quest led us to eight countries, where we slowly discovered treasure troves of precious material not seen for decades. And on these journeys, we also made another rare discovery – the "Lawrence people": enthusiastic, wonderful characters, many of whom have become cherished friends.

David Lean's epic masterpiece took longer to film than the duration of Lawrence's Arab campaign. Robert Harris's miraculous restoration required more time than did the making of the movie itself. And, the odyssey of our book project stretched across a greater time span than did the restoration.

But now, having completed the monumental task, we can lean back, content in the knowledge that – at last – "It is written."

L. Robert Morris
Lawrence Raskin

Damascus, Ontario
July 1992

CHAPTER • 1

THE LEGEND OF LAWRENCE

"COULD YOU GIVE ME A FEW WORDS ABOUT COLONEL LAWRENCE?"

— REPORTER TO LORD ALLENBY, ON THE STEPS OF ST. PAUL'S

His death occurred on an English road, in Dorset. He was riding a motorcycle powerful enough to satisfy his appetite for speed, and the time was early morning in the Spring of 1935.

With his death, the ballyhoo which hounded him through life was doubled. Had he, or had he not, a project for meeting and reasoning with Hitler? Was there, or was there not, a mysterious black limousine at the scene of the accident? Had he killed himself deliberately? Or merely been stung by a bee? In fact it seems most probable that he swerved to miss two boys on bicycles and was going too fast for it. But the world did not want an ordinary death for this extraordinary man.

An element of mystery there briefly was. When he was picked up from the road his papers identified him as a fellow called Shaw, recently discharged from the Royal Air Force with the rank of Aircraftman, the lowest rank of all, a bearer of coal scuttles and tender of air-camp pigsties. This unimportant person was taken to the Military Hospital at Bovington Camp.

But Mrs. Thomas Hardy, the widow of the great novelist, made anxious enquiries about Aircraftman Shaw; so did Mr. Winston Churchill; Augustus John, the

famous painter came in person. Artists of all kinds, high-ranking officers, men with titles and even crowns, awaited news. At length he was attended by the Surgeon and Physician to the King of England. On May 20th, the *London Times* announced:

> After a week of hope and fear, a commonplace accident has robbed the nation of one of its most remarkable personalities. Lawrence of Arabia is dead.

Shaw was the name he had taken when he had tried to escape from his publicity, his past, or himself, in what he called the "monastery" of an Air Force barracks. Now he was revealed as Thomas Edward Lawrence, illegitimate but well-loved son of Thomas Chapman, Irish baronet. And now his other names and titles were called over too: Liberator of Damascus; Hero of Aqaba; Uncrowned King and Kingmaker. To the Bedouin sheiks he was "Prince Dynamite" and "Destroyer," both for his exploits against the Hejaz railway and his own explosive energy.

To the ordinary Bedouin tribesmen, veterans of the First World War campaign against the Turkish Empire in Arabia, he was no man of mystery but a type they recognized, an iron-willed leader, brother-in-arms of Auda abu Tayi, chief of the fighting Howeitat. The "L" of "Lawrence" came adrift in their pronunciation and to them he was "El Aurens" or plain "Aurens." And this name, used with casual affection or respect, was a source of comfort to him while he was among them.

His own countrymen preferred the Legend to the man. There was substance enough in his life for a Legend,

"All men dream: but not equally. Those who dream by night in the dusty recesses of their minds wake in the day to find that it was vanity: but the dreamers of the day are dangerous men, for they may act their dreams with open eyes, to make it possible. This I did." T. E. Lawrence, in "suppressed" introduction to Seven Pillars of Wisdom. *Photo taken in 1918 by Lowell Thomas's cameraman, Harry Chase.*

1

Above: Thomas Edward Lawrence, circa 1900, age twelve.
Right: Two-room "study" bungalow in garden of Lawrence residence at 2 Polstead Road, Oxford. Built in 1908 for T.E.L. by his father, Thomas Chapman.

but romance was added. Did he love this Legend or detest it? "There's only one thing worse than being talked about," said Oscar Wilde, summing up the attitude of famous people to their fame, "and that is *not* being talked about." No doubt this was the case with Lawrence. One half of him was scholar, thinker, gentle and retiring. The other half was man of action, harsh, decisive, and it must be said flamboyant. Perhaps it was this second half he was in flight from when he changed his name to Shaw.

Now that he was dead the Legend grew unchecked and the suffering man was all but forgotten. The nation rang with eulogy. The king made public his grateful recognition. General Sir Ian Hamilton numbered him among the great who raise the level of human existence. Field Marshal Lord Allenby declared that he had left the pattern of a life well spent in service. Winston Churchill wrote most eloquently:

"In Colonel Lawrence we have lost one of the greatest beings of our time. I had the honour of his friendship. I knew him well. I hoped to see him quit his retirement and take a commanding part in facing the dangers which now threaten the country. No such blow has befallen the Empire for many years as his untimely death."

In the newspapers he figured as the Knight of Araby. He was a shining example to set before the young. And when the earth had received him, a young girl slipped through the lingering mourners and placed upon his grave a small bouquet of lilac and forget-me-not, upon the card of which was written "To T.E.L., who should sleep among the Kings."

Of course reaction followed. Hands were not wanting to tear down the image other hands had raised. Voices were not wanting to claim that there was Fraud in the Legend. Sensational books were written to show him in the light of charlatan, poseur, and worse. The arguments are long and complicated, any conclusion difficult. The glib solution is a shrug. He is a "mystery," a "paradox," a "puzzle" and "enigma." Let it be so; what man is not? But the makers of this film can testify that he is remembered very clearly by the Bedouin survivors of those not-so-long-ago campaigns, and by the simple name of "Aurens."

Meanwhile, what of the necessary man beneath all this blast and counter-blast of reputation? For that, the best, the only satisfactory piece of evidence lies in his own account of the Desert Campaign, his book *The Seven Pillars of Wisdom*.

Lawrence agonized over the preparation of this work.

Above Left: T.E.L. in Oxford University Officers Training Corps, summer of 1910, age twenty-two.
Above: Archaeologists T. E. Lawrence (age twenty-five) and Leonard Woolley at excavations in Carchemish, Syria, 1913.
Left: The five Lawrence brothers in 1910. Left to right: "Ned" (T.E.L., age twenty-two), Frank, Arnold, Bob, and Will.

debts incurred by the parent edition. But when that was done Lawrence withdrew *Revolt in the Desert* from the market, so far as he was able, and what it earned thereafter gave to charity. He seemed to turn away from the book, hating it. *The Seven Pillars of Wisdom* was not generally available until after his death. He himself never made a penny from it.

But George Bernard Shaw gave him enthusiastic encouragement in its preparation, H. G. Wells called it a great human document, E. M. Forster judged it a masterpiece but feared to tell Lawrence so lest he evoke a sarcastic reaction from a man whose friendship he treasured. Certainly it is unique.

The flesh of the book is its philosophical reflections and poetic descriptions. Its bones are the action. This begins with Lawrence's meeting with Prince Feisal and other Arab chiefs to unify their rising against the Turks; it recounts the taking of Aqaba by Lawrence's audacious

Yet, a true artist in this, he had no thought of what it might bring him. The First Edition was of 212 copies, for private subscribers only. Its beautiful printing and binding ran him heavily into debt which forced him to the publication of a hastily abridged edition called *Revolt in the Desert*. This was a best seller and paid the

strategy of attacking from the land instead of the sea; re-
lates the forays against the railway; and follows his triumphal ride to Damascus. This ride was interrupted by
an act of fearful carnage against retreating Turks at the
village of Tafas, of which more later. The book ends at
Damascus.

At Damascus, Lawrence's fortunes seemed to be at
their peak. But it was there that he broke off, fled from
Arabia and began that search for obscurity which led him
to the ranks of the Forces under an assumed name. Why?
Presently the Air Force discharged him, because his fame
as Colonel Lawrence was embarrassing to his officers. By
appeal to friends in high places he secured his reinstate-
ment, under yet another name. Why? It is in *Seven Pillars* if anywhere that we shall find the answer.

The book is sometimes mystifying, sometimes pain-
fully self-revealing. And both mystification and self-
revelation seem sometimes deliberate, sometimes unin-
tentional. Even admirers of Lawrence, writing about this
book, did so obliquely, as if averting their eyes. Moralists
recoil from it, and indeed they are warned at the outset:

> Some of the evil of my tale may have been
> inherent in our circumstances...We were a self-
> centered army without parade or gesture, devoted to
> freedom....As time went by our need to fight for the
> ideal increased to an unquestioning possession, riding
> with spur and rein over our doubts. Willy-nilly it
> became a faith. We had sold ourselves into its
> slavery...By our own act we were drained of morality.

Controversy rages about the alleged cruelty, even
sadism, of his campaign. Here he is on that very subject:

> What now looks wanton or sadic seemed in the
> field inevitable, or just unimportant routine. Blood
> was always on our hands: we were licensed to it...
> When there was reason and desire to punish we wrote
> our lesson with gun or whip immediately in the sullen
> flesh of the sufferer, and the case was beyond appeal.

Is this a confession or an excuse? One cannot tell.
Perhaps he did not know himself. Certain it is that he
shed a lot of blood, on one occasion needlessly and
dreadfully. But certainly also he hated bloodshed. He
reversed the 1914 strategy of seeking out and attacking
the enemy. His aim was to incapacitate, not to destroy.
The loss of two men caused him concern, the loss of

twenty (his own or the enemy's) was catastrophe. Early
in the campaign an Arab charge at a mountain pass wiped
out a Turkish force:

> ...these soldiers had been very young. The
> corpses seemed flung so pitifully on the ground,
> huddled anyhow in low heaps. Surely if straightened
> they would be comfortable at last. So I put them all
> in order, one by one, very wearied myself, and longing
> to be of these quiet ones, not of the restless, noisy,
> aching mob up the valley, quarreling over the
> plunder...

While one critic accused him of sadistic love of in-
flicting pain on others a second declared with an air of
discovery that Lawrence had a masochistic love of pain
inflicted on himself. The air of discovery is odd since
psychologists are agreed that the two emotions are one.
And in any case, here is Lawrence himself: He is
speaking of his torture at the hands of the Turkish governor of Deraa, who did not know the identity of his
prisoner.

> ...my flesh quivered with accumulated pain, and
> with terror of the next blow coming. They soon
> conquered my determination not to cry...I
> remembered the corporal kicking with his nailed boot
> to get me up...I remembered smiling idly at him, for
> a delicious warmth, probably sexual, was swelling
> through me: and then he flung up his arms and
> hacked with the full length of his whip into my groin.

This is plain enough. It is a little impudent after such
a revelation to claim any special shrewdness for the insight that Lawrence had a special attitude to his own
body.

This incident was a turning-point in Lawrence's life.
He quickly realized, he says "how in Deraa that night
the citadel of my integrity had been irrevocably lost." Utterly worn out, his love of the desert and his Bedouin
followers turned to revulsion. He sickened, he tells us,
of "that rankling fraudulence which had to be my mind's
habit: that pretence to lead the national uprising of
another race, the daily posturing in alien dress, preach-
ing in alien speech." He went to General Allenby and
"begged for a smaller part elsewhere." He had come to
realize the peril of his position as the English leader of
an Arab revolt, responsible to no one but himself, and

wanted "to pillow myself on duty and obedience." He was sick of the desert.

But Allenby had need of him, and persuaded him back. It can have been no small decision for Lawrence to quit the desert, and we should like to know how Allenby reversed it. But at this point Lawrence becomes exasperatingly brief. "There was no escape for me," he simply and sadly says. But the old straightforward idealism had gone. "I must take up again my mantle of fraud in the East." And a certain personal recklessness had taken its place: "I took it up quickly and wrapped myself in it completely. It might be fraud or it might be farce: no one should say that I could not play it."

That is all he says. We must make our own evaluation. But if it was farce it was bloody farce. Lawrence had a bodyguard. It comprised ninety men, outlaws and killers all. "They were," he says, "a wonderful gang of experts. . . . The British called them cut-throats but they cut throats only to my order." They were with him at the village of Tafas where the Arab army, newly raised by Lawrence at Allenby's behest, overtook a fleeing and demoralized Turkish column. The Turks had done their worst with the little place, and now the darker side of Lawrence's nature took control. He told his bodyguard: "The best of you brings me the most Turkish dead."

> By my orders we took no prisoners. . . In a madness born of the horror of Tafas we killed and killed, even blowing in the heads of fallen and of the animals." It went on all day and it became "one of the nights when men went crazy . . . and others' lives became toys to break and throw away.

It was with this deed behind him that he entered Damascus, the longed-for goal of the Arab Revolt. And there it ended.

The common enemy now gone, old tribal hatreds sprang into flame between the Bedouin leaders, and they despised the local politicals. They had conquered in the desert, but they could not run Damascus. The epitome of this failure lay, for Lawrence, in a Turkish Military Hospital, hopelessly broken down, in which the erstwhile enemy now lay, some dead, some dying, some long dead. As he labored hopelessly against such circumstances he felt, he says, that he would never again be clean. The British had their own intentions, and waited.

The Bedouin could not run Damascus but they had taken it, and at the peace conference their claims could not be ignored. Lawrence was called to Versailles to represent them, a much-admired, much-photographed, much-talked-of public hero.

The man himself? Thereafter began the intermittent, desperate search for obscurity, the Lawrence enigma which has filled a library of books.

This essay by Robert Bolt appeared anonymously in the 1962 Columbia Souvenir program.

Before the legend, there was a man. Lawrence, after all, is a hero of our own time, not some dimly perceived figure from a lost age. The details of his life may not be as readily available to us as they were to an older generation, but details—places and names and dates—there are in abundance. In themselves, of course, they explain very little. Even so, a brief and, insofar as possible, factual account of Lawrence's career may ease entry into a discussion of the films that career inspired. Actually, a factual account of Lawrence that does not in some way contradict another factual account is not really possible: the best one can do is point to those junctures where fact, fiction, and myth hopelessly intertwine.

T. E. Lawrence was born in Tremadoc, North Wales, on August 16, 1888. His father, a minor Anglo-Irish baronet named Thomas Chapman, had adopted the surname Lawrence after deserting his wife to live with his former housekeeper. Thomas Edward was the second son of this illicit but in nearly every other way unremarkable, conventionally bourgeois union. Indeed, so unremarkable was his family life that he probably did not discover his illegitimacy until well into his teens. Thomas's boyhood was marked by frequent moves—Scotland, Jersey, France, the New Forest—dictated by the senior Lawrence's restless nature. The family finally settled in Oxford where he attended the local high school and, in due time, the university. From an early age, Thomas exhibited a precociousness and intellectual curiosity that set him off from his peers. He became interested in the Middle Ages and traveled by bicycle and foot over parts of Europe and throughout the Near East, researching what would become his senior thesis, *Crusader Castles*. After taking a "first" in the Honors School of History, Lawrence went to the site of the ancient Hittite city of Carchemish, on the banks of the Euphrates, as a member of an archaeological expedition. While there he immersed himself in Middle Eastern culture and learned (well or poorly, depending on your source) Middle Eastern languages. The myth would have

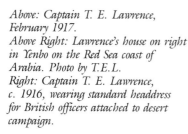

Above: Captain T. E. Lawrence, February 1917.
Above Right: Lawrence's house on right in Yenbo on the Red Sea coast of Arabia. Photo by T.E.L.
Right: Captain T. E. Lawrence, c. 1916, wearing standard headdress for British officers attached to desert campaign.

it that Lawrence spent more time spying on the Turks and the Germans than he did digging up artifacts. Certain proof for this is lacking, but we needn't doubt that any true-blue Englishman of Lawrence's generation, finding himself in a foreign and potentially hostile part of the world (in this case, the Ottoman Empire), would have instinctively kept eyes and ears open.

Soon after the outbreak of World War I, Lawrence, logically enough given his background and studies, was offered a minor position with British Intelligence in Cairo. A fairly nondescript second lieutenant assigned to making maps, he nevertheless had an impact on his superiors (negative as well as positive) disproportionate to his rank and duties. Soon, he found himself involved with a projected revolt of the Arab tribes against their Turkish masters. Here, conflicting testimony becomes particularly dissonant. Lawrence, depending on which account you follow, (a) personally chose Prince Feisal as the nominal leader of the Arab Revolt, but in fact led

the revolt himself; (b) was merely an unimportant liaison officer who transported gold from English coffers to Arab pockets; or (c) operated somewhere in between these extremes. Whatever his role, most accounts agree that Lawrence affected Arab dress, mingled freely with Bedouin tribesmen, was involved in the Arab conquest of Aqaba, and spent much of the Arab Revolt blowing up Turkish trains. What is certain is that Lawrence eventually came to be seen far and wide as the leader of the Arab Revolt, the uncrowned Prince of Mecca, a modern Arabian knight.*

The popular image of Lawrence as a romantic war hero was, to a great extent, created by American newsman and adventurer Lowell Thomas.

Thomas had originally journeyed to Europe seeking material which would help swing American opinion behind the Allied war effort. His search led him from the horrifying trenches of the Western Front to the relative calm of the Middle East. There, he was inexorably drawn toward the desert campaign, with its Arab guerrillas being led by an elusive British officer, T. E. Lawrence. Thomas was fascinated by this "shadowy Englishman among the desert tribes."

*These three paragraphs are extracted from an essay by Michael Anderegg.

In 1919, Thomas returned to the United States with miles of film and countless stills chronicling the Great War. However, Thomas sensed that Americans had quickly lost interest in the war. He wondered whether a new form of entertainment could be fashioned from this ostensibly documentary material, so as "to transport audiences to places they'd never imagined."

After weeks of editing the pictures, he secured a sponsor—the *New York Globe*—and then booked the Century Theater on Central Park West. "DIRECT FROM JERUSALEM, BERLIN, AND PARIS! LOWELL THOMAS! THREE WEEKS ONLY!" announced a banner in a display window full of war memorabilia at Lord & Taylor on Fifth Avenue.

The highlight of Thomas's show was the film shot by his cameraman, Harry Chase: it rendered the audiences spellbound. Included was the first aerial footage ever photographed in the Middle East. And, although Thomas's media spectacular at first presented a different "film lecture" each night of the week, it was only the Jerusalem program that had the "huge mobs" and that was favorably reviewed as "the most smashing picture...ever seen." In contrast, the shows about the Western Front, France and Flanders, or Serbia had comparatively low attendance.

When the engagement at the Century had finished, a wealthy Jewish group—including the Baron de Rothschild—convinced Thomas to book the gigantic Madison Square Garden. There, the show played to capacity

The Arab delegation to the Paris peace conference, 1919. Left to right: Rustum Haidar (Feisal's secretary), Nuri Said, Captaine Pisani, Emir Feisal, Lawrence, Feisal's slave, and Captain Hassan Kadri.

Lawrence enters Damascus, October 1, 1918, in "Blue Mist," his armored Rolls-Royce tender. Driver is S. C. Rolls.

for eight weeks. Nathan Straus—owner of Macy's—became taken with the Holy Land presentation, calling it "the most wonderful motion picture production I have ever seen." Straus chartered a fleet of double-decker buses to roam Brooklyn and the Bronx, advertising Thomas's "travelogue." Enthused at the capacity crowds night after night, Thomas started planning a nationwide American tour for the autumn.

However, fate intervened in the person of renowned British impresario Percy Burton. Scouting New York for new talent, Burton was thunderstruck at Thomas, "an American, telling of a British hero—Lawrence—of whom he, a Briton, had never even heard." Indeed, a British history of the Great War published by *The Times* in 1919 contained not a word about Lawrence in its section on the Arab campaign! Burton *demanded* that Lowell Thomas bring his show to London. Thomas jokingly agreed, on condition that two outrageous requests be fulfilled: a summer engagement at the prestigious Royal Opera House, Covent Garden, be arranged, and that a personal invitation from King George himself be extended! Burton retorted, "You don't want much, do you?"

A month later, Burton cabled: Covent Garden was booked, and the king was awaiting the show!

On the sea voyage to England, Thomas blended together his hitherto separate Allenby and Lawrence productions, calling the new show *The Last Crusade—With Allenby in Palestine and Lawrence in Arabia*. Sir Thomas Beecham, Covent Garden's foremost conductor, cordially greeted Thomas upon his arrival: "I say you have no more chance here than a snowball in the Jordan Valley."

Thomas's London show opened on August 14, 1919.

On stage was a "moonlight on the Nile" set borrowed from the opera *Joseph and His Brethren*. A dancer performed a "dance of the seven veils." In the background—accompanied by music of the Royal Welsh Guards Band—the Mohammedan call to prayer was heard, chanted by Thomas's wife. Thomas boldly announced "Here I am, and now come with me to the lands of mystery, history, and romance. . ." Then, with a running narration to accompany the film and "lantern-slide" show, Thomas created a sort of Arabian Nights spell. At the conclusion of the presentation, the audience rose and gave Thomas a ten-minute standing ovation. And Sir Thomas Beecham rushed up to apologize.

The next day, not a word about Thomas's extravaganza was to be found in the theater columns of London's multitude of morning papers. Instead, on their front pages, Thomas found "reviews full of such ardent tribute as to require even a prudent man to be helped down to earth." Indeed, London's most widely read drama crit-

American newsman–adventurer Lowell Thomas and Lieutenant-Colonel T. E. Lawrence, 1918.

ic wrote "This illustrated event is a triumphant vindication of the power of moving pictures. . . It seems almost a national misfortune that this series of wonderful speaking pictures should ever have to be withdrawn."

Thomas's show sold out its intended run immediately. Rudyard Kipling, George Bernard Shaw, and the Emir Feisal attended, along with "members of the royal family and both houses of Parliament, generals who had fought in the Middle East, theatrical stars, industrial tycoons, and the titled elite of Mayfair." One night, Prime Minister David Lloyd George appeared, together with his young cabinet minister Winston Churchill. After the show, Lloyd George announced to the press, "Everything that Mr. Lowell Thomas tells us about Colonel Lawrence is true. In my opinion, Lawrence is one of the most remarkable and romantic figures of modern times."

Thus, the legend of "Lawrence of Arabia" was born, a child of the cinema.

The overwhelmingly favorable response to his presentation caused Thomas to question the wisdom of returning to the United States at the end of August. Only one complaint had been raised, and that was from Lawrence himself, who had attended the show incognito. His life had been changed by Thomas's triumph. He could not venture out without being mobbed, and he was receiving a hundred letters a day, including marriage proposals. Lawrence would later complain that "Mr. Thomas made me into a kind of matinee idol." Lawrence, it seems, had become the world's first media-created superstar.

Thomas, however, suggested that the "reluctant" Lawrence "had a genius for backing into the limelight."

Finally, Lawrence left London for the solitude of Oxford. There, supported by a fellowship at All Souls College, he continued writing the account of the Arab Revolt which he had begun at the Paris conference earlier that year. Lawrence had been asked by the Foreign Office to attend the peace negotiations as an adviser and interpreter to Emir Feisal, who was there representing the Arab cause. Lawrence was deeply depressed during these months and was frustrated and angered at the unsatisfactory outcome. The carving up of the Holy Land by the British and the French served to reinforce his belief that he had betrayed his Arab friends. The diplomatic battles seemed to have drained his spirit even more than the military ones. However, he persevered with his book, saying that "the story I have to tell is one of the most splendid ever given a man for writing."

Lowell Thomas eventually decided to cancel his projected American autumn tour, thereby forfeiting

ROYAL OPERA HOUSE,
COVENT GARDEN.
PROPRIETORS . . . THE GRAND OPERA SYNDICATE, LTD.

Commencing Thursday Evening, August 14th, and Nightly at 8.30.
Matinees Wednesday, Thursday and Saturday at 2.30.
PERCY BURTON
(by arrangement with the Grand Opera Syndicate)
presents
AMERICA'S TRIBUTE TO BRITISH VALOUR
IN THE PERSON OF
LOWELL THOMAS
in
His Illustrated Travelogue of the British Campaigns :

With Allenby in Palestine

including
THE CAPTURE OF JERUSALEM
and
THE LIBERATION OF HOLY ARABIA.

Above: Cover of program sheet for Lowell Thomas's show.
Right: Depiction of The Palestine Film Lecture *at Covent Garden, from* The Sphere *magazine, August 23, 1919.*

thousands of dollars in deposits. The Covent Garden engagement was extended into the fall. In early October, Lord Allenby returned to England after serving as High Commissioner for Egypt after the war. The announcement that he and Lady Allenby would attend the Thomas show caused a sensation. The Welsh Guards greeted their entrance into the hall with "Hail the Conquering Hero" and the audience rose in a burst of applause.

Now, Covent Garden's opera season was about to begin, and Thomas was forced to move to the Royal Albert Hall. With a capacity of 6,000, it was the largest concert auditorium in the world. No extended engagements had ever been attempted there: Thomas's presentation successfully ended that tradition. Over a million people would attend his presentations in London alone. Thomas would later adapt his lecture material into *With Lawrence in Arabia*, the first Lawrence biography. The book sold more than 100,000 copies in England alone.

One Sunday, the Thomas home near Wimbledon Common had a surprise visitor. Lawrence had surreptitiously returned to London, having been given the free use of a friend's attic apartment at 14 Barton Street, near Westminster Abbey. Lawrence told Thomas about his continuing struggles to complete *Seven Pillars of Wisdom*. Later, on another visit, Lawrence casually announced that, while changing trains at Reading Station, the *Seven Pillars* manuscript had been lost.

By early in the new year, Lawrence had completed

the arduous task of preparing a hastily written second draft. He then decided to create a finely printed private edition of *Seven Pillars,* and commissioned artist Eric Kennington to create a collection of pastel portraits of the major Arab personalities of the revolt. The first time Kennington had in fact seen Lawrence had been on film, at Albert Hall. He later remarked, "Glorious photography, glamour and oratory. I came out drunk." Kennington, refusing to paint from photographs, visited Arabia for four months to obtain the required sittings.

Meanwhile, in order to obtain criticism of his work without fear of another "lost manuscript fiasco," Lawrence decided to produce copies of his third draft— now a huge 330,000-word document. He had the *Oxford Times* typeset the book in double-column newspaper style, and then had eight copies printed. This task was completed by July 1922. George Bernard Shaw and his wife Charlotte, together with many other friends, were asked to read and criticize this "Oxford Edition."

G.B.S. wrote T.E.L., "Confound you and your book: you are no more to be trusted with a pen than a child with a torpedo."

The published book would later thank "Mr. and Mrs. Bernard Shaw for countless suggestions of great value and diversity: and for all the present semicolons."

Finally, in late 1923, Lawrence's plans for a limited printing of his opus were arranged. He initially decided to produce only 100 copies which would be offered at the then astronomical price of thirty guineas (about a hundred times the selling price of books of the day!). Lawrence would oversee the book's actual production and distribution, and would act as editor of his own manuscript. By September 1924, proof copies of a number of chapters were being circulated for criticism. The first "final" sections would not be printed until early in 1925 and the complete books were not ready for the binders until late in 1926.

T. E. Lawrence's "titanic" epic, the lavishly illustrated *Seven Pillars of Wisdom* subscribers' edition, was now

Delegates to the Cairo Peace Conference visit the Pyramids on March 20, 1921. The outcome gave Lawrence some satisfaction as he helped secure a throne for Feisal in Iraq. Left to right: Clementine and Winston Churchill, British desert traveler–historian–archaeologist Gertrude Bell, T. E. Lawrence.

complete, and he had orders for all 200 copies of the increased printing.

Lawrence had made it clear that he had written his monumental autobiography to assuage his conscience and to ensure that the tale of the Arab Revolt was thoroughly chronicled. However, he was also adamant that *Seven Pillars* should never appear in a widely available edition during his lifetime: he was determined that he would not profit from any publishing venture which exploited his experiences with the Arabs, whom he felt he had betrayed.

However, in contrast to his earlier expectations that these sales would yield at least a small profit, the true cost of meeting his ambitious goals now threatened Lawrence's well-being. The books he had sold for about £30 each had cost him £90 each.

Lawrence was now £13,000 in debt, equivalent to about half a million dollars purchasing power in the 1980s. An effort to clear this debt was to lead to a bizarre encounter with the world of commercial filmmakers.

CHAPTER 2

THE EPICS
THAT NEVER WERE

"WE CAN'T JUST DO NOTHING."
"WHY NOT? IT'S USUALLY BEST."

—BRIGHTON AND ALLENBY, IN DAMASCUS

The 1962 Spiegel–Lean epic masterpiece *Lawrence of Arabia* was not the first attempt to dramatize the story of T. E. Lawrence's war adventures for the screen. It was merely the first *successful* one, and the striking exception to a lengthy and agonizing series of failed cinematic enterprises.

The earliest effort occurred in the fall of 1926.

The very first copy of *Seven Pillars of Wisdom* had just been delivered to King George V, the sole purchaser from whom Lawrence refused payment.

A strategy had been devised to start to clear his mammoth debt. The publisher Jonathan Cape offered Lawrence an initial payment of £3,000 in return for an abridged edition of *Seven Pillars,* to be called *Revolt in the Desert. Revolt* was to objectively describe Lawrence's Arabian adventures with all the "personal" aspects of his involvement ruthlessly expurgated.

In spite of this publishing prospect, a very immediate need for funds seems to have prompted Lawrence to approach a young British film producer, Herbert Wilcox, in the fall of 1926. In his autobiography, Wilcox described the unique event, which had taken place four decades earlier, when he was relatively new in the cinema industry:

A literary agent, Raymond Savage, had brought a young author to see me with the view of producing a silent film of a book he had just completed. The young author was slight and short, about 5 ft. 3 ins. at the most and not very prepossessing. However, Raymond Savage, being a top agent, would not have brought him had he not been important.

The title of the book meant nothing to me, but Savage suggested the author roughly outline his story and relate one or two of the more spectacular incidents.

In a hesitant voice, which became stronger and deeper as he went along, the author gave me an outline of his book which I found extremely interesting but not good cinema and in spots rather sordid. In particular he told me of the homosexual advances of a Turkish chief and how in desperation one night he fought him off with what he called "a knee kick," which resulted in the the chief being disinterested in homo or any other form of sexual activity for a week or so, and the author being scourged and tortured for his attack. Since he was a British subject, masquerading as an Arab, which

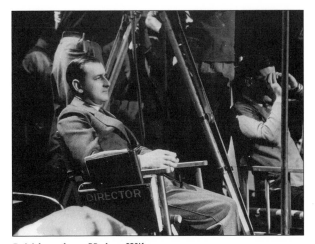

British producer Herbert Wilcox.

language he spoke like a native, his great fear was that during the torture he would cry out in English and not Arabic.

The book was *The Seven Pillars of Wisdom*—the author T. E. Lawrence.

I ventured the opinion that I could not see cinema audiences seeking entertainment being attracted to such a subject. Lawrence did not agree—neither did Savage. Lawrence told me that one day it would make an outstanding film. He failed to sway me—but how right he was.

Lawrence would never again display any real enthusiasm for a cinematic portrayal of his Arabian adventures. Indeed, only a year after Wilcox's rejection, British director M. A. Wetherell was contemplating a film project based upon Lawrence's newly published bestseller *Revolt in the Desert*. However, the royalties from sales of 30,000 copies had cleared Lawrence's debt, and he was not interested.

In August 1925, Lawrence had been permitted to transfer back to the RAF, on the promise that he would avoid all publicity. When *Revolt in the Desert* was issued in 1927, he had himself assigned to overseas duty in India. While stationed there he completed *The Mint*, a raw account of his experiences in the ranks: it was withheld from publication until 1955. Persistent rumors that the legendary Lawrence of Arabia was engaged in spy activity on the Afghanistan frontier led to his being recalled to England in 1929.

From 1931 onward he served as a designer and master mechanic of speedboats for the RAF, at various naval flying boat installations. T.E.—now Aircraftman T. E. Shaw—had become interested in development of a high-speed rescue boat to pick up downed airmen. He participated in the creation of a 30 mph thirty-foot cruiser,

Top: "Aircraftman Shaw" (T. E. Lawrence) on pontoon of De Havilland 60X Moth seaplane, early 1929, St. Helier, Isle of Jersey. Above: Captain Basil Liddell Hart. Left: Shaw/Lawrence, circa 1925, during his second period of enlistment in the Royal Air Force.

Above: British director M. A. Wetherell. Right: Cinematographer Freddie Young, twenty-five, and Wetherell, in Cairo in 1927 to film The Tragedy of the Kraskar.

which became the prototype for the WWII patrol torpedo (PT) boat. Lawrence documented his work in a superbly written eighty-page technical manual, *The 200 Class Royal Air Force Seaplane Tender*. Having somewhat recovered his health and mental outlook, Lawrence was now apparently content with this work.

Front and back of collectors' card, showing Leslie Howard, 1936, as Romeo. Text mentions his forthcoming role as T. E. Lawrence.

The year 1934 marked the beginning of the truly noteworthy attempts to film Lawrence's story. March of that year saw the publication of an authorized biography, *'T. E. Lawrence': In Arabia and After*, by famed military strategist Captain Basil Liddell Hart. In keeping with Lawrence tradition, even the book's title was to result in public controversy and discussion. The *Daily Express* in a story headlined NEW MYSTERY OF "LAWRENCE OF ARABIA"–WHAT IS HIS REAL NAME? remarked that "Liddell Hart . . . by putting the [subject's] name in quotation marks–thus 'T. E. Lawrence' as the title–. . .creates a new mystery." Lawrence actually insisted that Liddell Hart use this form since T.E.'s legal surname at that time was not Lawrence, but "Shaw." The *Express* instead dwelt upon a comment on the very first page of the book:

> The friends of his manhood called him "T.E.," for convenience, and to show that they recognized how his adopted surnames–Lawrence, Ross, and Shaw, whatever they were–did not belong.

"John Hume Ross" was Lawrence's alias while in the RAF from August 1922 till January 1923; "T. E. Shaw" was his identity from March 1923 onward. Lawrence feared that unwanted investigations into his murky ancestral background prompted by the publication of Liddell Hart's biography might represent a serious intrusion into his privacy.

Two months after the book was published, Raymond Savage again attempted to negotiate a Lawrence-related deal between a filmmaker and an author. He approached Captain Liddell Hart, now a celebrated biographer as well as a certified "Lawrence expert." Savage noted that film magnate Alexander Korda was interested in having Liddell Hart do the "scenario"–a detailed outline of scenes, characters, and situations–for a movie based upon Lawrence's abbreviated account of his adventures in

Arabia. Indeed, Liddell Hart had just read in the British press that *Revolt in the Desert* was to be produced by Korda for his company, London Film Productions, with Leslie Howard starring and Lewis Milestone directing.

A true giant of the British cinema industry, Alexander Korda would direct nearly 60 films during his lifetime, and produce, or have an association with, another 100! Included were such classics as *The Private Life of Henry VIII, Rembrandt, Lady Hamilton, The Scarlet Pimpernel, Sanders of the River, Things to Come, Fire over England, The Four Feathers, Conquest of the Air, The Thief of Baghdad, Jungle Book, The Third Man*, and his notorious, never-to-be-completed epic, *I Claudius*. In the mid-thirties, a great proportion of the 18 million people who attended British cinemas each week eagerly sought out the latest Korda film.

Liddell Hart, seeking his friend Lawrence's approval, drove down to the Hubert Scott-Paine shipyard at Hythe, near Southampton. On this June 2 visit, Liddell Hart was treated to a spin in T.E.'s experimental speedboat and was given a talk on Lawrence's ideas about the future of naval warfare. With regard to the Korda film, T.E. said–to Liddell Hart's surprise–that the project was

British film mogul Alexander Korda.

Basil Liddell Hart discusses "Lawrence films" with T.E.L. near Southampton shipyards, June 2, 1934.

"quite in order," since only an "authorized" film would prevent "uncontrolled" Hollywood versions with "sex-interest and sensationalism" from being made. Further, he approved of Liddell Hart as author of the film's scenario.

However, incredibly, Lawrence also added that he might later make a private effort to dissuade Korda from doing the film!

Lawrence had, in fact, already put these intentions on record in a letter he wrote on May 24 to Edward Eliot, a London solicitor, and one of the trustees empowered by him to handle all rights to *Revolt in the Desert:* "Tell your film negotiators that I'll be a very awkward pebble in the rock of their progress!"

Lawrence followed up with a letter to his bank manager, Lieutenant Colonel Robert Buxton, a longtime associate and another *Revolt* trustee, stating that "Savage is a nuisance with his film-greediness, but I suggest that Korda will not play. I am too recent to make a good subject—too much alive, in fact." T.E. made it very clear that, even if the ostensibly independent trust that he had appointed *did* sell his book rights to London Films, he "doubted if [those rights alone] would give them the power to put a lot of living people [in their film]."

In early June 1934, Liddell Hart visited Korda at the Elstree studios near London, and there discussed the film in broad terms. Korda also mentioned that he wanted to cover parts of Lawrence's life outside of the limits of

Revolt in the Desert, and that Liddell Hart's Lawrence biography would serve admirably in this respect. From that point onward, Liddell Hart apparently considered that both the adoption of his Lawrence biography as source material for the Korda film and his employment with Korda as a "Lawrence adviser" were a certainty.

As we shall see, Captain Liddell Hart was to become involved in every subsequent attempt to make a Lawrence film. On a wider scale, Liddell Hart (later Sir Basil) in fact functioned as a sort of "Lawrence bureau." He meticulously monitored and recorded all Lawrence-related activities for the next three decades. And he also was to be the driving force behind a fierce and loyal group of T. E. Lawrence aficionados who would sporadically mount vociferous press campaigns in defense of their hero's reputation.

Between July and November of 1934, Liddell Hart followed the extended dealings between Korda and the *Revolt in the Desert* trustees. Lawrence also monitored these ongoing negotiations, and apparently was resigned to the fact that the rights would be sold. He told Buxton in early July: "If they want to film the rotten book, they must." However, he asked that Buxton arrange to see a copy of the scenario before filming commenced, and to pass it along to him. Lawrence also asked him to preview the final film before any press or trade showings. And T.E. even made casting suggestions! Walter Hudd—who had played the Lawrence-based character, Private Meek, in Bernard Shaw's play *Too True to Be Good*—"was magnificent," said Lawrence, adding, "perhaps Leslie Howard might be more unlike [me], which would be an advantage!"

Finally, in December, Savage wrote Liddell Hart to

T.E.L. suggested that British stage actor Walter Hudd star as Lawrence of Arabia in Korda's Revolt in the Desert.

In October 1931, while walking in a London street, Shaw/Lawrence was accosted by photographer Howard Coster, who claimed that "you and Gandhi are the two people I want to [photograph]." Lawrence sat for a dozen exposures.

confirm that London Films and the *Revolt* trustees had agreed to terms.

The signed agreement specified that "all the motion picture rights throughout the world. . .are granted for a period of 8 years. . .including the right to exhibit the. . .motion picture by television (!) and any other process of distant transmission now known or hereafter to be devised." It was specified that the filmmakers must be British. The terms were to be £6,000 and 7-1/2 percent of the gross receipts. The trustees were to see the film before cutting. And if any dispute over "deviation from [the] approved scenario" arose, the arbitration would be supervised by the Right Honorable Winston Churchill. London Films also agreed that there would be "no departure from historical accuracy" and no inclusion of subsidiary events "likely to be objectionable or offensive by reason of their sentimental nature. . .and that no female characters otherwise than as members of crowds. . .shall be introduced." This final stipulation echoed Lawrence's conclusive comment in *Seven Pillars:* ". . .from end to end of it, there was nothing female in the Arab movement, but the camels."

Foreign language rights were granted in Danish, Norwegian, Czechoslovakian, Polish, Finnish, and Hebrew.

And rights to any songs derived from the work were conceded!

Liddell Hart hoped that a contract for his literary services would soon be forthcoming. However, at the end of January 1935, he received shocking news: *Savage curtly informed him that Lawrence had managed to persuade Korda not to do the film after all!*

This decision had been reached at a recent dinner meeting attended by Lawrence, Korda, and "*Revolt* trustee" Edward Eliot. There, Lawrence pointed out to Korda "the inconveniences his proposed film would set in my path. . .and [we] ended the discussion by agreeing that it should not be attempted without my consent." Obviously, such consent would not be forthcoming.

Moreover, Lawrence cleverly persuaded Korda *not* to announce that the film had been abandoned, since, as long as it remained on Korda's project list, other producers would "avoid thought of it."

Lawrence revealed even more details of this pivotal event in a letter written on February 4 to his other authorized biographer, the celebrated writer Robert Graves:

> I had not taken seriously the rumors that [Korda] meant to make a film of me, but they were persistent, so at last I asked for a meeting and explained that I was inflexibly opposed to the whole notion. [Korda] was most decent and understanding and has agreed to put it off till I die or welcome it. Is it age coming on, or what? But I loathe the notion of being celluloided. My rare visits to cinemas always deepens me in a sense of their superficial falsity [and] vulgarity. . . .The camera seems wholly in place as journalism: but when it tries to re-create, it boobs and sets my teeth on edge.
>
> So there won't be a film of me.

Savage was unwilling to accept defeat. He reminded Liddell Hart that Lawrence's influence extended only to "an official film approved by the Trustees." He asked if Liddell Hart would now be prepared to write a scenario based on his book alone, for possible use by another film company. Savage also expressed deep regret that his ten years of involvement—first with Wilcox and then with Korda—had come to naught at the very last moment. However, he suggested that there could be a faint chance that Lawrence might be persuaded to change his mind.

Shortly thereafter, on March 22, Lawrence visited Liddell Hart and gleefully explained how Korda had been

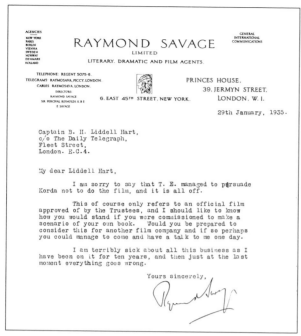

AGENCIES
NEW YORK
PARIS
BERLIN
VIENNA
SWEDEN
NORWAY
DENMARK
HOLLAND

GENERAL
INTERNATIONAL
COMMUNICATIONS

RAYMOND SAVAGE
LIMITED
LITERARY. DRAMATIC AND FILM AGENTS.

TELEPHONE: REGENT 5075-6.
TELEGRAMS: RAYMOSAVA, PICCY. LONDON.
CABLES: RAYMOSAVA. LONDON.
DIRECTORS
RAYMOND SAVAGE
SIR PERCIVAL REYNOLDS K.B.E
E. SAVAGE

6. EAST 45TH STREET, NEW YORK.

PRINCES HOUSE.
39. JERMYN STREET,
LONDON. W. I.

29th January, 1935.

Captain B. H. Liddell Hart,
c/o The Daily Telegraph,
Fleet Street,
London. E.C.4.

My dear Liddell Hart,

      I am sorry to say that T. E. managed to persuade
Korda not to do the film, and it is all off.

      This of course only refers to an official film
approved of by the Trustees, and I should like to know
how you would stand if you were commissioned to make a
scenario of your own book. Would you be prepared to
consider this for another film company and if so perhaps
you could manage to come and have a talk to me one day.

      I am terribly sick about all this business as I
have been on it for ten years, and then just at the last
moment everything goes wrong.

Yours sincerely,

Letter from Raymond Savage to Liddell Hart.

put off doing his *Revolt in the Desert* movie. Liddell Hart responded by mentioning Savage's bold new suggestion: a film based solely upon the Liddell Hart biography, thus bypassing both Lawrence's trustees and *Revolt in the Desert* altogether. With surprising detail, Lawrence then revealed that he already knew of "certain American companies" that were considering such a course of action and—astonishingly—added that he had no objection to the scheme! Finally, Lawrence suggested to

Liddell Hart that they might even work together on such an enterprise as it matured. Now it seemed that Lawrence had changed his mind: while he would not approve a film based on his own words, he might tolerate one based on someone else's.

At that time, Lawrence had just retired from the RAF, and was continually hounded by newsmen. He was unable to live peacefully at Clouds Hill, his little cottage in Dorset, because of their presence. Desperate, he fled his home, appealing to the Press Association and London photographic agencies to "call off their men." In April, he returned to Clouds Hill, seemingly free from harassment.

Another of his immediate concerns was the cost of running his powerful Brough Superior SS 100 motorcycle. He nicknamed it "Boanerges," meaning "sons of thunder." Lawrence's joy in motorcycling is described in his last book, *The Mint:*

> The burble of my exhaust unwound like a long cord behind me. Soon my speed snapped it, and I heard only the cry of the wind which my battering head split and fended aside. The cry rose with my speed to a shriek: while the air's coldness streamed like two jets of iced water into my dissolving eyes. I screwed them to slits and focused my sight 200 yards ahead of me on the empty mosaic of the tar's gravelled undulations. . . . A skittish motor-bike with a touch of blood in it is better than all the riding animals on earth.

Left: T.E.L. on Brough Superior "Boanerges," 1925-26. Above: Lawrence's cottage at Clouds Hill, Dorset, near Bovington Camp, where he was stationed in the Army Tank Corps. In 1923-25, Lawrence worked on Seven Pillars *there while off-duty. In 1929, Lawrence bought the cottage and improved it, intending to retire there.*

8. V. 35

No: wild mares would not at present take me away from Clouds Hill. It is an earthly paradise and I am staying here till I feel qualified for it. Also there is something broken in the works, as I told you: my will, I think. In this mood I would not take on any job at all. So do not commit yourself to advocating me, lest I prove a non-starter. Am well, well-fed, full of company, Calorious and unmixt — customed. News from China — NIL. Their area now a centre of disturbance. TES

Letter from T.E.L. to Lady Astor, written a month before his death.

Eric Kennington, *Seven Pillars* artist, recalled, "...the eyes gazed at the horizon as if in ownership...then the disappearance in a roar of dust. He was happy. He never looked back. Traveling twice as fast as his boats—nearly as fast as his brain."

Lawrence was not sure what his future would be, but contemplated another twenty years in which "to taste the delights of natural England, as has been my life's wish." In a letter to Liddell Hart, the previous year, Lawrence had wistfully expressed his longing to finally "taste the flavour of true leisure... May [life] be like...a great Sunday that goes on and on."

Lawrence still corresponded with many of his distinguished contemporaries, often writing on a small card imprinted with the announcement: "To tell you that in the future I shall write very few letters. T.E.S."

On May 7, Lawrence received a letter from socialite Lady Nancy Astor, then a Member of Parliament, who suggested that in the next government, he might be called upon to help reorganize Britain's defense forces. Lawrence immediately refused, suggesting that "wild mares would not at present take me from...my earthly paradise," and also declaring that "there is something broken in the works,...my will." He added that he was unwilling to take on any new tasks, "lest I prove a non-starter."

A week later, Lawrence received a letter from novelist Henry Williamson, proposing a visit to Clouds Hill in order to drop off a manuscript. That day, T.E. rode his Brough motorcycle down to the post office at nearby Bovington army camp, and sent a telegram in reply.

On the way back, Lawrence swerved his motorcycle in order to avoid two young cyclists he had overtaken.

He lost control and was thrown from his machine. Unconscious, he was eventually transported to the military hospital at Bovington Camp. There, he was tended by a Royal Army Medical Corps doctor who was later joined by Sir Farquhar Buzzard, the king's physician, as well as a London Hospital brain specialist and a London lung specialist. Having received severe brain damage, Lawrence lay in a coma for six days.

At 8:30 A.M., on May 19, 1935, he died.

Arnold Lawrence, told that his older brother had sustained irreparable brain damage, stated "it would have been a tragedy if he had recovered."

Lawrence once again was to dominate the nation's headlines. The *Daily Sketch* of May 20 trumpeted "TOO BIG FOR WEALTH AND GLORY: SIMPLE VILLAGE FUNERAL FOR UNCROWNED KING OF THE DESERT." *The Times* headlined "LAWRENCE DEAD: FATAL END TO CYCLE CRASH," and devoted nearly a full page to tributes. The lengthy *Times* obituary, written by Captain Basil Liddell Hart, commenced "If a tragic waste, it was none the less a fitting way in which T. E. Lawrence met his end. It was, I imagine, the way he would have chosen....To him, the sensation of speed was the one that never palled, seeming to free the spirit from the bondage of human limitations."

Lord Allenby broadcast a tribute, declaring that "[Lawrence] was the mainspring of the Arab movement. He knew their language, their manners, their mentality. He understood and shared their merry, sly humor. In daring he led them, in endurance he equaled, if not surpassed their strongest."

As the nation mourned, numerous theories were put forward to account for the tragedy. At the inquest on May 21, a witness to the accident insisted that a black

T.E.L on bicycle, February 26, 1935. Early that year, after his discharge from the RAF, Lawrence cycled around southern England.

17

Left: Lawrence was buried in the graveyard annex of St. Nicholas' Church, Moreton, Dorset, May 21, 1935. Above: Arnold Lawrence is immediately behind the coffin. A.W. arranged the funeral and chose the tombstone and inscription.

while George Bernard Shaw was in South Africa. Lawrence's mother Sarah and his brother Bob were steaming down the Yangtze River in China on a missionary journey.

On the very day of Lawrence's funeral, there appeared on the front page of the *News Chronicle* an article which pointed out that the rights to both *Seven Pillars of Wisdom* and *Revolt in the Desert* had been purchased by London Films. Alexander Korda was quoted extensively:

Colonel Lawrence and I discussed the film of his book some time ago and he asked me not to make the production until he gave his consent, or, he added jokingly, until he was dead. I agreed to respect his wishes. It was a part of the agreement with the trustees that the script of any film must be submitted to Colonel Lawrence for his approval. It was never my intention to make a romantic film about Lawrence. The idea was to present an historical record.

Colonel Lawrence was the greatest personality I have ever met, and I would never do anything which I believe would not meet with his approval. If his relatives or close friends object to the film being made, it will never be made by me and no one else will be allowed to make it. I could never contemplate such a thing.

This article was followed two days later by another report, in the *Daily Mail*. Korda quoted T.E. as having said that "he was done with 'Lawrence of Arabia' and wanted to forget him." The film magnate also begged off discussing

car was overtaken by Lawrence shortly before he encountered the cyclists. The two boys, when interviewed, swore that there had been no car.

The theme of the half-century-old mystery surrounding Lawrence's death has centered around the fact that he was an expert motorcyclist, and the overtaking of cyclists is not an unusual situation to encounter. Had they been hidden from him, until the last moment, by a dip in the road? Had he been sideswiped by the black car? Was Lawrence murdered: by British government officials, who knew that Lawrence was being courted by "undesirables"; by the Nazis, to prevent Lawrence from taking up the Prime Minister's call to reorganize Britain's defense forces; or by numerous other parties who could have had political quarrels with Lawrence: the French, the Zionists, the Bolsheviks, the Arabs, or the IRA?

The mystery of the circumstances surrounding Lawrence's death has never been resolved.

Lawrence's funeral was held at Moreton, Dorset, on May 21. The six pallbearers included Ronald Storrs (who as Oriental Secretary in Cairo had, in 1914, initiated the secret correspondence which led to the Arab Revolt) and Eric Kennington. Mourners included Winston and Clementine Churchill, Lady Astor, Siegfried Sassoon, and Augustus John, who created the most notable oil portraits of Lawrence. Allenby declined to attend,

Alexander Korda persisted in his attempts to dramatize Lawrence's epic story for the silver screen.

Scenes from "Lawrence of Arabia" ACE FILMS LONDON

Ace Films echoed Lowell Thomas with a modest cinema "documentary" presentation of Lawrence's exploits.

realized that year, and consisted primarily of black-and-white still photographs from the museum's collection.

On May 30, Liddell Hart met T.E.'s younger brother, Arnold Walter Lawrence, at lunch. As T.E.'s literary executor, A.W. would—for the next half-century—effectively assume the mantle of "keeper of his brother's legend." When told of Ace Films' approach, A.W. said that Korda had revived the idea of a Lawrence film and urged Liddell Hart to reserve himself exclusively as an adviser for Korda. Two weeks later, A.W. telephoned Liddell Hart, reiterating his request, but adding that Robert Graves would be asked to help, "on the dialogue side." Then, on June 24, Liddell Hart was stunned to hear that Graves had been asked to develop the entire scenario by himself! And, the following day, it became known that Siegfried Sassoon—a major literary figure and a Lawrence admirer from Oxford days—and Colonel W. F. Stirling—a colleague of Lawrence's during the war—had been added to the roster of scenarists for Korda's film.

Apparently "dumped," Liddell Hart complained furiously to the trustees. He argued that, if the "official" film was to have the scope which Korda envisioned, it must go beyond the limits of T.E.'s *Revolt in the Desert,* and "into the wider sphere that is only covered by my book . . . If you do not have either my advice, or legal access to my biography, then you either violate historical accuracy or infringe my copyright!"

Korda, made aware of Liddell Hart's tirade, invited him to discuss the problems in person at Isleworth Studios. Liddell Hart appealed to the *Revolt in the Desert* trustees for support, arguing that only a three-way agreement among them, Korda, and himself would ensure the

his future plans, somberly stating that "the death of Colonel Lawrence is so great a tragedy that it is not fitting to discuss the making of a film."

Liddell Hart later scornfully observed that the very next day after that article appeared, "Korda cabled Robert Graves, asking him to do the scenario for a Lawrence film"!

One week later, on May 29, Liddell Hart received a letter from the managing director of Ace Films. They had plans for producing a documentary entitled *Lawrence of Arabia,* and had been told by the curator of the Imperial War Museum that Liddell Hart was "perhaps, the best friend of Col. T. E. Lawrence." Liddell Hart was asked to help Ace "more accurately tell the story of [Lawrence's] great life." The thirty-six-minute documentary, directed by Ronald Haines, was successfully true historical representation of Lawrence's career. The trustees, however, replied that they must remain autonomous, and caustically advised Liddell Hart to approach Korda alone.

Thus, on July 6, 1935, an exasperated Liddell Hart wrote to Korda. Liddell Hart reminded the producer that T.E.'s approval had been sought and won, and that it seemed that all that remained was the formality of a contract. This would acknowledge that parts of his own book were to serve as source material for the film. Liddell Hart then warned Korda of the legal danger of stepping outside of the events covered by *Revolt in the Desert* and revealed that, by virtue of his role as a "consultant" to Lawrence, he had participated in the creation of that book as well.

Four days later, Liddell Hart received a polite reply from Korda's secretary: "Mr. Alexander Korda has asked me to thank you for your letter of July 6th, the contents of which are receiving his immediate attention."

Liddell Hart never heard from Korda again.

Meanwhile, the legend of *Lawrence of Arabia* was becoming an even more attractive property. The publisher Jonathan Cape ordered an immediate reprint of the hugely successful *Revolt in the Desert*. Lawrence's brother threatened Cape, emphatically restating T.E.'s insistence that *Revolt* had been published only to clear the original *Seven Pillars* debt, and that it must never be reissued.

A.W., however, offered an intriguing alternative: he proposed that *Seven Pillars of Wisdom,* with an introduction by himself, could appear for the first time in an edition generally available to the public. A jubilant Jonathan Cape agreed immediately and feverishly prepared for the immense effort. Sixty tons of paper, filling ten railway cars, together with three miles of binding cloth, were ordered for the first edition. Cape's printer, Alden Press in Oxford, was unable to handle the job alone. Duplicate plates were made, and the Cambridge University Press also began printing the book. Three binderies were required to handle the output of the two printers.

On July 29, 1935—less than three months after Lawrence's death—his 672-page epic autobiographical adventure, *Seven Pillars of Wisdom,* went on sale in the U.K. at a popular price. At the same time, a limited edition of 750 copies, each with four color plates, was published.

In the United States, Doubleday Doran issued a one-page prospectus, announcing that it too would publish

Liddell Hart was unsuccessful in becoming adviser to a Korda Lawrence film.

two editions of *Seven Pillars:* a regular edition, at $5.00, and a deluxe edition, limited to 750 copies, at $25 each. Both would appear in September 1935. In a second pamphlet, the publisher included two color reproductions of plates from the rare subscribers' edition, with a lengthy description of the book's history.

It was a remarkable success. By year's end, over 100,000 copies of *Seven Pillars* had been sold in England alone. In the United States, the book was on the best-seller list for several months. The saga of Lawrence's exploits was now exploding throughout the world.

In England, an appeal had been announced the previous summer seeking funds for a memorial to Lawrence. It was signed by Allenby, Churchill, and Bernard Shaw. Early in 1936, a magnificent bronze bust sculpted by Eric Kennington was unveiled in the crypt of St. Paul's Cathedral. The ceremony afterward included some of Lawrence's favorite music (by Purcell, Bach, and Beethoven), and an address by Viscount Halifax, who was chancellor of T.E.'s alma mater, Oxford University. The sculpture would later gain immortality in an early scene in the Spiegel-Lean film.

The years following Lawrence's death saw the beginning of what has been referred to by critics as "the

Ad in January 1937 National Geographic. Seven Pillars *had been the main selection for the Book-of-the-Month Club for September 1935.*

Lawrence industry." The first effort was a book entitled *T. E. Lawrence by His Friends,* compiled by A. W. Lawrence as a tribute to his late brother. It contained an impressive collection of essays by "friends," who included many of the most famous personages of the time: Bernard Shaw, E. M. Forster, Robert Graves, Lowell Thomas, Lord Allenby, Chaim Weizmann. Perhaps the most memorable accolade of all was penned by Winston Churchill:

> I deem him one of the greatest beings alive in our time. I do not see his like elsewhere. I fear that whatever our need we shall not see his like again . . . His name will live in history . . . It will live in English letters; it will live in the annals of war; it will live in . . . the legends of Arabia.

Alexander Korda now resurrected the Lawrence project by announcing that *Revolt in the Desert* would indeed be filmed that year, with Korda's brother, Zoltan (Zoli) Korda, directing. The first-ever Lawrence screenplay was to be written by American John Monk Saunders, who had scripted *Wings* (1927), winner of the first Best-Picture Academy Award, and *Dawn Patrol* (1930), which earned Saunders a Best Original Screenplay Oscar. Walter Hudd, who resembled Lawrence facially and whom Lawrence had once suggested for the part, was to have the starring role.

Saunders's script was finally approved by the trustees on December 29, 1936.

However, there were to be significant problems. T.E.'s colleague Colonel Stirling had earlier been hired as both technical and military adviser to the film. Stirling held discussions with both the Colonial Office and the For-

American publisher Frank Nelson Doubleday shared T.E.L.'s interest in fine printing. Lawrence often addressed his friend by the Turkish honorific "effendi," a play on Doubleday's initials.

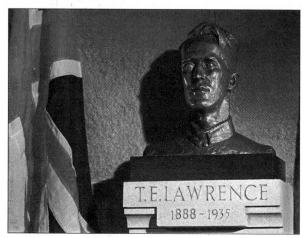

Bust of Lawrence, original sculpted by Eric Kennington in 1926. Sam Spiegel had a casting which was likely the one used in the film.

eign Office. The major issues, he discovered, were centered upon the film's potential to portray the Turks in an unfavorable light, as Turkey was now an ally of Great Britain. Stirling was ordered to permit the TransJordanian government to examine the screenplay for potentially objectionable situations. Additionally, it was suggested that no scenes be staged near the Arabian frontier due to the possibility that the filming might be mistaken for a real battle! However, potential problems were compounded by more realistic ones: Palestine, during most of 1936, was in the grip of a campaign of strikes, attacks, and murders by the locals, who were determined to drive out the British.

Thus, preparations dragged on into 1937. Another script had been prepared, this time by Miles Malleson. (Malleson—later Sir Miles—would eventually coauthor, and co-star in, Korda's 1940 epic *The Thief of Bagdad*.)

Brian Desmond Hurst—who spoke Arabic and had known Lawrence personally—was assigned to direct. Hurst had done significant research, and was about to set out for Jerusalem in order to scout locations for the film. As he was sitting in a seaplane preparing to take off, a launch pulled up alongside the plane. Hurst was told to return immediately to the studio. There, Korda explained that the governor of Palestine wouldn't countenance any large gathering of Arabs. Since the film unit would have to depend on the native population as extras in many scenes, the film would have to be put off.

Korda, experiencing one of his periodic financial problems, then sold the film rights to New World Films. They announced Harold Schuster as director, and American James Wong Howe as cinematographer, with Colonel Stirling continuing as adviser. New World were in turn

plagued by script problems, and within months, they had sold the rights back to Korda!

In October of 1937, Leslie Howard was yet again announced as the star, with William K. Howard as director and a new title, *Lawrence of Arabia*. Location shooting in Egypt was to commence immediately. However, after the Malleson script was examined by the Turkish embassy, objections were raised. Political pressure was then applied by the Foreign Office to suggest that Korda might be persuaded to "self-censor" the film. More realistically, it was requested that the film might be seen by both the Colonial Office and the Foreign Office before release. The film was again canceled!

The next year, 1938, John Clements would star in one of Korda's greatest successes. *The Four Feathers*, a truly epic film, was two years in the making and featured a final battle sequence in which Korda used 4,000 Arabs and tribesman. Clements was later to recall:

> Alex sent for me to make a test . . . for *Lawrence of Arabia*, and I said that the part of Lawrence . . . is already cast with somebody else, who had been advertised for years to play the part . . . [Korda] said, "Don't be silly. Come and make a test." . . . so I went . . . and I got the part. He said, "You must be ready to go to Arabia in six weeks." I said, "Yes, fine,

Author of first-ever Lawrence *screenplay, John Monk Saunders was married to Paramount star Fay Wray in 1928.*

Leslie Howard, announced as Lawrence for second time.

I'd love to do [it]," and nothing happened—I heard nothing for six weeks, eight weeks, nine weeks, ten weeks, and then somebody suddenly showed me a newspaper which said—headline: LESLIE HOWARD TO PLAY LAWRENCE OF ARABIA. Three days later Clifford Evans was to play Lawrence...then Robert Donat...then I was to play Lawrence of Arabia and then Laurence Olivier and nothing more was said and that was the end of that.

While they were filming *The Four Feathers* in the Sudanese desert, a telegram arrived from the head office with a startling request. It asked that when shooting was completed, John Clements, director Zoli Korda, the cameraman, and other unit members stay behind to shoot exteriors for *Lawrence of Arabia!*

Clements, Zoli, and the others ignored the directive and returned to England.

In London, Clements challenged Alexander Korda, "What's the matter with *Lawrence of Arabia?* Why haven't you made *Lawrence of Arabia?*" Korda's reply: "How can I make a film of *Lawrence of Arabia* when we are friendly with the Turks?"

In 1984, Jeffrey Richards and Jeffrey Hubert significantly expanded upon the details of the bizarre Korda affair, first investigated by Korda biographer Karol Kulik. They concluded that, in canceling the film at that par-

ticular point in time, "it is clear that Alexander Korda ultimately accepted the political situation."

Korda yet again sold the rights to *Lawrence of Arabia,* this time to the British subsidiary of Paramount Films. Korda, retained as an adviser to the production, was called upon to answer political objections to the film. His detailed reply is of interest:

Since [World War I], scores of war pictures have been produced showing the German or Austrian armies being defeated, and portraying characters of German or Austrian officers...in a somewhat unfavourable light. I am also quite sure that an equal number of pictures have been produced in Austria and Germany showing officers and soldiers of the French, British, or Italian armies in an equally unfavourable light. Still, I have never heard that one of these pictures has been banned on the same grounds for which the Turkish government objects to the production of a picture dealing with the life of the late Colonel Lawrence. If the principle on which we are asked to withdraw the production of this picture is accepted, the film industry will be faced with the complete extinction of all historical films, for no picture dealing with either ancient or recent history could be made without showing up some country or another in a light which may be regarded as unfavourable or unpleasant by that country.

John Clements, another Lawrence candidate, star of Korda's The Four Feathers.

Oddly, Korda, having made this articulate stand against censorship, then immediately capitulated:

> I am willing to exercise a restraining influence over the production of the film, and I can assure you that the Turkish troops will not be shown in an unfavourable light, and that we will not depict any atrocities on their part and...short of falsifying history, we will do everything in our power to ensure that this picture will not offend the national sensitivity of the Turkish people. I am also willing to preface this picture with a foreword...to the effect that the action of the film takes place during the Great War under the *old* Turkish regime...

```
FIRST SYRIAN:
     Then we must act alone!

FEISAL:
     I am at your mercy.  As an
     officer in Turkish service
     I must live at Military
     headquarters as the guest
     of Jemal Pasha.  Should
     any of you find yourselves
     in extremities and de-
     nounce me - I too shall
     find myself at the end
     of a rope.  For all our
     sakes be patient...


     SLOW DISSOLVE TO:


INTERIOR COURTYARD TURK-
ISH HEADQUARTERS DAMASCUS

Hanging by the neck from a
double row of scaffoldings are
a score of Syrians - members
of the Secret Society, their
hands tied behind their backs.
The dead swing peacefully at the
end of their ropes.  The dying
twist and spin crazily in con-
vulsive jerks.

Fresh victims are brought forward
by Turkish soldiers.  They stand
them on cartridge cases, slip the
nooses over their heads and kick
the support from beneath their
feet.  The doomed men look at
Feisal in last minute appeal. But
Feisal cannot speak.

                         CUT TO:
```

The Turkish atrocities in this excerpt from Saunder's 1936 script might have been politically unacceptable to the British film censors.

Thus, according to Richards and Hubert, Korda "balanced commercial and diplomatic considerations with great delicacy."

Once again, however, a *Lawrence of Arabia* film was not to be! Controversy over the script's portrayal of the Turks "in the blackest colors and shown in the most disparaging light" caused the British Board of Censors' president, Lord Tyrell, to suggest to the film's producers that there was no hope that a Certificate of Approval—without which the film could not be shown in the United Kingdom—would be granted.

The production was abandoned.

But not finally! In 1939, just before the war, Korda reacquired the rights and once again resurrected his *Lawrence* project. In deference to the Board of Censors, he offered to shift the emphasis of the film, devoting only about 45 percent to the Arabian campaign, during which "we will take care to show the Turks as heroic opponents"!

However, as Richards and Hubert later pointed out, "Although the Foreign Office was clearly reluctant to ban the project outright, it was prepared to embark upon a campaign of attrition against it."

In five years, Korda had announced the "imminent production" of *Lawrence of Arabia* half a dozen times. This time it really was the end.

Years later, Korda—who was knighted in 1942—recalled to his nephew Michael Korda that "Churchill was very worried because he felt it was important to have the Turks as allies when [World War II] came."

However, late in 1991, more light was shed upon the reason for Korda's ultimate abandonment of the *Lawrence* project. "FILM MOGUL KORDA WAS SECRET AGENT FOR BRITAIN," screamed a headline in Britain's respected *Observer*. Korda's family had just agreed to make public a secret FBI file on Sir Alex. The file suggested that Korda's 1942 knighthood was a reward from Churchill, not only for moral and financial support over the years, but also—remarkably—for "15 years of transatlantic espionage" under the cloak of his London Films organization!

A decade after the Korda fiasco, the legend of Lawrence of Arabia showed no signs of diminishing. With the passage of time, the story of his exploits had become an even more tantalizing target for the cinema industry. Thus, on the first day of September 1954, Captain Basil Liddell Hart received a telephone call which

Producer Anatole de Grunwald sought Liddell Hart as Lawrence *film advisor.*

heralded the beginning of his involvement in yet another *Lawrence* film odyssey.

Anatole de Grunwald, introducing himself as the famed producer of the films *The Way to the Stars* (1945) and *The Winslow Boy* (1948), revealed that he and British playwright Terence Rattigan were preparing a film script based on the adventures of Colonel T. E. Lawrence. In addition to his stage work, the forty-three-year-old Rattigan had written numerous screenplays, including *Breaking the Sound Barrier,* directed in 1952 by David Lean. Terence Rattigan was a particularly apt choice to do a *Lawrence* script. When Rattigan's family had lived in Cairo, from 1911–13, his father's greatest friend there was Ronald Storrs, T.E.L.'s close associate and mentor.

De Grunwald revealed that he was interested in acquiring the film rights to Liddell Hart's biography for his production company, Comet Films. He also somewhat brusquely added that, by virtue of having registered the subject with the British Film Producers' Association, he alone had exclusive rights to produce a film about Lawrence.

A meeting followed, and terms were quickly agreed upon. De Grunwald would purchase the film, television, and radio rights to Liddell Hart's biography for £3,000, to be paid upon signing. He instructed his solicitors to draw up a contract immediately, and to submit it to his

literary agent, David Higham. Liddell Hart was ecstatic at the news, and proceeded to ask Higham for income tax advice regarding his new windfall!

Events moved quickly at first. De Grunwald contacted Higham and further requested that Captain Liddell Hart be available as principal adviser and consultant to the production unit for a maximum of six months. A fee of 500 guineas was agreed upon for this service, with Liddell Hart to be available when production commenced. And, de Grunwald, added, on-site consultation in the Middle East, if required, would entail further "adequate compensation."

Higham and Liddell Hart mutually agreed that the terms were reasonable, with Liddell Hart's only concern that the time spent on consulting should be paid for at a rate commensurate with his usual per diem fees for writing.

Liddell Hart's confidence, excitement, and enthusiasm about the project grew: he was finally going to be adviser on a *Lawrence* film based upon his own book. In anticipation of a meeting with Rattigan and de Grunwald, he even went to see Rattigan's latest play, and complimented him on its "profundity."

In January 1955, Richard Aldington's *Lawrence of Arabia – A Biographical Enquiry* was published. It was a vitriolic attack on the Lawrence legend. The next month,

Playwright Terence Rattigan wrote 1957 Lawrence *script.*

The Mint, Lawrence's long-suppressed book on life in the army, appeared. So controversial was the book that—two decades after it was written–the general edition was riddled with blank spaces, indicating censored text. The expurgated material, mainly foul barracks language, could be read only by those who had purchased one of an expensive limited edition of 2,000 numbered copies. Lawrence was again in the news, yet again embroiled in controversy.

That April, Rattigan visited the Middle East to do some background work on his script for the *Lawrence* film. By the next month, news of the project had leaked to the London press. They speculated that Denholm Elliott, a young stage actor, would play Lawrence and mistakenly assumed that Korda's London Films was still behind the venture. Finally, at the end of May, the contract between Liddell Hart and Comet Film Productions was signed. The terms noted the agreed-upon sum of £3,000 as compensation to Liddell Hart.

In September, Rattigan flew to Hollywood to discuss the screenplay for William Wyler's upcoming film, *The Prince and the Showgirl.* Then, early in February 1956, the playwright went to the United States again and there joined stars Laurence Olivier and Marilyn Monroe at a New York City press conference to publicly announce the forthcoming film.

In England, Liddell Hart impatiently scanned the press for news updates about the *Lawrence* project: speculation brought Richard Burton and Alec Guinness into the running for the role of Lawrence. In June, having read a press report which suggested that Rattigan had finished the script, Liddell Hart wrote to him. Three weeks later, Rattigan's secretary apologetically replied, explaining that "with the advent of Miss Monroe, I'm afraid he has been extremely busy." Marilyn, with playwright husband Arthur Miller, had arrived in London in early July to start filming.

At Christmas, Rattigan again flew to Hollywood, this

time to commence work on a new screenplay, *Separate Tables,* and to continue work on the *Lawrence* script, which–in reality–was still incomplete. Back in England, in January 1957, Liddell Hart heard that de Grunwald had still not started production, and that because of instability in the Middle East he was unable to give any idea of when he was likely to start. The next month, Comet Films assigned Liddell Hart's agreement to the Rank Organization at Pinewood Studios. Through the press, Liddell Hart soon learned that Rank was expending vast amounts of money in preparing a film based upon his biography, even though he was still not yet in receipt of his advisory fee.

By the summer of 1957, Rattigan had finished both the *Lawrence* and *Separate Tables* screenplays. Early in 1958, the press were reporting an ever-expanding production for *Lawrence of Arabia* with the "biggest-ever budget of £500,000." It was also announced that Anthony Asquith would direct and Dirk Bogarde would star.

Asquith, called "Puffin" due to his slightly hooked nose, was the son of Herbert Henry Asquith. On August 14, 1914, Puffin's father–as Prime Minister of Great Britain–had formally brought his country into the Great War with Germany, the war which ultimately gave rise to T. E. Lawrence's star. Puffin Asquith's first great suc-

Above: In 1958, Dirk Bogarde was to star as Lawrence.
Left: Anthony "Puffin" Asquith was to direct.

cess as a director was the 1938 production of *Pygmalion*, which won a screenplay Oscar for T.E.L.'s friend and mentor George Bernard Shaw. *Pygmalion* was codirected by its star, former Lawrence "candidate" Leslie Howard, and edited by David Lean.

Filming in the Middle East was scheduled to start on April 7, 1958. Asquith and de Grunwald set out early in the spring, together with a cameraman, to scout locations. Eventually, they arrived in Baghdad. Asquith later related details of one of his Iraqi adventures with "Tolly" de Grunwald to his biographer, R. J. Minney:

> We had found a perfect spot on the fringe of Baghdad. I hopped around trying to select the right position for the camera. "Here!" I said. "We can shoot the King from here!"
>
> I heard a sort of gasp and turned to see what had happened to Tolly. Actually there was a large semi-circle of Arabs who had been watching us and on hearing me say "We can shoot the King from here," they completely misunderstood us.
>
> Tolly approached me and said "Let's pack it up and get back to the hotel." I hesitated, assuring him that it won't take more than a few minutes to finish. Tolly, however, suggested that it would be imprudent to stay where they were, pointing out that "some of those men are talking angrily to their neighbours, telling them in Arabic what you have said you would do to their King."
>
> I didn't think that it was really necessary for us to pack up and go, but perhaps Tolly was right. The atmosphere in Baghdad the next day made me uneasy. Tolly suggested that "we'd better go to Egypt and find some locations there. We can come back here when things settle down."

Ironically, that summer, the King of Iraq *was* assassinated.

In early 1992, Sir Dirk Bogarde recalled the chronology of the depressing final months of that *Lawrence* project:

On the 4th of February 1958, Asquith and de Grunwald met at Bogarde's home for "a heavy conference." The next Friday, Bogarde lunched at Pinewood with the costume designer and discussed the robes she was preparing. This was followed four days later by the final fitting of a blond wig that Bogarde was to wear. On Thursday the 16th, Bogarde was off to India for work on another film-in-progress. Back in England on the 27th,

he spent the afternoon with de Grunwald at Pinewood Studios.

"The conferences I had with de Grunwald were mainly about the locations, medical problems [jabs etc.] and how and where the Unit would be accommodated. A large Base Production Camp had been made available to us with showers, air conditioning, and so on. We would shoot in the desert within an hour or so of the Base. Remember, this was never to be Lean's panoramic thing.... We were not making a Technicolour blockbuster."

On Friday, March 14, the contract artists' rep at Rank phoned Bogarde to announce coolly that "*Lawrence* was now off." Bogarde was devasted.

The next day, Puffin Asquith and Tolly de Grunwald, returning from Iraq, were met at London Airport by Earl St. John, Rank's executive producer. He personally gave them the catastrophic message.

Bogarde reported to St. John's office at Rank's on Monday morning. Puffin and Tolly each had a half-hour meeting, with de Grunwald "hurrying out past [Bogarde] with an ashen face and no greeting." Bogarde fumed, "I was ashen too. With fury." When his turn came, St. John offered him no explanation and, as a substitute film, "a jolly comedy set aboard a cruise liner."

Liddell Hart was also in shock. His immediate reaction was to write to de Grunwald, angrily demanding the return of "the three hundred photographs that I lent you."

An explanation later emerged for the film's cancellation. A financial crisis had once again hit the British film industry: *Lawrence*'s £700,000 budget was simply too much.

Dirk Bogarde further described his *Lawrence* experiences in his 1978 autobiography, *Snakes and Ladders:*

> This was to be no monumental epic, rather the straightforward, if there could be such a term applied to such a man, story about Lawrence starting in Uxbridge and ending with his still-unexplained death on a lonely country road to Clouds Hill. I had never, in my life, wanted a part, or script, so much... Wig-fittings, costume-fittings and intensive research now occupied my time entirely. I thought of nothing else but the man I was to represent...I had read every book available on his work and life...

He also spoke to R. J. Minney about the project:

BRITISH SCREEN VISTA

'Lawrence of Arabia' Still on Way —Tax Cut, 'Mouse'—Addenda

By STEPHEN WATTS

LONDON.

IT would be understandable, and no reflection on Sam Spiegel or David Lean, if many a newspaper reader had decided that he would believe in a film about Lawrence of Arabia when he saw it. The project has been announced, postponed, abandoned and revived at intervals over more than twenty years.

The late Alexander Korda, with Lawrence's approval, wanted Sir Winston Churchill to write it and Leslie Howard to star. Jumping over a number of other starts and stops on the subject—in which the names of Laurence Olivier and Alec Guinness were canvassed for the screen Lawrence—we come up to 1956 when Terence Rattigan completed a script that his producer, Anatole de Grunewald,

announced was the best thing he had ever done. This enterprise reached the blueprint stage, with Dirk Bogarde lined up as the hero and Anthony Asquith as director, for the Rank Organization, but was shelved last year.

The present facts are as firm as may be. Negotiations are in progress with Prof. A. W. Lawrence for the rights to his brother's monumental book "The Seven Pillars of Wisdom," (the Rattigan script was based on Liddell Hart's life of Lawrence) and that they have reached an advanced state of agreement may be judged from the announcement that shooting is planned to start in North Africa next spring. The budget is £2,000,000, the schedule is for six months, and the film will be in color and, probably, Todd-AO. No star has yet been named.

A Spiegel-Lean Lawrence *project was first reported in* The New York Times, *June 21, 1959, with North Africa mentioned as a possible filming site. Horizon rep George Littledale visited Libya in late 1959, scouting desert locations for Horizon. Middle East expert St. John Armitage briefed him on the immense difficulties of operating in Libya, noting that "the potential in Jordan, not least the co-operation of the desert patrol, made better sense than Libya. As a consequence of our conversation, he took the Libyan venture no further."*

It was my greatest blow, and I think Puffin's. He had told me "No one can look like Lawrence, but you can probably make us feel how he felt." . . . After a great many conversations [with Puffin] and with Rattigan, my severe doubts about my ability to play Lawrence had been put to rest, a little, by Puff's sureness.

Bogarde also remarked that, with some hesitation, he had at one point asked director Asquith a very personal question about Lawrence: " 'Puff, tell me really and truly, . . .was Lawrence homosexual?' " The actor described Asquith's reaction: "Puffin's face was a study in white horror. The cigarette dropped its ash. With an unsteady hand Puffin removed it, then stubbing it out, he replied, 'Not practising.' "

Terence Rattigan promptly decided to convert the *Lawrence* screenplay into a stage play, *Ross—a dramatic portrait.* He finished it in February 1959, and then left on a three-month world tour.

In mid-June, shortly after his return, *The New York Times* quietly reported that producer Sam Spiegel and director David Lean were now in negotiation with Professor A. W. Lawrence for the film rights to *Seven Pillars of Wisdom.*

By October, *Ross* had been cast, with Sir Alec Guinness to star as Lawrence. As the authority from whom Rattigan's *Lawrence* film rights were derived, Liddell Hart was concerned that the playwright had *not* in fact purchased any stage rights to his biography. On October 28, Liddell Hart wrote to his literary agent, David Higham:

> I looked through the [outline] of *Ross*. . .[and] made note of a number of places where it is evident that Rattigan has drawn on my book . . . The main point, surely, is that he and Anatole de Grunwald together prepared a script for the intended film; that the film rights of my book were bought for this purpose; that they put out a lot of publicity that the script was "based on" my book (a fact that has been published repeatedly, and in papers all over the world); that it has since been announced that Rattigan has turned his script into a play for the stage. It would therefore seem hardly possible for him to argue that his stage play was not related to the previously intended film and that in adapting the script he did not utilize my book. In view of the connection between the two it would seem superfluous to have to prove laboriously that particular passages in the script of the play were derived from my book.

Higham consulted a solicitor, Lawrence Harbottle. He suggested that there was a moral ground for making an approach to Rattigan and asking for a copy of his play, but that either Higham or Liddell Hart should make the approach. Higham, in turn, suggested that Liddell Hart should carry out the deed.

Thus, in mid-November Liddell Hart wrote to Rattigan stating that "I would very much like to see [your script] since the press cuttings have mentioned that it is 'based' on my book." Ever the diplomat, Liddell Hart then tried to sway attention from his obvious attempt to compare the play to the screenplay: he volunteered to do "anything I can towards helping you ensure that the presentation of events and the man [in *Ross*] corresponds as closely as possible to reality."

Rattigan's secretary wrote back claiming that her employer was away in America. Liddell Hart wrote to

Higham: "the porter at my mother-in-law's flat—two doors away from Rattigan—told me that he had seen Rattigan's Rolls driving away." Before Higham could reply, Liddell Hart wrote back: "I have just had a letter from Rattigan, hand written . . . His stay in America seems to have been remarkably brief!" Rattigan, in his letter, claimed that "the production of the play is fairly imminent" and, therefore, all copies of the play were in use! But he would send the first of a new batch being printed to Liddell Hart.

Rattigan then rather convincingly argued that the play was quite different from the film: "I would like to meet the playwright who could deal with Lawrence's Arabian campaign—from Jeddah to Damascus—and use only *three* actors . . . To an historian, such economy might seem ridiculous. To a practising playright, it is a matter of pride." Rattigan suggested that lunch at the St. James' Club might be an appropriate venue for discussing the issue.

However, Rattigan had another problem, much more serious than a disgruntled author in search of his rights. The Lord Chamberlain, the great guardian of the British stage, had requested that Professor A. W. Lawrence, the perpetual protector of his brother's legend, approve the play before presentation was to be allowed. Rattigan had written to Robert Graves, the other major Lawrence biographer, complaining that A.W. had misinterpreted the play. Rattigan wrote back that "it *is* a little hurting that Hugh 'Binkie' Beaumont [London's most powerful theatrical entrepreneur], Sir Alec Guinness, Glen Byam Shaw [the play's director], the Lord Chamberlain's office, and myself should all be considered as being involved in some dark conspiracy to dishonour the memory of T.E.L.—five Aldington's, in fact, for the price of one—when, of course, our purpose is the exact opposite." Rattigan assured Graves that "I am genuinely anxious to make such changes. . .as I can which, without destroying the play's theatrical life, might bring it closer to the historical truth."

At the same time, Graves was corresponding with "the enemy," A. W. Lawrence. "Dear Arnie," he wrote, "It *is* a crooked story, isn't it?" Graves suggested that A.W. might "insist on removal of non-historical material where it misrepresents T.E." Or, he suggested, "you might insist on a foreword which notes that 'Playgoers are warned that this play is deliberately unhistorical, though the names included are historical. In particular, the characters of Ross and the late Colonel Lawrence as he really was, are dissimilar.' " Graves then revealed to A.W. that

"I have Rattigan's letter acknowledging, and indeed glorying in, the breaches of historical truth [in *Ross*]. Do you want this letter? To save time, I'll send it."

Liddell Hart—who had received from A.W. a copy of both Rattigan's letter to Graves, and Graves's letter to A.W.—responded to A.W., declaring that Sir Alec was "more capable of playing the part of T.E. than anyone whose name has been mentioned in the past." It was suggested that perhaps Guinness could personally help ensure that nothing untoward appeared in *Ross*. Liddell Hart then contacted Sir Alec, who was very reassuring. Guinness's attitude, including his feeling that the script was "basically sympathetic to T.E.," was communicated to A.W. by Liddell Hart, who also observed that Sir Alec appeared open to suggestions for script improvements.

Rattigan finally came forward with a script copy for Liddell Hart, and in doing so, the playwright admitted that he had "stalled." Liddell Hart also stated that Graves, who had recently shown interest in the Spiegel-Lean project, had softened his stand on the Rattigan script. Graves had also spoken to Guinness, and then told A.W. that "he's the gentlest and kindest man alive," suggesting that the actor would not want to misrepresent Lawrence. Graves also expressed his condolences: Sarah Lawrence, mother of T.E. and A.W., had passed away that month, at age ninety-eight.

After finally digesting the Rattigan script in detail, Liddell Hart admitted that "its jarring passages are not so numerous as they seemed at first sight" and he thought that "most of them could be corrected by relatively small cuts and changing of wording." He admitted, that "dramatically, it is a brilliant piece of work" and now urged A.W. to work with Rattigan, suggesting that "Rattigan's play might be a powerful antidote to [Lawrence detractor] Aldington."

A.W. replied that, while he appreciated Liddell Hart's work on his behalf, he was reluctant to approach Guinness without an invitation. Moreover, he was determined not to meet with Rattigan at all, lest he appear to be cooperating with the playwright.

Then, although the elaborate maneuvers surrounding *Ross* were far from resolved, an entirely new development was brewing, one which would dramatically impact Rattigan's intentions.

In November 1959, a rotund, cigar-chomping, tough-as-nails, wheeler-dealer of a man, producer Sam Spiegel, had achieved the impossible. Sam Spiegel had somehow convinced A. W. Lawrence to grant him the rights to make a film based upon *Seven Pillars of Wisdom*.

CHAPTER 3

SPIEGEL AND LEAN

*"ONE OF THEM'S HALF MAD.
AND THE OTHER–WHOLLY UNSCRUPULOUS."*

–DRYDEN ADVISING BENTLEY ABOUT
LAWRENCE AND ALLENBY, IN JERUSALEM

Producer Sam Spiegel's interest in T. E. Lawrence dated back to 1926, when he had read the limited "subscribers' edition" of *Seven Pillars of Wisdom*. After the immense popular and critical success of the first Spiegel–Lean collaboration, *The Bridge on the River Kwai*, the partnership had the challenge of conceptualizing a new venture that might conceivably top *Kwai*. Anything similar to it would be a gimmick. But the general theme was attractive: that of focusing closely on the situation of a solitary little man – like the eccentric Colonel Nicholson in *Kwai* – who was thrust by fate into an exotic environment at the focus of tumultuous events. "Our first choice," Lean said, "was to make a film of the life and death of Mahatma Gandhi." However, the producer–director team felt that there was something presumptuous in attempting to film the activities of a man widely believed to be a saint. "To dramatise you must simplify. To simplify, you must leave something out," Lean added. "To decide what aspects of Gandhi's life and personality could be decently left out and which retained was a responsibility which we found ourselves unwilling to accept."

At the end of work on *Kwai* in 1957, Lean met Spiegel in India to further discuss the Gandhi project. There the director learned that Spiegel instead wanted him to

Sam Spiegel and David Lean won seven Academy Awards for 1957's The Bridge on the River Kwai.

collaborate on *Lawrence of Arabia*. The two met almost immediately with *Kwai* screenwriter Michael Wilson to start drafting a shooting outline.

Spiegel's next movie project, however, would be Tennessee Williams's controversial *Suddenly Last Summer*, filmed in 1958–59. When star Montgomery Clift had severe problems delivering his lines, Spiegel secretly conspired to replace him. A screen test was arranged for a little-known actor, whom Spiegel had seen on stage. The producer asked the candidate to pretend to be a doctor performing an operation. Peter O'Toole faced the camera and ad-libbed, "It's all right, *Mrs. Spiegel*, your son will never play the violin again." Spiegel was not amused. Enraged, he swore that O'Toole would never work for him. In any case, costar Elizabeth Taylor ensured that her close friend Clift was not replaced. In the latter phases of *Suddenly Last Summer*'s production, Spiegel spent substantial time aboard his luxury yacht, *Malahne*, consulting with Michael Wilson on the *Lawrence* screenplay.

LOOKING FOR "LAWRENCE"

By early 1960, the news was about to become very public about the deal that Professor A. W. Lawrence had struck with Spiegel for the film rights to *Seven Pillars of Wisdom*. The inner circle of Lawrence watchers, however,

SAM SPIEGEL: THE PRODUCER

On first acquaintance, Sam Spiegel would probably satisfy the popular expectation of the more urbane type of film producer. He has charm, force of personality, is witty, dresses quietly. He speaks four languages fluently and two more sufficiently well to get his own way in them. He likes good living, knows where to find it in most parts of the globe, and delights in sharing it. He is stout, and has a Roman head in which the eyes are still mischievous when the expression is most senatorial. To give a good present and to drive a good bargain afford him equal satisfaction.

But he is also a scholar, versed in European literature and thought. His references in conversation range far in many directions. He is an arbiter of modern painting with a first class collection built up by himself. His respect for artists of all kinds is serious, though his judgment is sharp. He is an informed student of day-by-day politics.

His attitude on all these subjects is liberal and unattached, save that he is fiercely mistrustful of any creed which gives a man a license to persecute his fellows. It is the attitude of a cosmopolitan.

His parents, in Vienna, were booklovers and believed in a life lived earnestly. He was educated at the University there, and first came to the United States to lecture at the University of California at Berkeley.

The late Paul Bern, an M.G.M. Producer, heard Spiegel lecture at Berkeley, and engaged him as reader for original stories in French, German, Spanish, Italian and Polish. The world of films and filmmaking became Spiegel's passion and has been so ever since. Presently he was back in Europe, working for Carl Laemmle, re-filming Universal pictures for foreign distribution.

One of these pictures was the brilliant antimilitarist classic *All Quiet On The Western Front*. The European versions were banned in many areas, largely because of the growing power of the Nazi party. But Spiegel felt committed to this film. He fought the ban on all fronts, in all languages, in all circles. And in part at least he won. *All Quiet* was shown abroad, and in 1932 he had the satisfaction of presenting it to the Disarmament Conference at Geneva.

Elia Kazan, Budd Schulberg, John Huston, Robert Bolt, David Lean, Joseph Mankiewicz these and more, writers and directors of the first rank have joined with Sam Spiegel in forging the scripts and transferring to the screen some of the most notable pictures of our time. The actors and actresses who have starred in Spiegel films have achieved honor and fulfillment in their craft. Sixteen Academy Awards, literally hundreds of Awards from his peers in other countries and other Continents have honored films produced by this bold, venturesome man to whom the making of a motion picture represents the fulfillment of living.

A biographer of the motion picture industry would find it essential to include the productions of Sam Spiegel. From the early *Tales of Manhattan,* the list would go on to *We Were Strangers, The Prowler, The African Queen, On the Waterfront, The Bridge on the River Kwai, End as a Man, Suddenly, Last Summer* and, now *Lawrence of Arabia.*

Some of the qualities which have secured this success have already been listed. One more may be emphasised. He can identify talent at a great distance. If it is in the market-place he can bargain for it boldly. If it is obscure he can persuade it out of hiding. He can do this because he cares for it. And because he can usually offer talent a project worth working on. He hopes and believes that *Lawrence of Arabia* has been another such.

—From the 1962 Souvenir Program

had known of the film project for some time. In a casual postscript to a letter dated November 16, 1959, from Robert Graves to A. W. Lawrence, Graves had remarked, "I am very happy to hear that you are allowing Spiegel, David Lean, and Mike Wilson to make the T.E. film. It will be historical and heroic: the film of the year. The

Rank picture would have been a disaster." At the "Lawrence bureau," the morning mail brought Basil Liddell Hart an impressive invitation to what promised to be a very auspicious event.

At the gala reception, Columbia Pictures announced that Professor Lawrence had been paid "as much as he'll spend in a lifetime" for the rights to his brother's book. The *Daily Mail*, however, revealed that the fee was £30,000. Professor Lawrence was quoted: "It's been years since I last saw a film. I haven't the least idea whether or not I shall see this one."

The evening's highlight occurred when Sam Spiegel, clad in a red jacket with a glass in hand, interrupted the festivities by rapping on a table to demand silence. He proudly announced that American Method actor Marlon Brando had been chosen to play the coveted role of Lawrence of Arabia. A ripple of incredulous silence swept across the packed ballroom. Then a voice from the throng inquired, "Brando, you say. Will it be a speaking part?" Asked how he could make the mumbling, tough-guy Brando credible as the slight, easily blushing Lawrence, Spiegel replied, "In a way, they are very much alike. Both have that mystic, tortured quality of doubting their own destiny. In 1917, Lawrence was barely thirty. Brando is the same age. There is practically nobody else of international magnitude who could play the part."

Earlier in the evening, Spiegel had put on record the fact that "Sir Alec Guinness would have loved the part, but was about fifteen years too old." Had Professor Lawrence approved Brando? "That was not necessary," Spiegel replied. "He gave us blanket approval to do *Seven*

Mr. M. J. Frankovich
Chairman of Columbia Pictures Corporation Ltd.
has much pleasure in inviting
Captain B.H. Liddell Hart
to meet
Mr. David Lean, who will Direct,
and
Mr. Sam Spiegel, who will Produce,
"The Seven Pillars of Wisdom"
the story of Lawrence of Arabia,
a Horizon British Picture
at Claridge's on Wednesday, 17th February, 1960

COCKTAILS 5.30 P.M.
BALLROOM LOUNGE
CLARIDGE'S HOTEL
(BALLROOM ENTRANCE)

R.S.V.P.
COLUMBIA PICTURE CORPORATION LTD
142 WARDOUR STREET, LONDON, W.1.
GERRARD 4321 Ex. 20 or 37.

Pillars. No further objections are expected from him, nor is he entitled to one." Nonetheless, Spiegel added, "Professor Lawrence was anxious that the film should not damage his brother's reputation, that the story should not be ruined by love interest or other romantic treatment. We have no women in our film." But when an *Express* reporter asked, "Will a love affair be introduced into the film?" Spiegel coolly replied, "Surely the love of thousands of men for their leader is a great love story?"

Although Brando's spokesman in Hollywood protested that no contract had been signed, Spiegel was adamant. "He has agreed in principle. You can take it that he will play the part." Former Lawrence candidate Dirk Bogarde was more cynical. "There are so many actors knocking around who have at some time been going to play Lawrence that Alec Guinness and I decided to form a club. We have even designed a tie. Dark background with motif of burnoose and camel."

The *Express* also quoted Spiegel as suggesting that

A blond Marlon Brando dominated the 1958 WWII film The Young Lions.

Lawrence Row

I AM disgusted that Sam Spiegel wants Marlon Brando and not Alec Guinness to play Lawrence Of Arabia. Ridiculous! How would America like Guinness to play George Washington? Anyway Britain has more suitable actors than Brando. What about Richard Burton and Dirk Bogarde?— *David Legshan, Port Talbot, Glam.*

—Picturegoer and Film Weekly, *March 26, 1960.*

DAVID LEAN: THE DIRECTOR

This picture, says Lean, took hold of him in a way that no other has. He shares with Lawrence the capacity to drive himself, and the love of unfamiliar localities.

If he can drive himself he can lead others. He has those two contradictory qualities of leadership, humility and confidence. He will listen carefully to opinions from almost anyone as to how a scene is to be taken; but once he has decided on the way it is to be, it must be that way and no other. He can be most stubborn.

The ability to fix the spirit of a place on film has been stretched to the full by *Lawrence of Arabia,* but in Lean's own estimation this is incidental. His first intention is to tell a story.

Of his methods he himself says this: "I envy people who have flashes of insight and genius in solving picture problems. I have to work out every way to do a scene and then choose one which will serve the story purposes properly, and still not be expected by the audience."

The strategy of the unexpected gives his pictures their freshness and vigour. The adherence to "the story purposes" gives them their substance. His definition of a story is the classic one of something with a beginning, a middle and an end. He feels acutely the need of the artist to move with his times but he will not use devices, methods or themes until he understands them honestly and through and through, regarding it as trickery to do so.

The stars of *Lawrence of Arabia* accepted their roles in the picture without reading the script. That simple statement of fact is possibly the highest professional tribute that could be paid to Director David Lean.

The good actors—the most exacting in the profession—have learned faith in the man. They trust him for his intellect in the selection of subject matter that will be not only entertaining but meaningful and provocative to the public. They trust him for his mastery of the motion picture craft that will help them make their own performances memorable.

Alec Guinness has said "David Lean is the most meticulous craftsman in the industry, the most painstaking in every department."

His apprenticeship was arduous. He was born in Croydon, England and his family expected him to be an accountant. Instead he got a job making tea at Gainsborough Studios. He threw himself single-mindedly into every opportunity which offered, determined to equip himself as a Director who should know his job. He does. His films include *In Which We Serve, Great Expectations, Brief Encounter, The Sound Barrier,* and *The Bridge on the River Kwai.*

In person he is tall, thin, sinewy, sharp-featured. He has unusually large eyes which cloud as he retires into himself for long periods of thought and then as he emerges, will suddenly focus with startling penetration. "I try," says Lean, "to make clear a point and a point of view. People in the audience may differ with me, according to their own personalities and experience. All I hope for is that they take away with them something to think about and talk about."

Like Sam Spiegel, David Lean expresses ideas in motion pictures. He doesn't ask that the audience agree; only that it listen. These two men have been fortunate in finding each other. Their fight for artistic truth and integrity was challenged by *Kwai* and by *Lawrence.* Lean, like Spiegel, is a stubborn man in having his own way. One of the many remarkable things about *Lawrence of Arabia* is that two such stubborn men were able to agree on the making of it.

—*From the 1962 Souvenir Program*

Professor Lawrence "doesn't [even] know that Brando will be playing his brother." But an enterprising *Daily Herald* reporter had in fact revealed that news to A.W., who confessed that he had never even heard of Brando! However, the professor observed, "I think it will inevitably mean that the film will be a flop—in this country at least." The *Daily Telegraph* added that Professor Lawrence thought the film would start production in the Middle East in the fall of that year, 1960, and might run to three hours in length.

The *Daily Mail* added that Lawrence's brother had revealed why, after twenty-five years of refusing offers from film companies, he had suddenly decided to sell the rights to American Sam Spiegel. "Spiegel," he explained, "has done a first-class job of abridgment. It's the only really accurate film script of the book I have ever seen. For any one to cut down a book of between 300,000 and 400,000 words is a colossal task.... Spiegel's script doesn't lose balance, neither does it distort characters or incidents." The script which A.W. had read was a very early version by Michael Wilson.

Director David Lean and producer Sam Spiegel.

dell Hart on February 29, 1960, acknowledged the progression of *Ross* from screenplay to stage play, and formally granted Rattigan permission to make full use of the Liddell Hart biography in his manuscript. In return, Liddell Hart would receive 1 percent of the U.K., U.S., and Canadian box-office gross for all productions of *Ross;* 10 percent of Rattigan's rights for other country presentations of the play; and 10 percent of "other rights" income. But the agreement specifically excluded film rights to *Ross.*

Finally, the *Daily Express* casually mentioned, amid the flamboyant coverage of Spiegel's parleys with the press and the raging controversy over Brando's selection as star, that "the film...will be directed by Britain's David Lean."

Basil Liddell Hart, who did *not* attend the Columbia/Horizon celebration, anxiously devoured the daily newspapers. He immediately contacted A.W., commenting that "it is strange and disturbing that Spiegel should have chosen anyone so apparently unsuitable as Marlon Brando, to play the part of T.E., without any word to you. You have my sympathy over the way [Spiegel] seems to have changed his tone since the negotiations were finished." A.W. replied that he had retained one "check" on the Spiegel–Lean production: he could withhold permission to use the title *Seven Pillars of Wisdom* pending his approval of the finished film.

Liddell Hart added that Rattigan had telephoned to say that a copy of the revised script for *Ross* would soon be on its way. Later that month, the script indeed arrived. Captain Liddell Hart thought that the new version was "a great improvement as a more subtle and apt presentation of Lawrence."

A startling letter also arrived. Despite the playwright's earlier opposition, there had been a sudden change in attitude. Liddell Hart would indeed be compensated for the effective use in *Ross* of his ' T. E. Lawrence ' biography!

A contract to that effect, signed by Rattigan and Lid-

Thus, all was apparently in place for both a *Lawrence* film and a *Lawrence* play: Rattigan's *Ross* stage rights were legally derived from Captain Basil Liddell Hart's ' T. E. Lawrence ' biography. And Spiegel's *Seven Pillars of Wisdom* film rights originated from T. E. Lawrence's book of the same name, as obtained via purchase from the guardian of the *Seven Pillars* trust, A. W. Lawrence.

However, confrontation was brewing between the "Lawrence on stage" and "Lawrence on film" groups! Spiegel did not want *Ross* stealing publicity from his film. He cajoled A.W. to convince the Lord Chamberlain to formally withhold permission for portrayal of T.E. on stage. The professor's legal right to do this was quite simple: T.E. was his brother, and family members could – via the Lord Chamberlain's office and rules – prevent portrayal of deceased relatives on the English stage!

Rattigan countered instantly. If permission was not forthcoming to present *Ross* on stage, he would *televise* the play. Lord Chamberlain's jurisdiction was limited to the stage. Rattigan had won. In fact, it was soon apparent that his hasty turnabout in purchasing rights from Liddell Hart was calculated: the playwright needed to formally ensure that Spiegel – as a last, desperate measure to prevent *Ross*'s stage presentation – could not contend that Rattigan had no biographical source for his play other than *Seven Pillars of Wisdom*, whose rights resided in the Spiegel camp alone.

Captain Basil Liddell Hart.

Ross opened in London at the Theatre Royal, Haymarket, on May 12, 1960. The play was praised as a magnificent piece of storytelling and economic stagecraft. The *Sunday Observer*'s Harold Hobson called Rattigan, now in his fourth decade of writing for the English stage, "the brightest and wittiest of our dramatists" and said that by posing the central question of why Lawrence recoiled from his success, he had made him into "the uneasy spectacular symbol of the conscience of the West in the twentieth century. After both the great wars of our time, the victorious powers have been assailed by feelings of guilt."

The Spiegel–Lean film was entering preproduction and news of its progress was closely followed by the press. On March 31, it had been announced that forty-year-old Anthony Nutting had been hired, at a salary of £25,000, as an adviser to Spiegel. Nutting had gained notoriety during the Suez Crisis of 1956 by resigning as Britain's Minister of State for Foreign Affairs. With Nutting's intimate knowledge of the Middle East as background, his next project was to be a T. E. Lawrence biography and – by mid-1960 – that book was well under way. The press declared that, although "Mr. Spiegel's decision to hire Mr. Brando has already aroused tempers in this country, his decision to hire Mr. Nutting will arouse nothing but envy."

Nutting's job was to negotiate with Middle Eastern governments over issues of locations and logistics, and to take charge of public relations and promotions for the completed film. "I've had a lot to do with the Middle East and with government publicity," said Nutting, "so I have experience for both tasks."

In late August 1960, Captain Liddell Hart was pleasantly surprised when a letter from Horizon Pictures arrived. John Woolfenden, publicity director for the Spiegel–Lean production, wished to meet with him "to discuss the general subject of T. E. Lawrence, and also specific details of his life which are to be the subject of various newspaper and magazine articles now in preparation for outlets in the United States and Canada." A lunch date was suggested, with Woolfenden asking if the Rt. Hon. Anthony Nutting could also attend.

Nutting, in fact, had just returned to England after a publicity trip to the United States aimed at stirring up interest in the film. Spiegel sent him to "chat the thing up in America." He visited Columbia's top brass in Hollywood to "tell them how marvelous the film was going to be, and well worth their backing it." Nutting next went to "talk to all these dreadful women, like [notorious gossip columnists] Louella Parsons and Hedda Hopper." Finally, he made the round of the movie press, including *Variety,* to drum up interest.

Liddell Hart agreed to the luncheon, suggesting the last week of September, but also informed Woolfenden that it was not at all certain that the film abandoned by Rank or a film based upon *Ross* could not be made in the future. In either case, he suggested, he would have to advise those projects alone. Woolfenden assured Liddell Hart that his consultation would be limited to in-

Alec Guinness won praise for his role as "John Hume Ross" (Lawrence) in Terence Rattigan's Ross.

formation relating solely to upcoming publicity-related reports. Liddell Hart eventually asked to defer the meeting to October 12.

Before the meeting, however, a bombshell was to explode.

The *Evening Standard* of October 10, 1960, revealed that famed British producer Herbert Wilcox, who had rebuffed T.E.L. in 1926, was now—thirty-four years later—absolutely determined to make a Lawrence film! Wilcox had bought the film rights to Rattigan's *Ross* for £100,000! Laurence Harvey was targeted for the title role. This meant, the *Standard* added, that there were now likely to be two rival film versions of the story of Lawrence of Arabia in production. Although Wilcox would not comment further at the time, he later gave complete details in his 1967 autobiography:

Not only the film rights of *Ross* as a stage play, but the *screenplay* of *Lawrence of Arabia*, written by Rattigan were available—and I had £200,000 in my banking account.

Knowing that an American production company was in the market, I invited Terry Rattigan out to lunch [on September 8, 1960], and the conversation went something like this.

WILCOX: Are the film rights of *Ross* still available?

RATTIGAN: Well, they're on offer at $250,000.

(A quick reckoning produced a figure in sterling of £85,000.)

WILCOX: If I offered you £100,000 cash would you accept my offer?

RATTIGAN: You mean cash?

I assured him I did.

RATTIGAN: When?

I pulled out my cheque-book and made out the cheque for £100,000. I offered the cheque and held out my hand for a handshake. He shook hands but suggested the deal be completed by solicitors and accountants. It was—and [later would be] announced world-wide.

So great was the impact of this deal upon Wilcox's later life that he included a photograph of the canceled "unhappy £100,000 cheque to Terence Rattigan" in his book.

It was also reported that Brando had backed out of the Lean–Spiegel production due to delays on his film-in-progress, *Mutiny on the Bounty*. In any case, Spiegel felt that the *Mutiny* problems were indicative of Brando's transformation into a "difficult" actor and Lean believed that *Lawrence* would have become *Brando of Arabia*. Tony Perkins was briefly considered, but the fear of a *Psycho of Arabia* quashed that possibility.

Actor Albert Finney, who had recently completed the as-yet-unreleased film *Saturday Night and Sunday Morning*, was now touted as the likely replacement. Spiegel rationalized his new "choice": "*Lawrence* will make a star of an actor. For that reason, David Lean and I have

Three decades after rebuffing Lawrence, Herbert Wilcox paid Rattigan £100,000 for film rights to Ross.

● War for prestige between the two companies making films about Lawrence of Arabia (one starring Brando, the other starring Guinness) hots up.

The Brando group have just hired ex-Minister of State Anthony Nutting "as special assistant to producer Sam Spiegel."

I confidently await an announcement from the other lot that the Archbishop of Canterbury is being taken on as clapperboy.

—Sunday Graphics, *April 3, 1960.*

finally determined to forgo the established stars . . . and to choose an unknown, though necessarily brilliant performer. Our tests indicate that Finney has that rare quality."

These "tests" were unprecedented. Using the script by Michael Wilson, Spiegel shot over 1,400 feet of widescreen color 35mm film at a cost of more than £100,000. In several disparate scenes, Finney played Lawrence in full costume, on elaborate sets, with fully costumed actors playing Ali, Feisal, and Auda.

Anne Coates, the editor of *Lawrence*, recalled how Finney's extended screen test led to her selection: "I was lucky. I got the job, actually, through a fluke. I just bumped into a friend of mine in Harrods – the London department store – one morning. He was going to do the first assistant on the screen tests of *Seven Pillars of Wisdom* – it was called that then – for David. They had tested for a week, and needed an editor. So I asked this friend, 'Is anyone editing it?' because I was out of work at the time. He said, 'No.' So I said, 'Well, I'll ring up Monday morning.' I got the job, I cut the test for David. He liked my work and offered me *Lawrence*. I mean that's how you get on, how lucky this business is. Being at the right place at the right moment."

The tests impressed Spiegel, but not Lean. The direc-

Albert Finney starred as an "angry young man" in 1960's Saturday Night and Sunday Morning.

tor felt that Finney showed "indepedent" tendencies and might prove as difficult as Brando to control.

On October 12, Liddell Hart kept the luncheon engagement with Woolfenden and Nutting. There the main topic of discussion was the identification of the point in the Arab campaign where Lawrence's dream turned into a nightmare. "Was it before or after Deraa?" asked Woolfenden. "Or was the change primarily brought about when Lawrence discovered the disunity within the Sherifian family, so that there would be no united Arabia after all, whether the Allies kept or broke their pledges? Did the turning point have some deep psychological root?"

Liddell Hart replied by mail, after consulting his book and records: "Lawrence's disillusionment strongly developed when he learned [in May 1917] about the Sykes–Picot agreement [the secret plan between Britain and France to divide up the Middle East after the war], and was forced to lie to the Arab leaders. As to what happened [to Lawrence after he was violated by the Turks] at Deraa, I think the most probable conclusion is that it was a partial rather than a primary factor, deepening his feeling of losing personal integrity – perhaps through fuller self-revelation."

IT'S NOW A RACE FOR LAWRENCE OF ARABIA barked the headlines in the *Gloucester Citizen* of October 22, 1960. After recapping the background to the two Lawrence film projects, the article revealed that Sam Spiegel had also purchased the rights to Robert Graves's four Lawrence books and Lowell Thomas's *With Lawrence in Arabia*. The current cast list still had Albert Finney targeted for the title role, with Cary Grant as General Al-

"Brando of Arabia" in The Wild One *(1954).*

lenby, Kirk Douglas as "an American journalist," and Jack Hawkins as Colonel Newcombe, a British officer. Spiegel announced that "we will spend every dollar and pound to give us a picture which demonstrates the drama, the spectacle and the human relationships of T. E. Lawrence and the classic *Seven Pillars of Wisdom*. This will be a spectacle beyond the concept of any yet seen on the screen."

However, unbeknownst to the *Citizen,* Albert Finney had just issued a unilateral declaration of independence. The *Daily Mail* of October 10 reported that the brightest star in British acting had said, "No, thank you," to Spiegel's contract, worth £125,000. Spiegel had offered Finney a five-year contract. Finney wanted a three-year contract and script approval for future projects, declaring, "I will not compromise. . . I want to be an actor—not a marketable property like a detergent. You become a big cookie and somebody's investment. My freedom as an artist is more important to me."

Three decades later, Sir David Lean was to characterize Spiegel's offer to Finney as "a slave contract."

Thus, at the end of October 1960, Spiegel and Lean not only lacked a star, but they also had the rival Rattigan–Wilcox production to contend with.

Spiegel's lawyers had examined Liddell Hart's text and had decided that "all major dramatic incidents [in it] . . . must have been derived from *Seven Pillars of Wisdom* . . . so that any film which is based upon *Ross* [which derives from Liddell Hart's biography] would be regarded as an infringement of [Spiegel's] film rights to *Seven Pillars.*" Liddell Hart, commenting on these contentions, argued that much of the disputed material in *Seven Pillars* came from *Revolt in the Desert,* whose film rights had apparently been bought by Rattigan. Also, he reiterated that not only had Lawrence given him permission to use material from *Seven Pillars,* but also, when it seemed that a film was to be made by Korda, T.E.L. had approved Liddell Hart as the scenarist of choice!

"What is happening about your film?" Liddell Hart asked Rattigan. The playwright responded by noting that Wilcox's plans were somewhat incoherent, especially because of the threat of litigation by Spiegel. While Liddell Hart had faith that "every card of [Spiegel's] can be trumped" and Rattigan agreed, the dramatist also correctly suggested that the delaying action of the argument would make it difficult for Wilcox to raise money for his film.

With respect to their mutual disagreement, Rattigan told Liddell Hart that having sold film rights to *T. E. Lawrence* once—to Comet Films in 1934—he could

Lawrence film race is on
By DOUGLAS MARLBOROUGH

THE race to be the first to put a life of Lawrence of Arabia on film began in earnest yesterday, when Hollywood producer Sam Spiegel announced that he would probably sign Albert Finney for the title role.

Said Mr. Spiegel in New York : "He did a superb test for me, and one of the big advantages is that this boy really looks like the portraits of Lawrence."

Finney, 25-year-old actor from Lancashire, won critical praise for his performance in the new West End play *Billy Liar.*

Mr. Spiegel added: " Cary Grant will probably play General Allenby, Jack Hawkins will be Colonel Newcombe, Horst Buchholz will portray Sheik Ali, and I am negotiating with Sir Laurence Olivier to appear as Sheriff Feisal."

He said the film will cost between £2,000,000 and £3,000,000, and will be shot in Jerusalem and Akaba.

But there are to be TWO film Lawrences. In Britain Herbert Wilcox is also planning an epic on the desert adventurer. He is believed to want Laurence Harvey as the star.

Mr. Wilcox, who has paid playwright Terence Rattigan £100,000 for the rights of *Ross,* the West End stage success, starring Sir Alec Guinness as Lawrence, is in New York to sign up a director and stars.

It looks as though Mr. Spiegel has won the race to be first to get the cameras turning. He plans to start shooting in January, two months before Mr. Wilcox.

Daily Mail, *October 17, 1960.*

not sell them again! That is why, he contended, revenue from film rights to *Ross* were specifically excluded in the "other rights" section of the contract they had signed on February 29, 1960. "I am sorry," he added, and then proceeded to invite Liddell Hart to a 250th performance party for *Ross.* "I should love to see you . . . but will perfectly understand if you feel it isn't worth an uncomfortable journey from your comfortable home." Liddell Hart's lawyers also agreed that it was evident that there was no case to be made for film rights to *Ross.* They also suggested that he stay out of the feud between the Wilcox and Spiegel camps, even though his book was involved. "There does not seem . . . to be much point in voluntarily interfering between two dogs who are quarreling over a bone."

The legal battle between Spiegel and Wilcox was to rage on for months. Then in March 1961 Herbert Wilcox abruptly surrendered and sold his film rights in *Ross* to Sam Spiegel. Wilcox later recalled:

I [went] to New York to make a deal for world distribution and for casting the name part, since Guinness considered himself too old to play it. On arrival in New York, Sam Spiegel announced *Lawrence of Arabia* and threatened to injunct me if I attempted my film. I would have gone ahead and made *Ross,* defying Spiegel—and could have shown my film a year ahead of his since David Lean, although a great director, is very slow. However, the City [London's financiers] wanted no part of litigation, and so I had to let the whole subject drop since no distributor

39

would finance me with an injunction hanging over my head. Not a penny of the £100,000 did I recover.

And Liddell Hart, in declaring his allegiance to the Rattigan–Wilcox team during his discussions with Woolfenden, had also lost out. He would, after twenty-seven years of frustration, *never* be an adviser to a *Lawrence of Arabia* film.

But at last the way was completely clear for the creation of the Sam Spiegel–David Lean epic film *Lawrence of Arabia*. Now all they needed was a star and a script.

Lean recalled, "When Finney turned it down, I went to every cinema in London. I used to go to three shows a day, watching actors. And then one day I saw this film, *The Day They Robbed the Bank of England,* and there was Peter. On the screen, I saw this chap playing a sort of silly-assed Englishman, with a raincoat, casting for trout. And I said, 'That's it. I'm going to test him.' "

Asked what it was that attracted him to O'Toole, Lean remarked, "One of the first things about movie acting is a screen presence. Now don't ask me what a screen presence is. You know, you can put somebody up on the screen, and some people come – *VOOM* – out of it."

In 1960, Peter O'Toole – at twenty-seven years of age – was playing at Stratford-upon-Avon in three roles: Shylock in *The Merchant of Venice,* Petruchio in *The Taming of the Shrew,* and Thersites, in *Troilus and Cressida.* Previously, in 1954–55, O'Toole had studied at London's world-famous Royal Academy of Dramatic Arts. He then joined the Bristol Old Vic, a repertory company. In the next three years, he played some seventy-three roles, finally making his London debut in the Bristol Company's West End productions of *Oh, Mein Papa* in 1957 and *Hamlet* in 1958. O'Toole achieved his greatest stage success when he won the London Critic's Award for Best Actor of the Year, 1959, in *The Long and the Tall and the Short,* presented at London's Royal Court theater. It was this play, seen by Sam Spiegel, which had prompted O'Toole's disastrous *Suddenly Last Summer* screen test.

In London, O'Toole also met and, in late 1959, married Welsh actress Sian Phillips. Their first child – Kate – was born the next year. The O'Tooles formed a production company, Keep Films Ltd. It was their American business adviser, Jules Buck, who then convinced O'Toole that his nose should be altered if all avenues toward international stardom were to be kept open.

For Peter O'Toole's *Lawrence* screen test, David Lean – in contrast to the Finney extravaganza – set up a relatively modest one-day affair. O'Toole had dyed his

Peter O'Toole, as seen by Lean in The Day They Robbed the Bank of England.

hair blond and shaved off the beard he wore as Stratford's Shylock. In his "Arabian scene," he wore brown Arab robes, with a gold braid, supplied on short notice by Anthony Nutting. They had been given to Nutting by King Saud, and had also been used in Finney's test. Never worn by Nutting, the robes were eventually cut into squares by his wife for their dog to sit on.

David Lean recalled the test: "We went onto the set at Elstree, with some sand and desert backing, and Peter put on the clothes, and soon as he came on, he was wonderful." Halfway through the test, Lean stopped the cameras, saying, "No use shooting another foot of film. The boy *is* Lawrence."

On November 20, 1960 – nine months after the Brando headlines – Sam Spiegel and Columbia announced to the press that, *finally,* the star role in their epic was cast: Peter O'Toole was the man for the job.

After hearing his new contractee variously described as an unpredictable Irishman, a bearded young lion in need of a haircut, or simply "that wild man," Spiegel decided he'd better find out what manner of beast he had chosen to play the key role in his epic. Spiegel met with O'Toole and was told that his new star, while an admitted partier and partaker of the bottle, now intended

Peter O'Toole at his screen-test for Lawrence *on November 7, 1960. Lean's reaction was immediate: "The boy is* Lawrence.*"*

to settle down in a house bought with his acting fee. One of the contract provisions O'Toole finagled from Spiegel was that Sian would be brought to the desert once a month – at Horizon's expense. Spiegel now believed that O'Toole could – with the help of the proposed superstar "supporting cast" – carry off the film.

However, a more serious problem arose. O'Toole was apparently legally contracted to Stratford. His next play, Jean Anouilh's *Becket*, was to begin rehearsals in March 1961: £250,000 worth of tickets were already presold. Since *Lawrence of Arabia* was initially scheduled to film from January to May 1961, O'Toole could not possibly prepare for both projects.

Peter Hall, Stratford's producer, was incensed. He had even flown O'Toole to New York City to see the Broadway production in preparation for his role. Olivier starred and Anthony Quinn was King Henry II, the role targeted for O'Toole. (When *Becket* moved from New York to Toronto, Quinn was gone. He had quit on March 25 to play Auda in *Lawrence*, his contract bought out by Sam Spiegel. Olivier now played Henry, with Arthur Kennedy as Becket. A year later, *Lawrence* would again cause Kennedy to be called upon: he was to replace Edmund O'Brien, who – for reasons of health – had to abandon his role as Bentley!)

Jules Buck contacted Nutting and swore that there was no written contract between O'Toole and Stratford. Spiegel asked Nutting to "go down to Stratford and see Peter Hall and tell him to drop his injunction."

Nutting confronted Hall, saying, "I'm not denying that O'Toole probably made all sorts of verbal commitments to you. But there is nothing in writing." Hall replied, "Of course there's nothing in writing. We don't do that at Stratford."

Nutting snapped back: "Well, look, you are about to take out an injunction in the courts. No judge will look at you if you haven't got a piece of paper. You may have shaken hands with Peter O'Toole many times, but it is not a binding, legal commitment."

However, Nutting couldn't disuade Hall, who went to court and sought to prevent O'Toole from leaving the company. The judge told Hall, "Well, I'm sorry, but you haven't got a piece of paper. Out!"

Peter O'Toole was free of *Becket* – at least until 1964. Then he would costar in Peter Glenville's film with Richard Burton, who had starred as Mark Antony in Mankiewicz's *Cleopatra*. Ironically, O'Toole had declined that role, opposite Elizabeth Taylor, when he had accepted Hall's invitation to play at Stratford.

Peter O'Toole immediately started immersing himself in the three dozen books about Lawrence, nearly memorizing all 661 pages of *Seven Pillars*. He also sought out and spoke to many who had actually known Lawrence. Less than five weeks after he was chosen as *Lawrence*'s star, he would have to leave for Jordan to prepare for the physical aspects of the film.

Before filming could start, however, a significant problem would have to be resolved. There was no script. Lean had found that Wilson's screenplay was not suitable: it lacked continuity and was too American. Further, friction developed between Wilson and the Spiegel–Lean team. David Lean was very blunt: "Sam, it's not working."

Spiegel went to see Robert Bolt's acclaimed historical drama *A Man for All Seasons,* which had opened in London's West End in July 1960, and enthusiastically returned. He told Lean, "Baby, I think you better go and see *A Man for All Seasons*." Lean attended the play and agreed, "It's bloody well written."

They decided that Bolt should be considered. The screenwriter was summoned to see the producer at his tastefully ostentatious Horizon offices. Initially invited only to rewrite the dialogue, Bolt declined. The Spiegel countered with an interesting offer: a lot of money for a full rewrite—but it had to be done in seven weeks.

At screen test, O'Toole was also photographed in military garb. Lawrence hairstyle would change before filming began.

Bolt agreed, but his rapid reading of the script on the subway ride home convinced him that it was incomprehensible. He complained to Spiegel.

An agreement was reached whereby—as a test—Bolt would completely rewrite just one scene: the crucial early meeting between Lawrence and General Murray, a scene which Lean had labeled "a disaster to date." On the basis of the results, a decision would be taken by Spiegel. Writing started in late December 1960.

Bolt's initial research involved reading most of the Lawrence books available. However, he was soon to discard their contradictory tales in favor of Lawrence's own in *Seven Pillars:* "I took his account of what had happened or what he passionately wished had happened as true."

Bolt recalled that after "Lean returned from a trip [from Jordan]. . .when I had done the first twenty pages of my script, he said to Sam Spiegel 'Now, look. This is the sort of thing we require.' " In later years, Lean recalled his response to Bolt's writing: "It was simply wonderful. . .had a real style. . .You can't fake this sort of thing."

Bolt, too, they decided, was the man for the job.

Speigel and Lean now had the rights to Lawrence's book, the writer to transform that book into a screenplay, and the actor to portray Lawrence on the screen.

LOOKING FOR "ARABIA"

Now remained the question of *where Lawrence of Arabia* should be made.

Although the logical place was the very territory in which Lawrence had rallied and led the Arabs, this was not necessarily the case where Hollywood is concerned. The varied landscapes of California would have been the easiest choice. Israel's deserts could offer appropriate scenery and comfortable politics, since the movie industry has always had a large Jewish component.

David Lean, however, was from the start determined to opt for absolute authenticity and the breathtaking grandeur of Jordan.

Anthony Nutting recalled Spiegel's vacillation: "Sam simply couldn't make up his mind whether he was going to shoot the film in Jordan or in the Sahara or wherever. It was obvious that it *was* going to be Jordan—it *had* to be Jordan. But Sam took about nine months to make that decision."

Finally, Nutting informed his friend King Hussein that his country was being considered as a location, and that someone would be coming out to have a look.

Photographer Mark Kauffman was asked to create a "Lawrence" -like photograph. A day was required to achieve the desired pose. On November 18, 1960, Columbia issued the two photos juxtaposed on a single 8 x 10, and announced: Peter O'Toole is Lawrence.

In November 1960, David Lean made his first location scouting trip. Some officers of the Jordanian Desert Patrol had been assigned to assist Lean in his exploration by plane and jeep. Lean was overwhelmed: he had found a spectacular backdrop for his vision and was thrilled to find that the desert had changed imperceptibly since the days of Lawrence's adventures. He discovered remains of Turkish locomotives and twisted stretches of railway track which had been dynamited by Lawrence over forty years before. They still lay unrusted in the sun.

Lean returned to London determined that Jordan it must be. This presented many problems: a Jewish producer working in an Arabic country that had an economic boycott of Israel; a remote territory in which services and facilities were largely nonexistent. Fortunately, Jordan had an enlightened monarch in young King Hussein. And the country had a tremendous need of money.

Now Nutting had to switch hats, from Spiegel's "director of public relations" to his "Middle East diplomat." Nutting's friend David Niven had asked Hollywood writer Harry Kurnitz, "What's Nutball doing in the movies!?" Kurnitz replied, "He's the only man in the world who can persuade the King of Jordan that Sam Spiegel isn't really Jewish."

Robert Bolt was drafted into the RAF, but later joined the army and was commissioned as an officer. After three years' service, he returned to Manchester to obtain a degree, and became a teacher. He wrote a dozen radio plays, then quit teaching. A Man for All Seasons was his greatest stage triumph.

When Lean set out on his first location-scouting trip to Jordan, it was probably with images such as these in mind: (Above) Arab army on the march on the desert sand. (Below) Rolls-Royce armored cars at Wadi Rumm. Both photos World War I.

According to Nutting, this issue never amounted to much, as he convinced Hussein that *Lawrence* "was going to do a very good job for tourism—all those people who'd come flocking to see the beauties of Jordan after seeing the film."

Thus, King Hussein, great-grandson of Hussein, Sherif of Mecca, who launched the Arab Revolt in 1916, gave the film his blessing. This approval was quickly secured without even submitting a final script, in spite of the fact that some of characters in the story were the king's own uncles and grandfathers.

To Spiegel's great relief, Hussein promised to provide the complete cooperation of the Jordanian government and army.

But to Spiegel's great dismay, the proposed cost for

Jordanian Desert Patrol Officers, photos by David Lean, 1960.

44

Desert patrol at Wadi Rumm, photo by David Lean.

Mud flats with dust devil, photo by David Lean.

Wide angle shot of Wadi Rumm, photo by David Lean.

this "complete cooperation" soon arrived: the Jordanian army had put in a tender for a million pounds, for the hire of themselves and all their equipment. Sam Spiegel nearly had a heart attack.

Nutting and Spiegel set out for Jordan in an effort to solve the problem. Together with production manager John Palmer, they met at Horizon's Amman office with the king's representative, Gibran Hawa, Quartermaster General of the Jordanian army. Nutting led Gibran into a boardroom, slamming the door in Spiegel's face, and

locking it.

Spiegel beat on the door with his fists, screaming, "What are you doing? Let me in!" Nutting retorted, "Sam, this is *my* show. It has nothing to do with you. Just keep out of this. Sit down and I'll let you know when I've finished."

Gibran was very reasonable in negotiating details for a new proposal, more logically based on per diem costs of each item, and number of days the various items were required. The final figure amounted to £165,000.

Nutting came out of the room and jubilantly informed Spiegel that "from £1 million, we're down to £165,000." Spiegel's adviser was immediately "promoted from *baby* to *sweetheart.*"

Spiegel, ecstatic at having gotten the Jordanian army for a sixth of what he expected, immediately flew back to London.

Nutting's next task was to negotiate for the hire of the Bedouin and their camels for the big scenes. This was done with a Sherif Nasser, second-in-command of the desert patrol, who controlled and protected all the Bedouin and who therefore negotiated on their behalf. Nasser's asking price was astronomical.

Nutting inquired why, if the Jordanian army could be hired for £165,000, Nasser could demand such seemingly ridiculous prices for the hire of Bedouins and camels?

"You must think we're millionaires!" he exclaimed.

Panorama of Jebel Tubeiq, spliced together from three separate shots by David Lean, 1960.

Nasser replied, "Well that's *exactly* what we think!"

Nutting soon discovered that Sam Spiegel had secretly taken out a £1 million loan at the Arab Bank in Amman. Further, the director of the Arab Bank turned out to be none other than the same Sherif Nasser, also the king's uncle.

And the million? It was very simple why the army had asked for a million. An army hospital was being built and it was going to cost them a million pounds. And they obviously thought, "Well, these people are rich."

An embarrassed Nutting scolded Spiegel severely for not borrowing out of the country and importing chunks of capital as needed: "For Chrissake, you send me to Jordan, to do these negotiations for you—you don't even tell me where you're raising the money. A child of ten could have said to you, 'Don't raise the money in Jordan, raise the money anywhere else.' I thought you people were supposed to be good businessmen! You don't know anything about business at all! Not the slightest idea!"

Sam responded as he usually did in moments of crisis: he disarmed the enemy by having a "heart attack."

Sir Anthony Nutting recalled how Gibran Hawa later came over to England, and was greeted by Spiegel. Sam sweetly told him, "Now, Brigadier, because you have been such a wonderful friend to us all, and you have been so helpful, you must go and choose yourself a present. I suggest you go to Harrods."

Nutting gleefully described the finale: "This Quartermaster General went off—and what do you think he bought? You'll never guess in a million years! A grand piano! A grand piano!"

"The abstraction of the desert landscape cleansed me, and rendered my mind vacant with its superfluous greatness . . . In the weakness of earth's life was mirrored the strength of heaven, so vast, so beautiful, so strong . . . The essence of the desert was the lonely moving individual, the son of the road, apart from the world . . ." –T. E. Lawrence, Seven Pillars.

These snapshots were taken in November 1960, on a reconnaissance trip to Jordan. David Lean, along with John Box, pilot Wing-Commander Jock Dalgleish, and others, sought out and photographed potential shooting locations. Their guide was Lieutenant Aloosh, whom they called "The Desert Fox" (below). He had been personally selected by King Hussein for their mission, and was considered the best of Jordan's desert patrol. It was said that "Aloosh knew every place, every thing and everybody in the desert." On this trip, Lean discovered the spectacular backdrops he had envisioned for his film. Michael Wilson's early script had featured a climactic battle scene, which Lean had intended to film in the "lost city of Petra." However, it was accessible only by a long, narrow passage through the surrounding mountains (bottom sequence). This difficult access led to Petra's abandonment as a location.

47

In early autumn 1960, after Marlon Brando had turned down the starring role, an extravagant screen test was arranged for British actor Albert Finney. It was filmed at MGM's Boreham Wood studio, near London, by Geoffrey Unsworth (2001: A Space Odyssey). This previously unpublished frame from the test (top), shows Finney, at right, in one of the many elaborate scenes that were staged. The test contained dramatized studio sequences from the Michael Wilson script, intercut with monologues—extracts from Seven Pillars. Finney was offered the part, but negotiations broke down over the length of the contract. This screen test may be viewed at the British Film Institute in London.

In contrast, Peter O'Toole's test, on November 7, was a low-cost effort. (Stills taken at the test: left, and above.) Lean was immediately convinced that O'Toole was "the man for the job."

Costume designer Phyllis Dalton produced an impressive series of watercolor sketches in Jordan.

Top: Dalton's design sketch of Lawrence's Arab robes. One of these white robes was the centerpiece of a "Movies of the 60s" display at the Museum of the Moving Image, in London.

Bottom: Sketches of (left) Feisal's servant and standard bearer and (right) Auda's bodyguard. A sheikh's bodyguard was described as having a "kit consisting of innumerable weapons of all epochs, from the Saracen scimitar to the later Mauser automatic."

Howeitat tribe (Auda): Sheikh wearing farwah, four tribesmen.

Lawrence's servant Daud.

An unidentified Dalton Sketch.

Ageyl: Sheikh, servant, three bodyguards.

Juheina tribe: Sheikh wearing farwah, Sheikh, three tribesmen.

Brown/khaki/cream tribe.

Bodyguard.

Juheina tribe: Sheikh, servant, three bodyguards.

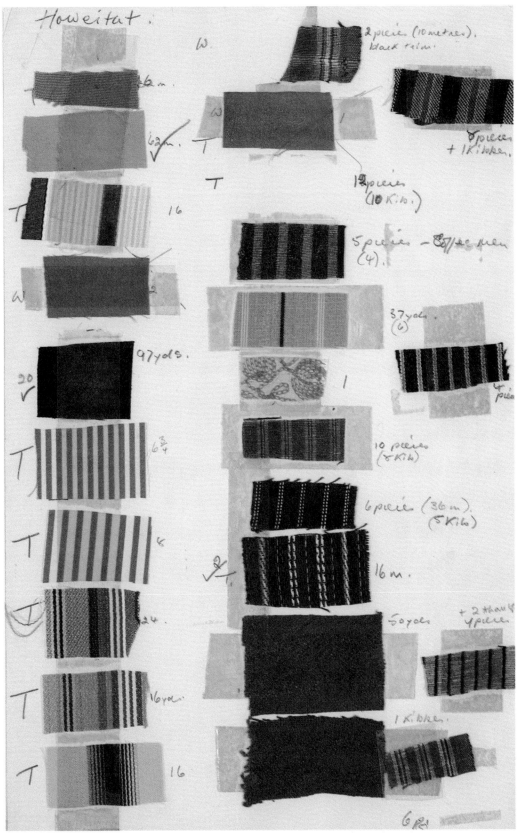

Phyllis Dalton taped samples of tribal colors onto page, as reference for textile merchants in Damascus.

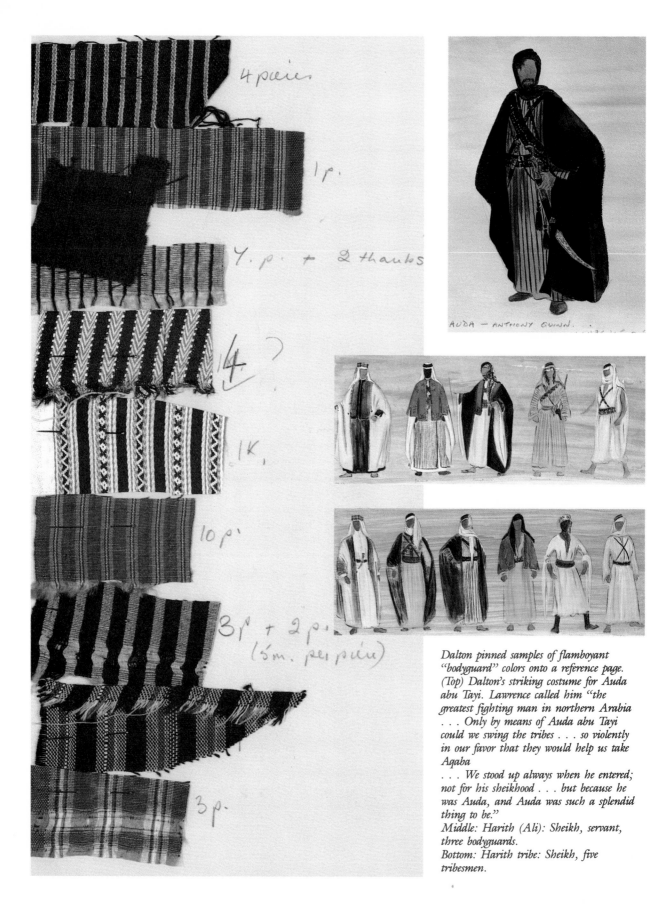

4 paies

1p.

4 p. + 2 thaubs

14?

1K.

10 p.

3p + 2p.
(5m. per piece)

3p.

AUDA — ANTHONY QUINN.

Dalton pinned samples of flamboyant "bodyguard" colors onto a reference page. (Top) Dalton's striking costume for Auda abu Tayi. Lawrence called him "the greatest fighting man in northern Arabia . . . Only by means of Auda abu Tayi could we swing the tribes . . . so violently in our favor that they would help us take Aqaba . . . We stood up always when he entered; not for his sheikhood . . . but because he was Auda, and Auda was such a splendid thing to be." Middle: Harith (Ali): Sheikh, servant, three bodyguards. Bottom: Harith tribe: Sheikh, five tribesmen.

Costume reference photographs provide a record to ensure visual continuity over breaks in filming.

Left: Early in the film, Peter O'Toole wears lieutenant's uniform in General Murray's office. T. E. Lawrence wrote, "A straight request [to leave Cairo for Arabia] was refused; so I took to stratagems. I became . . . quite intolerable to the Staff . . . I took every opportunity to rub into them their comparative ignorance and inefficiency in the department of intelligence (not difficult!). And irritated them yet further by literary airs, correcting split infinitives and tautologies in their reports."

Lower left: Property Master Eddie Fowlie tried "all kinds of things, even real ox blood," for O'Toole's costume after Deraa, then "just painted it on."

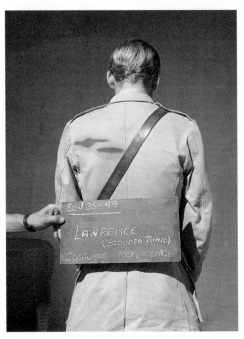

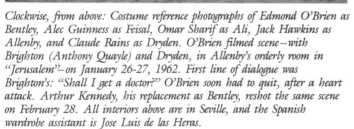

Clockwise, from above: Costume reference photographs of Edmond O'Brien as Bentley, Alec Guinness as Feisal, Omar Sharif as Ali, Jack Hawkins as Allenby, and Claude Rains as Dryden. O'Brien filmed scene—with Brighton (Anthony Quayle) and Dryden, in Allenby's orderly room in "Jerusalem"—on January 26-27, 1962. First line of dialogue was Brighton's: "Shall I get a doctor?" O'Brien soon had to quit, after a heart attack. Arthur Kennedy, his replacement as Bentley, reshot the same scene on February 28. All interiors above are in Seville, and the Spanish wardrobe assistant is Jose Luis de las Heras.

CHAPTER 4

PREPRODUCTION

"BEFORE THE GARDENS
MUST COME THE FIGHTING."

—FEISAL TO LAWRENCE, IN FEISAL'S TENT

The offices of Horizon Pictures in Dover Street, London, bustled with activity as filming of *Lawrence* was anticipated in the New Year, 1961. Lew Thornburn, Sam Spiegel's right-hand man, handled communications, correspondence, contracts, and nearly everything else.

LONDON: CAST AND CREW

Maude Spector was casting director and her roster was quickly expanding. Sir Alec Guinness, acclaimed as *Ross,* was obviously too mature to play a twenty-eight-year-old Lawrence on the Panavsion screen. But his enthusiasm for the film convinced Spiegel that *Kwai*'s "Best Actor" would excel as the Emir Feisal, leader of the Arab Revolt. David Lean, however, had quarreled bitterly with Guinness about the interpretation of Colonel Nicholson in *Kwai,* and threatened to quit the film when informed about his producer's choice. Legend has it that Spiegel then suffered yet another of his infamous "heart attacks." Lean offered "to give Spiegel anything he wanted if it would help him to recover." Spiegel instantly recovered, requesting that Guinness be confirmed as Feisal.

Anthony Quinn, after his smash hit *The Guns of Navarone,* agreed to play Auda abu Tayi, brigand chief of the Howeitat clan. Anthony Quayle, also in *Navarone,* was signed to play Colonel Newcombe (later Brighton) and Jack Hawkins, who had appeared in *Kwai,* would be General Allenby.

Lawrence's cast was truly international. Zia Mohyeddin, Pakistan's leading actor, would play Tafas, the guide who first takes Lawrence out into the desert. I. S. Johar, India's celebrated character actor, came from Bombay to play the key role of Gasim, whom Lawrence saves from death by thirst and later must execute to prevent a tribal blood feud. Johar would later become known as the only member of the troupe who had negotiated a deal that was more advantageous to him than it was to Sam Spiegel.

Michel Ray, then known as Britain's most promising teenage actor, and Malta's John Dimech were chosen to enact the two young desert imps, Farraj and Daud, who become Lawrence's personal servants. Ironically, Dimech – a waiter before *Lawrence* – would return to that vocation after the film. Egyptian actor Gamil Ratib would play Majid, the elegant young Ageyli desert fighter. Britain's Norman Rossington would play Corporal Jenkins. John Ruddock, veteran Shakespearean actor, was to be the elder of the Harith tribe.

Lawrence's principal crew would become the nucleus of Lean's filmic efforts for the next thirty years. His Oscar-winning cinematographer from *Kwai,* Jack Hildyard, was not available. Freddie Young, who had in 1941 photographed *The 49th Parallel,* edited by Lean, remembers how he was hired for the film which would earn the first of his three "Lean" Oscars, a Golden Globe, a British Golden Camera, and a French Prix d'Honneur: "Sam Spiegel rang me up and said, 'David would love you to photograph *Lawrence of Arabia.*' It wasn't a very long conversation. I said, 'O'K.' And that was it."

Although Property Master Eddie Fowlie had already worked for Spiegel before, on *Kwai,* he too recalls his first *Lawrence* encounter with the legendary producer: "Somebody said, 'Go and see Sam in Dover Street.' I went into this office. Sam always liked to have a big desk . . .a huge

Alec Guinness as Prince Feisal

Anthony Quinn as Auda abu Tayi

Jack Hawkins as General Allenby

Claude Rains as Dryden

Lawrence of Arabia's *cast would eventually be described as "all-star, all good." Sir Alec Guinness was famous as a master of cinematic disguise. Screenwriter Robert Bolt suggested that "if the audience had no advance information about the role of Prince Feisal, they'd have to take Feisal's fingerprints to discover that he is played by Alec Guinness." Anthony Quinn, of Mexican-Irish ancestry, had won an Oscar for* Viva Zapata! *and as Paul Gauguin in* Lust for Life. *Jack Hawkins had made a number of military films, including* The Malta Story, The Cruel Sea, *and* Kwai. *Hawkins would shave his head on top, with just enough thinned hair left to match Allenby photographs. Claude Rains, in his seventies when he joined the cast, had his first film assignment in a picture in which he was never seen:* The Invisible Man. *Other notable pre-Lawrence Rains roles included* Caesar and Cleopatra, Mr. Smith Goes to Washington, *and* Casablanca. *Anthony Quayle had performed on stage at Stratford-upon-Avon for nine years and was a veteran of numerous military roles.*

Anthony Quayle as Colonel Brighton

Indrasen H. Johar as Gasim

Gamil Ratib as Majid

desk occupying most of the office. I remember John Palmer, *Lawrence*'s production manager, standing to attention beside the desk. I didn't wait to be invited to sit down. I just pulled out a bloody chair and sat down in front of Sam's desk. He offered me a big cigar. And I said: 'Now you know I don't want those damn things.' Sam simply replied, 'Well, I want you to go out to the desert with David . . .' "

David Tringham, eventually second Assistant Director (A.D.), also had a Spiegel encounter: "Sam was right behind his great big desk. Very, very imposing. Very charming. He said, 'I hear you have a girlfriend in Paris.' I said, 'Yeah, yeah, I'm really missing her.' So he says, 'Give me her number. I will go and see her.' I said, 'Well, that's really nice, but um, um . . . She hasn't got a telephone.' " Tringham recalled with some amazement that the average age of the *Lawrence* A.D.'s was only twenty-five. Roy Stevens was about twenty-seven and Michael Stevenson was about twenty-two. "A principal crew that young, at that time, was very unusual," he suggested. He added that "the crew was not that well paid. I got £55 a week. In real terms, it was about half the salary of an A.D. in 1992. It *was* Sam Spiegel, you know. Night work. No overtime pay, nothing. Six days a week, including Sundays. Any hours, any time, anything. And so it was a pretty good deal—for the producers. They just said, 'That's the money, O.K.' It never even occurred to me to think it was little."

An art department was quickly set up on the fourth floor of an office in Berkeley Street, not far from Horizon Films. The department was a scene of bewildering chaos, with drawing tables littered with Arab swords and ancient rifles.

Like Anne Coates, Phyllis Dalton's first encounter with the *Lawrence* production was on Albert Finney's screen test. With only three days' notice, Dalton prepared a half-dozen costumes for the elaborate production. Afterward, John Palmer urged Spiegel to "make up his mind" and hire Dalton to do the costumes for the film. Finally, Sam said, "Ah, well, get the girl who did the test, O.K."

In October 1960, Dalton was finally hired. She did

Donald Wolfit as General Murray.

57

JAN. 2nd. 1961.

TO BE ORDERED FROM HAWKES FOR MR. PETER O'TOOLE

Sketch No. 1   4 Khaki drill jackets
                  4 pairs khaki drill trousers

Sketch No. 2   1 Khaki drill jacket (with fuller skirt for breeches)
                  1 pair khaki drill breeches
                  (This is only a sample to see if Mr. Lean approves)

Sketch No. 3   2 Khaki serge jackets (Major rank on sleeves.)
                  2 Khaki serge jackets (Lieut. Colonel rank on sleeves)
                  2 pair khaki serge trousers.

PLUS :-   4 caps as near type in still of Lawrence as possible - if in
doubt bring plenty!
Sam Browne belt and holster.
6 Dark khaki shirts   ) the stills show two different types
6 lighter Khaki shirts)
Plus more of each that can have shoulder pips in case we see him in
shirt and pants only.
Khaki socks
Assorted khaki ties at your discretion.
MEDAL RIBBONS - He actually had :-
         C.B. - June 4th 1917
         D.S.O. - May 13th 1918
         Knight Legion of Honour - 1916?
         Croix de Guerre - 1917/18?
According to all research and stills to date he appeared never to wear
them, but we'd better have them in case!!
Also in all photographs he never wore cap badge etc.
He should not look smart and slick in his uniform at all - the stills
are a good guide for this and just what John Bryan wants.

    I would also suggest - if you also think it a good thing - that we
have sent out here with the uniforms plenty of extra material, both the
serge and the drill which could cover us for extra uniforms doubles etc.
Also extra buttons etc., but you'll probably think of lots of extra
things which I've not remembered.

    Of the patterns selected - they are both from swatches given me by
Hawkes when in London. I have a hasty feeling that the drill selected
(called Mayfair) is one not in stock, but I chose it as it's softer
than the others and would look better when hot and sweaty! The second
choice is the one called "HULL", but it is stiffer --- so if "MAYFAIR"
is unobtainable can you find something as soft in exactly that colour
which Freddie Young has approved already.

    Just to double check - P. O'Toole's Knee boots are lace-up front
ones aren't they?

    I enclose three stills of Lawrence in uniform - hope they help!
         (C) Lawrence in cap.
         (B)   "   " kefia.
         (1) Full length with Col. Dawnay.

Costume designer Phyllis Dalton, in search of authenticity, ordered O'Toole's uniforms from Hawkes, which had made Allenby's uniforms in WWI.

HORIZON PICTURES (G.B.) LTD.

PRODUCTION: "Lawrence of Arabia"   DRESS CHART

2nd. Lieut. October 1914.   Character: LAWRENCE
Captain. March. 1916.
Major. August. 1917.   Artist:
Lt. Col. March 1918.

SCENE NO.	ACTION	COSTUME	NO.	SET
SEQUENCE A	Motorcycle crash	Sports coat / Polo-neck pullover / Goggles / (No cap)		Ext.Village D / Motorcycle
E	Long Shot of Lawrence walking through Jaffa Gate	Arab dress.		Ext. balcony D / Jerusalem
F	Covent Garden lecture - still of Lawrence in Arab clothes - Lawrence watches from beside the projector - Still of Lawrence in Bedouin woman's dress	Polo-neck sweater / STILLS / 1. Arab robes / 2. Bedouin woman's disguise		Int. Covent Garden N
H	In Bedouin woman's disguise, watches executions	Bedouin woman's clothes		Ext. Roman Arena, AMMAN. D
J	Map-making - interview with General Murray.	uniform. (drill or Col 4) / Drill with trousers Captain	✗ / ✓	CAIRO. D / Int.Map Section, / Brit.HQ. / Int. Office suite
K	Arrives at port of Yenbo on freighter - meets Capt. Harlan - enlists Tafas as guide.	Khaki - sweating (drill) / seabag / Sam Browne + revolver holster / uniform (rev. sets)	✗ / ✓	Ext.Deck of ship / Ext. Yenbo / Int. Shack D
L.	Trek to Feisal - Tafas killed by Ali Ibn el Hussein - Meets Col. Newcombe - they travel together	Khaki, very soiled / Arab headdress / as above.		Ext. Hejaz D / desert
M	They meet Feisal. Lawrence makes the acquaintance of Daud and Farraj - bombed by Turkish planes.			Ext. reception / tent. Late afternoon. / Ext. Bedouin / bivouac.

Dalton prepared dress charts for all characters, showing progression of costume during film. Lawrence sequences E, F, H, and K were in the original Wilson script and were never filmed.

not at all feel handicapped as a woman who would be designing military and Arab costumes for an almost all-male cast. Her lighthearted view was that "it takes a feminine woman to know what a man should look like in a very masculine way." Dalton started her research in England, making use of the resources of the Imperial War Museum and England's other great repositories of military history. She ordered dozens of photographs, many taken by Lawrence himself. Books like *The Arab of the Desert,* by H. R. P. Dickson, supplied much Middle Eastern design detail. And, of course, Dalton had color reproductions made of all the Kennington pastel sketches in the subscribers' edition of *Seven Pillars.*

Phyllis Dalton worked closely with of two of England's foremost costumers, Berman's and Nathan's: the former did many of the Turkish officer's uniforms. Some foreign army badges and buttons were re-created, while British Army regalia as well as British WWI uniforms were generally available off-the-rack. She discovered that a London military tailor named Hawkes had made General Allenby's uniform in the First World War. "They made Peter's lieutenant's uniform," she recalled, "tailoring it deliberately not to fit, and then bashed it through a wash-

ing machine!" To save money, Dalton bought English khaki fabric for the Turkish soldiers' uniforms and sent it on to Jordan for tailoring.

Another *Lawrence* researcher was the Baroness Marie

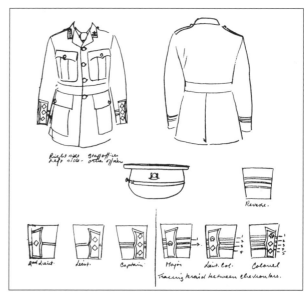

Dalton's sketch of a British army officer uniform, circa 1917, with insignia of various ranks, aided Hawkes in fabrication of costumes.

Budberg, whom Spiegel had cannily hired a year *before* the rights to *Seven Pillars* were finally secured. The baroness, one of Britain's leading researchers, was to amass the mountain of facts which scriptwriters would normally require once the project was formalized. In the course of her research, Budberg even visited the Imperial War Museum to view the rare footage that Lowell Thomas's cameraman, Harry Chase, had shot during the Arab Revolt.

Meanwhile, at his home in Surrey, Robert Bolt worked on the *Lawrence* script, night and day, but initially made little progress. He was under intense pressure from Spiegel and Lean who, he later complained, had "taken him over body and soul": a script *had* to be delivered, and quickly. Bolt became consumed by the project. Eventually, he made a radical decision: he decided to reject all of the contradictory research material on Lawrence, to accept *Seven Pillars* as fact, and to consider it as his sole source. He thus attempted to invade the mind of the man who acted out the events of the Arab Revolt, and who later wrote about them in such a distinctive manner. This proved to be his *key* to the enigma of Lawrence of Arabia. Years later, Bolt would be asked whether, through *Seven Pillars*, "he had *really* penetrated Lawrence's mind." The screenwriter impishly replied, "Who knows?"

And Peter O'Toole's ongoing personal research into Lawrence's background and motivation seemed never-ending. The actor visited Lawrence's birthplace in Wales and even sought out the site of Lawrence's death in Dorset. However, the more that O'Toole learned, the more confused his perception of Lawrence became. "It was impossible to find any two men who could agree on Lawrence," he complained.

AMMAN HEADQUARTERS

In late 1960, Jordanian offices for Horizon Pictures were established in the capital city of Amman, in a house which was formerly the Indonesian embassy on Jebel (Mount) Luweibdeh. This was to be communications headquarters for all personnel, material, and messages being sent from London. A sense of informality and camaraderie developed in the relaxed, informal atmosphere.

Costume Design

For Phyllis Dalton, December 1960 in Jordan meant time to do drawings and check reference material. Dalton recently recalled that she entered the *Lawrence* project as a costume designer who "tries to get away with as few sketches as possible" but ended up—because of the immensity of the project—doing the most design sketches of her entire career!

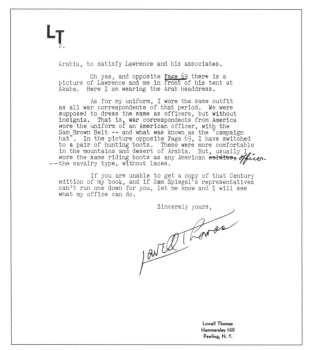

Phyllis Dalton wrote journalist Lowell Thomas in America to inquire about his costumes while in Arabia: "Most particularly we are anxious to establish whether you wore a specific uniform as a privately-sponsored war correspondent before America's entry into the war, and if this changed after that date." Thomas replied in a roundabout but informative manner.

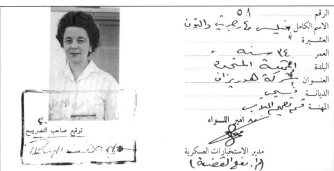

Phyllis Dalton, like other cast members, required a Jordanian work permit. At her drawing board in Amman, she produced dozens of sketches and designs.

The khaki material Dalton had previously ordered in the United Kingdom had arrived, and tenders were issued for fabrication of the Turkish soldiers' uniforms. Design information about these uniforms was lacking: old photographs showed Turkish officers and a few men, but with poor detail. And she had almost no information at all about the *backs* of the uniforms. Many of these problems were resolved on a research trip to Istanbul, with Anthony Nutting providing letters of introduction. The Turks—the losers in the conflict to be portrayed—were in fact extremely helpful. Through museum visits and photographs sent via diplomatic channels, Dalton was able to obtain what she needed. The Turkish soldiers' costumes were intentionally made ill-fitting for dramatic purposes.

As almost none of her photographic research material was in color, Dalton had waited until her arrival in Jordan before starting to design the Arab costumes. She knew that she must experience firsthand the local ambience before putting brush to paper or scissors to fabric.

The styles of the contemporary clothing, little changed in forty years, as well as the colors, textures, and patterns of the markets and the landscape, all provided her inspiration. In collaboration with the design ideas emerging from the art department, Dalton decided the "look" of the costumes and assigned each tribe a slightly different color scheme. She concedes that these distinctions were subtle and tended to merge onscreen, especially when masked by sand and dust. Besides, she said, "the audience really identifies more with the tribal leaders than with the tribesmen themselves."

Her only "cheat," she recalled, was Auda's striking outfit of black and blue and copper—a Dalton invention created by visualizing "how marvelous it would look in the desert when he made his sudden appearance."

She made many shopping trips to Damascus, said to be the oldest city in the world, and even today a sprawling labyrinth of ancient markets. Dalton dashed

in and out of the shops "terrorizing the vendors with my bargaining . . ." Part of the difficulty was the diversity of material available. It required determination to keep track of the dozens of bales of cloth that were set before her. "You sit there like a pasha," she quipped, "and they bring you things and bring you things to look at . . . and

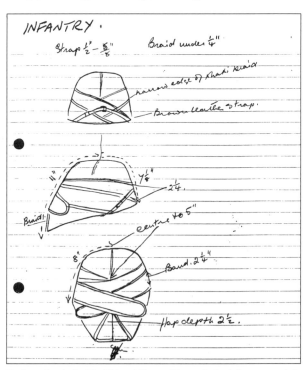

Dalton sketch for Turkish soldier uniforms derived from extended archival research, including Museums in Turkey.

Left: Turkish soldiers on the march, 1917. One of Dalton's actual research photos.
Below: As an economy measure, Dalton ordered cloth for Turkish soldier uniforms from England, but had costumes sewn in Jordan.

you haven't got time to actually concentrate on anything." Dalton was accompanied by her trusty scissors—for snipping samples—and by her assigned army officer, Captain Guessous, who functioned as guide and interpreter. Dalton, racing about the Middle East in the blazing midday sun, seemed to have become one of the famed Victorian lady desert travelers, whom she so admired.

Costume *design* was in fact not the major problem. Dalton's biggest annoyance was in getting the tailors in Damascus to produce a dozen or so duplicates of each

Imperial War Museum, London, was the source of most historical photographs relating to the Arab campaign.

intricately embroidered costume. These duplicates were required for major characters, to account for wear, different looks at different stages of the film, or for use by a stunt double.

For example, the long embroidered silk shirt of Peter O'Toole's white outfit was created in London, and then embroidered in Damascus, to ensure an authentic look. Dalton would approve a sample and then find—to her frustration—that she needed to order as many as two dozen to get just six approximately the same: the enterprising tailors would decide to progressively "improve upon" the original design.

As well, many *Lawrence* costumes were bought off-the-rack in Arab markets. Baggy trousers and shirts, for example. A problem with some of these goods was that

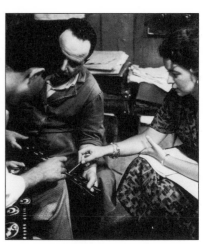

Left: The markets of Damascus, in early 1961, were the source of most of the material for the Arab costumes. Center: Phyllis Dalton in fabric warehouse, bargaining with merchants. Right: Intricate embroidery required care in specification and execution.

they were made too well: they were too thick to "age" properly. Thus many of the "abayas" or cloaks had to be made of specially woven thinner material. A not-so-obvious advantage of a Middle Eastern production was that all of the Arab clothes were loose and very easy fitting. "It's not like fitting Faye Dunaway for seven hours," Dalton remarked.

A wardrobe hut was later established down in Aqaba. On specific location sites, the production manager would make available a large marquee tent, which provided space for racks. For laundry facilities, they required water and electricity—often at a premium in the desert.

A thin line sometimes existed between the costume and props jurisdictions. For example, who would do the jewelry, or the eyeglasses, or the bandolier that a weapon goes on? Is it wardrobe or is it props? Dalton laughed: "Better make sure there isn't a gap. Doesn't really matter who does it, as long as it's done."

A Royal Romance

King Hussein welcomed the money brought into his country by the production: in twelve months the com-

Estimate from Jordanian supplier for fabrication of leather bandoliers.

In her notebooks, Dalton sketched designs, recorded measurements of the principal actors, and noted comments for various costumes.

Sam Spiegel, second from left, and Production Manager John Palmer, right, await audience with King at Royal Palace in Amman.

David Lean, left, and Sam Spiegel, center, in conversation with King Hussein of Jordan.

pany would spend more in Jordan than the sum total of a year's income tax revenue!

Hussein also took an active interest in the activities of the film unit. And vice versa: at Horizon headquarters, Toni Gardiner—the switchboard operator—would often run up to the roof to watch Hussein buzz the office in his Hawker Hunter fighter jet.

On May 1, rumors started that "His Majesty is going to marry—and it's an English girl." It soon was revealed that Toni Gardiner was that girl! Toni, it seems, had been taking Friday afternoons off to watch the king—an enthusiast for all things mechanical—wheeling around a go-cart track he'd had specially built at the military airport. They had met, and a secret relationship had developed.

At Aqaba, the announcement of the pending marriage caused a barrage of celebratory gunfire in the streets. Many there thought at first that it was an Israeli invasion. The joy was quickly curtailed when the populace became aware that the future bride was British. The wedding would take place on 25 May 1961. Then, Toni became known as *Mouna el Hussein*, the desire of Hussein.

Sir Anthony Nutting recalled, "King Hussein whisked her away, to the everlasting detriment of the telephone exchange at Horizon Pictures. We never got another call through . . . She was the only one who knew how to work the telephones!"

AQABA BASE CAMP

It was also vitally necessary to establish a "location headquarters," which would be the operating base for the shooting unit. Aqaba, some 250 miles south of Amman and Jordan's only port, was picked as the logical spot. Heavy equipment could thus be shipped by cargo vessel, through the Suez Canal to the northern tip of the Red Sea, and unloaded at the Aqaba docks.

The scruffy military town lay at a particularly interesting point geographically. Three other countries could easily be seen from Aqaba. To the immediate west lay the twinkling lights of bustling Eilat, at the southernmost tip of Israel, and only a few miles further west, stretched the Sinai desert of Egypt. A short distance to the south of Aqaba was the Saudi-Arabian border.

Aqaba was about to be transformed. A smiling Welshman named Phil Hobbs would become the "Conrad Hilton of the Desert," with "holiday hotels" springing up under his supervision in some of the world's unlikeliest places. If you wanted fried scampi and iced beer in the remote dunes of Jebel Tubeiq, or an outlet for your electric razor in the wild canyons of Wadi Rumm, or even a change of sheets on the searing mud flats of El Jafr, Phil Hobbs was your man. There was only one catch. You had to be a member of the film cast or crew.

It all started when the Hobbs Catering Service was established in the late forties to take care of motion picture location units, beginning with a mobile canteen in London and gradually extending to the far corners of the earth. Hobbs and his assistants spent seven months in Ceylon feeding the *Bridge on the River Kwai* troupe, and the same length of time on the Aegean island of Rhodes, solving the food problems of *The Guns of Nava-*

rone unit. They had worked from Ireland to India and now were being asked to supervise all the living accommodations for the *Lawrence of Arabia* company, which was to film in places where only Bedouin and their camels had previously trod.

With construction foreman Pete Dukelow and his assistant Freddy Bennett, Hobbs started to organize the administration or basecamp from scratch at an unused Army barracks near the warm waters of the Gulf of Aqaba. A sixty-seven-acre site near the docks was rented for the erection of a part Nissen Quonset hut, part canvas-tent "city," to house all the required production facilities.

Hiring a local labor force, and aided by a Jordanian Army detachment, Hobbs, Dukelow, and Bennett cleaned out old sheds, converted them into shops and offices, set up a lumberyard and carpenter shop, piped in water from two desert wells, installed three sets of showers, washbowls, and flush toilets, and put up thirty-four British Army two-man tents which had originally been developed for use in India.

Phil Hobbs, legendary caterer and hotelier.

Water from one of the wells proved a little salty, so it was diverted to the showers and toilets. The other well provided acceptable drinking water, tested and certified by the company medical officer, Dr. Eustace Shipman.

Quarters were soon established for production and publicity offices; art, wardrobe, and makeup departments; camera and sound equipment maintenance shops; props and set-dressing department; paint and plaster shops; post office and transportation headquarters; and a camel parade ground.

To provide for recreation, a British labor staff augmented the original working force and began setting up a Beach Camp about a mile away. A quarter-mile of sand-dune waterfront was bulldozed and leveled, palm trees were moved, and property master Eddie Fowlie employed a band of local laborers to do nothing but pick up stones and broken glass for a week, to ensure safe swimming on the new bathing beach, near which nasty coils of barbed wire separated Israel and Jordan.

The Beach Camp also required showers and toilets, which were set on concrete bases. Battered Nissen huts, acquired from a former Brit-

Left: Entry to Horizon Pictures Aqaba Base Camp, 1961. Center: Horizon's Aqaba Administration Camp. Right: Part of tent "city" at Horizon's Aqaba Beach Camp.

In 1917, during the Arab Revolt, the British Army set up HQ on the same Aqaba beach.

ish Army depot, were reconditioned, painted, set on concrete floors, and converted into dining hall and canteen. Others were partitioned into living quarters for the actors. In addition, one- and two-man caravans (trailers) were towed in and set up alongside the new twenty-four-tent "city," so that, at a moment's notice, all linen, supplies, and personal belongings could be wheeled out and sent to advance shooting sites.

Fowlie, as usual, fashioned his own unique quarters by "joining two or three tents to form quite a nice 'chalet.'" He also grew nasturtiums all around it, as "they grew easily on the beach, and David used to like nasturtiums." Other "characters" in the crew soon began to emerge. Makeup man Charlie Parker, a Canadian, had his tent moved to the far end of the camp when it became apparent that each night he and his wife would have an "evening chase round and round" the tent.

In the center of the tent area were some solid prefab buildings, imported from England. Here, Lean and O'Toole lived. Eddie Fowlie recalls that "O'Toole broke his hand there. . . He punched a door in one night 'cause he couldn't get in . . ." Another "building," the hospital, had its roof covered with aluminum foil by the doctor, to keep it cooler.

And of course, the bar. In Aqaba, it was a *big* one, in a huge tent with a wooden floor. It had comfortable chairs and low tables. There, Phil Hobbs set up his first desert catering operation.

What started as a recreation camp soon became a complete "home away from home" for actors and production personnel, as the troupe grew in size from an original 75 to a total, at one point, of 403. Of that number, nearly 300 were Jordanians, hired as assistants in virtually every department, from camel veterinarians to "bat-

men" (personal servants).

The Beach Camp so impressed King Hussein upon one of his visits, that he ordered a government commission to draw up plans for Aqaba's future development as a tourist resort.

Spiegel of Arabia

One of Anthony Nutting's major problems was getting Sam Spiegel into the various countries of the Middle East. When asked his religion, Spiegel always insisted on replying "Jewish." Nutting told him, "Well that's very stupid. You won't get into an Arab country like that."

Before one trip to Egypt, Nutting took Spiegel's passport to the embassy in London, and persuaded his friend the Egyptian ambassador to have his consul-general personally deal with the situation. Nutting filled out Spiegel's visa form, entering "Anglican" for "religion," and simply asked the consul-general to copy it out.

When Spiegel later asked, "How'd you get the visa?" Nutting replied, "Well the consul just wrote you down as an Anglican."

"You wrote me down as an Anglican?" asked Sam.

Nutting reiterated, "No, I didn't, the consul did."

"How did the consul do it?" asked Sam, persisting in his quest for more details.

Nutting replied, "Sam, just shut up! Here's your bloody visa."

Lean and Spiegel show off their equipment to King Hussein during one of his visits to Aqaba Camp.

65

Nutting later pointed out that similar strategies were employed on several other occasions.

Sam Spiegel's yacht—*the* place to be in the sixties—was often moored off Aqaba. On one occasion, Spiegel was invited to come ashore to stay at the king's summer palace there. Spiegel—aware that he would be in the midst of "the enemy"—invited David Lean to accompany him, insisting, "You're going to stay here with me tonight, baby." A reluctant Lean replied, "Don't be so silly, Sam, you can stay here by yourself. What's the matter?"

Spiegel of Arabia.

As usual, Sam prevailed and Lean remained overnight. However, they were assigned separate rooms. Sam insisted, "You're sleeping in my bedroom." David retorted, "No, I'm not. I'm not going to sleep in your bedroom. That's ridiculous. You're perfectly all right alone."

"No, no, no, no, I want you to stay with me tonight, baby," Sam demanded. Lean later recalled, "All I needed to do was sleep in the same bedroom as Sam—as if I didn't have enough of him during the day!"

Again, however, Lean gave in and agreed to share Sam's bedroom.

Before retiring, Lean opened the doors onto the balcony, and said, "Sam, come out and get some fresh air." Sam—because his mother lived in Israel—asked, "David, where do you think Eilat is?" David replied, "Eilat. I'm not sure, Sam, but I think it's over there," and pointed into the night. And with this, Sam screamed, "Don't point! They'll shoot!"

The king had paid a visit to the yacht, and in return, he had invited Spiegel and Lean, and a few others, to come to dinner at the palace at Amman. The paranoid producer begged his colleagues to avoid discussing religion or politics. But, to his horror, a crew member asked the king, "What is Ramadan?" As the king was explaining that it was a Moslem month of daily fasting, Spiegel interjected, "Oh, that's just like *our* Lent."

To the consternation of all, Spiegel continued his preposterous ploys of crying or feigning "heart attacks" in moments of dire stress. Perhaps the most infamous

Spiegel "performance" would occur well into production. Spiegel had himself strapped to a stretcher and flown by Red Cross helicopter to the desert where filming was in progress. There, attendants carried him to the dismayed Lean's side, where Spiegel croaked, "Don't worry about anything, David—not the budget, not the schedule, not my health. The picture—the *picture* is all that counts!" Whereupon he was whisked (stretcher and all) back into the helicopter, which vanished into the blazing desert skies.

The Script

In Aqaba, David Lean and Robert Bolt continued their struggle with the script. Barbara Cole, who would be responsible for "continuity" when filming started, typed the document. Lean and Bolt, together with Anthony Nutting, were all at that time trying to fathom what had happened to Lawrence in Deraa. To depict him after this critical event, a consensus on its significance was essential.

Nutting felt the key to "rooting out how this thing came about" was more research. The 1926 subscribers' edition of *Seven Pillars* was not sufficient since Lawrence had told Charlotte Shaw (wife of George Bernard Shaw) that his account therein was not true. The breakthrough

David Lean and Sam Spiegel inspect construction.

came when Nutting, with publicist John Woolfenden, sought out a rare 1922 "Oxford Edition," which contained a more graphic description of the Deraa incident, an account at that time not known to the general public.

One of Lawrence's biographers, psychiatrist John Mack, was later to review all the known evidence:

In a report to General Headquarters on June 28, 1919, Lawrence claimed that "[The Turkish governor] Hajim Bey. . .an ardent paederast. . .tried to have me. I was unwilling and prevailed with some difficulty. Hajim sent me to the hospital. . ."

In the original handwritten manuscript of *Seven Pillars,* preserved in Oxford's Bodleian Library, Lawrence described the Bey's "fawning" attempt at seduction, at which point Lawrence kneed him in the groin. Brutal attacks by soldiers followed. This is the description excerpted herein in Bolt's essay of Chapter 1: ". . .my flesh quivered. . ."

It is, however, in a letter to Charlotte Shaw, that Lawrence unquestionably refers to a sexual surrender of some sort: "For fear of being hurt, or rather to earn five minutes respite from a pain which drove me mad, I gave away the only possession we are born with—our bodily integrity."

Bolt would remain in Jordan until shortly after filming began. Even then, the script was unfinished. He returned to England, describing the Spiegel–Lean production effort as the biggest job since the building of the Pyramids. Life out there in the desert, he claimed, was "a continuous clash of egomaniacal monsters wasting more energy than dinosaurs and pouring rivers of money into the sand."

Peter O'Toole

Although it has been suggested that one of Nutting's tasks was to tutor Peter O'Toole in the ways of "a young Edwardian gentleman," Nutting claims that "it would never have happened, because the one thing Lawrence never pretended to be was an English gentleman." Nutting recalled that his main job with respect to O'Toole was that he "had to keep old Peter off the bottle and that was not too difficult, as it turned out. What I said to him was, 'Look, if you don't stay sober, you're going to leave Jordan on your ass. I'm not going to tolerate this sort of behavior that I'm told you usually give out. . . .You're the only actor we've got, and if you get bundled home, then there's no film. That's the end of the film, and that's probably the end of you. So you'd better behave yourself. You're going to learn to ride a camel.' "

O'Toole had arrived in Jordan early in 1961 to start training with Sergeant Hamdan Hamid of the Jordanian Desert Patrol. The art of riding a camel usually requires a minimum of six weeks to master. O'Toole was also determined to learn the Arabic tongue and customs, to familiarize himself with Bedouin dress, and to continue his research on Lawrence.

American photographer Mark Kauffman, there to take the pictures which would eventually appear in the souvenir program and in *Life* magazine, reported O'Toole "initially developed a nasty cyst on his backside." He refused to complain. His resourceful solution was to pad the camel saddle all around with pink "Dunlopillo" foam rubber pads obtained from the props department. This innovative technique was immediately adopted by the Bedouin, including the tough officers of the Desert Patrol.

O'Toole also learned about the delicate art of desert conversation. At first, the Bedouin seemed—to him—hardly hospitable, sitting for hours on end without saying a word. With their guns and daggers they represented a formidable sight, and O'Toole feared that they might be planning "some untimely end for me." Finally he was comforted by the realization that the Bedouin never speak unless they have something important to say.

Eventually, O'Toole was considered nearly as proficient as the Bedouin who had been born to the camel saddle. Guinness and Quinn were mercifully spared the

Peter O'Toole was first principal actor to arrive in Amman, Jordan, February 1961.

King Hussein greets O'Toole at the palace. They found that they had much in common, and Peter made many visits.

Peter O'Toole with camelry tutor, Desert Patrol Sergeant Hamdan Hamid, at Aqaba basecamp.

crash course in camelry, since they arrived much later and were mounted only on Arab horses. Most of the other main actors—Mohyeddin, Johar, Ray, Dimech, Ratib, Rossington, Ruddock—also underwent six weeks of training in camel riding and Arab folklore, before finally heading out to the first location.

Omar Sharif

Sam Spiegel's first choice for the role of Ali was French actor Alain Delon. He, however, had blue eyes and couldn't tolerate the brown contact lenses he would have had to wear: Lean demanded an actor whose dark hair and eyes would contrast with Peter O'Toole's blondness and blue eyes.

A month before shooting was to start, and having

found no one who satisfied these requirements, Lean gave Sam Spiegel carte blanche. Spiegel contacted Maurice Ronet, another French actor, who signed a contract and then flew to Jordan. True, Ronet was dark. As for his eyes...

As soon as David Lean saw him he phoned Spiegel: "He won't do—he's got green eyes."

"It's too late," Spiegel replied, "he's hired. You'll just have to make do."

David Lean wouldn't admit defeat. He called his assistants. "Get me photos of every Arab actor—there's got to be one who's just right!" Lean spotted Sharif's image,

O'Toole learns the agonizing art of camel riding at Aqaba Camp. Neighboring Israel is just beyond the barbed wire.

Actress Sian Philips visits husband Peter O'Toole in Jordan.

Pakistani actor Zia Mohyeddin (with beard) and Second Assistant Director David Tringham (right) relax with Jordanian assistants.

and said, "If this guy speaks English, send him out."

Sharif, then an Egyptian actor, was contacted by Columbia Cairo, and consented to have his photo sent to Sam Spiegel in Hollywood. Ten days later, he was called, told Spiegel was in Cairo, and asked, "Could you be at his hotel in half an hour?"

Spiegel—as usual, smoking an enormous cigar—was impressed by Sharif's fluent English. Sharif, in fact, also spoke French, Greek, Italian, Spanish, and Arabic. Sam

T. E. Lawrence, pictured in 1917, mastered the art of camel riding.

Spiegel watched Sharif, and Sharif watched Spiegel. Spiegel asked if Sharif would "like to do a screen test for a second part, one that we've still got to write?"

Sharif recalled, "I'll never forget it. Sam Spiegel came into Nasserland and got me an exit visa. I mean—I, an Egyptian, can't get it—and here comes a Jew—from I don't know where—who gets it for me. He was so smart and clever and devious."

Three days later a small private plane dropped the actor off in the Jordanian desert where "all I could see was a post, standing straight and alone. But soon the post moved and came toward the plane. It was David Lean. He looked me over unashamedly, from every angle. Movie people have a nasty habit of undressing you with their eyes—I had to get used to that. Once the inspection was over, he put his arm around me and finally said something: 'Let's go get a costume.' "

Lean quickly fitted Sharif with a black robe, and then tried first a beard, and then a mustache on the clean-shaven Sharif.

"That's it. What you needed was a mustache," said the director. A real mustache would become part of Sharif's persona for the rest of his career.

Sharif then did a scene with O'Toole, with Sharif playing Tafas, the guide, and then another scene, with Maurice Ronet: Ronet played Ali and Sharif was Auda. Ronet, who knew Sharif, said, "Oh I hope you get the 'part,' because then you can help me with my English."

These screen tests were sent to Spiegel, along with an evaluation from David Lean: "As you'll see for yourself, the stand-in for Quinn is a real Arab who can act."

The decision came quickly. The *Arab* would play the Arab. Ronet was gone. Omar Sharif was Ali.

Unknown to Lean, Sharif–with no agent and no lawyer–had signed "a slave contract" with Spiegel for seven films. He would receive only £8,000 for *Lawrence,* about half what O'Toole was getting. Sharif would make £8,000 a film up to and including *Funny Girl.* "Sam Spiegel," Sharif commented, "made the money. I didn't."

Sharif recalled: "When I was introduced to O'Toole, they said, 'Mr. O'Toole, this is Omar Sharif.' And he replied, 'Omar Sharif. No one in the world is called Omar Sharif. Your name must be Fred.' Now I'm known as Cairo Fred." O'Toole was right. Sharif was in fact born Michel Shalhoub and before one of his earlier films he had changed his name.

Sharif, although Egyptian, was a "city boy." He had never been to the desert. He had never ridden a camel. He too required a course before shooting started. He remembers: "I'm a horse rider since I was four. So it was easy for me. The first couple of weeks were diabolical. But I had icicles in my blood. I was very good. I had a terrific camel–a small, female racing camel. She was wonderful–a beauty. I lived with her for twenty months. Her name was Alia."

Freddie Young

Shortly after Young was engaged to do *Lawrence,* he was flown out to Amman, Jordan, for preliminary discussions:

> David had already made an extensive reconnaissance of the desert through which Lawrence had journeyed. He now sent me off to look at some of the areas he had chosen for filming so that I could examine for myself the scenery and conditions under which we would be shooting the initial phase of the picture.
>
> First I went to Aqaba Base Camp. From there, by plane, jeeps, and footslogging we went to Wadi Rumm, a fantastic desert of towering red mountains, and then on to El Jafr, with its miles of white mud-flats and the blinding glare and duststorms we came to know so well. After about ten days in the desert I returned to Amman, and the following day caught a plane to Rome, where I had to arrange for lighting equipment, generators, and other apparatus to be sent out to Jordan. Then I returned to London to report.

Egyptian actor Omar Sharif was tested on location, and hired to play Ali ibn el Kharish.

Sherif Ali ibn el Hussein (tallest, at left), was young Harith Sheikh who played role in Arab Revolt. He was model for the character played by Omar Sharif.

David Lean had decided to shoot the picture in Super Panavision 70mm. He felt that *Lawrence* must be a prestige picture and that "quality should shine out of it. 70mm gives a superb picture on a screen and . . . the big frame has an impact and a quality which . . . is unbeatable. And I don't believe there is any substitute for true quality."

Freddie Young then set off to pick out the equipment:

> This necessitated flying to Hollywood to decide with Robert Gottschalk, President of Panavision, on the selection of the massive 70mm cameras, together with all the accessories and lenses.
>
> When I left David, he had said, "I want to get a *mirage,* Freddie. I don't know how in bloody hell we'll do it, but I want you to think about it." I was walking around the plant with Gottschalk, and I saw

Cinematographer Freddie Young, left, with Sam Spiegel and John Palmer at Aqaba camp.

this long lens—shaped like a fire-hose nozzle—on the desk and I said "Bob, what's that?" And he said, "It's a 482mm [extreme telephoto] lens." He gave me the idea that I should put that in my equipment. He said, "Good, glad to get rid of it. It's very seldom used." When I got back to David. I explained to him that I had got this long lens, and that this would enable us to get a close-up of a mirage.

Already I could see that the requirements of the film would be very complex and varied. I had spent two hectic weeks in Hollywood, dashing backwards and forwards between the Panavision offices and workshops, and Columbia Studios, where I tested cameras and added to the equipment all I thought we might need for a long and arduous period of work far away from civilization in remote parts of the desert. I lay awake at night, tired after an exhausting day, trying to think of some item which I might have forgotten and later on would need desperately.

Another busy week in London fixing my crew and equipment, then back to Jordan for final preparations, 'reckies', script reading and discussions, sorting out our gear, getting acclimatized, and testing cameras.

Property Department

The most visible evidence that a major film was in preproduction at Aqaba camp was the "props" compound, rapidly filling up with the "things" that David Lean would require to populate his images.

Eddie Fowlie, nominally the property master on *Lawrence,* was also David Lean's right-hand man, and would become his best friend. Fowlie was literally a jack-of-all-trades, and master of *all.*

Given the script, Fowlie would start "breaking it down." Typically, he would lie in bed from about four to five in the morning, thinking things out. Then he jotted down all his ideas, making a complete "prop breakdown." He would go through the script and underline everything which was an "essential prop," each of which he would have to find or make.

And then he would delineate anything that had to have *action* associated with it. For example, if a man had an "object" and he was going to hit somebody with it, Fowlie would need to know that, in case that object had to be made in a soft way. Next, he'd underline everything which required some *effect.* For example, striking a match. "It's got to strike, and the flame's got to be the right size, and so forth," explained Fowlie. Finally, he'd make a separate list at the side of the script of "all the stuff that I think I'm going to require for each set." Fowlie noted that collaboration with production designer John Box was an ongoing process.

Considerable preplanning was often necessary. A good example was the multitude of flags which helped give the riding sequences such impact. Fowlie explained:

> For flags, I usually just age them down with spray paint, or various acids, or bleach them out. For the *Lawrence* banners I made them very early, and put them all out in the weather, for weeks and weeks and weeks, blowing in the wind, and the sun, to get them a lovely bleached color. That's done for real. That's what you see in the picture. All the flags, all the flags throughout the picture. There were a lot of flags. And I find them very important. . .to have things in the top of the frame like that. I always try to do things that reach above the rest of the set—put something in the top of the frame. With the wind, it gives you that lovely motion. And David seemed to like the ones that were translucent, that you can see through. Kind of a gauze effect, wiping across.

"All those things on the camels—saddles, tassels—we made 'em right there in my prop making shop," Fowlie pointed out. The designs were based on historical photographs researched by John Box's art department.

"Slowly, I'd start to gather all the 'essential props' which are written into the script. I start to get the stuff, the essential things, together: the swords, the daggers, the stuff that's in the script, the stuff which the director has to O.K. And, hopefully, eventually I'll get David to come and see them all. All laid out in the prop room, which I've built. A prop room with shelves and tables and work benches and everything. And I'll lay out an

Above: Property Master Eddie Fowlie's compound at Aqaba Camp. Shelter for Lean's Rolls Royce in left background. Right: Props Truck: Fowlie, with property supervisors, brother Dave Fowlie and Tommy Raeburn, and chief makeup artist Charlie Parker.

exhibition of all the stuff.

"At Aqaba we had a huge prop compound in fact, with rooms inside it . . . David Lean would come and he'd say, 'Yes I like that' or 'don't like it . . . yes that's great' and then I stick a label on them and I say 'This is Ali's sword for the particular sequence of such and such a scene number,' and then it's all labeled up and it goes into the 'essential prop' truck. And all that is then looked after by my 'standby prop man.'

"And even if I'm not going to be on that set that day, I'll be there the first crack of the morning and make sure everything is ready for that day's work. But those things have got to be looked after, kept in good condition, repaired, polished, cleaned . . .or dirtied, whatever is required, covered in blood or whatever."

The strangest items found in Fowlie's prop department were "hundreds and hundreds of throwaway needles and syringes! They were for Sam, in case he required any injections. Sam shipped his *own* packages of hypodermics out for his private use. Never used them, but, I mean, that was the way it was gonna be. Sam was gonna have his own stock."

Fowlie recalls that *Lawrence* did not have a restrictive budget. For example, he had "more assistants on *Lawrence of Arabia* than I've ever had before or since. Normally I maybe take one, but on this occasion I took, in total, twelve. They were making props and they were in various parts of the desert. *Lawrence* was a big deal. Also it had to be correct, and damned good stuff. You had to be right, bang on. *Land of the Pharaohs* (Fowlie's first

film) didn't matter: who remembered what it was like three thousand years ago?"

Fowlie, Pete Dukelow, John Box, and David Lean were among the first into the desert, together with John Bryan. Bryan, one of the top designers in England, had done many of Lean's previous films, but had to leave the desert due to poor health. John Box, art director, then received his big break, and was promoted to production designer, with John Stoll hired to fill Box's position.

Production Design

John Box recalled the role of his team in *Lawrence of Arabia:*

The Art Department's main task is to provide the background behind the actors, and help tell the story in pictures that move. The all important factor is *atmosphere.* We are brought up to think in terms of decor, lighting, props, wardrobe, visual rhythm of contrast and style, and camera lenses, but never before have I been so conscious of them as I was during the making of *Lawrence of Arabia,* probably because of the extraordinary technical clarity and ability of David Lean.

In these deserts are the paths of many a prophet; and in the same area went Lawrence, to rise to great heights and to come crashing down. These deserts breathe history, and the efforts of man to find a fundamental philosophy. They are magnificent in their scale and variety. They can be romantically beautiful and awe-inspiring in their cruelty. This was the atmosphere we had to capture and instill right through to the end, even into the interiors of Cairo, Jerusalem and Damascus, because it was in these surroundings that Lawrence tried to find his true self. . .

We also had to create a classical quality in our story. To achieve this there must be clarity of intention, and then visually a directness of approach however complicated a scene might appear in the reading. There had to be a basic simplicity, and anything extraneous had to go however much one might be attracted by its beauty or its interest. Once we had decided on how to do a set or setting, then we had to concentrate all our efforts right down to the last detail in order to create the background and surroundings to Lawrence's life, whether in Jordan or far away in Spain. It had to be real, and if the costume designer and the art department have succeeded to any degree then an audience should never be aware that we were at work on the film, and accept everything as part of Lawrence's life, however dramatic it may seem.

Our part of Lawrence's life has been described as "a dream of high ideal, that turned into a nightmare." Therefore, when we came to the desert for the first time, our backgrounds in themselves had to be magnificent, romantic and inspiring in their scale and color. At the same time, at certain moments, the desert itself should warn us of the future. The scale had to put man in his place, against his surroundings, and at the same time accentuate his awareness of himself and his ambitions. This mood had to be with us until the big train derailing sequence, by which point the Bedouin had come to look upon "El Aurens" as some form of god, and Lawrence had started even to think of himself in the same terms.

From the train derailment onwards, the camera had to tighten slowly on Lawrence and examine him carefully through his doubts, his agonies, and finally in his apparent failure. The background had to change with Lawrence; there was no place for the vast scale setting, unless it helped to extenuate Lawrence's very personal problem.

Lawrence started his journey in Arabia and made his way to Jordan, and then into Syria, deviating only to return to Cairo across the Sinai desert from the southernmost point of Jordan, to take the news that Aqaba had fallen. The script required that, besides the

deserts we see Cairo, Jerusalem, Damascus, Aqaba and Deraa. The film runs for 3 hours 40 minutes approximately, and during this time we see many different settings. We never went back over old ground – except to Cairo, where we introduced General Allenby (which anyhow meant new set-dressing in order to create a new atmosphere in a previous set for the purpose of introducing a very important character dramatically), and to Aqaba to launch the second half of the film, and again to introduce a new character, Bentley. All this taxed our ability to the utmost, as, within a comparatively small area, we had to create the sense of the changing terrain, within vast overall distances, and give the audience a sense of what is required from a man to cover these distances, and live in such places.

It was clear from the start that to achieve these factors *Lawrence* was going to be physically an extremely difficult film to make. It has been called a "big" film, an epic – it had to be, it was an epic story we had to tell, and there was no other way to do it, to achieve the sense of the man himself.

Production Designer John Box.

SYNOPSIS OF "LAWRENCE OF ARABIA"

Most readers of this book are aware that films are not usually shot in the sequence found in the script. The next chapter describes the making of the movie in the chronological order in which it was filmed. For this reason, we provide a brief synopsis:

Lawrence of Arabia portrays that moment in WW I when a brash young British officer joins the Allied conflict in the Middle East, and plays the pivotal role in uniting the Arab tribes into an effective fighting force. British Intelligence sees the Arab Revolt against the Turks in 1916 as a possible wedge between Turkey and her German allies. Young lieutenant T. E. Lawrence, who knows Arabia from pre-Army days, is granted leave of absence from British Army HQ, Cairo, to investigate the revolt. This leave is grudgingly granted by General Murray at the instigation of Dryden, civilian head of the Arab Bureau.

Lawrence sets out across the desert to find Prince Feisal, a leader of the revolt. On the way, his guide is killed—in a nomadic quarrel—by Sherif Ali, chief of a rival tribe. Lawrence spurns the newcomer's offer to accompany him. Arriving at Feisal's camp as it is being strafed by Turkish planes, he hears Colonel Brighton, liaison officer, insisting that the Arabs adapt to modern warfare. Lawrence, however, recommends that they fight traditionally, using innovative guerilla tactics.

In a bold stroke, Lawrence, with Feisal's approval, persuades Sherif Ali—who has joined them—to aid in an attack from the land on the strategic Turkish port of Aqaba. This involves the feat of crossing the treacherous Nefud desert in order to unite with Auda abu Tayi and his Howeitat tribesmen. On the journey, Lawrence infuriates Ali when he courageously turns back to rescue Gasim, a shifty Arab who has fallen from his camel. The now respectful Ali urges him to discard his Army uniform for the white robes of a Sherif.

The initial meeting with Auda is not propitious. Just as the formidable chieftain is won over at the prospect of capturing Turkish gold, a Howeitat is killed by Gasim in a tribal squabble. To save the expedition, Lawrence intervenes and executes Gasim. They capture Aqaba, but when no gold is forthcoming, Lawrence writes Auda a promissory note.

With Farraj and Daud, his servants, he sets out across Sinai to inform his generals and get the money. On the journey, Daud loses his life in quicksand. In Cairo, Lawrence's triumph is recognized by Murray's successor, General Allenby. The general shrewdly recognizes that Lawrence's idealism can be turned to military advantage, and promises arms and money—everything except artillery, which might give the Arabs independence.

Lawrence's further successes in ambushing troop and supply trains result in "El Aurens" becoming a legendary name among the tribes. These exploits are witnessed by Bentley, a tough, cynical American war correspondent who glamorizes Lawrence in his dispatches. After each raid, however, more and more Bedouins retreat into the desert with their booty and Lawrence's force dwindles. Having promised Allenby that the Arab Revolt would be in Deraa before the British are in Jerusalem, Lawrence goes in disguise to scout the Turkish stronghold. He is captured, beaten at the order of the sadistic Bey, and flung on a rubbish heap where Ali rescues him.

Lawrence emerges from the experience acutely aware that he is no superman and would have betrayed his friends to stop the torture. His will is broken. He retreats to Jerusalem, to ask for reassignment. It takes all of Allenby's diplomacy to persuade Lawrence that *he* is the person to lead a newly-equipped Arab force on Damascus. After a bloody slaughter of Turks outside the village of Tafas, Lawrence and his Arabs enter Damascus. By the time Allenby, Brighton and Dryden arrive, squabbling has already broken out among the tribes. Allenby sits back to await the inevitable: the collapse of the United Arab Council, and with it, Lawrence's dream.

Unable to unite the Arabs and no longer wanted by the British, Lawrence finds he has been promoted to colonel simply so that he can have a cabin to himself on the boat home. The Arabs and the British acknowledge their debt to Lawrence, but—at the end—Feisal suggests to Allenby, "We are equally glad to be rid of him, are we not?"

On the road leaving Damascus, Lawrence looks in vain for a friendly face. There is nothing but endless desert.

CHAPTER 5

ON LOCATION

*"THE ENGLISH HAVE A GREAT HUNGER FOR
DESOLATE PLACES."*

—FEISAL TO LAWRENCE, IN FEISAL'S TENT

JORDAN: Jebel Tubeiq

While the Aqaba base camp was being established, however, reconnaissance units were far out in the desert selecting camera set-ups for the first shooting location. This remote wilderness recommended itself by virtue of its brilliant red sand dunes and stark black mountains.

Jebel Tubeiq is situated over 250 miles due east of Aqaba, near (or even over!) the Saudi Arabian frontier: a spot so desolate that even the Bedouin avoid the place, for the nearest water is 150 miles away. It was discovered through aerial reconnaissance by director David Lean and production designer John Box, and until photographs and sketches of the area had been made by this duo and their associates, it had been unmarked on any map. In 1960, it had been without rain for seven years.

Jebel Tubeiq had been uninhabited since the seventh century A.D., when a band of monks abandoned a monastery which they had established there, in what must have been the world's most remote hideout. Since then, there had rarely been a sign of human life, except for perhaps an occasional camel caravan en route to Mecca. Until the arrival of the film troupe, T.E. Lawrence was undoubtedly one of the very few white men ever to have laid eyes on the region. Paleolithic rock carvings in the same area are said to date back 12,000 years.

The reconnaissance units lived in "reckie" camps consisting of three to four 165-pound tents, sleeping six to a tent on folding camp-cots. Phil Hobbs was there, too, fighting to keep sandstorms from ripping tents to shreds, learning that all seams and stitching would have to be reinforced, deciding that all future camps would

need mattresses or the crew would shiver all night in the bitter cold despite daytime temperatures up to 125 degrees. This was an experiment in living conditions as well as in location scouting.

Phil Hobbs, along with construction foreman Peter Dukelow and his assistant Fred Bennett, had to organize the feeding and housing of a seventy-three-man, mostly British crew, together with 120 Jordanians. Every drop of water, every grain of food would have to be trucked in over trails that did not yet exist.

Hobbs's first task was to hire 2400-gallon tanker trucks, formerly used for hauling kerosene, to bring in water daily from the El Hasa oasis, over a hundred miles away. There are no roads between El Hasa and Jebel Tubeiq. The water trucks cut their own trails.

Within a week, a small "city" sprang up at Jebel Tubeiq. The living and working facilities for the population of 203 consisted partly of tents, partly of wheeled caravans.

Hobbs's food supplies were partly provided by Jordanian farms near Ma'an, 150 miles to the west, and partly by frozen packages shipped every second week from London and Denmark through the Mediterranean and the Suez Canal to the unit's Aqaba camp on the Red Sea. Ground transportation from there to Tubeiq was partially pioneered by the first convoy of their Land Rovers and Austin Gypsies to make the 250-mile trek. The original mobile kitchen at Tubeiq gave way to a complete cook-tent as personnel grew, and a generator truck provided electricity both for the tents and the refrigeration units.

The company's eight-place Dove airplane ferried actors, technicians, and petrol supplies. To supplement transportation, the Royal Jordanian Air Force supplied a four-motor Heron, later supplanted by two thirty-two-place Dakotas (DC-3s).

To supply each member of that troupe with food, drink, living quarters, and tools during the first three-month period required the equivalent of a fully loaded thirteen-ton truck.

Shooting at an elevation of 2,500 to 3,000 feet, cameraman Freddie Young and his crew might be faced at any moment with a sudden sandstorm, heat mirage, or other atmospheric conditions sufficient to drive men crazy. The schedule worked out in such a way as to permit periodic rest periods back at Aqaba. The heat might be just as extreme there, complicated by high humidity, but at least one could go swimming and eat food without sand in it.

This advance shooting unit became known as "Lean's Mobile Maniacs." A dedicated group of artists in every line, they knew that their constant discomforts were the price of authenticity.

John Box recalled the challenges of their first location:

> The production problems were considerable and the demands on the unit enormous, but here we got our desert, and this we had to have.
>
> In Jebel Tubeiq and all the other desert areas we found it very difficult to put over the feeling of the intense heat in which Lawrence worked, and in which we had to work. The desert is very dry, and any

moisture dries immediately, thus you do not see damp sweaty clothes when out in the open. (This method of showing heat has become almost a film cliché.) If there had to be perspiration, it had to be put on by the make-up man. Dust helped and it was with us in large quantities; it naturally settled on the actors, their clothes and their beasts. The intense blue sky of Arabia doesn't give a sense of intense heat on the screen, and therefore many shots were backlit with the strong shadows very much in evidence. Backlighting was particularly successful when the floor of the desert was basalt (a hard black stone with no color in it). This basalt gives off a pronounced heat shimmer, and in these areas there were excellent mirages. The larger basalt boulders are cruel, and I think helped us most in the effort to emphasize personal endeavor. The actual temperatures in which we, the unit, worked in Jordan were very high. I can remember telling the General commanding the Bedouin forces that it would be necessary for us to work in southern Jordan during June, July and August. His only comment was, "It will be terrible for the camels." They survived.

The opening sequence with Tafas leading Lawrence to Feisal's camp was the first to be shot here. Two factors had to be established: first, a romantic background, and second, the vast scale of Arabia. This Jebel Tubeiq did for us, also showing the audience quite a deal of sand which, I suppose, is the accepted notion of desert in the western world. At the same time we started to reveal that there are many more facets to the desert than just this.

"Every morning we would be waked at 5:30 and we'd go to his trailer. And every morning we'd see the same sight: planted in the midst of that trackless immensity, a chair bearing a man. It was David Lean studying the horizon. He'd already been there, alone, motionless, for two hours. He had to have his ration of the desert every day."—Omar Sharif

One of Spiegel's fleet of three planes arrives in Tubeiq, with camera crew, for start of film adventure.

Above: "Eva Monley was sort of a 'production help' to John Palmer, who organized practically everything. She certainly was a character . . . She always wore two different colored shoes. It was her trademark. Eva involved herself very much in the 'transport department.'"—Eddie Fowlie

Center Left: Water, at three dollars per gallon, had to be hauled across 150 miles of desert in giant trucks. These were converted oil tankers that had been washed out: they roared constantly back and forth for three months. "Physical discomfort," director David Lean had said, "is the price of authenticity."

Left: At the Tubeiq location, it was quickly discovered that the tents had to be reinforced to prevent ripping in the violent sandstorms. Here, Second Assistant Director David Tringham runs for shelter.

Left: The production unit had a two-man medical staff, headed by Dr. Eustace Shipman.

Below: Spiegel was usually on his yacht, moored in the Red Sea. Here he confers with Lean on one of his infrequent location visits.

Bottom: First Assistant Director Roy Stevens.

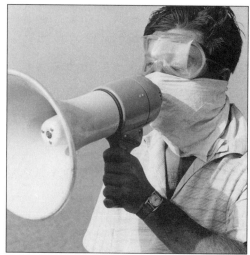

"He wasn't the youngest of the camera crew, but Freddie Young could stay up all night and out dance them. He had more energy than the rest of them put together!"—Phyllis Dalton

Right: The radio crew adopted code names for their far-flung communications network: headquarters in Amman was "HORIZON 1," Base Camp in Aqaba was "HORIZON 2," and the current shooting location was "HORIZON 3." Brian Coates, an Assistant Director in the early days of the film, at left, behind operator.

One of the first things that Peter Dukelow built at Tubeiq was the bar. It consisted of "some bits of plywood and bamboo and had straw mats hung around the walls." Beer and soft drinks were available from 5:30 p.m. to midnight, and a gramophone pumped out Johnny Mathis tunes. At left, pouring drink, is Cliff Richardson (Special Effects). In striped shirt, at bar, is rigger Tim Murphy, in charge of scaffold construction.

"The first night in the desert I turned on my little Zenith short-wave radio to try and find some news. And just as an enormous sun came up over the horizon— it made my hair stand on end — the music from Bridge on the River Kwai came on. And I thought, 'Christ, if that's not a good omen . . .'

"My personal campsite, about twelve miles away from the unit, was very close to where we were going to shoot the initial scenes. So I thought, 'Well, I'll be ready to greet David first day of shooting.' And so, near to my truck, just before you arrived at the site, I put down some artificial grass, a square of it, a lawn. And I put down some nice beach furniture, a table and chairs, and a nice umbrella over it, and an English teapot with tea and tea service, and laid it all out there. When David drove by, I invited him to stop and have English tea on the 'lawn.'"—Eddie Fowlie

Barbara Cole, Freddie Young and David Lean examine script in early days of shooting.

Lean loved the desert: "I used to sometimes go out at night. If there was no moon I'd walk across the flats and see the vague shapes of these pyramids—not man-made, but wind-made. And countless stars that one's never realized before. When you're in the desert, you look into infinity. It's no wonder that nearly all the great founders of religions came out of the desert. It makes you feel very, very small."

Director Lean discusses first scenes in desert with Peter O'Toole and Zia Mohyeddin, who plays Lawrence's guide, Tafas.

"David is the most determined man I ever met in my life. He would have his way. He was absolutely 101 percent determined. And I don't care what you did, how you went about it. In the end, David would have it his way. Not other way. I wouldn't give a damn even if Marlon Brando was the actor. David would have it his way and not Marlon Brando's way."
—Eddit Fowlie

Below: Dalton's costume reference photos for the "Journey" sequence, filmed the last half of May 1961.

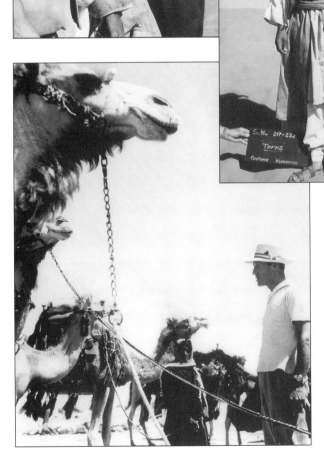

Jeremy Taylor, "Master of the Horse" (or, in this case, Camel). Eighty camels and riders were chosen from 1,500 inspected by Taylor, together with Lean, chief stunt man John Sullivan, and veterinarian Dr. Raif Asharif.

John Woolfenden, director of publicity, was there on May 15, 1961, to describe the first day of shooting for *The New York Times:*

Up the face of an almost perpendicular sand dune, in the desert vastness of Jordan's Jebel Tubeiq, a 500-foot ski-lift now has been built. It has been rigged out of a complex of metal poles, wooden platforms, ladders, block and tackle combinations, and at least half a mile of rope. Its purpose is to lift both personnel and material to the top of the blood red dune, for the current shooting of the career of the British World War I writer-soldier-mystic. The equipment works like a charm. But there is something about being hauled through sand on a rope that causes Mr. Lean and most of his cast and crew to prefer climbing unassisted.

Although summer has scarcely started at Jebel Tubeiq, the heat radiates like the proverbial blast furnace from the unique vermilion sand which rises in drifts from the desert floor to a height of a thousand feet. Cast and crew wear goggles, for not only does the dazzling color hurt the eyes after a prolonged gaze, but also the sand itself, blown by the "khamsin," or desert wind, stings like birdshot.

An entire morning is consumed taking two complete Panavasion cameras, parts, reflectors, sound-recording equipment, and all the paraphernalia of color filming to the lip of the first dune. There is a second 500-foot stretch of sand above it. Scores of green canvas bags, filled with sand have been set into the face of the lower dune to provide steps.

You then look down the far side of the dune onto a wood and metal track that was hauled up piecemeal and assembled the day before to provide traction for what is known as a "Wickham dolly." This is a camera mount on wheels that rolls along the track, but that on this occasion is hooked to another block and tackle since it must be pulled uphill, time after time, through rehearsal and "takes" by a dozen men running backward. Small wonder that at the end of the day, members of the *Lawrence* troupe drink one cold (they hope) beer, eat a dinner brought by refrigerated ship and truck from London, and fall exhausted into bed.

At the moment, however, they have work to do. Below the track, in a second cup-like depression, Peter O'Toole and Pakistani actor, Zia Mohyeddin, as the guide Tafas, await the signal to ride their camels into view.

Director Lean, burned almost as black as the surrounding volcanic buttes after more than six months of preparatory work in the southeast Jordanian wastelands, waves his hat for the camels to advance. His assistant, Roy Stevens, signals frantically for a moment's delay. He has spotted a white plastic drinking cup, being whipped by the wind right into the camera's line of view.

The riders touch the necks of their camels with thin wooden guide sticks. But Lean wants a special effect of the wind blowing the sand from the top of the dune. It creates an unearthly golden light as the grains whirl and eddy in fantastic patterns above the red sand carpet. Midafternoon shadows are creeping down the face of the upper dune. There is probably half an hour of shooting time remaining. The wind suddenly comes in gusts, the hat is waved again, the camels advance, the camera swivels on its platform, and the dolly is hauled smoothly across the track. Mr. O'Toole dismounts at the edge of the precipice and his camel kneels, as the script requires. Mr. Mohyeddin's mount refuses, though he tugs desperately at its neck and repeats the guttural Arabic kneeling command. There may yet be time to try it again.

Mr. O'Toole and Mr. Mohyeddin start once more.

Cameraman Freddie Young resights through his viewfinder. Continuity girl Barbara Cole wipes her goggles and checks her shorthand notes. At the last second, a bright blue beach umbrella is set up over the second camera, which is nearly cooking its film in the shimmering heat. Mr. Lean bites his lip and tensely awaits the right second to start. Here comes the wind again.

The camels behave like a team this time since the kneeling has been eliminated until a later sequence. The actors perform with split-second precision, dismount, and scan the route ahead. For the first time, Mr. Lean permits himself a smile as he waves to the camera to "cut." A dedicated perfectionist, he glows for a second in the congratulations of a dedicated crew.

There may be ten months of such work ahead, with a crisis every hour, but the first scene for the multimillion-dollar *Lawrence of Arabia* is in the can.

Left: A primitive pulley system was used to lift equipment, in this case a light, up the dunes. You would pull down on one rope, and it lifted the equipment up on the other.

Below: Gaffers haul heavy electrical cables from generator truck to shooting location.

"It's hard to go up those sand dunes. You took one step up and slipped back half a step," noted David Tringham, ascending dune on "ski lift" behind O'Toole.

Shooting locations were usually miles away from base camp at Tubeiq. This helped prevent tire tracks, footprints, and plastic cups from littering Lean's landscape. Tringham recalled: "Each day, Roy Rossotti (Assistant Art Director) would scout and mark the best route from camp to the next day's filming site. The following morning, all our trucks would line up beside each other and—at a given signal—would race to the first marker. From there on, we had to drive in single file. The winner's prize was the joy of not having to swallow red dust all the way. David's vehicle, of course, always left five minutes before the race began."

"I hope the money men don't find out that I'd pay them to let me do this."—David Lean

David Tringham (at right, with clapper-board) remembers the early days of shooting: "I was the second assistant, you know, and at first we didn't have radios. One day, I was sent to a nearby dune, with a red flag and a green flag, just in case a jeep would come along. But there wasn't a road. They weren't coming that way. There was no traffic as far as the eye could see. And I thought, 'I'm the most highly paid stopper of non-existent traffic that ever existed.' You'd sit there, just sit there and think, 'Well, this is what it's like working on a David Lean film. This is what it's like on the big ones.'"

Eddie Fowlie recalls: "First we'd play a scene, and of course the sand's all kicked up, so you've got to put all the sand back for 'take two.' If anybody put a foot on it—it was murder. Or if one of those bloody plastic cups blew out, I had to have all kinds of long canes to rescue the stuff. And to get rid of footprints, we had 300 locals with palm fronds and all kinds of soft brooms. Sometimes we'd even drag mats across or use big tennis court brooms to keep the desert clean. One tool I made was a huge powder puff on the end of a long cane, to do the final touches. Also, a little fan, to get the ripples back in. It was a tremendous effort. We'd waste quite a lot of time keeping the desert virginized."

David Tringham was also concerned with this problem. "They'd roped off some desert, and we went there next morning, and somebody'd walked straight across it. And they had these very distinct footprints. So, David said, 'I want to find who that is. I want a shoe inspection.' They never did find out who it was."

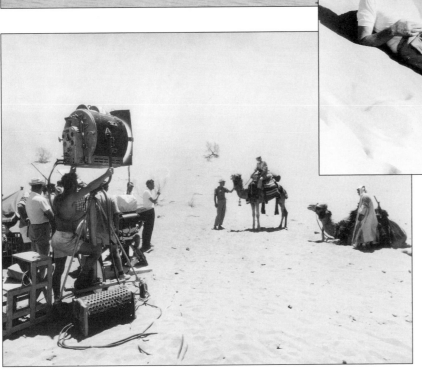

"...O'Toole dominates the film. He is on camera for 218 minutes, and he spins off now with arrogance, now with resignation—a record 648 lines. It is the longest speaking part in the history of movies."—Saturday Evening Post, *March 9, 1963*

Opposite and above: Freddie Young sets up day-for-night scene with Lawrence and Tafas. Tringham recalls, "David said to Peter, 'You're in the desert, and you're hungry. But you've got to keep your culture, your civilization, your Englishness. You're holding this thin arrowroot biscuit . . . very delicately. And you just sort of nibble it, don't munch it . . . Eddie, have we got enough of these biscuits?' Eddie growled, 'Don't worry about it, David. I've got a gross of biscuit boxes for you in my dump. All kinds.' "

Eddie Fowlie remembers, "In the script, Tafas was eating 'rancid mutton fat.' For this 'Bedu food,' I think I used chunks of marshmallow with a bit of color on 'em. Easier for the actor to do a few takes that way."

Above: A series of publicity stills were taken at Jebel Tubeiq to accompany newspaper articles—to appear later in 1961—about the filming of Lawrence.

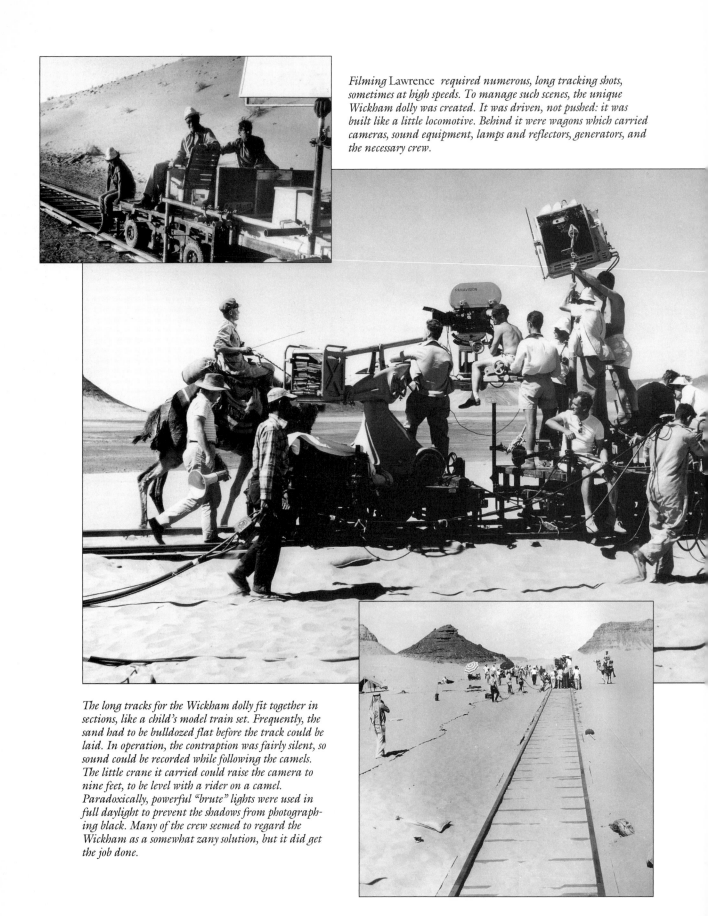

Filming Lawrence required numerous, long tracking shots, sometimes at high speeds. To manage such scenes, the unique Wickham dolly was created. It was driven, not pushed: it was built like a little locomotive. Behind it were wagons which carried cameras, sound equipment, lamps and reflectors, generators, and the necessary crew.

The long tracks for the Wickham dolly fit together in sections, like a child's model train set. Frequently, the sand had to be bulldozed flat before the track could be laid. In operation, the contraption was fairly silent, so sound could be recorded while following the camels. The little crane it carried could raise the camera to nine feet, to be level with a rider on a camel. Paradoxically, powerful "brute" lights were used in full daylight to prevent the shadows from photographing black. Many of the crew seemed to regard the Wickham as a somewhat zany solution, but it did get the job done.

Top: O'Toole's hair received the attention of A. G. Scott ("Scottie"), the Hairdressing Department.

Omar Sharif arrived at Tubeiq to begin the "raiding party trek" scenes the last week of June 1961.

"No director gets the same performance out of anybody that David did. Doesn't matter who it is. I don't care who it is. Nobody gets the same performance as David did. David was always ready to fire a bloody actor and replace him. Nothing deters David."—Eddie Fowlie

Right: Phyllis Dalton inspects costumes of tribesmen during filming of "Raiders Trek" sequence.

Below: Charlie Guerin, wardrobe master.

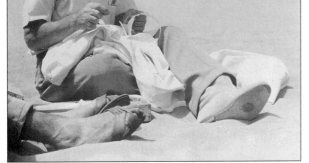

Above: Arab tribesmen photographed during WWI Arab Revolt.

Left: Jordanian extras portraying their ancestors in Lawrence.

Top: Peter O'Toole, Sam Spiegel, and David Lean relaxing on set.

Bottom: Filming trek sequence in which Lawrence, Ali, and fifty raiders are heading for Aqaba.

Top: Sound mixer Paddy Cunningham.

Inset: Peter showing chief stunt man John Sullivan how to double as Lawrence.

By now, in a tribute to Peter O'Toole's prowess and stamina, the Bedouin were calling him "El Aurens," the same name they had once given Lawrence. It was almost as if he had somehow assimilated Lawrence's masochistic pleasure in driving himself to exhaustion.

"You know," O'Toole quipped to photographer Mark Kauffman one day, "if someone had just given that bloody Lawrence a cigarette, a bottle of whiskey, and a woman forty-four years ago, none of us would be in this bloody place today."

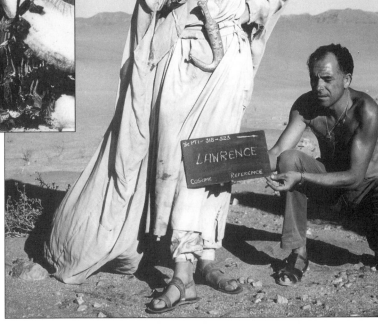

Top: Wickham dolly: Jeremy Taylor leading Lawrence and Ali's camels.

Above: Freddie Young taking light meter reading of inquisitive friend.

Right: Costume reference photo for Lawrence in a scene where he drops compass during journey across Sinai.

The "quicksand" scene, the last to be filmed at Tubeiq, was shot at the end of June. Eddie Fowlie—seen below in "pit" handing a drink to Peter—described the scene: "They built the usual 'porridge pit' and it was a disaster. The boy wasn't sinking, and the sand was becoming a lumpy mess. I made a box, a four-foot cube, in the ground, with a big rubber 'iris' on top. I went down into the box, and held the boy up by the legs, then slowly pulled him down, with all the sand coming in on top of me."—Eddie Fowlie

Bottom left: Crew with wind machine.

Bottom right: Barbara Cole with John Dimech (Daud), discussing his sandy demise.

JORDAN: El Jafr

From Jebel Tubeiq, the troupe moved bag and baggage to an identical camp on the El Jafr mudflats, where all roads end and only old caravan trails extend into the hinterland to the east.

John Box recalled:

This was the second area we used in Jordan. The mudflats were white, absolutely flat, and stretched as far as the eye could see—nothing could have been more simple and nothing more awe-inspiring and fascinating. Driving at night on these mudflats was a very peculiar experience, as you could swing the steering wheel around as much as you liked, but you never seemed to change direction, as there was absolutely nothing to give you a sense of direction, nothing in your lights for miles and miles.

During the day, as the sun got higher over the mudflats, vast mirages would appear around you. Mirages do not take the form of cities and palm groves (this is a mirage of the imagination), but are physical in so much as the tiny particles are reflecting back the sky. The mirage can often appear as a blue lake, or sometimes just as a jelly of nothingness that disrupts the distances and horizons. Objects are reflected in these mirages, and a man becomes elongated to twice his height; at the same time the heat haze being given off causes a walking man to appear as an eerie, bobbing, dancing object.

David Lean from the start wanted to introduce Ali to the picture, and to Lawrence, with such a metaphysical atmosphere. Ali had immediately to bring with him the real and the unreal of the desert life. Ali was *revealed* to Lawrence through a mirage at Jafr. The dancing, black apparition came out of the mirage and became stark reality, cruelly shooting down Lawrence's guide Tafas for drinking at his well. Lawrence was brought face to face with the age-old Bedouin law of the desert, the law based on survival in such places.

We also shot what we knew as the Gasim sequence at Jafr. On the trek to Aqaba, Lawrence, Ali and the raiding party had to cross the 'sun's anvil,' the very worst of the desert, and cross it by night because of the impossible heat during the day. Again the mudflats of Jafr provided the starkness and the harshness for the ''anvil'' as the sun changed from a fiery red to a merciless white and Lawrence retraced his steps back to find Gasim, and at the same time accepted the challenge he had given to himself.

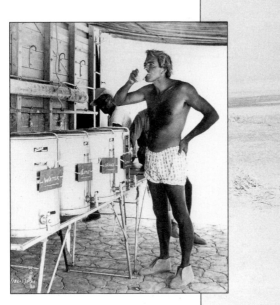

The script calls Jafr "a burning, fiery furnace." Eddie Fowlie, like the others, constantly sought relief. Only David Lean seemed comfortable.

In a telegram, Spiegel threatened to "sweep away and replace the whole crew" if they couldn't work any faster. Lean had himself filmed in a sand storm with a broom and sent a 70mm reply.

"...we had that delicious thrill 'Friend or enemy?' of meeting strangers in the desert..."
—T. E. Lawrence, Seven Pillars

July 1961 was spent at El Jafr, where the first scene shot was the now legendary arrival of Ali at the well.

Top left: "David would say, 'Come on, Freddie, we'll go on a reckie,' and we would go miles to pinpoint the location for the next day's work. Of course, we had arguments, but it was all to do with the best way to shoot a scene. Once shooting starts, the relationship between the director and cinematographer is very close, and at the end of the day, we were good friends."—Freddie Young

Top right: Young, Cole, Lean, Ernie Day (camera operator), Box, and Ken Withers (focus) at test of "mirage lens."

"Our film relationship gradually revealed itself in affectionate behavior which was in fact a reflection of the everyday life that Peter O'Toole and I were living. I'm convinced that the fraternal feeling that sprang up between us was one of the great things to come out of the movie. You know, Peter and I never speak a kind word throughout the film, and yet people come out feeling that we loved each other."—Omar Sharif

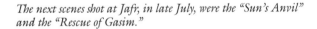

George of Arabia

The next scenes shot at Jafr, in late July, were the "Sun's Anvil" and the "Rescue of Gasim."

Top: Another Lawrence innovation, for both tracking and static shots, was the CAM-EL (CAMera-ELevating vehicle), a truck with a hydraulic platform, like a forklift, in front. A camera could be placed on it and raised. In addition, there was a roof platform for filming, and inside were film changing, storage, and washroom facilities. The Americans called it "The Blue Goose."

Bottom: "Is it the blood? The desert has dried up more blood than you can think of."—*Auda abu Tayi.* "Same desert, new war, more blood. An editorial cartoon, an analogy. Here Margaret Thatcher has slipped from the saddle just like poor and unfortunate Gasim. George wonders what has happened to her. 'God knows,' is the reply. Besides, wasn't it written in the London Times? Somehow I can't imagine President Bush going back for her. However, I believe Ronald Reagan would have. He believed in movies, and so do I."—*Calvin Grondahl*

(Grondahl's "Desert Storm" cartoon was syndicated in December 1990.)

"... Gasim was not there ... the miserable man was lost. This was a dreadful business, for in the haze and mirage the caravan could not be seen two miles, and on the iron ground it made no tracks: afoot, he would never overtake us. Upon me lay the responsibility of him ... My shirking the duty would be understood, because I was a foreigner: but ...I should make it impossible for myself if I claimed, simultaneously, the privileges of both societies ... I turned my unwilling camel round, and forced her, grunting and moaning for her camel friends, back past the long line of men, and past the baggage into the emptiness behind.

"... Not a long death—even for the very strongest, a second day in summer was all—but very painful; for thirst was an active malady; a fear and panic which tore at the brain and reduced the bravest man to a stumbling babbling maniac in an hour or two; and then the sun [would kill] him."—*T. E. Lawrence, Seven Pillars*

JORDAN: Wadi Rumm

After three weeks of filming on the scorching mudflats of El Jafr, a three-day rest period was decreed and the Bedouin extras were permitted to visit Ma'an, the nearest town. They were then taken in Mercedes trucks, through miles of talcum-like sand and dust to the next location, Wadi Rumm.

The entire Jebel Tubeiq camp had been moved there, and another camp was established at El Quweira, site of Jordan's largest desert camel market.

John Box:

Wadi Rumm, the third main area used in Jordan, was called "Ram" in the book of Genesis. It is about twenty miles northeast of the head of the gulf of Aqaba and separated from it by an arid range of mountains. It was entirely different from the other areas, with its towering red cliffs rising two or three thousand feet from the pink, sandy floor of the desert. It was grand, romantic, but more sympathetic to man than Jebel Tubeiq, partly because of its color, and partly the feeling that there might be help behind the towering cliffs. The emphasis was vertical, rather than exposing vast lateral distances. We used it accordingly.

Feisal's camp, filmed at nearby El Quweira, had to have a melancholic atmosphere to emphasize the hopeless position he found himself in during his fight to achieve independence from the Turks. His camp was large, but the setting not very dramatic. Feisal rode out of the dust and smoke caused by the Turkish bombs to stop and ponder on his hopeless position; then, being aware of a presence, he suddenly looked up. Lawrence and Feisal came face to face for the first time. Destiny was at work. The smoke and dust gave us the atmosphere, not the terrain.

We used another area of Rumm for the Well which lay at the far side of the Nefud desert, and which was a sanctuary to the raiding party at the end of the trek. It was at this Well that Ali came to accept Lawrence and gave him the robes of an Arab. There followed the scene in which Lawrence paraded himself in these new white garments in solitude, only to be rudely disturbed by Auda. David Lean revealed Auda, the big warrior of Southern Jordan whose name is famous

John Box, Production Designer, surveys the glories of Wadi Rumm.

to this day, by the use of his camera. The camera movement was all important to create surprise. The background was important for Lawrence, but technique with a moving camera introduced the character of Auda.

The camp of this large, expansive man of the desert, and his tribe the Howeitat, was set in Wadi Rumm itself. We shepherded the Bedouin into areas to form with their black tents the pattern and design we wanted beneath the towering, skyscraping cliffs of Rumm. But, the nocturnal interior scenes of Auda's tent were later shot in Spain, at night, since we had to have more lamps there than we had in Jordan. Auda had been won over to the cause. The following morning, the original raiding party, now joined by eight hundred of the Howeitat, set out on the last leg to Aqaba in high excitement. We used the most visually romantic and large-scale parts of Rumm, together with the trilling of the Arab women, to accent and heighten this mood.

A total of nearly 3,000 Bedouin men were employed in the Quweira and Rumm sequences, with 1,600 of them, plus their wives and children and livestock, appearing at Auda's camp at the extreme south end of Wadi Rumm. Here, at the base of fantastically carved and eroded buttes, the Bedu, from every part of Jordan, set up some 350 black goat-hair tents and resumed the life that they have lived since Biblical times, except that now it was being filmed.

The Bedouin women, however, were not permitted to appear before the cameras. It is believed bad luck to permit another man to own a picture of "your woman." When women were needed in order to provide an authentic picture of the camp life, 20 of them had to be "imported" from Aqaba — members of a Christian church whose priest gave them special permission. This was the first time they had ridden in a plane, the first time they had earned money, the first experience they had had with a motion picture. And the Bedu men, whose own women had disappeared, as ordered, into the hills, flocked around to watch the newcomers.

With more than 1,400 of Jordan's finest camels and Arabian horses to be fed and watered, in addition to supplies being provided for the tribespeople, water requirements alone now soared to some 35,000 gallons per day.

"I felt at first glance that this was the man I had come to Arabia to seek— the leader who would bring the Arab Revolt to full glory. Feisal looked very tall and pillar-like, very slender, in his long silk robes . . . His hands were crossed in front of him on his dagger."
—T. E. Lawrence,
Seven Pillars

Top left: Sir Alec Guinness arrived in Jordan July 15, 1961, to play Emir Feisal, seen in WWI photos, top right and left center. The Daily Express *criticized Sir Alec's first riding lesson (top center), and noted several faults, including "His feet are pointing outwards instead of forwards." Guinness was not pleased.*

Left: On July 29, filming started at Wadi Rumm, with exteriors of "Feisal's Second Camp," and the pivotal "In whose name do you ride?" sequence.

During August 1961, the scenes "Lawrence meets Brighton," and the "Bombing" and "Exodus" of Feisal's camp were filmed in the region.

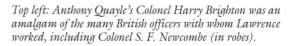

Top left: Anthony Quayle's Colonel Harry Brighton was an amalgam of the many British officers with whom Lawrence worked, including Colonel S. F. Newcombe (in robes).

Top: One of Horizon's transport fleet, a DC-3, together with WWI British Tiger Moths disguised as Turkish warplanes.

Above: Snapshot panorama, by Phyllis Dalton, of Feisal's first camp, before the "Bombing" scene (left).

Bottom: Visualization sketch by John Box, and filming of the epic "Exodus" scene in which Feisal's camp moves south to escape further aerial bombing by the Turks (see also page 130, top).

99

Like the British officers relaxing in Aqaba in 1917 (right), the crew used their Aqaba camp for recreation in 1961, between bouts of desert filming.

At Jebel Tubeiq, the crew took a "weekend" only every three weeks. But, from Rumm, the crew could commute to Aqaba every day. Top left: Freddie Young with AD's David Tringham and Michael Stevenson. Dalton called the impish boys "the funniest comedy team you ever saw, doing brilliant takeoffs of everyone on the film."

Center left: Gamil Ratib with Sharif, who watched all 102 films shown at the camp's outdoor cinema. Center right: John Dimech. Bottom left: Anthony Quinn arrived at Aqaba in late August to play the role of brigand Howeitat chieftain Auda abu Tayi. Bottom right: I. S. Johar and Quinn.

Left: T. E. L.'s 1921 photo of Auda abu Tayi (right) and son (left).
Below: Columbia 1962 publicity photo shows
Quinn, with Kennington portrait of Auda from 1926 Seven Pillars.

T. E. L. wrote of Auda: "He saw life as a saga . . . all personages in contact with him heroic . . . When Auda dies, the Middle Ages will be over." In early September 1961, O'Toole was filmed receiving his robes, and meeting Auda. Center left: Make-up chief Charlie Parker, "a brilliant character," was creator and custodian of "The Nose." Center right: King Hussein meets "Auda." Left: T. E. L. in Aqaba, 1918; Peter O'Toole with new robes in Wadi Rumm (see page 120).

"We were riding for Rumm . . . We looked up on the left to a long wall of rock, sheering in like a thousand-foot wave . . . the other side straightened itself to one massive rampart of redness. They . . . must have been a thousand feet above us, [and] ran forward in an avenue for miles . . . this processional way greater than imagination. The Arab armies would have been lost in the length and breadth of it, and within the walls a squadron of airplanes could have wheeled in formation. Our little caravan grew self-conscious, and fell dead quiet, afraid and ashamed to flaunt its smallness in the presence of the stupendous hills."
—*T. E. Lawrence,* Seven Pillars

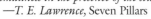

In mid-September 1961, the entry to, and departure from, Auda's spectacular camp were filmed in Wadi Rumm.

"It took 3 weeks to build that camp. Up on a hill, Johnny Box put a 'viewing' frame, and said, 'Dress me a set to fit that frame.' I kept going back to that damn thing to look through it, so that no tent was hidden behind another one. It was such an enormous set that I had to drive around in a jeep to organize it."—*Eddie Fowlie*

Top: John Box sketch for Auda's camp. Center right: Photo by T. E. L., 1917.

"There were two other sorties made in Jordan with a small film unit; one was to an area known as 'H.4' in the north-east of Jordan on the border with Iraq, to shoot eyelines of a particularly awesome desert; and one other to a peculiar, desolate terrain known by us as 'White Rock.' It was here that we shot the eerie opening sequence of "Crossing Sinai," on September 28, 1961. This was the last scene shot in Jordan." —*John Box*

Interlude

The mounting expenses of filming in Jordan had finally emptied Spiegel's pockets to the point that he insisted a less expensive location must be found to finish *Lawrence*. The chosen country was Spain, apparently the site of another stash of Spiegel's frozen funds. Moreover, Spain had areas which could masquerade as desert, and Moorish architecture which could evoke the look of Middle Eastern cities.

An interlude in England would allow the cast a respite from the rigors of desert filming. Robert Bolt could now complete the second half of the script, and the crew could move from Jordan and start to set up in Spain. Guinness and Quinn both left to work on other films in the interim. Spiegel demanded that Sharif accompany him to England, for fear that his new star might be detained back in Egypt without another exit visa. O'Toole became Sharif's guide to English pubs, nightlife, and the London West End theatres. The main exodus from Jordan, by air, was on October 1, 1961.

Native Jordanians had been convinced that no white man could live through a desert summer. The *Lawrence* cast and crew had proved them wrong. Despite dehydration in the heat, despite dysentery, despite the fact that the crew members had lost an average of fifteen pounds in weight, they returned exhausted but triumphant, and were given a six-week rest period to recuperate.

Eddie Fowlie recalls that one of the final shots in Jordan had involved camels in the usual spectacular desert panorama. David Lean remarked, ''Bloody well match that somewhere else in the world!'' Lean, in fact, didn't want to leave the desert at all, and stayed in Wadi Rumm for some time after cast and crew had left.

Fowlie's job was to coordinate the transport of all the equipment to Spain. Spiegel chartered a tramp steamer and almost everything—including trailers and generators and the ''star'' camels and horses—was loaded aboard. The strangest and most fragrant part of the cargo was about 100 stuffed camels. Fowlie had bought the skins from a slaughterhouse and had stuffed them with straw, to be used ''just in case'' Lean needed them in shots after battle scenes.

Top: "SEE WHAT O'TOOLE BROUGHT HOME . . . ONE GENUINE BEDOUIN," read the headline in the Daily Mail *of October 3, 1961. O'Toole had returned from Jordan to his wife Sian, and daughter Katie, accompanied by his "friend, bodyguard, servant and guide," Salim Ismail Mahmoud. "We met in Aqaba last February during my first week out there. Since then we've been inseparable," said O'Toole, at his London home.*

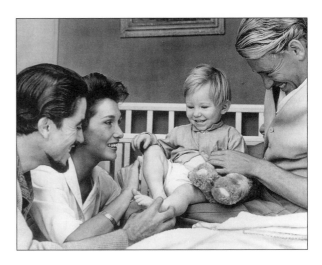

When O'Toole of Arabia returned

ACTOR Peter O'Toole, pictured above, returned from the desert where he has been filming as the star in "Lawrence Of Arabia" and visited friends for a few drinks. But he took too many, magistrates at Bristol, were told.

Police said that after they stopped his erratic drive down a Bristol street at four in the morning, O'Toole staggered from the car and said: "Okay Skip. Let's go to the station. I'm drunk."

O'Toole, aged 28, was fined £75 and disqualified from driving for a year for driving under the influence of drink.

ROBERT BOLT LEAVES GAOL

PLEDGE GIVEN TO AVOID FILM DELAY

DAILY TELEGRAPH REPORTER

MR. ROBERT BOLT, 39, the playwright, was working on the script of the film "Lawrence of Arabia" yesterday at a secret address outside London following his release from prison on Wednesday because his absence might delay the production.

He had served 14 days of a month's sentence he received for taking part in Ban-the-bomb demonstrations in Trafalgar Square on Sept. 17.

Mr. Bolt agreed to sign recognisances for his good behaviour after a visit from Mr. Sam Spiegel, producer of the film, at Drake Hall, in Staffordshire, the open prison where most of the anti-bomb demonstrators are serving sentences.

MONEY FOR CHARITY

According to members of the Committee of 100, Mr. Bolt asked the prison authorities for permission to work in prison, and offered any payment for charity. Prison regulations made this impossible.

Mr. Spiegel said yesterday: "I told Bolt it was absolutely necessary that his work should continue. There had already been a delay for almost three weeks, and it could have caused serious trouble if prolonged."

An executive of Horizon Pictures, who are making the film, said that a unit was on location in Jordan shooting scenes there. Scriptworkers normally worked some months ahead of production, but if there had been any further delay, it might have caused difficulties.

A member of the Committee of 100 said: "I believe Robert Bolt only signed the recognisances because of what Mr. Spiegel told him. He made every effort to get permission to work in prison, and other demonstrators understand why he has had to do this."

SPAIN: Seville

Seville had been chosen for all the city sequences simply because the original buildings involved in the story had long since been obliterated. Those ancient cities had expanded and modernized, but the Moorish-Arabic architecture of southern Spain was an acceptable alternative.

Thus the Capitania at the Plaza de Espana, the immense semi-circular concourse of buildings erected in Moorish style for the Iberian-American Exhibition of 1929, became Allenby's Cairo headquarters. The Teatro Lope de Vega, the casino built for the exhibition, became the council chamber of the Damascus Town Hall. And the nearby basement of the Peruvian Consulate on the Avenida de Maria Luisa became the Arab Bureau's mapping room in Cairo, where Lawrence started his military career.

Allenby's private apartment was set up in the Pabellon Mudeja of the Plaza Americana, and his entry into Jerusalem was filmed in front of the Archaeological Museum. A large private residence, the famed Casa de Pilatos (built in 1519 as a replica of Pilate's house in Jerusalem), was converted into Allenby's Jerusalem headquarters. Sections of the Alcazar, the 11th century Arabic fortress, represented parts of Damascus.

For a change, cast and crew lived and ate in modern hotels, apartments, and restaurants, instead of tents and trailers, and did not have to fight the flies to reach the food. Water was available at the nearest faucet. To a British main unit of sixty-five technicians, plus eighteen actors with speaking parts, were added an equivalent number of Spanish craftsmen. Up to 2,000 local extras were employed for such scenes as Allenby's entry into Damascus.

John Box recalled:

From Jordan we went to Seville to do what amounted to our interiors for Cairo, Jerusalem, Deraa, and Damascus. We never built any sets at any time in a studio, except for a small piece later created for the crypt of St. Paul's in England.

We chose Seville for its inherent eastern atmosphere, brought to it by the Moors. Granada has the same qualities with its Alhambra, but nothing like the variety of buildings we found in Seville.

We embellished them, added to them, changed an architectural emphasis here and there, and generally brought the atmosphere we wanted into the existing structures. It cost quite a lot of money to do so, but the script demands on us were very considerable in the number and size of the interiors required, and in the little shooting time on each set. I don't know where we would have got the vast amount of stage space that would have been needed under studio conditions. We didn't have to spend money on building walls; we had natural finishes which made our world a real world. Obviously, props also played a very big part in creating the places. On several occasions the most important part of the set was the part seen through windows. In Allenby's quarters in Damascus we went for the palms in a Seville park with a view of a tower amongst these palms. The walls of the room were of lesser importance, because the emphasis in the dialogue was on Lawrence and what he was doing in the town hall. The tower represented the town hall, and the green palms (in contrast to the arid deserts) were to suggest the prize that Damascus was to both Arab and English.

When we first conceived Seville, the unit was in Jordan finishing that location, and I was terribly worried about the possible requirements of the cameraman regarding rigging for his lamps. I had had the experience of shooting in real interiors before. In fact, any rigging we did was minimal, and when one remembers that we were shooting in colour on 70mm negative, I acknowledge the sheer technical ability of Freddie Young. I am still amazed.

Besides the interiors, two main exteriors were done in Seville; first the Damascus road, with eight hundred Spaniards trained and dressed to represent the Imperial British Army advancing to Damascus, and second, the town of Deraa, where Lawrence is apprehended and taken to the Turkish Bey. Deraa in reality was a wretched place, so we picked a terrible slum of Seville, using the rear sides of existing houses, adding our bits of Arabia to them.

On December 18, 1961, camera work resumed in Seville. There, Jack Hawkins reported as General Sir Edmund Allenby, commander-in-chief of British forces in the Middle East from 1916-18. Sir Donald Wolfit was cast as General Murray, Allenby's inept predecessor. Sir Alec Guinness returned to the cast from *The Mutineers,* as did Anthony Quayle. Anthony Quinn rejoined the stellar roster after completing the title role in *Requiem for a Heavyweight,* filmed in New York. Claude Rains arrived from Rome to play the role of Dryden, the astute and scholarly civilian head of the Arab Bureau, British Intelligence division in Cairo, who launches Lawrence on his Arabian adventure.

After Edmond O'Brien took ill, Arthur Kennedy came from Hollywood to take over the part of the opportunistic American war correspondent, Bentley, whose dispatches and photographs from the Middle East put Lawrence on the international map. José Ferrer (best ac-

tor Academy Award, 1950, *Cyrano de Bergerac*) came from India to portray one of the most maleficent heavies in screen history, the Turkish Bey, governor of Deraa, at whose orders the captured Lawrence was flogged. Also added to the cast were Howard Marion Crawford as the British medical officer who, not recognizing Lawrence, slaps his face at the Turkish Hospital in Damascus, and Fernando Sancho as the Bey's brutal sergeant.

The cast of *Lawrence of Arabia* had now attained epic proportions.

The first month in Seville, all the 'Cairo' scenes were filmed: "Murray's and Allenby's Offices" (see page 113), the "Map Room," the "Officers Mess" ("He likes your lemonade."), the "Mess Courtyard," "Dryden's Office" (blowing out the match), and "Lawrence's Return to Cairo."

Top left: Mad's April 1964 parody, "Flawrence of Arabia," displayed surprising insight into the enigma of Lawrence. Note substitution of Allenby for Murray. Above: A. G. Scott doing Hawkins's "hair."

"Officers Mess," where Lawrence's irreverent attitude to military protocol and senior officers is first shown.

Box's sketch of "Map Room," where Lawrence's masochistic nature is first revealed: "The trick is not minding that it hurts."

The last week of January 1962, "Jerusalem" scenes were filmed in Seville: Lawrence's return to Allenby after Deraa, the "Seduction" scene (Allenby beguiles Lawrence into returning to the Arabs), and Edmond O'Brien's short stint as Bentley (see p. 54). February 1962 saw Seville transformed into "Damascus": "Allenby's quarters," the elaborate council chamber of the "Damascus Town Hall," the various parting scenes at the story's end, and the "British Staff Officers' Strategy Session." On February 28, Bentley's "Jerusalem" scenes with Dryden were redone with O'Brien's replacement, Arthur Kennedy.

Far left: Lieutenant Colonel T. E. Lawrence, Cairo, 1918.
Left: According to costume designer Dalton, O'Toole's Jerusalem uniform is typical of all his intentionally ill-fitting British officer's garb throughout the film.

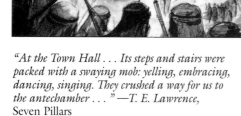

"At the Town Hall . . . Its steps and stairs were packed with a swaying mob: yelling, embracing, dancing, singing. They crushed a way for us to the antechamber . . ." —T. E. Lawrence, Seven Pillars

Above: Box's sketch of "Council Chamber."

Left: Hawkins, 1962; Allenby and Feisal, 1918; Guinness, 1962.

"It was fitting the two chiefs should meet . . . in the heart of their victory; with myself still acting as the interpreter between them . . . They were a strange contrast: Feisal, large-eyed, colourless and worn, like a fine dagger; Allenby, gigantic and red and merry, fit representative of the Power which had thrown a girdle of humour and strong dealing round the world." —T. E. Lawrence, Seven Pillars

In early March 1962, José Ferrer spent a week in Seville in his role as the sadistic Turkish Bey. Sharif recalled Lean's suggestion that José "do a sort of 'sexual cough,'" which, according to one critic, "voluptuously punctuates one of the most daring homosexual scenes of indecent assault ever to be filmed decently." Sharif called Ferrer's performance "sublime."

O'Toole said that he learned more in a few days working with Ferrer than he had in all his years at drama school. Ferrer said, "If I had to be judged by only one performance, it would be my five minutes in Lawrence. They are my best work."

Left: Lean and Fernando Sancho.

SPAIN: Almeria

Claude Rains and José Ferrer had completed their roles in Seville. Jack Hawkins had finished also, except for an opening sequence to be shot later in the year in England.

On March 19, 1962, after three months in and around Seville, another major move was made 350 miles to the southeast, to the port of Almeria, which became the base for additional exteriors in the region.

Overnight, a special train carried personnel from Seville to the new location, while a forty-eight-truck convoy moved props, costumes, and technical equipment. A second freight train carried the same trailers which had been used in the Jordan desert, plus three vintage 1916 Rolls Royces and motorcycles of the same period.

On March 20, equipment was set up some twelve miles east of Almeria, on the road to Nijar. The following day, camera work resumed. The interior scenes in both Feisal's tent, and then Auda's tent, were filmed. For the former, British actor Henry Oscar had come to Almeria as the Reciter of the Koran.

Shooting sites near Almeria became known simply as "Kilometer 20" or "Kilometer 24," indicating their distance from the port. In some cases, however, nearby villages such as Rambla de Tabernas, in the Sierra Almahilla, or the tiny fishing community of Carboneras, lent their names to the locations.

In a canyon near Tabernas, a sudden flash flood resulting from unseasonal heavy rains in the mountains to the north, came near to wiping out the Lawrence shooting site at one point. A wall of water between three and four feet high swept down between the canyon walls, sent principals, extras, camels, and horses scrambling up the precipitous hillsides, and inundated David Lean's caravan before it could be towed to safety, and before Gasim could be executed.

In another canyon, three kilometers north of Carboneras, where the dry bed of the Rio Alias becomes an alluvial fan stretching to the sea, the entire town of Aqaba, Jordan, as it was in 1916, was reproduced. It consisted of some 300 separate false-front buildings and a quarter-mile-long sea wall. It was necessary to recreate Aqaba in Spain, since the original—in Jordan—had completely changed.

Behind the mammoth set, half a mile square, a

Turkish Army camp and parade ground were laid out, and on the hillsides overlooking the town, four forty-foot Turkish cannon were built on concrete emplacements. It was the fact that these cannon faced the sea and could not be turned around that permitted Lawrence and his attacking Arabs to capture Aqaba from the rear.

In the harbor, created for the film, two iron-ore freighters from Almeria and some four dozen fishing boats from nearby villages lay at anchor. Here, Arthur Kennedy, as the American correspondent Bentley, arrives in his quest to find Feisal and Lawrence.

The thunderous Arab charge of 150 camels and 450 horses down the wadi and through the Turkish camp, brought crowds of sightseers to the hillsides, villagers from as far away as 100 kilometers, coming by donkey, mule, farm horse, bicycle, and cart to witness the greatest free entertainment of their lives.

As at Seville, extras were found among the Andalusian gitanos or gypsies, most of whom are descendants of the Moors and are Arabic in appearance.

In the sand dunes near Cabo de Gata, railroad track was laid for the sequences depicting Lawrence's attacks on the Turkish trains. A German and a Belgian locomotive of the period, each with tender, eight passenger carriages, fourteen horse cars, two luggage vans, and a guards' van were acquired from RENFE, the Spanish national railway system. They were taken out of service from the Almeria, Alhama and Santa Fe line, then loaded by crane onto trucks for transshipment to the shooting site, where an access road one mile long had to be built. Then intricate plans were laid to blow engines and tenders sky-high, and to wreck the carriages for climactic scenes. This was one of the most critical explosive operations attempted on the film, as a second take would be impossible.

Tests made by construction foreman Peter Dukelow, who blew up the bridge in *Kwai,* and special effects expert Cliff Richardson, showed that a mere ten pounds of guncotton would cut the rails ahead of the speeding locomotive. Another ten pounds of gunpowder would blast the broken rails aside, sending the engine and its tender careening off the track, their momentum making them plow through the sand on heavy steel plates buried below the surface. The carriages were dragged crazily behind until they toppled into a telescoped mass of wreckage. Engineer Emilio Noriega had set his mechanism at full throttle and then jumped away from the direction of the falling cars.

Camels brought from Spanish Sahara for these scenes were shipped folded, their legs drawn up under them, to prevent seasickness. They were then given a day's recuperation and exercise before proceeding overland to the shooting sites, a short trek from the coast.

Three of these camels had the unique experience of working in the snow on the slopes of Mulahacen, Spain's highest mountain, at altitudes from 7,500 to 9,000 feet, for scenes depicting Lawrence and a handful of followers struggling through mountain passes in wintry weather. Lack of snow in Jordan the year before had caused the scene to be switched to the Sierra Nevada, where the Panavision camera had to be mounted on a specially built sledge with ski-type runners.

John Box elaborated his artistic concerns:

> The terrain in the Seville area was not suitable for exteriors, and the weather being unreliable in the spring, we moved to Almeria. It has very little rain—the nearest one can get in Europe to desert conditions. In no way could it compare pictorially with Jordan in majesty, size or color, but we had already got our big vistas, and we decided that it would be foolish to try and compete with Jordan. We kept the camera much tighter, and were anyhow mainly shooting locations for the second half of the film, which was dramatically much closer and more intense.
>
> There were two main exceptions to this. First, we had to do the taking of Aqaba, visually the climax to the first part of the film. After many headaches we found a wadi leading to the sea, built our Aqaba, and I think the dramatic point was made.
>
> Secondly, we had to build about two and a half miles of railway line in the sand dune area of Almeria. This had to represent the Hejaz railway that runs from Damascus to Medina in Arabia, the railway that Lawrence raided with such success. The dune area was very limited in size, and we were just able to squeeze in our railway line, but we were helped in our three railway sequences by the strong winds from the sea that blew the sand all over the place (including all over the railway lines, so they had to be continually cleared) and by a haze that hangs around in the area; thus we got an impression of far bigger desert distances than were really there. We shot several other sequences in Almeria that were meant to be in Arabia, by using purely atmospheric conditions, such as sand blown up by wind machines that shrouded out figures and obscured distant background. The deserted

hutments at the end of the Sinai desert were merely an old ruined farm building near a main road, to which we added our pieces to give us our design. We scraped away the tufty grass, spread sand and white salt, shrouded the whole in whirling white smoke and Fuller's earth; in the backlight we had planned, I think we achieved the impression that we were on the edge of Sinai. The colors were matched very carefully to samples from the real area.

The interiors of our tents were shot in Almeria. They were erected out in the open on waste ground. The rigging was difficult and had to be carefully planned to allow for "floating" tent walls. We had made attempts to shoot Feisal's tent in Seville, but unusual rain and floods washed out this effort. We had trouble from wind in Almeria at first, but learned by experience to overcome the problems it brought.

From the very start of the film camels had a very important visual part to play. A limited number were shipped from Morocco to Spain. The saddles and other dressing for the beasts, we had brought with us, as the Jordanian equipment is completely different from the North African. The horses used in Almeria were Spanish and carefully picked to match the Arabian breed. We had brought the saddle dressings from Jordan and some were remade in Spain.

Cameras began rolling in Almeria on March 21, 1962. Sequences in the first seven weeks included: the interior scenes in Feisal's and Auda's tents (see p. 118); Bentley's meeting with Feisal in Aqaba; and three sets built on a windswept hill at "Kilometer 24"—"Aqaba" after the conquest (left, and Box sketch above), the night exterior in "Deraa," and the Turkish hospital in "Damascus" (below).

"I stepped in, to meet a sickening stench: and, as my eyes grew open, a sickening sight." —T. E. Lawrence, Seven Pillars

"John [Box] designed an authentic 'hospital' set, and said, 'Shit it up in your usual way.' So I got cow's guts from the abattoir, and put all this crap all over the walls. And a lot of rotting fish, so there were flies everywhere. When Peter came onto the set, he didn't have to act sick."—Eddie Fowlie

Left: Middle Eastern hospital, 1917.

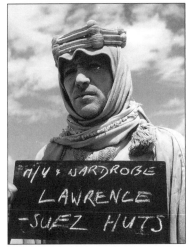

Above: Box sketch of "Suez Hutments" (see p.125).
Far right: Camels cruising from North Africa to Almeria. Below: A flash flood foiled the first attempt to film the "Execution of Gasim." Three days later, on May 15, 1962, the troupe enjoyed a First-Anniversary-of-Shooting party, complete with fireworks, at the yacht club in Almeria.
Below right: Around the corner from "the Gasim Gulch," "the Oasis" was built from scratch, including imported trees. It flourished, and is now found on maps of the region.

"It must be a formal execution, and at last, desperately . . . [I] laid the burden of killing on myself. Perhaps they would count me not qualified for feud. At least no revenge could lie against my followers; for I was a stranger and kinless."—T. E. Lawrence, Seven Pillars

Two weeks after the flood, the "Execution of Gasim" was filmed.

"I think they both thought they were Lawrence and they were jealous of one another! They were both deeply involved in it, weren't they? Both their lives were wrapped around that character, for a long time. They had to 'become' the man."—Eddie Fowlie

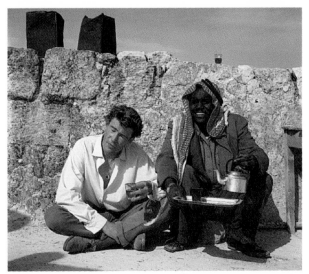

In early 1961, cast and crew started to arrive in Jordan. Production headquarters was set up in Amman, the capital, and the location base camp was built in Aqaba. Top left: Peter O'Toole strolls through the Amman marketplace, trailed by a publicity photographer. Top right: O'Toole's wife, actress Siân Phillips, visited him during his training sessions in Aqaba. O'Toole, here seen riding his favorite camel, Shagran, commented on the dangers associated with his new skill: "After a few nasty spills, you just don't tumble off a nine-foot beast at thirty miles an hour." Center: Besides mastering the art of riding a camel, O'Toole was also determined to learn the Arabic tongue and familiarize himself with Bedouin customs. Here, he samples Arab tea and, in a nomad tent, inspects the evening's dinner. Left: Barbara Cole, who worked on script continuity for David Lean, inspects props in Fowlie's "dump."

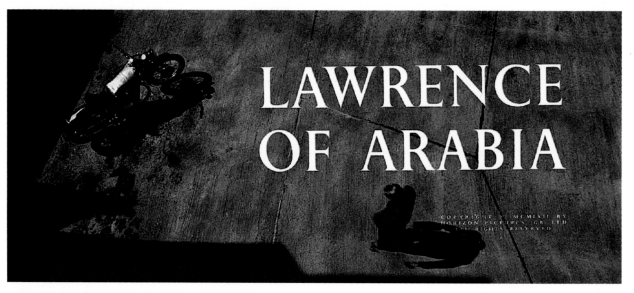

Almeria, Spain, June 24, 1962: Lean and O'Toole prepare to film the "Main Title" scene, which will introduce O'Toole as Lawrence. From 3:40 to 4:05 P.M., the cameras rolled. The shot was done five times. Only "takes" 3 and 5 were printed. The start of "take 5" is shown on an anamorphic frame (left), which is used for 35mm prints. These squeezed frames are expanded to "widescreen" during projection. Compare them with the 70mm frame above. Michael Anderegg, in his brilliant 1984 essay, observed: "By casting the virtually unknown O'Toole as Lawrence, Lean complicates the categories of actor, role, and identity. Since, in the cinema, character and actor cannot easily be distinguished, O'Toole, with no 'star' persona to interfere, at once embodies and individualizes Lawrence. And O'Toole is supported by well-known stars whose very presence insures immediate identification . . . These casting strategies also contribute meaning to a subsidiary but related theme: Lawrence, the young upstart lieutenant, takes over the Arab revolt supported by the older and more experienced Allenby, Feisal, and Auda, just as O'Toole, the young upstart actor, takes over the film."

Above: General Murray's office, in Cairo, was decorated to show that his heart was really with the fighting men in the trenches of Western Europe. To him, the Middle East was just "a side show." Photo on Murray's desk is of the real Allenby, taken two years after this scene was supposed to have taken place!

Below: General Allenby's office, formerly Murray's, was initially "dressed" with fishing rods and hunting gear. David Lean objected, ordered the set emptied, and the marble floor polished to a dazzling shine. Lean then called for a desk and four chairs. He told Fowlie: "I want nothing else. This is the desert."

"The main thing David knows when he's shooting a scene is the last shot: and the first shot of the next scene." —Omar Sharif

At a time when dissolves and fades were the accepted way of changing scenes, Lawrence made striking use of direct cuts. Above: One of the most famous cuts in cinema history: Lawrence extinguishes the fire of the match to enter the fire of the desert. Top right: Ali presents Lawrence with new robes: "They are good for riding. Try!" Right: Lawrence and Farraj arrive at the Suez Canal.
Opposite page. Top left: Auda: "I must find something honorable." Cut to wheels of horse-train locomotive. Bottom left: Turkish Bey, to Lawrence: "You are a deserter . . . but from which army? Not that it matters at all. A man cannot be always in uniform!" Top right: Lawrence to Ali: "Trust your own people! And let me go back to mine . . ." Bottom right: Lawrence to Allenby re the allegiance of the Arab Army: "The best of them won't come for money. They'll come for me."

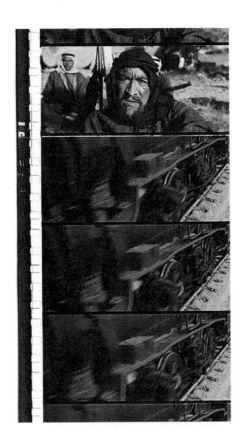

Tafas leading Lawrence to Prince Feisal.

"*Only David could have made* Lawrence of Arabia. *Even with the wonderful backdrop of the desert and the camels . . . anyone else would have missed it. They wouldn't have got it right like David did.*" —*Eddie Fowlie*

"*. . . I can think of few complexly-staged movies . . . in which*

the camera is so consistently ready—advancing, backing away, rising, sweeping—to reveal the essence of the action . . . and perhaps none that produces as many images of frightening natural sublimity, so many scenes of landscape as spiritual alienation." —*David Denby,* Premiere.

"*The size, the immensity of the desert, it's in David's soul.*" —*Anthony Quinn.*

Sharif's entry into the film out of a mirage has been described as the greatest debut scene in cinema history.

Omar Sharif: "The night before the 'well scene' I decided to practice my moves: with the camel, the water bucket, the cup, and the rifle. And I am glad I did it, because I discovered that when I was pulling the water bucket up, the rifle would slip off. So the next morning, I had it sewn onto my costume. The scene went smoothly, and Lean—learning of my efforts—said: 'Omar, if you can't speak your lines or act the scene, I will stay five months with you till you get it right. But if you can't handle your props, I have no time for that. That should not be done on my time, that should be done on your time.' "

Phyllis Dalton: "David would spend a great deal of time getting it perfect, and then, getting it more perfect [below]. I'd come on the set and think it all looked wonderful. And then we didn't shoot for another eight hours 'cause they were getting it even better."

Eddie Fowlie: "I remember painting the desert with truckloads of colored powder. Dumping sacks in the bloody wind machine and blowing it across."

Barbara Cole: "The touchy camels could never hit their marks. When the script said, 'He brings his camel to a halt', we knew we were in for a day's frustration."

"Feisal was passionately fond of Arabic poetry and would often provoke recitations . . . Auda's tent [was] a huge hall seven poles long and three wide." —T. E. Lawrence, Seven Pillars.
Both tent scenes were filmed in a field near Almeria. Fowlie dumped red earth outside to simulate Wadi Rumm. For years afterward, he would see the red patch as he drove by. Now, it's all gone, under the white dust of a cement factory.

". . . from end to end of it, there was nothing female in the Arab movement, but the camels."
—T. E. Lawrence, Seven Pillars.
Lean and Bolt honored Lawrence's observation by creating nearly four hours of film with not one word spoken by a woman. But women there were:
Top left: At Wadi Rumm, Howeitat women are heard ululating to inspire the warriors onto victory. These women were chaperoned by Phyllis Dalton.
Large frame: Women watch Arab army departing Auda's camp for Aqaba.
Left: Howeitat girl was seen at the beginning of the sequence inside Auda's tent. There, Auda complains: "You trouble me like women."
Bottom: Lawrence's account of an Arab tribe on the march, describes "camels swaying curiously, like butterflies, under the winged and fringed howdahs, of the women." In the film, during the "Exodus" from Feisal's camp, a slender, delicate, bejewelled hand is seen emerging from one colorful howdah. It belonged to Second Assistant Director David Tringham.
"In a film where women are conspicuous by their absence, Lawrence—pale, effeminate, a blond and blue-eyed seraph—becomes a surrogate woman, a figurative white goddess." —Michael Anderegg
Top right: Women's powder room at Jebel Tubeiq.

119

"Suddenly, Feisal asked me if I would wear Arab clothes . . . I agreed at once, very gladly; for an army uniform was abominable when camel-riding, or when sitting about on the ground; and the Arab things . . . were cleaner and more decent in the desert . . . I took a stroll in the new looseness of them . . ." —T. E. Lawrence, Seven Pillars.

"Lawrence is now an Arab. At the same time, he looks like no other Arab in the film; rather than taking on the identity of his comrades, he assumes a visually unique role . . . Here, in particular, we sense the actor behind the role. Lawrence and O'Toole seem to be both reveling in and in awe of the part they are playing, uncertain of what to do next but at the same time aware that from now on there is no turning back: destiny calls. The moment is privileged: Lawrence will never again seem at once so winning and so vulnerable." —Michael Anderegg

"The clothes were so comfortable I practically turned into a transvestite! I thought I'd literally end up running around in a nightie for the rest of my days!" —Peter O'Toole

"There entered a tall, strong figure, with a haggard face, passionate and tragic. This was Auda, and after him followed Mohammed, his son, a child in looks, and only 11 years old in truth." —T. E. Lawrence, Seven Pillars.

September 3–9, 1961, Wadi Rumm. Slate Numbers 450–492. For the memorable scenes in which Auda enters Lawrence's adventure, a young boy—the only significant child in the film—was required. Kamal Rashid, son of a Jordanian Army major, was chosen. He was an expert rider and a big hit among the crew. But he wasn't an actor. Lean gently spent considerable time coaching a performance out of him. During these scenes, according to Daily Continuity Reports, numerous takes were required due to: poorly arranged kaffiya, fluffed line, boy rode around wrong bushes, horse snorted over dialogue, voice too weak, horse-plume covered Auda's face, too much wind, camel moved in background, fly crawling on Peter's nose, boy looked at director, salute not warm enough, boy has slight American accent, gun didn't fire, camel sat down, Bedouin looking at camera, background smoke covered action, smile held too long, eyes blinked, too solemn, bodyguard wearing wristwatch, horse restless, Lawrence's skirt caught on dagger, boy's horse turned back to camera, horse-handler's head in frame, and camel misbehaved.

"In my opinion, Aqaba . . . would be best taken by Arab irregulars descending from the interior without Naval help . . . Unfortunately for them, the enemy had never imagined attack from the interior, and of all their great works, not one trench or post faced inland. Our advance from so new a direction threw them into panic." —T. E. Lawrence, Seven Pillars.

In fact, there was no battle: the Turks quietly surrendered. Left: "Then we raced through a driving sand-storm down to Aqaba . . . and splashed into the sea on July the sixth [1917] . . ." —Photo and quote, T.E.L.

Eddie Fowlie: "The Turks only fired one shot and that guy fell down in the front. The stunt men wouldn't do it, so we gave this Gypsy about 5 quid and he did it. He rolled himself up in a ball and let the horses go over . . ."

Eddie Fowlie: "Can you imagine. John Box and I came to this dry river bed, and he looked at it for a minute. And then he said, 'OK, let's put it here.'" By the 1960s, the real Aqaba, in Jordan, was too modern to masquerade as Aqaba in 1917. In Spain, at Playa del Algorocibo, near Carboneras, local workers constructed 300 false-front buildings to create Lean's 'Aqaba' (top). In 1992, the site was visited with Eddie Fowlie, who has lived nearby since Lawrence was filmed. Bottom photo reveals that Lean's 'Aqaba' site has itself undergone modernization.

Opposite page: "I decided to go across myself with a party of eight, on the best camels in the force." –T. E. Lawrence, Seven Pillars.
Lawrence covered the 150 miles from Aqaba to the Canal quickly and uneventfully, reaching Suez in 49 hours. The film's "Quicksand" scene was dramatic fiction, and Daud, in fact, later "died of cold". Preparations for this sequence, including wind machine and brooms, are shown. Photographer Kauffman recalled that "after the shot, Fowlie bobbed up out of the box, like a sandy sea monster."

Above: "We reached . . . forts and barbed wire . . . falling to decay . . . on the Asiatic bank of the Canal . . ." –T. E. Lawrence, Seven Pillars.
John Box explained: "The deserted huts are revealed through eddying sand, and must have a metaphysical quality. The desert is taking over. The line to the door is most important. Lawrence must go to it, as if it were inevitable." The scene was shot on the arid plains of Almeria, at an abandoned farm building. The location is presently occupied by a service station beside a superhighway.

125

"There followed a terrific roar, and the line vanished from sight behind a spouting column of black dust and smoke a hundred feet high and wide. Out of the darkness came shattering crashes and loud, metallic clangings of ripped steel . . . There succeeded a deathly silence . . . as the now grey mist of the explosion drifted from the line towards us, and over our ridge . . ." —T. E. Lawrence, Seven Pillars.

Lean had originally wanted to shoot the trains in Jordan, but had to settle for Cabo de Gata, in the dunes of southern Spain. Fowlie recalls that they had to build the track, truck in the trains, and remove dozens of Gypsies and thousands of shrubs, before shooting could begin. His propmen "stole a locomotive one night, drove it down the line, and nearly wrecked it. In the morning, we discovered the damn thing at the wrong end of the track." Win Ryder, Sound Editor, in pursuit of perfection, made a special trip to Almeria to record the authentic clatter and hiss of the steam locomotives.

". . . there was a yell from the Arabs, and . . . sounding the women's vibrant battle-cry, they rushed in a wild torrent for the train . . . like wild beasts, to tear open the carriages and fall to plunder . . . Travelling became an uncertain terror for the enemy. At Damascus, people scrambled for the back seats in trains, even paid extra for them. The engine-drivers struck." –T. E. Lawrence, Seven Pillars. Top: David Lean rides the Chapman crane as the crew sets up for Lawrence's triumphal parade across the train tops.

"David asked me, 'What's it about this desert that you find so wonderful?' And I said, 'Well, I suppose . . . it's clean.' And he said, 'That's a wonderful line.'" —Sir Anthony Nutting

On May 2, 1962, at a mud flat near Tabernas, Spain, Scene 59 of Part II of the script was filmed:
"BENTLEY: What is it, Major Lawrence, that attracts you personally to the desert?
[Lawrence looks the disreputable figure up and down with insulting deliberation and says]
LAWRENCE: It's clean."
Top left: T. E. Lawrence and Lowell Thomas, Aqaba, 1918. Top right: Peter O'Toole and Arthur Kennedy, Tabernas, 1962. Right: Eddie Fowlie and assistant, Tabernas, 1992. Veteran newsman Lowell Thomas told an interviewer after seeing Lawrence of Arabia, *"The only true things in it are the sand and the camels." Although accurate historical names were used for most major figures in the film, Lowell Thomas was the conspicuous exception—becoming "Jackson Bentley" in the script.*

"Auda . . . had been wounded thirteen times; he himself had slain seventy-five men, Arabs, with his own hand in battle . . . Of the number of dead Turks, he could give no account: they did not enter the register." —T. E. Lawrence, Seven Pillars. This display of Auda's temper precedes the "Bodyguard" scene, and was filmed in Morocco.

"Lean fills Lawrence of Arabia *with flamboyantly theatrical shots . . . breathtaking vistas of Middle Eastern topography . . . He takes great pains to formalize the real world until it begins to resemble an impossibly elaborate studio set. Lean's remarkable pans and tracks, his complicated zooms, his compositions revealing the mysterious mirages of the desert, his dramatic visual surprises . . . are all directed toward establishing Arabia Deserta as a series of fabulous backdrops for Lawrence's exploits." —Michael Anderegg*

"David always said: 'Every frame is important. Every frame.' You could stop the projector, take a frame out of it, and make a picture to put on the wall. Every frame is a beautiful picture.

In Lawrence of Arabia *he must have had over a quarter of a million bloody good pictures." — Eddie Fowlie*

Crew members were often asked to perform small roles: the truck driver
(second from top) who drove Lawrence
and Farraj to Cairo after they crossed
Sinai was First Assistant Director Roy
Stevens: "We didn't have any British
actors in Spain for those little parts.
When I discussed it with David, he
said, 'We'll get them from the crew.'
David liked to see his 'Dedicated
Maniacs' in the film. He said, 'OK,
Roy, you can be the driver.' David
knew, that'd embarrass the hell out of
me." And when Lawrence and Farraj
enter Cairo Headquarters, the Sergeant (bottom) who stops them is
played by Construction Assistant Fred
Bennett: "You can't take him in
there, sir." Later, in the patio of the
Officer's Bar, Lawrence has "seduced"
Allenby into parting with more gold
and weapons. One of the officers gazing at the scene (top) is Screenwriter
Robert Bolt, with pipe: "Well, you see,
it was David's idea, and I said I'd do
it. No rehearsal. No pay. Just a bit of
fun." David Tringham, Second Assistant Director, remembers a day in Jordan: "They wanted to set up for the
shot of Lawrence bringing back
Gasim. They said, 'You go, David.
You can ride a camel. It's too hot to
bother Peter. Take a radio and we'll
tell you when to stop.' Well, I rode a
mile out and the radio didn't work
and I got so thirsty I finally thought,
'Oh, to hell with it. I'm going back.'
So I turned my camel and he saw his
friends back there, and went mad.
Galloping, four legs off the ground.
But I managed to hang on and get
back to the camera, screeching to a
stop in a cloud of dust. And I said,
'I'm sorry, but I didn't know how long
I was supposed to stay out there.' And
David said, 'Don't worry, that was
very very good, dear. We were filming
and we've got it all!' They never did
send Peter out. I was the dot on the
horizon."

"The sword also means clean-ness & death." Embossed inscription, within crossed swords, on front cover of Seven Pillars of Wisdom, *1935 edition.*

Peter O'Toole: "When I was first given the Arab robes, David said, 'There's something missing here, Pete. What do you think a young man would do alone in the desert if he'd just been handed these beautiful robes?' I said, 'Can I have a think?' So I went to my tent and jotted a few things down on paper, and then a jeep arrived to take me back to the set. Then David said, 'There's your theatre, do what you like.' Well, I did all sorts of things. But the one idea I had was that anyone in this position would want to look at themselves. There's no water or mirrors in the desert, so I had the idea of pulling out my knife and looking in the blade. I can still hear David from behind the camera saying, 'Clever boy.'"

"Twice in the film, Lawrence looks at his own reflection in the blade of his knife. In the first instance, he is still relatively innocent. . . . He studies the image reflected back to him in puzzled admiration, not quite believing that he has been able so thoroughly and drastically to change his identity. The second time . . . the context is very different. Lawrence, after giving the order to take no prisoners, participates in the massacre at Tafas. The white robes are now soiled with blood, and the face Lawrence submits to reflective scrutiny seems to be that of a madman. Neither the man nor the role is recognizably what they were before, and Lawrence can now only retreat from heroism, put aside his Arab dress, and return to England, and the absurd, perhaps not entirely accidental death with which the film began." —Michael Anderegg

Eddie Fowlie: "He's a transparent figure, you know. He's like a phantom in the world. He's like a phantom in the desert! Nobody ever really found the real Lawrence . . . David always tried to give this 'transparency' to him. . . . he was deliberately aiming at transparency . . . He wanted Lawrence's costume made transparent . . ."

Phyllis Dalton: "In nearly all of David's films, he'll want something floating and see-through. Diaphanous. He loved that. I don't know if you noticed it, but later in the film, Peter's robe is thinner—different fabric. It was one of David's whims. I think it was probably psychological, a symbolic thing."

Eddie Fowlie: "David always said that he didn't do things with 'symbolism', but of course, he did. You might call them 'subtleties' if you like. But they were there, and they were suggestive to the subconscious. I don't think it occurred to him that he was doing anything unusual. He doesn't quite realize that he's doing it. Something in his own subconscious would suggest it."

Top: Lawrence as "Sun-God." For Lean, this triumphant moment replaced the scene he had been unable to film in Petra.

Large frame: Script, Part II–Scene 244: "CLOSE SHOT: The SCREEN is momentarily MAUVE, the mauve of Lawrence's banner: it passes out of picture, disclosing LAWRENCE."

Center: Eddie Fowlie: "It was before the scene when Allenby and Feisal are negotiating in Damascus. David said to me, 'Do you think you can get that desk to come up like a mirror? Because I would like to have Lawrence reflected in it. It's . . . It's a ghost.'" John Box: ". . . and there's the scene of . . . Lawrence's reflection in the desk, which underlines how he has no substance."

Second from bottom: Lawrence departs Damascus, leaving only his shadow.

Bottom: Closing scene of film: Lawrence is being driven away from Arabia. He has just watched Arabs, mounted on camels, receding into his past. Now, as a British soldier on a motorcycle roars past, Lawrence—barely perceptible through a dusty windshield—mistily contemplates his uncertain future.

In June 1962, Almeria, the three train
sequences (see pp. 126-27) and the "Taking of
Aqaba" (see pp. 122-23) were filmed. Above:
Explosion on tracks, photographed by T. E. L.,
c.1918. Right: During this scene, many of the
horses escaped into the dunes.

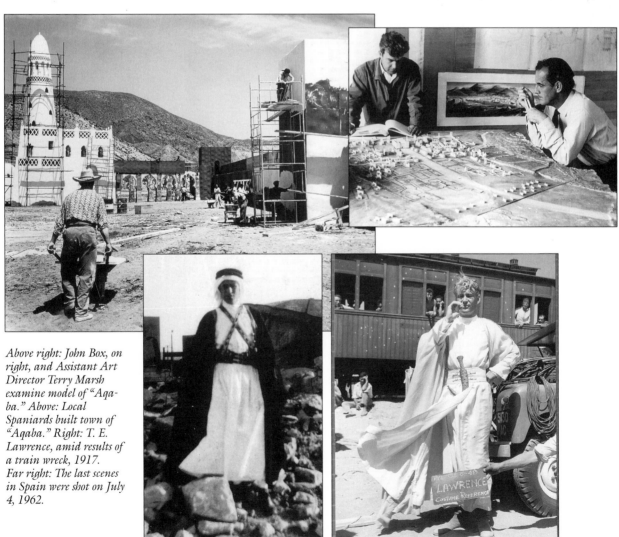

Above right: John Box, on
right, and Assistant Art
Director Terry Marsh
examine model of "Aqa-
ba." Above: Local
Spaniards built town of
"Aqaba." Right: T. E.
Lawrence, amid results of
a train wreck, 1917.
Far right: The last scenes
in Spain were shot on July
4, 1962.

MOROCCO

In July 1962, shooting was finished in Almeria. The production team packed up yet again for its final major location move, to Ouarzazate, Morocco, on the south side of the towering Atlas Mountains. Here, on the arid mudflats, the bodyguard scene was filmed, followed by the final bloodbath battle, which saw the annihilation of the remnants of the Turkish Army.

Once again, every piece of equiment had to be packed and shipped by freighter from Almeria to Casablanca, then transported south through Marrakech by truck convoy over a 10,000-foot-high mountain pass. Personnel were flown from Malaga to Tangier to Marrakech in four chartered planes, then driven to Ouazazate.

Through the cooperation of King Hassan II and his brother H.R.H. Prince Moulay Abdallah, the Royal Moroccan Army supplied 600 calvary, 500 members of the Camel Corps, 800 foot soldiers, and 180 mules, plus field kitchens, cannon, and 1,000 rifles of the period. Of this group, 400 infantrymen, 400 cavalry, 300 camelry, 200 cannoneers, and kitchen help represented the Turkish forces. Among the Arab forces were 100 of the famous Blue Men, nomads from the Sahara.

John Box recalled:

Ouarzazate was our last location before we returned to England. We had made extensive 'reckies' (reconnaissance trips) to find a suitable location for a very important battle sequence known as the 'bloodbath.' This had to be in a desert terrain, not grand, in fact rather miserable, but still desert, flat, open, with a sense of size. What is more, it had to have a floor that was 'good going' for camels and horses. We eventually lined up to shoot the 'bloodbath' with an Arab force of over 800 men (mounted on camels and horses) and a Turkish force of 1200 men with carts and mules. We concentrated on our long shots first so as to reduce these numbers as quickly as possible; the wear and tear on men and their animals, as always in these scenes, has to be taken into account, and more so when you are in desert conditions.

In general terms, the plan for the 'bloodbath' sequence was based on the intention to create the impression of slaughter and carnage by building up tension in the first place and then unleashing one army against the other. But once contact had been made

David Tringham with Moroccan nomads, the famous "Blue Men of the Sahara," who were to be transformed by Dalton's colorful costumes into "Lawrence's Bodyguard."

between the two opposing forces, we aimed to get to the final dramatic point as quickly as possible to show the desolation of the battlefield. Lawrence had indulged in an orgy of killing, and we had to show the effect this had upon him. Stunt men were very important to the scene, but 'stunts' in themselves were not wanted except as seen in passing; they helped to create an overall impression of slaughter taking place. Our most important ally in getting power through suggestion was the dust, which we knew we would get in abundance, and it was decided to make as much use as possible of its shrouding and atmospheric effect combined with backlight; the key shots were planned for as late in the day as possible.

The following cable was received late Friday evening, August 17, 1962, in the Casablanca Horizon office, and forwarded the next morning to production manager John Palmer in Ouarzazate:

PLEASE EXTEND MY HEARTIEST THANKS AND APPRECIATION ON THIS LAST DAY OF SHOOTING FOR FIRST UNIT TO EVERY MEMBER DEPARTING FOR HOME STOP AM FULLY AWARE OF THE TREMENDOUS EFFORT SPENT ON PICTURE BY EVERYONE AND HOPE THAT THEY WILL BE PROUD OF THEIR ACHIEVEMENT STOP WISH THEM ALL A SAFE VOYAGE HOME AND HOPE TO SEE THEM ALL UPON THEIR ARRIVAL LONDON

BEST REGARDS
SAM SPIEGEL

HORIZON PICTURES (G.B.) LTD.

CALL SHEET

PROD. No. H.P.6. LOCATION/STUDIO No. 11

PRODUCTION: "LAWRENCE OF ARABIA"

UNIT CALL: 7.00 leave base
7.30 on location

DATE: Saturday, 28 July 1962

SET: EXT. TAFAS VILLAGE & TURKISH COLUMN

LOCATION: TAFAS VILLAGE, OUARZAZATE

ARTISTE	CHARACTER	MAKE UP	LEAVE	READY ON SET
PETER O'TOOLE	LAWRENCE	7.30 on set	7.00	8.00
ANTHONY QUINN	AUDA (stand by at Hotel from 9.00)		7.00	8.00
OMAR SHARIF	ALI	7.30 on set	7.00	8.00
M. HABACHI	KHITAN	On Set	7.30	8.00
STAND-INS : R. Stoddard for Mr. O'Toole		As required	7.30	8.00
J. Gaffney for Mr. Quinn				
J. Michel for Mr. Sharif			7.30	8.00
DOUBLE : MARIO DE BARROS for LAWRENCE			7.00	7.30
JIMMY LODGE for AUDA		7.00	7.30	8.00
STUNTMEN: All Stuntmen under instructions of F. Hayden			7.00	7.30
CROWD: 3 Arab children			8.00	8.30
12 Arab Women		6.30	7.20	8.00
9 Special Artistes			On Location	
20 Lawrence's Bodyguards			7.30	8.00
2 Ali's Bodyguards / 4 Auda's Bodyguards			6.30	7.30
350 Cameman / 500 Arab Horsemen			7.00	7.30
800 Turkish Soldiers / 20 Turkish Officers			7.00	11.30
200 Turkish Muleteers / 10 Donkeymen			11.00	11.30
CAMELS : Lawrence's Camels and Double; Ali's, Majid's Camels			7.00	7.30
20 Lawrence's B.G. Camels; 2 Ali's B.G. Camels			7.00	7.30
200 Army Camels; 150 Civilian Camels; 62 Raiding Party Camels			7.00	7.30
HORSES : Auda's Horse; 350 Army Horses; 100 Civilian Horses			7.00	7.30
5 Auda's B.G. Horses; 20 Turkish Army Horses (11.00 for 11.30)				
MULES / DONKEYS : 200 Mules; 10 Donkeys			11.00	11.30

PROPS: As breakdown Page 24A-D; Bandoliers; Banners; Daggers; Swords, etc.
Verey Lights; Signal Flags; Village Debris, etc. Dummies; 4 Artillery Pieces;
32 Wagons; 6 Hotchkiss; Turkish Column Transport, etc.
SFX : (Liaison with Army) 600 Turkish Rifles; 1000 Arab Rifles as already issued;
200 Lee Enfield Rifles; Smoke & Dust.
PROD. : (Liaison with Army) 7 W.T's with Operators; Loud Hailers; Army Ambulance from
7.30 a.m.; Vet required; P.A. System 7.30; All availabel water bowsers required.
All Army Liaison Officers - 7.30 a.m. on Set.
CAMERA DEPT. : 2nd Camera Unit required; Chapman Boom reqd.; 2nd Camera Car required.
CATERING : Breakfast in Hotel from 6.30; Lunch from 3.00; Running Buffet on Set 11-12 noon
TRANSPORT: Car for Mr. Lean from 7.00; Car for Mr. Sharif from 6.55; Car for Messrs.
Thompson, Davies, Fox and Wilson 6.45 (Casbah). -

Transport for 400 Civilian Crowd at 8.30 a.m. as arranged.
ALL OTHER TRANSPORT AS ARRANGED.

Bus for 12 Women Service et Sports 6.15, Royal 6.20, then M.U. College. Leave 7.20 with
Women and Stand-ins, then to Service et Sports for 12 Special Artistes, all to set by
8.00.;
Car for Messrs Beale (Casbah) 6.30, then to Gite 6.45 for Wairelese Personnel.

257-260 (24*)

Gite d'Etape.
Ouarzazate.

29th July 62.

Dear Ann,

This is the most awful place God made. It has no charm at all to make up for the heat and dust. The days are very hot - our thermometers do not record higher than 109 in the shade and it is much hotter than that. At least in Jordan we had relief at night but here it hardly cools off at all. We are all longing for the day we pack and say farewell to the lousy hills and Casbahs of Ouarzazate.

The whole thing is summed up when one learns that this is where the French Foreign Legion were sent as a punishment. I now understand all those Somerset Maugham stories about the goings of on of Colonial Administrators. Just hope that the stuff we shoot here is really worth the huge effort.

About Slate 1296 and 1296B. It really isn't any good at all and probably should have been junked but since it involves 1000 men with horses and camels and is quite an operation I thought it had beeter be devolped and put on records - since it is conceivable that one day someone will say 'Let's look at that attempt' and by then people would have forgotten that they said 'Absolutely useless'.

The local Arabs are not a bit keen about whipping up enthusiasm and who can blame them. But I think it has at last penetrated that unless they do we will all stand out there until we dehydrate. Everybody is on their knees at night trying to enthuse something into them. We were all xx very cast down too when we first tired tracking shots and realised that once again we had to train the camels before we could get anywhere. Now - we pray - we are over the initial grind of getting everybody accustomed to the mechanics and life will be a bit easier.

The people are taking in their harvest here and manually beating the wheat from the chaff - the wheat dust is blown all over the place and people who have never had hay fever in their life have swollen eyes and runny noses. Poor Grace who suffers from Asthma can hardly breathe.

Don't be a bit surprised if you see a strange face suddenly popping up where another has been. If the camels dont go sick or die the men do and we practically rip their costumes from them as they fall in order to at least have the same colours in the same place. So many of the Unit were going sick at first that we counted on using their bodies in the Tafas Village. We felt they would like to make that last contribution to the film. Most of us went deaf when volunteers were asked for to stay on with the 2nd Unit - we are more than happy to let the keen new recruits have a ball by themselves. Hope you are gathering your strength for the final rush - I will come round handing out pep pills and strong black coffee.

Hope to see you sooner than you expect,

Luv,
Barbara

P.S. Did you hear that 'Of course it's never happened before' we have days that are completely clouded over - and a flash flood that made a river of the Arab Army Assembly set and washed away the track and one lamp.

"Fellows were very proud of being in my bodyguard, which developed a professionalism almost flamboyant. They dressed like a bed of tulips, in every color but white; for that was my constant wear . . ." —T. E. Lawrence, *Seven Pillars. The "Bodyguard" scene, the first in Morocco, was begun July 18. Top: T. E. L. with his bodyguard, Aqaba, 1918. Above: Letter from Barbara Cole to Anne Coates. Top right: Call sheet for "Tafas Village Massacre" scene. Center right: Setting up crane shot of Arab army entering "Tafas village." For this scene, the numerous extras were given directives from the surrounding hilltops by means of bugle calls. Right: For the beginning of the "No prisoners!" bloodbath sequence, the camera crane used here as a stable platform—was braced against wind vibration.*

ENGLAND

The battle sequences completed, there remained only the opening scenes of the Robert Bolt script to be filmed in England, including Lawrence's fatal motorcycle crash (in Chobham, Surrey) and the 1936 Lawrence Memorial Service at St. Paul's Cathedral.

Shortly before the premiere, producer Sam Spiegel penned—for the first and only time—an articulate and fascinating essay on his *Lawrence* adventure:

A film is the result of a combination of minds applied to the subject in hand, and my own mind was fascinated by the subject of Lawrence of Arabia long before I began to produce a film about him.

Lawrence's combination of introspection and adventure is unique among men of our times or, indeed, of any other times. Most of the adventurers who have remained legends throughout the years have been either men of action, like Marco Polo, Columbus, Buffalo Bill, or Robin Hood, or adventurers of the spirit and the mind, like Galileo or Martin Luther or Einstein. Lawrence was an unprecedented combination of the two qualities, an adventurer both in action and in spirit.

He has remained a legend in our lifetime because he achieved some of the secret desires that are common to many people. Almost every human being is a frustrated philosopher or a frustrated adventurer. Everyone would like to be a little of both and very seldom has the opportunity to be either. So it is easy to become identified, wishfully, with Lawrence, and identification with the personality on the screen is the most exciting thing for an audience. It need not happen in an intellectual way; sometimes it is purely emotional, sometimes even subconscious. Our object was to weave Lawrence's introspection into the film obliquely, through action and through disputes and arguments that arise out of the action. In such a way we could present the thinking man and the adventurer at one and the same time. Lawrence had almost every contradictory trait that could possibly be found in the same human being. On the one hand he was a thinker and a poet, but on the other he carried poetry sometimes to the point where he was prevaricating. He was attacked for distorting facts, but I do not believe that he was ever a liar: he was a poet who colored things with his own impressions. He was a modest man and yet he was inclined to attract a

tremendous amount of attention and publicity. His attitude to religion was in one sense almost agnostic, and at the same time he imagined himself to be a prophet. Frequently he was close to that moment in which man sees himself as the demigod.

To him the desert personified the birthplace of all religion, and there he felt that it was possible to approach the unknown in the most secretive way. Yet he was delighted that there were witnesses to his communion.

It would have been unsatisfactory to make a film about Lawrence with a conventional plot construction. It had to be a progression of character rather than a progression of story.

. . . But before any of our work could begin, there had to be a common viewpoint shared by three independent minds, Lean's, Bolt's, and my own. Each of us had his own concept of Lawrence, so initially some friction was inevitable. If we had compromised, making various concessions to each of our attitudes, the result would have been a contrived film. We had to take time to wrestle with our doubts and arrive at a common point of view. Any film worthy of being called a good one (and I hope, modestly, that *Lawrence of Arabia* will be) must begin with this kind of friction.

However, although we reached agreement among ourselves on the concept of *Lawrence*, our intention was not to resolve everything for the audience. We want the audience to become co-author with us, contributing its own impressions of what Lawrence was like as a human being and a human dilemma. It is this emotional involvement that makes a picture successful. So we leave a few questions unanswered and set the audience searching for solutions. One of the great mysteries of Lawrence was his retirement into an anonymous existence. We have not dwelt on that phase of his life. We have supplied some information that will lead people to ask themselves why he chose one way out instead of another. Just as Bolt and Lean and myself began with a friction of viewpoints that had to be talked out, we like to think now that any three people leaving the cinema after seeing the picture will have three different attitudes toward it. The important thing is that everyone should be sufficiently intrigued to want to supply an answer. So we have not tried to resolve the enigma of Lawrence but to perpetuate the legend, and to show why it continues to haunt us after all these years.

CHAPTER 6

POSTPRODUCTION

*"YOU'RE AN IMPORTANT
PART OF THE BIG PUSH!"*

—ALLENBY TO LAWRENCE, AT JERUSALEM HEADQUARTERS

During the autumn of 1962, the final phases of filming *Lawrence of Arabia* continued. Activity on four other major fronts also proceeded with much urgency: editing the film, creating the musical score, organizing the Columbia Pictures promotional campaign, and—in the inner circle of *Lawrence* watchers—preparing a strategy to attack the film.

EDITING

Anne V. Coates functioned as much more than an editor on *Lawrence*. She was partially responsible for scheduling many of the tasks required for the final prepa-

Anne V. Coates, editor, Lawrence of Arabia.

HORIZON PICTURES (G.B.) LTD.

Inter-Office Correspondence

| From | ANNE COATES | To | SAM SPIEGEL ESQ | Date | 28.5.62. |

c.c. Messrs David Lean
John Palmer
Subject LAWRENCE OF ARABIA – Lew Thornburn
Proposed Finishing Schedule Wyn Ryder

This schedule is worked out on the assumption that 1st Unit shooting finishes on July 15th, 1962.

July 15th	End of Shooting
July 30th	Rough cut running
Aug. 6th-10th	Post-sync Dialogue
Aug. 20th-23th	Post-sync Dialogue
Aug. 31st	Fine cut running
Sept. 3rd	(Start sending music measurements of Part I (Start sending reels for duping
Sept. 6th	All titles, special effects and opticals of Part I ordered.
Sept.10th-14th	Effects recording Part I.
Sept.10th	Start sending music measurements of Part II
Sept.13th	All titles, special effects and opticals of Part II ordered.
Sept.14th	Music measurements complete.
Sept.17th-21st	Effects recording Part II
Sept.24th-28th	Music recording Part I
Sept.24th-28th	Effects recording.
Sept.26th	Start sending reels for Neg. cutting.
Oct. 1st	Start dubbing
Oct. 2nd - 4th	Effects recording
Oct. 2nd - 5th	Music recording for Part II
Oct. 29th	All reels sent for Neg. cutting.
Nov. 13th	View silent answer print.
Nov. 16th	3 - Track stereo dub complete.
Nov. 23rd	4 - Track stereo and 35 mm and F.V. dubs and transfers complete.
Nov. 23rd	Send show print for striping and 6 track stereo recording.
Nov. 30th	View final show 70 mm print.

Coates's projected "finishing schedule" as of May 1962. Final "show 70mm print" was to be ready on November 30.

ration of the film. As early as March 1962, she had drawn up a "rough finishing schedule," which then anticipated June 29 as end of shooting; July 13 as rough cut running; August 24 as fine cut running; with scene timing (for music), titles, music recording, dubbing, negative cutting, and, eventually, final prints to follow on Novem-

139

ber 30. In the revised May 28 version of Coates's completion schedule, end of shooting and rough cut had each moved two weeks later. The criticality of the situation was emphasized in a July 6 letter from Lew Thornburn, Horizon's representative in London, to Sam Spiegel: "In view of the immutability of [the December 10 Royal Premiere], everybody . . . must start *now* to fight a battle against time. I have no doubt that this battle will come to a crashing climax towards the end of November when every minute in every twenty-four hours will be hotly contested." On July 29, 1962, Barbara Cole—still on location in Morocco—wrote to Coates, also about their desperate time constraints: "Hope you are gathering your strength for the final rush—I will come round handing out pep pills and strong black coffee. Hope to see you sooner than you expect."

In September of 1962, in the midst of editing, Anne Coates took time to describe her unique experience in an unprecedented special issue of the British *Journal of the Society of Film and Television Arts,* the first ever devoted entirely to a single film:

> Owing to the fact that we had a Royal Premiere in December, we had to have the film fine cut, sent for negative cutting, music written and a six-track stereo dub completed in under four months. Even under normal conditions—cutting the film to keep abreast of the shooting—this would have been quite a formidable task, but under the particular conditions attendant to the shooting of *Lawrence,* on paper the finishing schedule seemed impossible.
>
> During the first six months of filming in Jordan, David Lean was unable to see a single foot of rushes as he was shooting in the middle of the desert. So having no chosen takes to work with I was unable to do very much cutting, though of course I ran rushes with Sam Spiegel in London and we kept the unit fully informed of the results of their work.
>
> Upon the completion of shooting in Jordan and before the unit moved to Southern Spain, David Lean came to London and we saw something like ten hours of rushes and cut sequences, and due to his remarkable powers of selection, by the time he went to Spain a week later [October 1961], I was able to start rough cutting all the material. I had very much hoped to be able to show him these cut sequences when I finished them—but by that time he was too engrossed with the shooting in Spain and consequently I was unable to work on them much further.

> However, from then on I took rushes down to Spain once a month, so I was at last able to keep more or less up to date with the cutting. These runnings were a little on the hectic side to say the least of it, as in Seville we had fixed up two old projectors in the local school to run in interlock with a makeshift bar, and when things went at all wrong the projectionists were helped out by the teacher priests! Not the ideal way to judge rushes, but certainly better than nothing!
>
> For me these trips were extremely interesting as it was the first time I had been able to see any of the film being shot. In the usual way I think it is most important for the editor to spend as much time as possible on the floor, since one is able to assimilate a lot of the mood of the film and the director's intention. In fact, I don't think this remote way of working is particularly good for the film and I much prefer being with the unit.
>
> At the very end the unit moved from Spain to Morocco [mid-July 1962] to finish the shooting. Once more it was impossible for me to take rushes out, so when David eventually arrived back in England in the middle of August I had about two and a half hours of cut sequences, none of which he had seen, and nine hours of uncut rushes. These had piled up because the last sequences shot were battles, which were covered by three or four cameras.

Coates described how the editing task had become an exhausting marathon:

> And now the work really began—day and night, seven days a week. Myself and my cutting crew of four moved into cutting rooms in London, so that David, who was already very tired, would not have to travel up and down late at night between London and the Studio, and we had a theatre at our disposal. The dubbing crew under Win Ryder stayed at Shepperton and had now grown to four dubbing editors and their assistants, and a music cutter. This arrangement worked extremely well on the whole, but of course a lot of strain was put on the crews to see that trims and sequences were in the right place at the right time. We had three black and white dupes taken off all reels and dupe transfers from the sound.
>
> The film is in two halves with a ten-minute intermission, and we all decided that since the second half was shorter and more straightforward, it would be

better to finalise this first. A little unorthodox, but we had to bear in mind getting the reels off for negative cutting, music scoring, and effects laying as soon as possible. And, we had to take into account that this was the first 70mm film that Technicolor had handled in this country. Anyway we started sending the first of the ten reels of the second half off for negative cutting on September 24—two days ahead of schedule—and in fact we ran two reels of answer print at the Odeon before we finished cutting the rushes of the first half! As you can imagine, it was very exciting seeing the first reels in 70mm, as of course we had been cutting in [reduced definition] 35mm CinemaScope. Previously, we had had only a few selected scenes in 70mm for special showings for the heads of Columbia. It is also interesting to note that when we had our first cut of all the material the film ran three and three-quarter hours, only five minutes more than the final length. This is unusual even in a normal film, let alone one of this size. This was partly due to the fact that we fine cut sequences as we went along, but mainly to the extremely well-constructed and executed script.

In midautumn, the postproduction unit was involved in sound mixing and most of the reels had been "negative cut." However, the entire three hours forty minutes of the picture had not been seen in one consecutive run-through.

Later Anne Coates would recount details of *Lawrence*'s arduous editing process, and some of the innovations introduced in the film.

For example, the projectionist at the pre-premiere showing would complain, "I know you did this film in a hurry...but surely you could have got the sound in synch with the picture."

Coates explained: "They'd never seen that done before—we'd never 'pre-laid' sound, as they now call it. There was no word for it then—laying the sound track ahead of the visual cut." Thus, as the camera closes in on Lawrence's tortured face after he executes Gasim, we hear the frantic sound of the alarm bell rung by the Turkish lookout to warn of the charge on Aqaba prior to the start of the new scene itself. And, when an exhausted Lawrence—feeling responsible for Daud's death in Sinai quicksand—stares blankly across the Suez Canal at the motorcycle rider who has questioned his identity, we hear the nerve-jarring tram bell before we cut to the chaos of Cairo.

Anne Coates was also responsible for the final form of what has become, perhaps, the most famous transition scene in film history: the blowing out of the match to plunge Lawrence into the desert. Lean has admitted that this was Robert Bolt's invention—it appears in the script—but there it was written as a dissolve, not a cut.

She remarked: "I take a lot of credit for the direct cutting, because David was still really into opticals [dissolves]. He hadn't done very much—if any—direct cutting. He'd always used dissolves and fades and things—and they were in the script. And I suggested that he go and see some of the French cinema, Chabrol and that sort of thing. You know we were doing a lot of that in those days, the 'Nouvelle Vague.'"

Coates declared that the actual frame that the famous scene was cut on was hers: "I did it twice, actually. I did it once and showed it to David and he said, 'That's great, but I think you could make it greater.' So I went away, and you know, I had a little fiddle with it and altered it a couple of frames or something like that—a couple of frames to an editor is very important. Timing something like that—to an ordinary person, it wouldn't mean anything. And anyway, I altered it and he came back and said, 'Great. Perfect. That's it.' And that's how it stayed.

"But you know, the idea for doing it originally, I can't even remember. We worked—such very close collaboration, David and I, and we also worked extremely long hours together, and got extremely tired. Worked seven days a week. For me it was an enormous strain, because I was quite young then, and less experienced, and working with the master editor in the world. It was a constant strain on me. Actually, I was very worried. David could never understand it. He thought I should not be so worried. I'm still worried. I think when you cease to worry, you cease to be any good at what you're doing.

"David has a lot of say in the way his film is cut, obviously. And...he was doing cutting on scenes, and I was doing cutting on scenes, and I was altering his stuff and he was altering my stuff. I mean, the last word in the editing is David's, but then the last word in any film is the director's. He has a more acute feeling for editing because he was a very famous editor, and he had marvelous ideas. But in four months, there's no way one single editor could have actually cut that film. You had to have two people. Maybe more."

Coates pointed out that Lean "had a very good visual idea of how he wanted [the film] to look." Although "he had much looser ideas with the action and desert scenes...he gave me explicit notes as to how he want-

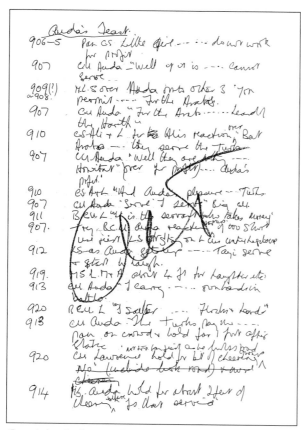

Coates's handwritten cutting notes for "feast in Auda's tent."

ed the dialogue scenes. Sometimes, you couldn't do exactly what he wanted."

Another task associated with preparing the film for presentation was the creation of projection "test loops" and "test reels" to ensure proper calibration of picture and sound on the 70mm projectors to be used in cinemas showing *Lawrence*.

Finally, on November 14, 1962, Lew Thorburn was able to confirm with Anne Coates that the total length of the 70mm version of *Lawrence of Arabia* was precisely 24,975 feet. The editing was complete.

COMPOSING

Now the composer's crucial role in *Lawrence* was about to swing into high gear.

Lean and Spiegel had originally planned to ask British classical composers Sir William Walton (Olivier's *Henry V*) and Malcolm Arnold (*The Bridge on the River Kwai*) to write the *Lawrence* score together. Composer Arnold reminisced:

> I was to do all the dramatic music and conduct and coordinate everything. Sir William Walton was to

write the patriotic British music and [Russian composer] Khachaturian [*Sabre Dance*] [was] to write the Arabian music, on which he was an expert. I went to see the film with William Walton and we both thought it was terrible and turned it down.

Susana, Lady Walton, recalled a slightly different version:

> . . .after seeing the rushes and drinking a fair amount over lunch, they [William and Malcolm] decided that it [*Lawrence*] was a travelogue needing hours of music, and declined. This deeply offended David Lean, an old friend of William's, and provoked an irate phone call from Paris from Sam Spiegel, the producer, who berated William for his failure to understand commercial cinema.

Editor Anne Coates recalled the rather peculiar incident in more detail:

> We had about two-thirds of the film cut, I suppose. Something like that. And Sam Spiegel rang up and said that Sir William Walton and Malcolm Arnold wanted to come and see the rough cut, and that David had said it was all right, and that they were going to write the music at that time. Malcolm Arnold. . .came with William Walton. . .and saw the film. . .with me and my first assistant.
>
> We loved the film. We thought it was just the

Memo from Lew Thorburn to Anne Coates: official length of 70mm Lawrence of Arabia *print is 24,975 feet.*

greatest movie, you know. And so had everybody who'd seen it so far, which were a few people–Sam's friends had seen it, and Fred Zinnemann had seen it, and people like that had seen the odd bit.

Anyway, Malcolm–I don't know the politics behind it–but Malcolm Arnold had had one or two drinks before he came, and he proceeded to send that picture up from the beginning. He was going, "funny little musical instrument" goes here, [in a high voice] "plink plink plink" noises and [low voice] "bang," "boom" and all this sort of thing, all the way through the film. And Willie Kemplin, my assistant, and I were absolutely furious. And–anyway, he and William Walton kept laughing and nudging each other, you know, absolutely behaving like two schoolboys.

At the end of the picture Sam rang me from Paris and said, "So what did they think of it? Did they think it was great?" And I said, "Well, I'm not quite sure." And he said, "Well I want to speak to Malcolm."

Malcolm was saying, "I'm not speaking to Sam, no way." And I was pretty young then, and Sam Spiegel was pretty fierce. He said, "Put Malcolm on the phone to me or your job's on the line." And I said,

David Lean and Maurice Jarre discuss Lawrence *score.*

"I'm sorry Sam, but he won't speak to you. He says he'll give you a call next week."

And Sam said–he's shouting down the phone at me–"I insist upon speaking to him tonight. What did they think of the film?"

I'm not going to say that they obviously hated the whole movie, which they apparently did. And next thing I know, they turned it down.

At that point, Sam Spiegel went to Paris to see Maurice Jarre, who had just composed the score for *Sundays and Cybele.* Spiegel invited Jarre "to see the greatest movie ever made: *Lawrence of Arabia* . . . a great film . . . a very long film."

Spiegel then revealed his latest plan. He wanted three composers: Russian composer Aram Khachaturian for the Arabic music; British composer Benjamin Britten for the British military band music and British music; and Jarre to coordinate and write "the dramatic music." Although Jarre thought it was a somewhat strange procedure, he was happy at the idea of collaborating with the two great musicians. Jarre later learned that Bernard Herrmann had also been a candidate, but had been rejected for demanding a salary of $50,000: "equal to half of what Lean got for four years' work on the film!"

Jarre went to London in July, eager to see the film. He was told that "it was impossible since the film was not edited yet." He wasn't informed, however, that the film's opening–the Royal Premiere–was less than five months away. However, Jarre read up on Lawrence, including *Seven Pillars,* and began to consider possibilities for the music.

In the middle of August, Sam Spiegel summoned Jarre to his office, and said, "Maurice, I have bad news. Khachaturian cannot go outside of Russia, and we obviously cannot record the music there, and Benjamin Britten asked for one year to write a third of the score, because he has some other work."

Maurice Jarre was delirious with joy at the possibility that he alone would do the score. With Sam Spiegel off on a trip to New York, Jarre watched forty hours of the film during a single week. "I was so excited," he remarked, "because it was beautiful, you know. But the film didn't make much sense after each screening. It only came together at the end. Nevertheless, it was amazingly beautiful."

At the end of August, Spiegel returned to England, with a shock for Jarre: "Maurice, I have good news. I have just signed an American composer who is going to write 90 percent of the music. You are going to write 10 percent of the original music and you are going to orchestrate and do all the arrangements on the film."

Jarre was depressed at the new allocation of tasks, but even more so when it was revealed that the composer was Broadway's Richard Rodgers *(Oklahoma!, Victory at Sea)*. Jarre then asked, "Am I supposed to go to New York, or is he coming to London, or what?" Spiegel's reply: "He's going to send you his themes from New York." Jarre probed further: "Did he see the film?" Spiegel said, "Well, he does not need to see the film. He is writing the themes from the script."

Eventually, the themes arrived—by mail! In Rodgers's absence, a British pianist was hired. Jarre described what happened next: "We were in a little room—David Lean, Sam Spiegel, myself, and the pianist, and he started to play the 'love theme' of *Lawrence of Arabia!* And then there was the 'Lawrence theme,' and then something that sounded like *In a Monastery Garden* or *In a Persian Market Place*—something like that—it was really funny!"

At one point the pianist, playing "the military British theme," turned to David Lean and he said, "This is really an old British tune, you know," and he continued to play without looking at the score sheet. Lean stopped the music and said, "Sam, what is this rubbish? It is ridiculous! You took me from my work in the editing room, where I am very busy, just to hear this stupid thing? What is that?"

Spiegel, who until now had kept his protégé Jarre isolated from Lean, asked if Jarre had written anything that could be played for Lean. Jarre replied, "Yes, I have been working a lot, but it is only musical ideas." Spiegel gave the go-ahead, and Jarre played what would become the haunting "Lawrence theme." Lean approached Jarre,

Autograph sketch of Lawrence *music, by Maurice Jarre.*

put his hand on his shoulder, and said, "Great! That's exactly what I want! Sam, that's what we should have—this kind of feeling. Why is this chap not going to do it?" At that point Sam said, "Well, Maurice, you have a Superman job to do because we have to deliver the film by December. . ." And it was already the beginning of October.

Jarre then had only about five weeks to compose the music and record it! He toiled in a little office in Berkeley Street, essentially living there: working all day long and all night, taking some naps on a couch every hour for about ten minutes, or every two hours. Since the second part of *Lawrence* was edited before the first, Jarre also had to compose the music for it first. "It was double work," he emphasized, "as you have to imagine what's happening before."

During this period, Jarre worked very closely with Lean:

"At times there were conflicts about musical points between Spiegel and Lean, and I had to do two versions for the same sequence. For instance, the sequence which begins under the tent the day before Lawrence decides to go to Aqaba. It begins with the cord dangling in front of Feisal's tent and continues with Lawrence going into the desert with the two kids and spending the night thinking. Musically, you have to show how his decision came about intellectually. I thought of a passacaglia because it is a musical form which fits the intellectual process. I told this to David Lean and he thought it was very interesting, but Sam hated it when I showed it to him. He asked me to redo it. So I did it, but I told him I liked my first idea better. So there was a battle on this sequence and, as usual, David Lean's version prevailed.

"Sometimes at night, after our conference, Sam called me and told me not to listen to David and do it his way. It was strange! *Lawrence of Arabia* taught me a lot about

144

what you have to do when you're caught between a strong producer and a strong director to keep the balance."

However, Jarre added, "Sam Spiegel was a very good producer and supervised everything organizationally and artistically."

Jarre—who had previously orchestrated his own work—was asked to to work with Gerard Schurmann, who had worked on *Exodus* for composer Ernest Gold. "The orchestration," explained Jarre, "is 50 percent of the score. It gives the score its color."

Schurmann recalls that initially he was approached by Spiegel to cocompose with Jarre. He met with David Lean and saw a few edited reels of *Lawrence*. "The sheer beauty of what I saw bowled me over," he declared.

Schurmann and Jarre got acquainted, and spent time in daily visits to the viewing theater, often followed by dinner and stimulating conversation with David Lean in the evening. Schurmann and Jarre at first got on well together. However, Schurmann soon sensed that Jarre had "little experience of composing or orchestrating anything appropriate for the kind of large symphony orchestra of close to one hundred players that we were going to employ." Thus, things at first did not run smoothly between them. Jarre felt that Schurmann was wasting too much time in detailed questioning regarding the notations for orchestrations that Jarre made on his sketches. Schurmann felt that Jarre—with only a few weeks left—might not be able to finish the score in time. In that event, Schurmann might not be paid for his work.

A solution, unacceptable to Jarre, was to have Schurmann write some of the score. Jarre approached Spiegel and insisted that "I took this assignment, and even if I don't sleep one night, I will finish it. I will write all the music myself. I have done difficult things, timewise, in French films, so it's not the first time and I can do it. I will do all the music myself, so you have to pay this guy for the work he is doing, because it's not fair. He's not going to write one single note."

It was then agreed that Schurmann would take full charge of the orchestrations and reduce his input of original music. Spiegel had been impressed especially by Schurmann's vast experience in producing superb orchestrations for large-scale films, like *The Cruel Sea* and *The Vikings,* as well as *Exodus,* and was pleased with the compromise. Schurmann, however, was annoyed because his change in status would entail, potentially, a large loss of royalties. However, Spiegel "soothed [him] down with his expressed belief that [Schurmann] would in any case

Orchestration page of Lawrence *music, by Gerard Schurmann.*

still be required to contribute a fair amount of original music." This was not to be the case: "In the event, I did not compose anything for the film," Schurmann has observed.

Jarre recalls, "After this was cleared up, everything was fine, as [Schurmann] was a good musician, he was very correct with me, and I remember we went to have dinner when the score was finished."

More controversy centered around the recording of the score. Spiegel thought there were too many foreigners in the film credits and wanted to add more British names. Horizon had retained the London Philharmonic Orchestra to record the soundtrack. Jarre agreed that Sir Adrian Boult, their musical director, could conduct.

Jarre, however, asked that he be allowed to rehearse the orchestra first. Boult agreed. On the first day of recording at Shepperton Studios, Sir Adrian came in after Jarre's three-hour rehearsal. Although his conducting pleased Jarre, it soon became evident that Boult was simply unprepared to cope with the unfamiliar task of pacing the music to the "streamers" (visual film cues).

"Oh?" Boult said. "No, no, no. Wait a minute." Boult then called Sam Spiegel and complained that he had never conducted in this [synchronized] manner. "Sam, I never did that. I cannot do that. This young man seems to know what he is talking about, so I think he should do it himself." So, Jarre recalls, "He put his baton on the desk and did not conduct one single bar of all the score!"

Maurice Jarre noted that the resultant sound, recorded with three microphones, one for ambience, one right, one left—no digital, no Dolby—was marvelous.

Yet another controversy was to be associated with *Lawrence*'s musical score. Jarre agreed to accept Boult's name on the screen credit—for purposes of British content regulations. The credit thus reads MUSIC BY MAURICE JARRE; PERFORMED BY THE LONDON PHILHARMONIC ORCHESTRA, CONDUCTED BY SIR ADRIAN BOULT; Jarre recalls, "I remember David Lean saying he never saw anything like that: somebody with a credit for conducting and he didn't conduct a single note!" However, the composer insisted that "there's no reason why I should give up some royalties on the sound track album." On the sound track, therefore, the credit reads CONDUCTED BY MAURICE JARRE.

PUBLICITY CAMPAIGN

Columbia/Horizon were determined to make *Lawrence of Arabia* an unforgettable theatrical experience. They prepared a special "Souvenir Program" to be sold at showings of the film.

The elegant forty-page book—created by famed New York graphic designer Henry Wolf—is a work of art. Two special pages reveal—via cut-out windows—portions of large photos on the page following. The first window

shows Lawrence's eyes embedded in a grandiose presentation of Churchill's famous quote, with the next page bearing a stunning color portrait of O'Toole as Lawrence. The second of these pages contains the script excerpt of Lawrence giving Bentley his reason for loving the desert: "It's clean." These lines are followed by a cut-out window which reveals a tiny image of Lawrence and his servants heading into a Sinai sunset. The full splendor of the desert panorama is revealed when the page is turned.

Also included are two impressive color foldouts, extensive essays on "The Legend of Lawrence" and "The Making of the Picture," a map of the locale where Lawrence's exploits took place, biographies of the cast and crew, production credits, a chronology of Lawrence's life, and—surprising in a film program—an extensive bibliography.

Special white-leatherbound versions were prepared for presentation to VIPs, including Queen Elizabeth II and John F. Kennedy. The Kennedys had visited Sam Spiegel aboard his yacht, the *Malahne,* before JFK became President.

Jesse G. Levine, a Columbia promotion executive who shared the excitement of being involved in the release, years later commented to David Lean that "our program, in contrast to the standard, superficial moneymaking piece of flummery that attended most roadshow presentations of the period, was a literate, interesting and artful piece of craftsmanship." David Lean replied, telling Levine—confidentially—that it was outstanding for

Timing sheets showing synching of visuals to music.

the genre because he had induced Robert Bolt to write it. Lean also remarked that "Bolt, of course, wanted no writing credit for the booklet, no souvenir program added to his corpus literati, nor any calls offering more such work." The book's production credits read simply TEXT BASED ON MATERIAL SUPPLIED BY [unit publicist] JOHN R. WOOLFENDEN.

A hastily prepared four-page, advance information "Campaign Book" was issued by Columbia U.K. In addition to showing, for the first time, an early version of the notorious "dark head" advertising motif [not appearing in the program], it listed accessories available to exhibitors—stills, giant linen banners, and photographic blowups of five shots from the film—at sizes up to 72″ x 40″. The booklet gave technical and cast credits, a short version of the film's story, and offered a selection of a dozen small advertisement variations ("ad mats") which were available for newspaper insertions.

THE ATTACK

While the postproduction teams whipped *Lawrence of Arabia* into its final shape, the inner circle of T. E. Lawrence watchers anxiously sought out any information which would hint at the film's content.

In midsummer, A. W. Lawrence had obtained an incomplete copy of the script and then had written to Sam Spiegel. The producer was reminded that final approval for use of the title *Seven Pillars of Wisdom* was contingent upon an endorsement by A.W., and a copy of the finalized script was urgently requested. A.W. added that, on the basis of what he had read, "to say that I am extremely disappointed is a gross understatement." He contended that the scriptwriter made "singularly little use" of *Seven Pillars,* and that he had "distorted the passages he has used. . . From opening. . . to the end, almost every event in this script is either fictitious or fictionalised."

Lawrence's brother concluded his letter with a warning: "I have objections so strong that I may eventually feel obliged to consider whether to make them public."

Three weeks later, on August 22, 1962, Spiegel wrote back, expressing "disappointment. . .as both the scriptwriter and ourselves had made every effort to follow as closely as possible the film treatment which I had originally submitted and which you not only approved, but praised wholeheartedly." Spiegel offered to show some sections of the film to A.W., and then to arrange a meeting with Robert Bolt.

On September 5, Bolt wrote to Lawrence's brother. The playwright lamented that, on the basis of A.W. hav-

ing read his script and an article published in *The New York Times Magazine* earlier that year,

> You. . .have concluded that my attitude towards Colonel Lawrence is hostile, belittling and indifferent. That I am distressed by your judgment is not of much importance, but I must state firmly that your judgment of my attitude is quite mistaken. My attitude to this, my principal protagonist, has been of admiration throughout and increasingly of interest and sympathy. . .it is simply not in me to deploy twelve months of nervous effort and concern about a figure to which my attitude was anything but of the deepest interest and respect.

Bolt also expressed hope that the finished product—the film—would favorably modify A.W.'s judgment. Ironically, the day that Bolt drafted his letter, Spiegel had arranged a private showing at which A.W. viewed more than half of the completed film.

He was enraged.

A.W. wrote to Spiegel, declaring that it was no longer necessary that a final version of the script be submitted: "If it were in my power to do so, I would prohibit use of the present title *Lawrence of Arabia* because in the character so designated in your film I can see very little consistent with my brother, and an overwhelming amount utterly inconsistent with him; this impression, which I derived from reading the script, was not merely confirmed but intensified by viewing corresponding pas-

One of first pieces of art produced for Columbia Lawrence *campaign: used as decoration in various ads.*

sages in the film." A.W. suggested that viewers of *Lawrence of Arabia* will "accept the portrayal without question," while viewers of a film titled *Seven Pillars of Wisdom* might compare it to the book and "share my opinion that it both travesties the book and misrepresents the principal figure.

"I cannot," A.W. declared, "appear to sanction a claim that this film might represent the book." T. E. Lawrence's

FROM DEC. 11TH ODEON *Leicester Square*
PHONE: WHI. 2688

After five years...
the first motion picture
from the creators of
"The Bridge On
The River Kwai"

Columbia Pictures presents
The SAM SPIEGEL–DAVID LEAN Production of

STARRING
ALEC GUINNESS
ANTHONY QUINN
JACK HAWKINS
JOSE FERRER
ANTHONY QUAYLE
CLAUDE RAINS
ARTHUR KENNEDY
AND INTRODUCING
PETER O'TOOLE
as 'LAWRENCE'

LAWRENCE OF ARABIA

WITH
OMAR SHARIF as 'Ali' · SCREENPLAY BY ROBERT BOLT · PRODUCED BY SAM SPIEGEL · DIRECTED BY DAVID LEAN
PHOTOGRAPHED IN A HORIZON BRITISH PRODUCTION IN
SUPER PANAVISION 70° TECHNICOLOR*

SEPARATE PERFORMANCES
Evenings 7.15 p.m. (Doors 6.30) Matinees: Weds, Thurs & Sats 2.15 p.m. (Doors 1.30) Sundays at 6.30 p.m. (Doors 5.45)
ALL SEATS BOOKABLE

First U.K. ad for booking reserved seats for Lawrence *at Odeon Leicester Square.*

brother then formally withdrew permission for Spiegel to use the title *Seven Pillars of Wisdom,* thus forfeiting £5,000, the final portion of his rights fee.

A.W. then wrote to Liddell Hart, amplifying his feelings about the Spiegel–Lean production. After playfully disclosing that Spiegel's lawyers were unaware that copyright did *not* apply to film titles—Spiegel and Lean could have used *Seven Pillars of Wisdom,* after all—A.W. called the script "a feeble piece of nasty fiction-'psychology'. . . [which] distorts everything."

The inner circle quickly organized their campaign. "It is difficult to think of any way of attack which will not help to advertise the film," A.W. remarked. Nonetheless, he devised a tentative plan, and proposed it to Liddell Hart:

> Obviously, about December 10, I ought to write a letter to the *Times,* and maybe some cheap paper (such as the film audience might read, e.g., *Daily Mail*) would serialize bits of *Seven Pillars* to call attention to discrepancies. (A Penguin [edition]. . . is too far advanced for anything to be printed on the cover.) *Of course, the film will soon be forgotten (especially since it needs a wide screen, and so can't become a repertory standby)* . . . Perhaps the multitude that will say "Oh, what a horrid man" will forget too. [Emphasis ours]

Liddell Hart, not having seen the film or the script, begged off proffering advice. A.W. decided to request a few changes to see if Horizon would respond. His short list included the scene when Lawrence tells Allenby that he killed two men and enjoyed it, and the fact that Lawrence's motive for entering Deraa was converted from "reconnaissance to despairing bravado." A.W. and Liddell Hart also proposed preparing a complete compendium of suggested alterations "in

148

case [Spiegel] should show willingness [to respond]."

However, by mid-November, alterations to the film seemed an outside possibility, they thought, and the publicity approach might have to be used. A.W. had persuaded Penguin to cease distribution of display cards for the *Seven Pillars* paperback which "appeared to advertise the film far more than the book." And there was no further communication from Spiegel: A.W. did not even receive an invitation to the premiere!

Liddell Hart decided to write to Robert Bolt.

There followed a most remarkable exchange of letters by two of the great intellects of the twentieth century. Captain Basil Liddell Hart, an extraordinary military strategist, author, close friend, and biographer of T. E. Lawrence, and—as operator of the "Lawrence bureau"—completely informed about every aspect of Lawrence of Arabia. And Robert Bolt, a brilliant playwright whose acclaimed *A Man for All Seasons* would eventually be studied in schools alongside works of Shakespeare.

Liddell Hart knew that any references to the script would not be in order until A.W. had personally heard from Spiegel. Thus, the subject under discussion would be Bolt's article in *The New York Times Magazine* of February 25, 1962. However, the exchange would soon stray into an exploration of *Lawrence*'s two controversial themes: sadomasochism and homosexuality.

21 November 1962
Dear Mr. Bolt,

A friend of mine has sent me, rather belatedly, a clipping...of your article "Clues to the Legend of Lawrence." I read it with keen interest, and agree with many of your wider reflections on the historical background of the period.

In regard to Lawrence himself, much of your interpretation is very discerning, but I think it is off the mark in at least two important respects—perhaps because you have relied too much on, and read too much into, what he wrote in *Seven Pillars of Wisdom*.

Thus...you draw the deduction that he was "homosexual by nature" even if not "homosexually active." While a number of passages in *Seven Pillars* may appear to support such an idea, none of the friends with whom I discussed his personality during the nineteen twenties and thirties ever took that view. Moreover, it is surely significant that none of his many friends whom I knew had homosexual traits.

He was also far more friendly with women than you suggest, and several were of the really feminine type whom homosexuals do not usually like....

A more important point is your deduction that he was sadistic...I think that here, and in using the compound term sado-masochism, you fail to distinguish between masochism, which he had markedly, and sadism, of which there was much less even the normal degree in his composition.

You seem to me to have been unduly influenced by his account of the [no prisoners] sequel to the Turkish atrocities in [the village of] Tafas, and his horrified revulsion from it subsequently. If he had had experience of battle with British troops on the Western Front he would have known that even they could easily turn into blind and bloodthirsty "killers" when their blood was up, and with much less justification than in the Arab case after Tafas. Moreover some of the most highly respected commanders, normally quite humane, encouraged such killing, with bayonet or hand-grenade, of surrendering Germans.

On the question of his truthfulness you are nearer the mark, but I learned to differentiate between his airy "Irishness," or fondness for "smoke-screens," and his exceptional accuracy when it was a matter important for history. When I tackled him on this ground, I found that his evidence was usually confirmed when checked from other sources....

Yours sincerely,

Basil Liddell Hart

P.S. I would like to take the opportunity of saying how greatly I enjoyed your play, *A Man for All Seasons*.

Bolt's reply was prompt, polite, and persuasive:

22 November 1962
Dear Captain Liddell Hart,

Thank you for your letter of yesterday...I don't have a copy of the *New York Times* article but I must have written very carelessly indeed if it gave you the impression that I am one of Lawrence's "knockers."

It would be impertinent for me to attempt controversy with you on this subject. On the questions of fact I defer to you absolutely. And you are correct in thinking that my only real source is *Seven Pillars of Wisdom* and still more dangerously, my own interpretation of it. When asked to write the film I concluded, after some thought: *"I will take* Seven Pillars, *I will ignore all other opinions, I will assume it to be a true account of what happened to him and assuming it to be true will ask myself, 'What kind of man is it to whom this happens and who then writes about it in this way?' "* [Emphasis ours]

On the question of his homosexuality (of nature, not practice), and sado-masochism, while I would still recommend anyone to take your opinion rather than mine, I may without impertinence offer my argument perhaps.

As I said in the article, I don't find the first question very interesting. But I must say that in *Seven Pillars* I find a very strong homosexual colouring, over and above the specific hints which you refer to. There is a sort of delicate, loving, half fastidious, half squalid self-examination, a superfluity of lyricism over and above the content, a failure of the emotion to flow from himself to any outer object, which I associate with that condition. Of course these are dreadfully vague terms, but then a man's inner nature is a dreadfully vague thing, and opinions on it, even the opinions of his closest, even the opinion of himself, can hardly be more than opinions. But it must be obvious to any objective person that your opinion, since you must have been close to him, is of more worth than mine who has only approached him through his book. You will be pleased to know that we have made nothing of the matter in the film, though we felt bound to make a reference to it which would be picked up by those already aware of the controversy, and will be missed by anybody who isn't.

The other question, that of sado-masochism, is more crucial, and one I feel prepared to make more of a fight for. (Unhappily it is an even more equivocal trait than the other one.) I don't confuse masochism with sadism except insomuch as clinical psychiatrists do. One of the few postulates upon which all psychologists appear to agree is that sadism and masochism are very closely linked indeed. Not that one is a repressed form of the other but that they are associated products of a common source almost always found together. I share the literary man's distaste for and jealousy of psychological jargon. However, let me speak more commonsensically. I think any psychiatrist

would say that if as you say Lawrence was "markedly" masochistic then, at some level or other, he must also have been sadistic. This does *not* mean that his compassion and concern for others was in any way hypocritical; on the contrary it means that it was inspired by real horror, a degree of horror which an averagely constituted person would probably find excessive. But in everyday terms: when I meet a man with a *passionate* hatred of cruelty and destruction, I feel pity as well as respect, because I sense that he is wittingly or unwittingly at war against something which he knows too much about. When you say that he had "less than the normal" amount of sadism I think, with respect, that you strengthen my case. In short I think that Lawrence was sitting on something. Again this does *not* imply any kind of hypocrisy. He was rightly, nobly, courageously and sensitively avoiding something impermissible.

To put it a little nearer to the knuckle: when we find a man with a detestation of violence and suffering (i.e., a man with "less than the normal" degree of sadism) who works himself (for whatever reasons) into a position where he is absolutely bound to be surrounded by and to dispense violence and suffering, and that position not an ordinary one to which any man might be drafted but a most exotic and unlikely one, then it is only reasonable to wonder if there was not some contradiction in his nature, about this matter.

To descend to actual fact (as represented in *Seven Pillars),* I cannot think your account of [the village of] Tafas is adequate. It was, in plain terms, a war-crime. You know the book far better than myself and you will remember that it was done at his instigation, included the murder of men already taken prisoner, became so hysterical that even animals and wounded were slaughtered too, and, most significant of all, that it went on all day. That it was triggered by justifiable anger is really not here or there for it obviously became an orgy in itself ("One of the nights when men went mad". . ."other's lives became toys to break and throw away" and so on.) Nor is it any excuse that other men behaved as badly elsewhere. Indeed excuse and blame seem to me beside the point. We have here a fact, a terrible but also deeply interesting one. *How did a man who was quite clearly not, as you say, a sadist but the contrary, come to do this, and having done it to write about it in that rapt poetical manner?* [Emphasis ours]

One of the things that have most irritated me in accounts of Lawrence has been the tendency of writers to put this Tafas business down as one incident among others and walk away from it. It simply won't do. Unless we are to assume a literal stroke of madness, a medical aberration, then we have to have a picture of the man which will embrace the incident properly. It seems to me to do less than justice to the man to whitewash this; all whitewashing belittles; it denies the man his whole stature and by implication lessens the pain (the inner pain I mean) which he must have borne. And as you say, he suffered horrified revulsion afterwards. Of course he did. And before, too. That is my point.

I see that I have let myself be carried away and seem almost to be instructing you. Excuse that. In the film, in dramatic—and therefore crude—terms I have tried to show this contradiction in him, show what it cost him, show how use of it was made by the Generals and Politicians who needed him in order to perform the duties society had imposed on them, show how War and nothing else was the villain of the piece, in taking this fine and hardy man and turning his own best qualities against him, filling him as you say, with revulsion for himself.

You have so much more authority than me in this matter that I almost hope you will not see the film lest it offend you. But if you do, I shall be grateful if you will tell me, making allowance for the necessary simplicities of drama, what you think of it. And thank you for taking so much trouble with a stranger.

Yours sincerely,
R. O. Bolt

Liddell Hart responded a week later:

27 November 1962
Dear Mr. Bolt,

I much appreciated the way you took my comments on your article in *The New York Times Magazine*, and your illuminating explanation of how you arrived at your conclusions, while the open-minded tone of your letter encourages me to continue the discussion.

In regard to what you say about the "homosexual colouring" of Lawrence's phrasing in *Seven Pillars*, that colouring seems to me to be a product of the particular literary style he adopted in writing the book, rather than natural to himself—plus an attempt to reach and show, understanding of what his own upbringing and composition made foreign to him.

On the second and more important question, that of "sado-masochism," your exposition of the matter is also very interesting. But while you share my doubts about the tendencies of psychologists, you seem to give their theories more credit than is justified, especially as to sadism and masochism being "very closely linked." In my observations of, and discussions with, Lawrence I found little sign of their combination—and it has also been rare in other cases known to me.

In regard to what you say about Tafas, I have carefully reread the chapter about this in *Seven Pillars* and found nothing to support the charge that the killing "was done at his instigation" apart from the sentence: "By my order we took no prisoners, for the only time in our war." I have long regarded that sentence as an example of his rather masochistic tendency to self-accusation—for it is hard to imagine that in the fury of that moment any "order" given by him could have had the slightest additional effect in spurring the Arabs to take vengeance—or in stopping them if he had tried to restrain them before their blood-lust was slaked.

Elsewhere in these three pages, about the Arabs' revenge for the Turkish atrocities in Tafas, his use of the word "we" reads to me as a product of his self-identification with the Arabs, and thus instinctive self-accusation over the massacre. In discussing the matter with a number of his friends who were with the Arab forces in the advance—particularly Stirling, his companion most of the time—I found that they did not take his implied participation very seriously. Stirling and he shared the same car, "Blue Mist". . .and rode in it throughout these days except for a few brief interludes on camelback. So it is evident that Lawrence cannot have taken a hand in the "all day" killing—sitting in a car that was bumping along a desert track made that a practical impossibility.

With the Arabs, it was more than a one-day orgy of killing—they went on killing every Turk they could all the way from Deraa to Damascus, and without any such excuse as at Tafas. Hubert Young related how he saw Lawrence trying to prevent such a killing, but in vain. The Arabs were completely out of hand—even of his hand. But it is very characteristic that he could saddle himself with responsibility for what he could not prevent. To his friends, that was one of his most maddening characteristics, and carried so far as to seem masochistic.

I appreciate what you say in the last paragraph of the letter. I have not had an invitation to see the film, but hope to have the chance of doing so later and will certainly send you my comments as suggested.

But I have now had an opportunity of reading, rather hurriedly, the copy of the script that was sent to A.W., and in view of what you said in your letter I made some notes, on Sunday, before returning it yesterday.

It is, as I expected, a brilliant dramatic presentation of events and personalities, and should make a very striking film.

From a historian's point of view, I naturally regret the extent of the departure from the historical record of events. It seemed to me that in some respects the extent is more than dramatic necessity requires, when the theme is handled by a playwright of your calibre. I also noticed that some important factual errors which could have very easily been corrected, and only wish that I had seen the script in time for that. It may be that they have been corrected in the final script. (If you have a spare copy I would welcome it.)

A point that puzzled me was why several of the leading personalities are telescoped into a compound figure—as I had imagined that a film allowed more scope than the stage for keeping personalities distinct if they are interesting in themselves and in the part they played.

As regards Lawrence himself, I was glad to find that the script touched very lightly on the "homosexual" question, and is not likely to mislead viewers in that respect if the actors go no further than the script.

On the other hand, I was sorry to see how much emphasis is put on his supposed sadism in a series of passages... From what I have said earlier in the letter, you will realize why I am convinced that you have "got him wrong" there. It is all the more pity because very slight alterations or excisions in the script would have sufficed to correct the impression....

With renewed thanks for your letter.

Yours sincerely,

Captain Basil Liddell Hart

Bolt required only two days to draft his incisive, stunning response, making it immediately clear that it was his final retort:

29 November 1962
Dear Captain Liddell Hart,

Thank you very much indeed for your courteous and stimulating letter of the 27th. I must come back just once again, as briefly as may be: there is no need whatever for you to reply.

You refer to your own knowledge of T.E. and to things said to you by common friends. Against this knowledge I make no appeal, nor would wish to. Any such appeal by me would be plain silly. As I say, my filmscript is an effort at a dramatic interpretation of the story and the man as shown in *Seven Pillars*. It's not an effort to clear up the "Lawrence mystery," which I should think a quite forlorn endeavour for anyone so unskilled in biographical techniques as me.

So far as *Seven Pillars* goes there seems to be one point where we clash, but that is a crucial one. This is the massacre at Tafas and the importance to be given it. As you point out, such terrible behaviour may be taken as quite normal among Beduin advancing an ancient, hated enemy and under provocation. One would have taken it they they were simply out of hand if Lawrence had not specifically stated otherwise. One would have thought that he watched helplessly and horrified, or tried without effect to intervene. But not only does he not make any such claim, he says, "By my orders." It quite plainly takes responsibility to himself. If you say that, knowing Lawrence and the circumstances as you do, you simply don't believe that he *was* responsible then it does seem to me (how can I put this politely?) that you are saying that he has lied. I see no evidence in *Seven Pillars* for this. And it's a very strange kind of lie for a man to tell.

In this description of the deed you tell me that by "we" he really meant "they." Well, what can I say? You knew him and I didn't, but he was no mean writer and "we" is what he says. And in perhaps the most dreadful incident of all he definitely states that he was personally present and active: "Just one group of Arabs, who had not heard our news, took prisoner the last two hundred men of the central section. Their respite was short.

I had gone up to learn why it was...(being "not unwilling" that they should be spared. But another

152

Turkish atrocity was discovered, the work of these men now taken prisoner) . . . They said nothing in the moments before we opened fire. At last their heaps ceased moving." Now you have authority, as a friend, to say that this can't be true. But I submit that there can be no doubt what it *says*. And nobody wishing to give the story of Lawrence as portrayed in *Seven Pillars* can simply pass by such a thing, if he wishes to be half way honest.

In short, you have a knowledge of Lawrence over and above the knowledge which he gives us in his own account. You have your own picture which you can compare with his self-portrait, and where they do not tally you can say "here my picture is true and Lawrence's is false." But for *me* to have formed an opinion of his nature and then, whenever his account ran contrary to it, to have said "oh well, that's a lie" would have been outrageous I think. Like those irritating scholars who have a theory about Shakespeare and where they run against a passage of Shakespeare which upsets their theory say "this is the work of an interpolator."

With great respect therefore, I must think it was my duty to take Lawrence as meaning what he says, not something else, in these pages as elsewhere. If I am to assume that he was lying wherever his statements are inconvenient to me, I have no right to take him as truthful when his account fits in with some theory of my own. The whole thing would become questionable, a quicksand of fantasy, which is the view of Aldington, not of myself.

I therefore had to form a picture of the man which would embrace, and not reject, this very shocking, this quite impermissible deed. I take it that it happened. I can find no "excuse" for it. I am shocked by it and should be. *But,* I must not take refuge in my shock or enjoy my indignation; I must bring every effort of understanding to bear so that I can comprehend how the seeds of this can be carried in a man who elsewhere reveals himself as gentle, sensitive, and compassionate. I found, or thought I found, clues to his dual nature in his treatment of suffering, his own and others, throughout the book.

Another long letter, I'm afraid. But I'm deeply engaged in this. I will defer instantly to anybody like yourself in the matter of what Lawrence was. But I'll defend my interpretation of what he *says* he was as being a dignified and responsible one, without

denigration on the one hand or prevarication on the other.

Yours sincerely,
Robert Bolt

P.S. I don't even have a copy of the script myself! For some reason, film people seem to love to make them rare. But I think it's going to be published and it will give me pleasure to send you one then.

About the collapsing of many characters into one I too thought that the sprawling medium of the film would allow them to make separate appearances, but it isn't so. It turns out to be a medium requiring as much economy as any other. Thus, "Dryden" (my composite for all those civilian intellectuals in and about the Arab Bureau) has only time to make four brief appearances. To have divided these between all the individuals he represents would have fragmented his part beyond the patience of an audience. Similarly, my "Colonel Brighton." Like all dramatic media, it's powerful but crude. Not like etching with a silverpoint but like splitting logs with an axe. Get it in the right place at the right angle and the log flies apart like magic: get it wrong and an ugly mess results. Pity we workers in such a field.

It is noteworthy that Bolt's 1961 interpretation of Lawrence's character, as portrayed in the film, is generally supported by biographical material which has appeared during the last thirty years. In particular, the eminent psychiatrist John Mack's Pulitzer Prize-winning *A Prince of Our Disorder* (1976) explores and defines the relationship between Lawrence's inner life and his exploits.

On November 29, 1962, the premiere loomed less than two weeks away. A.W. told Liddell Hart that Bolt's script was a "brilliant misrepresentation of events and personalities." And, he complained, "The press are starting to bother me." He made a statement, explaining that Bolt's script was very different from Michael Wilson's "treatment," which three years ago convinced him to sell the rights to *Seven Pillars*. A.W. asserted that "episodes inspired by the book have been fictionalised and completely imaginary episodes have been inserted; the distortions and inventions build up the character attributed to my brother with the aid of invented dialogue." He explained that he had thus denied the use of the title *Seven Pillars of Wisdom* and returned £5,000 to Horizon.

Three days before the premiere, Bolt offered Liddell

Hart two "of the few remaining seats." Liddell Hart turned down the offer, later telling Terence Rattigan that he felt "it might be some embarrassment in publishing my criticism of the film, or that Sam Spiegel might find some way of exploiting the fact of my attendance."

The first full screening of the completed film was held only one day before the premiere, on Sunday morning, December 9, 1962, at the Odeon Leicester Square. Until then, no one—not even David Lean or Anne Coates—had seen the picture all the way through from beginning to end. This showing—arranged because the Sunday evening press showing was oversubscribed—was attended by friends and family of the cast and crew.

In the intermission, the first instance of what was to become a worldwide *Lawrence of Arabia* phenomenon was born: everyone wanted cold drinks, but there were none left! The supply had quickly run out.

The Sunday evening showing—for press, cast, and crew—was attended by David Lean and Anne Coates, with an enormous party following. Anne Coates related her account of the proceedings:

"My assistants and I had been working day and night, literally seven days a week 'til midnight, to get the picture ready. Sam did a very clever thing: he made a date with the Queen, that was impossible to make, absolutely impossible on paper to have it ready in time. 'Cause he thought he'd be really clever and David would have to have it ready, and he had to have it finished. And we were working incredible hours, and so we got there early, and we got ourselves some really good seats. It was the press show, it wasn't the Royal Premiere or anything.

"And then they started running out of seats. They'd invited a lot of VIPs, and the manager tried to move my boys out of their seats—and I said, 'No way do you move them. Without them you wouldn't even have a movie here tonight. They all stay in their seats.' And then it was really embarrassing, because I didn't know him very well, but he was pretty rude. And I was quite rude back.

"And the following night, the premiere night, I went to Sam Spiegel's party over at Grosvenor House. I was sitting at the *same* table as the manager of the Odeon Leicester Square!"

CHAPTER 7

PREMIERES, REVIEWS AND OSCARS: 1962 AND 1963

"IN TEN DAYS I'LL BE BACK WITH THE GOLD."

—LAWRENCE TO AUDA, ON DEPARTING FROM AQABA

The Royal World Premiere of *Lawrence of Arabia* was held on Monday, December 10, 1962, at 8 P.M. It was a charity performance, the tickets ranging in price from 1 to 25 guineas (about $4.00 to $100). The first public showing was to be at the Odeon Leicester Square in the heart of London's West End entertainment district. The Odeon—with a capacity near 2,000, Britain's largest cinema—was built in 1937, and is distinguished by an all-black granite façade, with a ninety-foot tower. The magnificent interior of the cinema was adorned in the art deco style, with swirling lines, sweeping arcs, and mythical figures flowing across the auditorium walls toward the proscenium arch around the giant screen.

In the weeks before the long-awaited premiere, Peter O'Toole had been tracked down by the London press. "Short of searching every ale-house and tavern in town, there's nothing you can do but wait for him to surface," they complained. They also predicted that "this Irishman is going to explode across the screens of the world as a star of glittering proportions." The press wondered how fame would affect the star called "the wild one," the actor who had audaciously recommended to King Hussein that the best idea for bolstering his country's economy would be to "bottle the River Jordan" for sale to Christian tourists. O'Toole, who was being heralded by the press as "the most fantastic new actor of our time," had—they claimed—been "tamed by the desert."

However, an obviously "untamed" O'Toole spent the two days preceding the premiere in the home of a friend, *Daily Mirror* film writer Donald Zec. "Peter O'Toole," Zec noted, "hair down, tie loosened, and feet up, talked

as uninhibited as he drinks . . . He poured out large measures of self-revelation and salty four-letter word observations laced with beer, whiskey, brandy, milk, and a dash of bitters. He is a grinning, raucous, yet most eloquent mixture of affable anger and ferocious goodwill."

Cover of ticket application form for Royal Premiere. Note music credit to Richard Rodgers.

155

by trumpeters of the Royal Horse Guards—arrived and entered the foyer, resplendent in a full-skirted dress of white silk faille, and wearing a diamond tiara, necklace, and bracelet.

O'Toole puffed away at a large cigar until someone nudged him in the ribs, announcing, "Here comes the Queen." The star then discreetly discarded the cigar into the hands of a friend behind him, and O'Toole—along with members of the cast and crew—was presented to Her Majesty and the Duke of Edinburgh. The *Daily Mirror* reported that "as other stars chatted with the Queen in a discreet hush . . . there was a guffaw from O'Toole and the Duke." O'Toole was quoted afterward, "I'm sorry, but I cannot tell you what it was that we were laughing about. It is more than my life is worth."

Above: Exterior of Odeon Leicester Square, December 10, 1962. TONIGHT AT 8 P.M. ROYAL WORLD PREMIERE—Right: Splendid art deco interior of cinema was, unhappily, modified in the mid-sixties.

"Sam Spiegel," O'Toole declared, "expects all of us to wear our decorations [at the Royal Premiere]. I have a Star of David and a St. John Ambulance gong. That should have 'em rolling in the aisles . . . I lost two stone [twenty-eight pounds] in the picture. I sprained one ankle, cracked another. My thigh muscle was ruptured, my groin was torn, my back dislocated, and my skull cracked . . . I sweated it out for two years in the desert digging inside myself to find the right chemistry of this gent called Lawrence."

Zec asked O'Toole, "Supposing this film really clicks. I suppose it will be Hollywood, a Cadillac, a press agent, and a blonde-filled swimming pool?" O'Toole shot back, "Hell, no! When I'm in the chips, I'll be back to [Ireland] in the morning! I don't want much money. Just enough to keep me in suffocating luxury for the rest of my life."

Then O'Toole was gone, "heading for tonight's arc-lit foyer, the royal handshake, and . . . *Lawrence.*"

The long-awaited evening had arrived. In addition to the usual throng of show business luminaries, the ambassadors of Jordan, Morocco, Spain, Iran, and the United States attended. Queen Elizabeth II—heralded

In the next few days, most British newspaper critics were exceptionally kind:

David Lean's *Lawrence of Arabia* makes all previous screen-deserts seem as false as the Aldershot sandboxes with which I was once taught tactical warfare in theory. Here is the desert in blistering bloody fact—with the sun rising like an obscene white egg to become a ball of flame. . . . Noon mirages make distant horsemen look as though they had been written in water. Winds are solid and hit one like a club.
—Paul Dehn, *Herald*, December 11, 1962

David Lean's *Lawrence of Arabia* is an extraordinary

156

film. . . .The splendours of the desert scene, rock formations, sky, and endless sand are caught, as in Lawrence's own descriptions, to perfection. That we really feel "the scalding tempest of the sun's rays, parching the eyeballs from the glowing sand" is a measure of the wonderful photography. . . .Two long hours are needed to take Aqaba, albeit spectacularly, and if this pace had persisted we would not be in Damascus until next week. . . .But after the interval the treatment changes with exciting results. The raids on the Hejaz Railway, the key scene of Lawrence's degradation at Deraa, the massacre at Tafas village, and the final capture of Damascus are all splendid scenes, but now used to interpret Lawrence's character. . .

The duologues between Allenby and Lawrence have the cut and thrust of the best theatrical writing . . .[O'Toole] achieves a facial likeness which should satisfy Lawrence's admirers: a splendid pair of blue eyes. That he is far too tall matters little. So completely does he seem to understand the complex character, so skillfully does he register the painful progress from the heroic to the hopeless. . .Alec Guinness's Feisal is gentle urbanity itself. Omar Sharif brings a romantic aspect to the part of Ali; and Anthony Quinn makes Auda an equally picturesque old rogue, one of several studies recalling the Kennington pastel portraits [done for *Seven Pillars*].

–Patrick Gibbs, *Daily Telegraph*,
December 11, 1962

Peter O'Toole, a brilliant Lawrence, carries with total credibility all the contradictions, from the shambling "outsider" in the officers' mess to the confident "Sherif El Aurens" by the desert campfire and even the horrified, blood-soaked wretch on the road to Damascus.

–Yorwerth Davies, *Guardian*,
December 11, 1962

Lawrence of Arabia is an unprecedented kind of multi-million-dollar super spectacle. . . . Here is an epic with intellect behind it. An unforgettable display of action staged with artistry. A momentous story told with moral force. What on earth has wrought this miracle? The makers.

Producer Sam Spiegel is a man of culture as well as finance. David Lean is a director who goes out to the

Lobby of cinema in Newcastle, showing special Lawrence *decor.*

wild place to meditate on his films, much as prophets used to contemplate unworldly things. Scriptwriter Robert Bolt is our subtlest playwright of men's emotions.

And I think that Allah, in the shape of F. A. Young's Technicolor camerawork, poured down his blessing for the two years of filming. . .

An unbeatable team!

Peter O'Toole. . .brings to life the film's vision of a flawed warrior who is corrupted by pride, soured by the empty victories, and betrayed finally by the jubilant jump of his heart every time he kills—so that he ends his career elbow-deep in needlessly spilt blood.

. . .If this British film isn't loaded with every Oscar there is, then justice . . . will have deserted Hollywood.

–Alexander Walker, *Evening Standard*,
December 13, 1962

Some critics begged to differ. The *Daily Mirror*'s notorious William Connor (pen name "Cassandra") observed, in a scathing review, that:

. . .history is put through the mangle and comes out tattered, torn, and largely unrecognisable. . . . history as written by Columbia Pictures and Professor Sam Spiegel is not for me.

. . .Allenby's discussion of his military plans conducted at the top of his voice in an officer's mess is

157

a splendid lesson in military insecurity. Turkish agents in Cairo would have had to have earplugs not to have heard him. . . . Anthony Quayle is superb as the puzzled, baffled Colonel Brighton, although his task may have been made easy in this film in which there is so much to get puzzled and baffled about.

. . .The credit for this picture lies completely with the technicians rather than with the actors, director, and script writer. The superb and truly magnificent camera and lighting work by F. A. Young. . .are among the finest ever captured through the lens.

. . .The camels (God bless them. . .) were great, and I shared the expression on their faces, which was one of unlimited enthusiasm.

. . .The length of the film—four miles, five furlongs, eight chains, one perch, three yards, one foot, and six inches to be exact—seemed interminable. . .

. . .I predict the utmost success for *Lawrence of the Odeon.*

(We must point out that—with furlongs, chains, and perches measuring 660, 66, and 16 1/2 feet, respectively—Cassandra's sarcastic description of the film's length exactly equals Horizon Pictures' precise calculation of 24,975 feet!)

The *Sunday Observer*'s respected critic Penelope Gilliatt claimed that:

. . .in the performance Peter O'Toole gives, there seem to be at least ten incompatible men living under the same skin, and two or three women as well. . . . When he puts on a Sherif's robes for the first time and does an entranced ballet with himself in the desert, it made me think more than ever that one of the reasons for Lawrence's passion for Arab life might well have been that it allowed him to wear a skirt. . . . I suspect that Robert Bolt's dialogue has been pared down to the bone to get in so many acres of blood and sand; everyone has been so conscientious about packing in as many insights as possible between massacres.

The inner circle also saw things differently. On December 13, Basil Liddell Hart finally saw the movie, and jotted down his "Notes on Seeing the *Lawrence of Arabia* Film":

Early scenes of the British Army are farcical. Photography wonderful. Peter O'Toole is good—*as*

Peter O'Toole. Silly exhibitionist dance on donning Arab clothes.

Brilliant production. . .and brilliant dramatic fiction—an appalling perversion of history [and] the characters of Lawrence and Allenby. Hope viewers don't take it as truth. The film is much worse than Bolt's script, with Lawrence portrayed worse still, in depicting maniacal blood-lust.

Liddell Hart's letter to *The Times,* published on December 15, was forthright:

The film called *Lawrence of Arabia* raises in acute form the question of how far history and personality can justifiably be twisted to serve a dramatic purpose.

The photography is superb, the production brilliant, while Peter O'Toole gives a most vivid performance of the principal character as conceived by Robert Bolt, a gifted psychological playwright. Yet to anyone who knew T. E. Lawrence, it rarely bears any resemblance to him in manner, speech, or behaviour.

He then spoke of the Tafas village "blood-lust" incident, giving many of the same arguments invoked in his letters to Robert Bolt. He also called attention to the fact that Gasim, an Arab who actually *was* rescued from the desert by T. E. Lawrence, and Hamed the Moor, whom Lawrence actually executed to defuse a tribal blood-feud, were combined into the single character of the film's "Gasim." Finally, Liddell Hart suggested that Allenby's character was distorted, since the general is portrayed as being "devilishly intent to let the chaos [in Damascus] continue for Britain's political advantage—whereas. . .he did not arrive in Damascus until order had been restored."

Professor A. W. Lawrence was interviewed for the *Sunday Observer* of December 16:

. . .The film. . .is above all a spectacle in which skillful directing, visual splendor, and music, sugarcoat the script's bitter treatment of character and events. . . .

The film's Lawrence has more than any one man's share of psychological aberrations. . .there are demonstrated narcissism (in his first Arab robes he dances with his shadow), fantastic chivalry (he stands immobile for an injured Turk to shoot at him), the crudest exhibitionism (he parades like a peacock along

Earliest American poster, December 1962, with original "dark head" artwork (27x41 inches).

Odeon Leicester Square, London, England: 8 P.M., December 10, 1962. Royal World Premiere of Lawrence of Arabia. *Peter O'Toole and David Lean meet Her Majesty Queen Elizabeth II.*

O'Toole's nervousness prevented him from sitting through to the end of the presentation. He finally watched the entire film twenty years later: on a hotel television in Amman, Jordan.

Columbia Pictures prepared a special "Souvenir Program" to be sold at showings of the film. The elegant 40-page book is a work of art. (See this and following two pages.)

In June 1961, Mark Kauffman, assignment photographer for Life *magazine, was on location in the dunes of Jordan. He had been asked by Columbia to bring back some unusual pictures which could be used to promote the film. In one scene, Lawrence chases Farraj, running toward Daud, who is caught in quicksand. David Lean, filming them running toward the camera, suggested, "Mark, you can sit under the Panavision." Kauffman, however, envisioned his own impressionistic image and chose to shoot the scene from the side. He wanted a blurred effect, but the combination of the blazing desert sun and the film he was using would not permit a slow enough shutter speed. Freddie Young came to the rescue by offering Mark one of his neutral density (darkening) filters. "It worked perfectly," said Mark. "It was one time where what I had envisioned came out exactly as I'd hoped." But the next day, David Lean was very cool to Kauffman, because "I'd dared to ignore his direction."*

A year and a half later, at the New York premiere, Kauffman met Lean in the lobby. They both spotted the display of souvenir programs, which featured Kauffman's photo on the cover (right). Kauffman recalled, "Lean put his arm around me, and said, 'Now I see what you were doing.' "

Page 3 of the program (below) has a die-cut window, through which O'Toole is seen peering from page 5 (below right).

All of the photographs in the program were taken by Kauffman and Ken Danvers, the Production Stillsman.

LAWRENCE OF ARABIA

"I deem him one of the greatest beings alive in our time. I do not see his like elsewhere. His name will live in  **English letters; it will live in the annals of war; it will live in the legends of Arabia."** *—Winston Churchill*

Page 9 of program: Guinness as Feisal.

Page 27: Quinn as Auda, at "Charge on Aqaba."

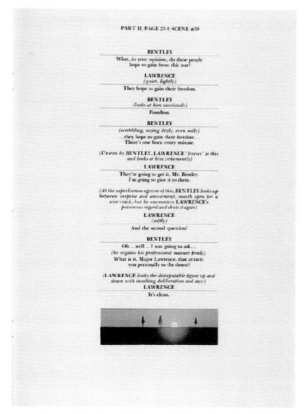

Page 29 and 31: Second die-cut window, through which is seen . . .

. . . Lawrence, Farraj, and Daud, crossing Sinai.

Foldout, tipped in at page 15 of program: "No prisoners!", photographed at Ouarzazate in Morocco.

Foldout, tipped in at page 21 of program: "The Trek to Aqaba," photographed at Jebel Tubeiq in Jordan.

Many variations of the "Souvenir Program" were produced over the first few years. There were at least three American editions, one of them trimmed slightly smaller for inclusion with the sound track recording, in a special boxed set. For the British program cover (right) a slightly different, less "impressionistic" photo from Kauffman's "Quicksand" shoot was inexplicably chosen.

The program was also published in several foreign language versions, including French, Spanish, German (below), Italian, Japanese (below right), and some Scandinavian languages. Typically, these had similar content to the American editions, but with different covers and photographs.

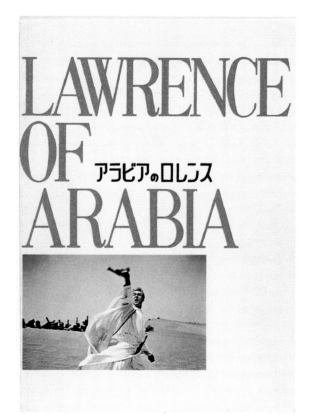

Second U.S. poster, used only in early 1963, until the Academy Awards (27x41 inches). Note, disappearing "dark head."

Immediately after the April 1963 Academy Awards, new posters appeared proudly announcing Lawrence's seven Oscars. An American poster (left, 28x22 inches) shows an effort to improve the controversial "dark head" motif by making the face lighter. A post-Oscar British poster (below, 40x30 inches) shows the "Lawrence-on-camel" artwork shrinking to extinction. None of the early promotional artwork included Omar Sharif, whose impact on audiences was not anticipated. Sharif, his popular success enhanced by an Oscar nomination, would appear on most subsequent artwork—often to the exclusion of Lawrence's other "stars."

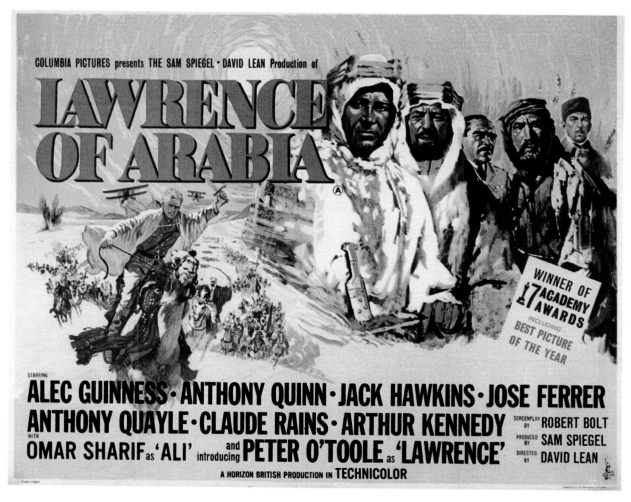

Original North American lobby-card set, 1963 (all 11x14 inches), consisted of title card and seven scene-cards. This title-card (top left), used in the province of Quebec, was crudely changed to French by over-painting. Note that the scene card on the lower left has the photo reversed, a recurring phenomenon in promotional material.

167

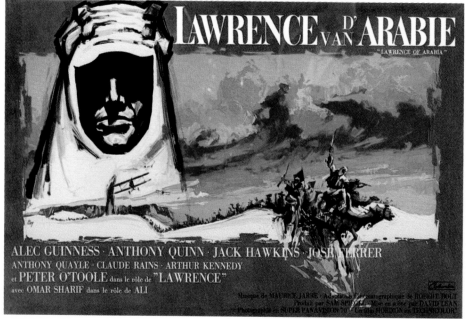

*Top left: U.S.A., 1962
(14x36 inches).
Top center: U.S.A., 1963
(14x36 inches).
Top right: U.S.A., 1970
(14x36 inches).*

*Left: Original Belgian
poster, 1963 (21x17 inches).
Note trilingual title, in
French, Flemish, and
English.*

*Note that the 1970 poster
on this page, and the Spanish, Japanese and French
posters on opposite page, have
included Omar Sharif. On
all of these except the French
poster, Sharif's image has
replaced José Ferrer's.*

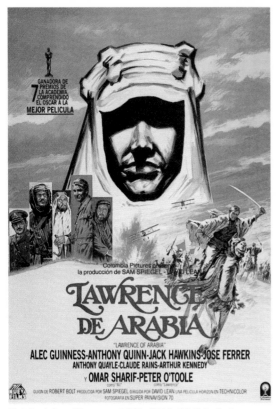

Original Spanish poster, 1963 (27.5x39.5 inches).

Japan, 1971 (20x28.5 inches).

France, 1971 (23x30.5 inches, and 47x63 inches).

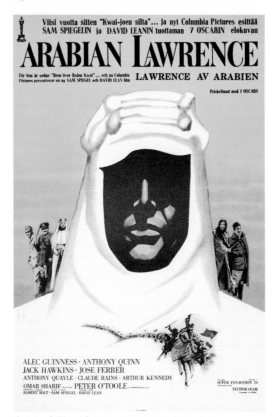

Original Finnish poster, 1963 (16x24 inches).

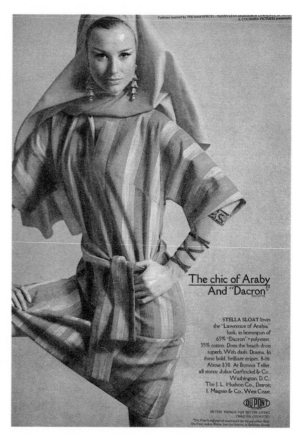

Even though there are virtually no women in Lawrence, fashion designers, always eager to seize ideas from the movies, attempted to capitalize on the film's success. This influence spread across the fashion world . . . In clothing, "The Look" was a fluid line borrowed from the robes worn by Lawrence. In 1963, many top designers offered Arabic fashions, from bedroom to beach to ballroom. Vogue's January issue called the trend "Desert Dazzle." Dupont termed the Lawrence look "the chic of Araby" (above). Elizabeth Arden (left) described their new "Chic Sheik" cosmetics shades as "a color oasis for the woman who has wearied of winter": they warned users to exercise "caution or you may end up betrothed to a chieftain."

The June McCalls—in "How to be Sheik on the sand"—alerted readers to the exotic appeal of Lawrence-inspired beachwear. This short-lived fad consisted of sand-colored swimsuits, to be worn with "desert headdresses." Ads in Women's Wear Daily publicized a "Little Lawrence Beach 'n' Bath Burnoose" for children. Many of the season's turban-like hat styles claimed inspiration from Lawrence, as did the designer of a dazzling evening gown he called "Desert Sunset." Even hair stylists joined the caravan. One chief of coiffure sat through the film twice and came up with "two Lawrence hairdos. One was a turban of hair. The other featured hair combed straight down at each side of the head, to meet under the chin like a hood."

Journalist Jeanette A. Sarkisian opined: "How long will the Lawrence Look last? About as long as it takes to make another film. The next epics [are] on the horizon . . . which suggests that American women will soon fold their tent dresses and quietly pack them away."

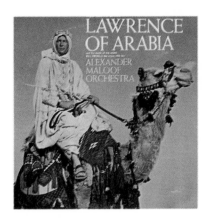

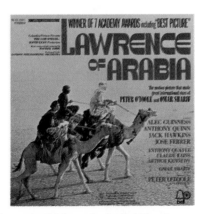

Prior to the 1990s, analog sound recordings were available on twelve-inch vinyl discs, known as "records" or "LP's." Large sleeves provided ample space for artwork: Lawrence was no exception. Some examples from the authors' collections: Top left and center, center right, and bottom right are identical sound track albums with variations on artwork. The sleeve notes pointed out that Maurice Jarre imported an Ondes Martenot—an early electronic musical instrument—from France. So unique was this instrument that special musicians capable of playing it had to be flown in from Paris. It was used primarily in the desert sequences, its unusual sound adding "romance and mystery" to the score. Win Ryder, Lawrence's sound editor recalls, "I hate electronic music but this was marvelous. The three ladies who played them looked as though they could have been playing in the Palm Court Orchestra in Brighton, for Ladies' Tea. It was like a dream."

Center left is one of many collections of movie themes, featuring Lawrence music. Bottom center, "Jazz Impressions of Lawrence of Arabia": the sleeve notes remind us that "a great score is only made greater by a great jazz interpretation." Bottom left, entitled "Lawrence of Arabia and the Romance and Mystery of the Arabian Nights," endlessly alternates between the Lawrence theme and Scheherazade: the performers responsible were not mentioned. Top right, "Original Theme from the Movie Lawrence of Arabia" performed by "Bill Ewing at the organ with the Alexander Maloof Orchestra." Sleeve notes posed the question, "Was he hero or charleton [sic]?"

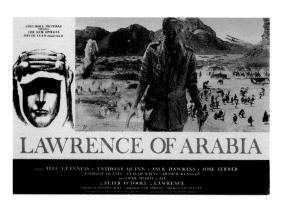

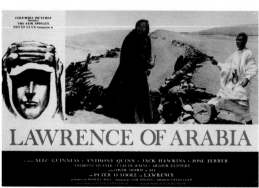
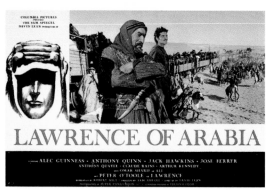
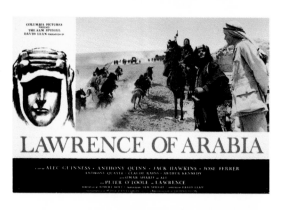
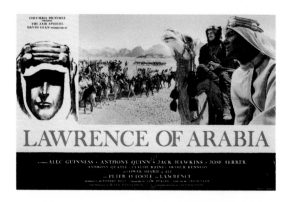

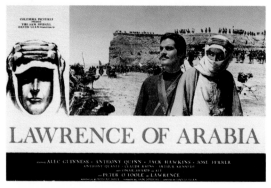

This set of 1971 posters (all 26x18 inches) was manufactured in Italy for British and North American distributors. The incredible collection consists of collages of black and white photographs, skillfully hand-tinted in fanciful colors, with characters and scenes inexplicably rearranged in bizarre juxtapositions.

First Mad *movie parody "cover story", April 1964.*

DELL Comic book, U.S.A, 1963.

Star Cin-Roman, Italy/France, July 1965. The entire story of the film, in 288 black-and-white production stills.

M Inc., U.S.A., November 1990. "Examines the heroics of T.E.L. and his imprint on today's geopolitics."

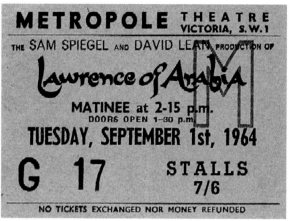

Reserved seat ticket for London cinema, 1964.

Perhaps the most unusual item of memorabilia in authors' collection is a custom-made chocolate bar wrapper, produced for one particular theater in Toronto, 1963.

the roof of a train . . .).

. . .The real key to the hero is sadism—a trait a good many Englishmen could have observed in T. E. Lawrence if it had existed. He tells Allenby he had "enjoyed" killing two Arabs. . .[*Seven Pillars*] record's Daud's death "of cold" and nobody's in any quicksand.

. . .The fiction here prepares the audience for a grand-scale glutting of blood-lust upon a mob of Turks . . .

. . .I do not want to give the impression that I consider the Lawrence of the film entirely untrue. So far especially as determination, courage, and endurance are concerned, he is comparable. . .with the man [Mr. O'Toole] purports to represent.

. . .I need only say that I should not have recognised my brother.

On December 17, Basil Liddell Hart sent a message to Cassandra, praising his review and requesting half a dozen extra copies of the *Mirror*. Three days later, he mailed "warnings" to many of T.E.'s former friends, calling attention to his letter in *The Times* and to Cassandra's review in the *Daily Mirror*. "I saw the *Lawrence of Arabia* film . . ." he told them. "While brilliant in photography, it depicted T. E. Lawrence as struggling with sadistic impulses and eventually giving full vent to them at Tafas—where Peter O'Toole depicted him as murderously maniacal in expression and the whole of his right arm, as well as his dagger, steeped in the blood of the Turks he killed."

Omar Sharif and Sam Spiegel at New York premiere.

Lady Allenby wrote a short letter to *The Times:* "Is there any way in which a film company can be stopped from portraying a character so inaccurately as that of the late Field Marshal Allenby in . . .*Lawrence of Arabia*? . . .What can one do? What is the remedy? Or isn't there one?" Liddell Hart replied, ". . .your letter . . . most valuably reinforces A. W. Lawrence's and my earlier protests."

Air-Commodore Sydney Smith, who was T.E.'s superior officer at Plymouth, wrote Liddell Hart: "I dislike the. . .film. As you say, the photography is good. . .*but* it is all so unreal."

And David Garnett—editor of a collection of T.E.'s letters, and an adviser to the film—also offered an opinion: "I went and sat through. . .*Lawrence of Arabia*. It is, of course, an outrage. Not a single thing I wrote was made use of. . .I came out of my preposterous association with Spiegel with clean, though not—I am glad to say—empty hands."

Finally, at year's end, Professor A. W. Lawrence informed a *Daily Mail* columnist that £12,500 of the £17,500 he had received for the movie rights to *Seven Pillars* would go to various charitable organizations. He termed the film "an unholy marriage between a Western and a psychological horror."

THE AMERICAN PREMIERE

The American premiere of *Lawrence of Arabia* took place at the Criterion Theater, New York City, on December 16, 1962. The American press also embraced *Lawrence* and Lean with enthusiasm. The New York papers were on strike, so reviewers read their opinions on the radio:

> Brilliantly produced, artfully directed, skillfully performed. . .Will rate high on the list of all-time classics of the screen.
> —Frank Quinn, *New York Mirror*

> Four stars. . .If there were more stars in my Christmas pack, I would gladly give them to *Lawrence of Arabia*.
> —Kate Cameron, *New York Daily News*

> One of the all-time great films. There may never have been in film history a movie which so deftly combines an epic grandeur of scene and action with surpassingly fine and subtle details of character. A picture to place ahead of *Kwai* and *West Side Story* as an award-winning grand slammer, if there's any justice!
> —Archie Winston, *New York Post*

175

The main exception, but the one which has prompted the erroneous legend that *Lawrence of Arabia* was not well received in 1963, was that by Bosley Crowther, the then-influential critic of *The New York Times:*

> Like the desert itself, in which most of the action in *Lawrence of Arabia* takes place, this much-heralded film about the famous British soldier-adventurer, which opened last night at the Criterion, is vast, awe-inspiring, beautiful with ever-changing hues, exhausting, and barren of humanity.
>
> It is such a laboriously large conveyance of eye-filling outdoor spectacle. . .that the possibly human, moving T. E. Lawrence is lost in it. We know little more about this strange man when it is over than we did when it begins.
>
> . . .Why Lawrence had a disposition to join the Arab tribes, and what causes his streak of sadism, is barely hinted at in the film. The inner mystery of the man remains lodged behind the splendid burnoosed figure and the wistful blue eyes of Mr. O'Toole.
>
> The fault seems to lie, first in the concept of telling the story of this self-tortured man against a background of action that has the characteristics of a mammoth Western film. The nature of Lawrence cannot be captured in grand Super Panavision shots of sunrise on the desert. . . .
>
> The fault is also in the lengthy but surprisingly lusterless dialogue of Robert Bolt's overwritten screenplay. *Seldom has so little been said in so many words.*
>
> . . . It is, in the last analysis, just a huge, thundering camel-opera. [Empasis ours]

Oddly, the first paragraph of Crowther's review—along with its quite negative conclusion—was excerpted in whole for publication in New York ads touting the film. It is his "camel-opera" capsule comment, however, which lives into posterity. However, in complete contradiction to Crowther's "too many words" contention, renowned American screenwriter Robert Towne (*Shampoo, Chinatown*) would—in a 1991 *Esquire* article entitled "Why I Write Movies"—extol Bolt's *Lawrence* screenplay for its verbal economy:

> Consider this: In *Lawrence of Arabia*, Lawrence, in flowing white robes, sits on a truck in the middle of the desert giving a press conference. He's ten feet tall on the screen and overwhelmingly immaculate. He faces a grimy-looking reporter [Bentley] who scratches his beard and asks snidely, "Just what is it, Major Lawrence, that attracts you to the desert?" Lawrence glances distastefully at the dirty reporter and offers a two-word reply: "It's clean." It is not the text but the context that gives this reply its full force. Those two words in a novel or even on the stage would be mildly amusing at best, but on the screen the effect is as overwhelming as the figure of Lawrence and the desert looming behind him. Those two words *are* the scene. There is no speech, long or short, about Lawrence's need to seek remote places of the earth in order to avoid the corruption inevitably found in its more populated areas. Only a clean man, a dirty reporter, a big desert, and two little words "It's clean."
>
> It's a movie. What else do you need?

On December 17, an excited David Lean wrote to Barbara Cole from the St. Regis Hotel in New York, with first news of critical reaction to the American premiere:

> . . .The film has been a wild success so far, with a standing ovation at the press show. The papers are on strike. . .[but] they do a sort of criticism on TV—the [news]paper critics—and all are tremendous *except* the most revered critic. . .Bosley Crowther, who tears it to bits! I couldn't care less. The Premiere last night was fantastic with everyone talking in superlatives. . . .
>
> When Fred Zinnemann got back to Hollywood after the N.Y. show he sent me a wire: "You're a bloody poet." Then, this morning I met a man who was with Fred, [Richard] Brooks, and Joe [Joseph L.] Mankiewicz. . .after the N.Y. show, and [he told me] that Joe said that the three of them were going to put through a resolution to the Screen Directors Guild to bar me from working in the future. Very sweet. They seem to think it's one of the best directed pictures ever made, and Fred rang me up last night and said, "You don't know what you've done."
>
> . . .Sam has just popped in to tell me that the N.Y. box office is jammed with queues bigger than they've ever had . . . and that a T.V. personality has just gone on the air saying that anyone who misses *Lawrence* will be depriving himself of one of the greatest experiences of his life. . . .And the Columbia stock has gone up from $14 to $25.

The advice given by another Hollywood giant has become legend. The evening *Lawrence* opened in New York, the story goes, David Lean was walking down Fifth

Avenue with David O. Selznick. Selznick put his arm around him and said, "David, I've had *Gone With the Wind* for twenty-six years, and all through the years people have been trying to cut it. I would never let them. Tomorrow morning you're going to start getting phone calls from other filmmakers and people telling you the film is too long. It's got to be cut. Don't do it!" Sure enough, the next morning, Sam Spiegel called and said, "Baby, you've got to cut this picture."

This warning, as we shall see, signaled the beginning of the *Lawrence* cutting controversy.

Lawrence gathered momentum, with reserved-seat presentations opening in Boston, Philadelphia, and Los Angeles on December 21.

Very early that morning, Omar Sharif and Peter O'Toole—in Los Angeles for the premiere—attended a performance given by the controversial comedian Lenny Bruce in a small theater near Sunset Boulevard. They introduced themselves to Bruce: "We may still be unknown, but tomorrow our names are going to be heading the list of [review] credits on *Lawrence of Arabia*." With Peter and Lenny quite high, but Omar sober, they followed the comedian to his apartment, where he "shot up." They were promptly interrupted by the police, and all three were thrown into a jail cell. Sharif recalled the incident:

> I called the Beverly Hills Hotel, where I knew Sam Spiegel was staying. I asked for his room.
> "Mr. Spiegel doesn't want to be disturbed."
> "It's very important."
> Finally, the switchboard operator rang his room. A sleepy voice:
> "What is it? What the hell do you mean waking me up in the middle of the night?"
> I came right to the point. "Sam, we're in jail—Peter and I."
> From the other end of the line came a firmer voice. "*What? In jail?*" The prospect of his fourteen-million-dollar extravaganza coming out minus its two stars woke him up completely.
> I repeated, "We're in jail."
> "Why? What did you do?"
> "They arrested us, with Lenny Bruce, for having drugs."
> The great Sam Spiegel went into a panic. "Just stay put, Sharif."
> He didn't have to worry about that—we weren't going anywhere.

> Barely half an hour had gone by when he arrived, flanked by at least six lawyers. Very dignified men with hats and briefcases who immediately entered into a big conference with the cops. Well out of our range, of course.
> The confab seemed to last forever. Finally a policeman opened the cell and said:
> "Okay, you two can beat it."
> Peter reacted quickly. "What? And leave Lenny in the clink? Then I'm not going!"
> Peter had become pals with Bruce. When you're in the clink, you make friends easily.
> "Don't be ridiculous," Spiegel said. "Bruce has a police record—they can't release him just like that."
> "I don't give a damn," Peter retorted. "I'm staying with him!"

Eventually, they were all let free. "It must have cost Spiegel an arm and a leg," said Sharif.

That evening, Omar Sharif and Peter O'Toole entered the Beverly Hills cinema, dazzled by famous movie stars such as Elizabeth Taylor, Shirley MacLaine, Richard Burton, and Gregory Peck.

Omar Sharif remembered:

> . . .our names appeared in big letters on the giant screen. . . .We watched the audience reaction. . . .Right from the start the spectators seemed spellbound. I felt the silence become gently oppressive.
> [My] first scene was silent—so was the audience. . . . The black spot takes shape—it's Ali, the man who would become the friend of Lawrence of Arabia. It was I, the actor who'd been unknown five minutes before. The impossible had happened: a supporting role had boosted itself to the height of the leading one. A film had "discovered" two actors, had made two stars.
> . . .When the curtain came down, Peter and I found ourselves the focal point of that theater full of celebrities.
> . . .Elegantly dressed men and women came over to congratulate us. A sea of glossy mink and sable on undulating bodies carried me into a banquet room. I felt like Alice in Wonderland.

The New York City "radio reviews" were followed shortly by the out-of-town newspaper and magazine assessments. All were enthusiastic:

...Despite the grandeur of the backgrounds, despite the vast scale of its action, it is essentially the exploration of this man's intricate intelligence, and—yes—soul.

The hero, Lawrence, is still a matter of speculation, nearly half a century after his exploits in the Arabian desert, and his influence is still apparent in the emergence of Arab nationalism. Lean's direction and Robert Bolt's screenplay attempt to explore the most secret recesses of this bewildering man's mind and soul and to make the inner storm explicit in graphic terms. They succeed.

...No comparison is altogether exact, but what Lawrence did is roughly comparable to a situation that might arise if the U.S. State Department were to send an obscure second lieutenant into Castro's Cuba with orders to come back in a few weeks with an intelligence report on anti-Castro elements, only to have the second lieutenant raise a revolt, appoint himself field marshal-saint, capture Havana, and then present the U.S. government with a Cuban government appointed by him.

...Lean's direction is demanding. He is determined to convey the harshness and the beauty of the desert which so profoundly changed Lawrence, which fired him in his final mold.

...Never before, in any film, has the desert been so magically captured. Part of this is the imagination of the director. Part of it is the means available to him, the film process—Super Panavision 70—and his cameraman, F. A. Young. This Panavision process has a matchless definition of image, making possible shots of desert and mountain immensities against which are placed humans in long, long perspective but perfectly clear. The photography of a desert mirage is probably the first time this phenomenon has ever been recorded on film.

These technical achievements may seem minor in a film essentially of story, and they would be minor if they were not matched in the telling of the story itself. They are significant in their evidence of an attitude that runs throughout the production, of a determination to make *Lawrence* superior in every way to anything even remotely similar attempted before. This is done.

Bolt's screenplay is lean and terse. It is subtle and sinuous. It manages to take a half dozen antagonistic philosophies and make them acceptable without compromise or easy reconciliation. Lean's direction, a

Peter O'Toole, Mrs. Lean, and David Lean at Los Angeles premiere, Decemberr 21, 1962.

vast conception of many troublesome ideas, is reined tightly. As noted above, the film is long, and in hammering with finality at the spectator the effect of the desert, the spectator is left somewhat exhausted. Only half-humorously, one theaterman noted at the intermission: "I don't know about the box office on this picture, but I'd settle for the beverage concession." It has that effect.

Peter O'Toole is a major star with this one role. A handsome, sensitive actor, he moves with grace and speaks with charm. His self-torture is great and it is conveyed with compassion. A young Egyptian actor, Omar Sharif, is splendid as his desert tutor and friend. The rest of the cast is a roll call of the best British and American talent available—available for the best.

Lawrence of Arabia is an adventure, a spectacle, a searing story of man's fallibility and culpability. Somewhat rarer, it also has dignity. It is stately and honorable, without loss of motion, in the sense that life has motion. It is distinguished in every way.

—James Powers, *Hollywood Reporter,*
December 21, 1962

How rare it is for several disparate talents to be simultaneously at their best. Yet here we have a screenplay by Robert Bolt that, if it fails to explain its mysterious protagonist, at least presents a number of eloquent clues to the mystery; a stunningly handsome production by John Box; a haunting musical background by Maurice Jarre; exquisite camerawork by

Fred A. Young, whose prolonged, almost lovesick views of the Jordanian desert and of camels racing are among the most beautiful shots I've ever seen; and— most important—brilliant, passionate direction by David Lean.

—*The New Yorker,* December 22, 1962

So faithful is it to the truth of Thomas Edward Lawrence that a viewer leaves the picture with no idea whatever of what Lawrence was really like. . . . [Spiegel and Lean] concede an intermission, but offer no pat solutions, no cheap uplift, only an honest presentation of the phenomenon of Lawrence, and, appropriately, a bibliography of twenty-five suggested books in the souvenir program. . . .The cast, too, is not only all-star, but, for a change, all-good.

—*Newsweek,* December 24, 1962

I can't remember a previous film in which visual beauty has been provided as generously as here.

—Hollis Alpert, *Saturday Review,*
December 29, 1962

Lean. . .works with a sensitivity to form and color that he has never shown before—it is as if the desert, like a gigantic strap of white-hot steel, had burned away a northern mist that has always obscured his vision. Time and time again the grand rectangular frame of the Panavision screen stands open like the door of a tremendous furnace, and the spectator stares with his eyes into the molten shimmer of whitegolden sands, into blank incandescent infinity as if into the eye of God. It is a mind-battering experience with the absolute. . . . In his performance, O'Toole catches the noble seriousness of Lawrence and his cheap theatricality, his godlike arrogance, and his gibbering self-doubt; his headlong courage, girlish psychasthenia, Celtic wit, humorless egotism, compulsive chastity, sensuous pleasure in pain. But there is something he does not catch, and that something is an answer to the fundamental enigma of Lawrence, a clue to the essential nature of the beast, a glimpse of the secret spring that made him tick. But then the script does not catch it either. People who knew Lawrence did not catch it. Lawrence himself did not seem to know what it was. Perhaps it did not exist.

—*TIME,* January 4, 1963

In 1989, Jesse Levine—who was involved in the film's promotion—was to recall that there was an interesting story behind the 1962 advertising art, a story which reflects the societal racial viewpoint of those years. He commented on the "strong, shadowy figure"—a head, almost full-ad-size, clad in a "kaffiyeh" [head-cloth], with its mysterious face almost fully obscured by deep shadow—which was the centerpiece of all original advertising artwork, including the sound track album. Levine explained.

Quite simply, the picture had opened soft in some of the first tier of major cities immediately after the U.S. premiere in New York. There was agitated conjecture and analysis about the disappointing grosses.

However discerned, the story was that the almost completely shadowed face in the ad art was being mistaken by the public for a black man. Adding the prevailing "wisdom" of the times to the reality of the public's response—that people would not pay to see a movie about a black man—a new ad campaign was rushed into the breach with Lawrence in flowing white burnoose, uncovered blond head, scimitar and/or pistol in hand, all against a battle-and-gore background.

I cannot say with certainty whether the change was born of market research or internal conjecture, but all of the above took place. A blood-and-guts action campaign has always been standard practice in the industry whenever the original ad campaign didn't support the picture.

Happily [in 1989], the acceptance of black heroes on screens large and small is now commonplace.

The original head was, in essence, one of the best pieces of art I'd seen in industry advertising, reflecting perfectly the mystery and enigma of the title figure. It has since become one of my prime examples of an ad campaign being intellectually and artistically on the nose but ineffectual as the selling device it was intended to be.

Lawrence of Arabia was a class act from inception to opening, and Sam Spiegel, its producer, is also due enormous credit for his vision, his organizational talents, and not least for the wisdom to leave David Lean alone to create his masterpiece. And, astute showman that he was, he even induced Columbia Pictures to increase the salaries of those responsible for advertising, publicity, and promotion in major cities of

Above Left: Artwork for initial Lawrence of Arabia *ads and posters featured the "obscured black face" and paintings of major stars.*
Above Right: Lightened versions of the controversial face were prepared, and used in later ads.
Below Left: The new "Lawrence with scimitar" motif was first combined with the original artwork.
Below Right: The darkness diminishes and evenually disappears.

Superb paintings of Alec Guinness, Anthony Quinn, José Ferrer, Jack Hawkins, and Peter O'Toole were prepared for promotional material. Omar Sharif, then a complete unknown to Western audiences, was not included. Bottom Left: After Sharif's Supporting Actor Oscar nomination, posters were updated to include him. Bottom Right: The posters later featured him, along with Peter O'Toole.

The Unique Film Experience

The motion picture that made great International stars of
PETER O'TOOLE and OMAR SHARIF

One of the most honoured pictures of all time
WINNER OF 7 ACADEMY AWARDS including BEST PICTURE!

The SAM SPIEGEL · DAVID LEAN Production

LAWRENCE OF ARABIA

ALEC GUINNESS · ANTHONY QUINN · JACK HAWKINS · JOSE FERRER
ANTHONY QUAYLE · CLAUDE RAINS · ARTHUR KENNEDY
Omar Sharif and PETER O'TOOLE in 'LAWRENCE'

SCREENPLAY BY ROBERT BOLT   PRODUCED BY SAM SPIEGEL   DIRECTED BY DAVID LEAN   PANAVISION   A HORIZON BRITISH PRODUCTION IN TECHNICOLOR

Columbia Pictures Presents The SAM SPIEGEL · DAVID LEAN Production of

LAWRENCE OF ARABIA
STANDS ALONE!

The motion picture that made great International stars of
PETER O'TOOLE and OMAR SHARIF

UNANIMOUSLY ACCLAIMED AS "ONE OF THE ALL TIME GREAT FILMS!"
WINNER OF 7 ACADEMY AWARDS including BEST PICTURE!

Starring ALEC GUINNESS · ANTHONY QUINN · JACK HAWKINS · JOSE FERRER
ANTHONY QUAYLE · CLAUDE RAINS · ARTHUR KENNEDY with OMAR SHARIF as 'Ali'
and PETER O'TOOLE as 'LAWRENCE' Screenplay by ROBERT BOLT Produced by SAM SPIEGEL
Directed by DAVID LEAN   PANAVISION   A HORIZON BRITISH PRODUCTION IN TECHNICOLOR®

U.S. and Canada during the months they toiled on the openings. Thus, amid the usual stream of good, bad and indifferent movies through the years, *Lawrence of Arabia* was a thrill to work on, with bonus attached.

Immediately after the Los Angeles premiere, director David Lean wrote to screenwriter Robert Bolt. It was their first written correspondence ever. Lean was brimming with enthusiasm for the fruits of their first collaboration:

December 23, 1962
My dear Robert,

I have thought about you such a lot these last couple of weeks and have wished so much you could have been here. Now that the rush and excitement is over, I will try and give you some idea of what it was like.

. . .this film of ours has knocked the top filmmakers sideways. In short, they all say they have never seen anything like it. They keep saying it's quite new–and can't quite put their finger on it.

As I think I told you, the top American moviemakers are more generous than anyone in the world, and they have given us their praise on a plate. Don't quite know how to describe it to you at this distance but among the real ravers are Willy Wyler, Billy Wilder, Fred Zinnemann, Richard Brooks, Joe Mankiewicz, and the great old-timer, King Vidor. They have all been round here to deliver their feelings in person, and all of them say that the film has such an impact that they can't start to pick out special scenes for mention because in a way they can't describe it took hold of them as a whole. I know that will please you. They are so bloody generous that every one of them has said words to the effect, "It's out of our class"–and really mean it.

. . .George Cukor rang up. . .to say that he just can't get the film out of his mind. "I don't know what it is, but I've never seen anything like it." Then [he] went on and on about your sense of a whole.

In New York, the audience broke out into applause about ten times during the first half of the film. After that they were somehow caught up in a grip and stayed quiet as mice. The Hollywood audience was the best of the lot. They clapped two or three times but had an attentiveness far beyond London and New York. It was a sort of rave show and at the dinner afterwards it was rather wonderful because I knew that everyone present thought we had done something very substantial for the film medium. Wish you could have been here because you could not have failed to be very proud.

. . .Billy Wilder went on and on about the film last evening. . . .Billy says he thinks the film is a tremendous piece of work and [he said] "if my heart had been really touched by Lawrence as a human being, I would put it up into the first movie Sistine Chapel stuff. But it wasn't." I find that interesting because I think he's right in that we could have done that. Lawrence; not the Chapel. Wonder if that rings a bell with you. Came thumping in on me as he said it and, apart from our feelings about Lawrence as the human being he was, I think the rush of the second half is more than half responsible. No point in chewing over it now, but I find it interesting. Funny. Like you, I started off against Lawrence and then gradually started to swing round. As an audience, I feel like Ali about him now. I have a feeling that, given the time to be alone with him a little more, we could have gone a stage further and given the audience real compassion. Don't trouble to comment on all this. You must be busy enough. It's been the greatest and the most exciting adventure of my movie life. My life, I think. Yes. I know. I have never worked along anyone of your caliber before and it's a great reward to know that you are happy about the interpretation. Forgive me, but you know Robert, we *must* work together again. . . .You have such an eye and feel for this medium that I think it would really be a shame to ignore it. . . .I'm just about at the top of my form and, looking around me, I see how age shrinks the mental and physical capabilities of those in my particular job. This film of ours has so fired me that I'm–for the first time–anxious not to allow too long to go by before making another attempt on something ambitious. People keep telling me–all except Columbia of course–that I ought to do something small and have a comparative rest. But in five or six years I can do something small and do it all from a chair. To hell with it while I have the physique. . .

However, it also appears that the pressures to cut their masterpiece had already become very real, and that– contrary to legend–Lean himself had already begun to consider possible scenes for deletion. *In fact, at least one copy of the film had already been cut.* The version Lean had seen in Hollywood, he told Bolt, had eliminated the spectacular two-minute entry sequence into Auda's camp, cutting directy from Auda's invitation to "Dine with me in Wadi Rumm!" to the close-up of a little girl preceding in the feast scene. Lean's comment: "It doesn't come off very well."

On December 28, 1962, David Lean—under increasing pressure to shorten all copies of the film—formalized his thoughts on cutting his masterpiece in a seven-page memorandum, entitled "*Lawrence* Cutting Comments." This document would herald the beginning of the progressive slashing of the film over the years to come.

Another subject of discussion between Lean and Bolt was the proposed publishing of the *Lawrence* screenplay by Heinemann. The director was to write a short foreword, and Bolt had prepared an Introduction and an "Apologia."

Bolt's introduction discussed the difference between a narrative account of a simple event—his synopsis of the event was: "early one morning Tom met Dick and Harry on the beach but, to his dismay, they ignored him totally"—compared with a filmscript of the same event "which might be split into a dozen separate scenes." These scenes were in fact written by Bolt, by way of example.

The playwright then revealed that it would be a "rigged" version of the *Lawrence* screenplay that would be published, instead of the actual document: "The script...is tedious to read. It lacks the speed and urgency of the very images it is specifying. Therefore...I've collapsed the 'multitudinous' scenes into narrative paragraphs...which [describe] what we hoped the audience would *see*."

Bolt's "Apologia" was an essay which extended the thoughts and ideas previously raised in the letters exchanged with Basil Liddell Hart. This essay is a quite formal document, however, and lacks the urgency, spontaneity, and dynamism of the original correspondence.

In any case, Bolt's "rigged" *Lawrence* script was never published.

After Christmas, Sam Spiegel—who had read A.W.'s comments in the British press—wrote to *The New York Times,* defending his film's interpretation of T. E. Lawrence:

> I did not want to be drawn into a controversy with Professor Lawrence. I quite understand what the movie must mean to someone who has lived in the

shadow of a legend of an older brother for some fifty years. Professor Lawrence did not want family skeletons rattled. He wanted to preserve the Lawrence of Arabia legend in Victorian cleanliness. But anyone who dramatises the life of Lawrence of Arabia cannot ignore that he was illegitimate or avoid the conflict of this man who was aware of homosexual tendencies but did not want to commit himself to homosexuality. This was a man who became involved in all sorts of masochism as the result of his conflicts.

The producer further contended that A.W. had not known T.E.L. under wartime conditions, and thus was incapable of understanding the sadomasochistic side of his brother's nature. Spiegel continued:

> I don't think that Professor Lawrence realizes that his brother was narcissistic enough to create a curtain of mystery as part of his sense of humour. If any man was capable of planting false footsteps, it was Lawrence of Arabia.
>
> Professor Lawrence's only concern was that we be faithful to *Seven Pillars of Wisdom* as much as possible. But if we had just followed the book, we would have been just a set of photographers. We think that life should imitate art, and not the other way around.
>
> We did not try to resolve the legend of *Lawrence of Arabia*. We tried to perpetuate it.

Miami Beach and—in early 1963—Chicago, San Francisco, and Detroit were added to the list of venues.

THE CANADIAN PREMIERE

Lawrence of Arabia invaded its third country on January 30, 1963, when the film opened at the Odeon Carlton in Toronto.

There, many of the issues hotly debated by Bolt, Liddell Hart, Spiegel, and A. W. Lawrence were to be viewed from a startling new perspective.

"THAT'S THE WAY IT WAS," SAYS A MAN WHO KNOWS claimed the headlines of a story in the now-defunct *Toronto Telegram* the day after the premiere. Peter Worthington, currently editor emeritus of the *Toronto Sun* and *Ottawa Sun* newspapers, wrote:

> The clock turned back forty-five years for George Staples last night to the day in the desert when he was a trigger squeeze away from killing Lawrence of Arabia.

A tiny man with a big memory, Mr. Staples attended the premiere of *Lawrence of Arabia* and re-fought—for four hours anyway—the day of the Arab Revolt when he was a cavalry troop commander.

He was leading a troop of Middlesex Yeomanry, closing the net on the retreating Turkish army when he joined up with Bedouin hordes, led by Lawrence.

"It was blistering hot and we were all edgy, when suddenly around a sand dune rode about ten Arabs on camels," Mr. Staples recalled.

"Just as we were about to fire, the Arabs stopped. And out of one of the flowing white robes came a voice with an Oxford accent.

"He said: 'I'm Lawrence. . .where's Barrow?' [General Barrow, the divisional commander]

"He acted as if the whole world should know who he was. He was terribly self-opinionated, but would have to be to do the job he did.

"I had quite a shock, I don't mind telling you, when I realized I might have given the order to shoot him down!"

The year was 1918 and Lawrence was leading the Bedouins on a bloody dash to beat the British army to Damascus. The Arabs were slaughtering all Turks, taking no prisoners.

Mr. Staples, seventy-two years old, watched the film like a drill sergeant searching for flaws in a recruit. He found very few.

"It was just like I remembered it—especially General Allenby [Jack Hawkins] who was incredibly like the 'Old Man' was in real life," he said.

"I was shocked at first to see Lawrence played by such a big actor [Peter O'Toole, six foot five]. Actually, Lawrence was a thin little chap about my size—five feet five.

"But I soon forgot the size, as the actor seemed to have Lawrence's personality and mannerisms—remarkable."

At one point, the movie has Lawrence leading a massacre of retreating Turkish troops. Mr. Staples, who arrived on the gory scene shortly after the depicted incident, said it was dead accurate.

"But the film didn't show too clearly why the Turks were all slaughtered," Mr. Staples said, his gentle voice hardening as memory carried him back through the years.

"The Turks had just gone through an Arab village. And if you had seen what the Turks did to the women, children—everyone—you'd understand how Lawrence and the Arabs must have felt."

Of course the Toronto audience hadn't seen the Turkish village scene *in its shocking entirety,* for it already had been severely censored. It was restored only in 1989. Worthington continued:

> The brother to Lawrence has written that he would never have recognized his brother from the film version.
> Mr. Staples disagrees.
> "I don't think [A.W.] knew the Lawrence of Arabia we in Arabia knew. The man in the film WAS very much like the Lawrence we campaigned with."

After Toronto, other U.S. and Canadian cities quickly followed with *Lawrence* openings: Phoenix; Washington D.C.; Salt Lake City; Montreal; Vancouver; Memphis; San Diego; Dallas; St. Louis; Denver; Houston; Providence; and Atlanta. By late June 1963, seventy-six cinemas across the United States and Canada would be presenting the film, with nine more openings scheduled for June, twenty-three for July, and eighteen for August.

Lawrence of Arabia had now conquered England *and* North America. This third, most massive wave—to be accompanied by a second publicity blitz, including a new American campaign booklet of epic proportions—would be triggered by a remarkable event: *Lawrence's* unequivocal triumph at the Academy Awards ceremony in April.

35TH ANNUAL ACADEMY AWARDS

The Sam Spiegel–David Lean production of *Lawrence of Arabia,* with ten nominations, dominated the ceremonies honoring the films of 1962.

To Kill a Mockingbird had eight nominations. And *Mutiny on the Bounty,* the film which had prevented Marlon Brando from playing Lawrence, had seven.

The Academy Awards ceremony, at the Santa Monica Civic Auditorium, got under way at 7 P.M. on April 8, 1963. Bob Hope, the perennial master of ceremonies, had been replaced by Frank Sinatra. A radical procedural innovation was also established. As reported in the *New York World Telegram and Sun,* "The presenters. . .were neither aspiring starlets all a-tremble nor producers' girlfriends nor 'cute' newlyweds with the giggles. They were former Oscar winners, stars of enduring fame whose presence restored a certain aura of respectablity to Oscar night."

One of the highlights of "the Oscars" has traditionally been the fashions flaunted by the attendees. In 1963, the *Lawrence of Arabia* look was "in." "The *Lawrence* in-

184

fluence covers the fashion world as sand covers the Sahara," proclaimed industry leader *Vogue* magazine. Their pages announced that "*Lawrence* inspires the Arab look–chic sheik." Ads declared "Desert Dazzle: Night and Day," unveiled garments "reflecting all the chic of Araby," and touted "Sheik: a lip shade only the chic will know." Flame-haired actress Arlene Dahl noted that her own Oscar gown and cape of white chiffon "was directly inspired by Peter O'Toole's dramatic white Arabian costume." Presenter Rita Moreno displayed a Vidal Sassoon Cleopatra haircut and another celebrity wore a dress inspired by Omar Sharif's black costume.

Actress Shelley Winters started the formalities by reading the nominees for Best Achievement in Sound: *Bon Voyage, Lawrence, The Music Man, That Touch of Mink*, and *What Ever Happened to Baby Jane? Lawrence of Arabia*'s first Oscar–for John Cox the sound director– was accepted by Robert Wagner.

After the Special Effects award was won by *The Longest Day*, Karl Malden read the nominees for Film Editing: *Lawrence, The Longest Day, The Manchurian Candidate, The Music Man,* and *Mutiny on the Bounty. Lawrence*'s editor, Anne Coates, "never expected to win the Oscar; it seemed very unlikely. So I was away on holiday with my family. They'd had a pretty rotten time while I was on *Lawrence*. . . the only time my son saw me was if he came to the cutting room. So I thought they deserved a holiday." Her award was accepted by Robert Stack.

After the Documentary awards, and a medley of Eddie Fisher songs, Ginger Rogers announced the "original" Music Scoring nominees: Jerry Goldsmith for *Freud*, Maurice Jarre for *Lawrence*, Bronislau Kaper for *Mutiny on the Bounty*, Franz Waxman for *Taras Bulba*, and Elmer Bernstein for *To Kill a Mockingbird*.

Maurice Jarre recalled:

> You are a kid in Lyons, France, living under the Nazi occupation. Not much to eat, not much to smile about. But one dream to hold on to: "I am going to be a COMPOSER someday."
>
> Fade out.
>
> Paris radio announces that you have been nominated for an Academy Award for the music for a film called *Lawrence of Arabia*.
>
> The excitement you feel is somewhat dampened when you hear the lugubrious voice of the producer telling you, "Baby, you haven't got a chance. The competition is ferocious."

> Okay.
>
> So you go to bed like Harry Truman and the next thing you hear is the Paris radio announcing: "You have WON!"
>
> Wrestling my Oscar from the reluctant grip of Sam Spiegel was perhaps the most difficult task of all.

Jarre's Oscar was accepted by film composer Morris Stoloff.

After the "Adapted" Music award (*The Music Man*), Rita Moreno announced the Supporting Actor candidates: Ed Begley in *Sweet Bird of Youth*, Victor Buono in *What Ever Happened to Baby Jane?*, Telly Savalas in *Birdman of Alcatraz*, Omar Sharif in *Lawrence*, and Terence Stamp in *Billy Budd*. Ed Begley's Oscar was accepted by– Ed Begley. Observing the paucity of winners present to accept their Oscars, he simply stated, "I'm not Ed Begley."

After the Cartoon and Live Action Short Subject awards, Eva Marie Saint announced the nominees for Costume Design. Phyllis Dalton, for *Lawrence*, was not among them. *The Wonderful World of the Brothers Grimm* captured the Oscar. It seems that Dalton's efforts had been so successful that almost everyone thought that the Arabs were simply wearing their own clothing! David Lean would later write to her:

> Between you and me, I blame Columbia and Sam for not somehow getting you nominated for your wonderful job. You did it so beautifully that I think they failed to realize every costume was an original by you . . .
>
> I was at a party the other night given by Vincente Minnelli and met Cecil Beaton. He was absolutely raving about your work on the film– . . . [he] thought you had done one of the best and most subtle designing jobs he had ever seen on any film–and . . . took it as a sort of enormous back-handed compliment to you that none but the truly discerning were conscious of your art behind the reality.
>
> I still haven't found a subject [for a new film] . . . when I do, I will come a-running to you.

Lean was true to his word. Phyllis Dalton would design *Doctor Zhivago*'s costumes and win an Oscar.

Robert Goulet sang a medly of Oscar-nominated songs, and the Supporting Actress (Patty Duke in *The Miracle Worker*) and Foreign Language Film award (France's *Sundays and Cybele*, the movie that had led Spiegel to Jarre) were announced.

The Oscar for Achievement in Art Direction/Set Direction for Black-and-White films was won by *To Kill a Mockingbird*. Gene Kelly then read the Color nominees: *Lawrence, The Music Man, Mutiny on the Bounty, That Touch of Mink,* and *The Wonderful World of the Brothers Grimm*. The Oscars for *Lawrence's* John Box, John Stoll, and Dario Simoni were accepted by the popular husband-and-wife acting team of Anne Jeffreys and Robert Sterling.

After *The Longest Day* was awarded the Cinematography award for Black-and-White films, Donna Reed announced the nominees for Color: *Gypsy, Hatari!, Lawrence, Mutiny on the Bounty,* and *The Wonderful World of the Brothers Grimm*. Freddie Young was filming *The Seventh Dawn* in the jungles of Malaya; his Oscar was accepted by Carol Lynley.

Then *Days of Wine and Roses* was awarded the Best Song Oscar.

The Direction award was at hand. Joan Crawford read the nominees: Frank Perry for *David and Lisa,* Pietro Germi for *Divorce—Italian Style,* David Lean for *Lawrence,* Arthur Penn for *The Miracle Worker,* and Robert Mulligan for *To Kill a Mockingbird*. David Lean—who only five years previously had become the first British filmmaker to win as Director—accepted his second Director's Oscar, stating simply, "This Limey is deeply touched and greatly honored. Thank you."

The Oscar for Screenplay "based on material from another medium" was next presented, by Bette Davis, to Horton Foote for *To Kill a Mockingbird*. Lean later remarked that "I blame Sam and Columbia almost entirely for Robert Bolt's loss because he was entered in the category for a script from another [medium]—which I think is quite wrong. *Freud* was listed as 'original' and if that's original, surely *Lawrence* is too." *Divorce—Italian Style* won for "original" screenplay.

Three major awards ended the evening.

On Oscar night, Peter O'Toole was performing in London's West End. Sam Spiegel had offered to "buy out the house" so that O'Toole could attend the ceremonies, but it was obviously not possible to reach all of the ticket holders beforehand. Sophia Loren read the nominees for Actor: Burt Lancaster in *Birdman of Alcatraz,* Jack Lemmon in *Days of Wine and Roses,* Marcello Mastroianni in *Divorce—Italian Style,* Peter O'Toole in *Lawrence of Arabia,* and Gregory Peck in *To Kill a Mockingbird*. Gregory Peck accepted the Best Actor Oscar to shouts of "Bravo!"

David Lean later would later comment "I spoke to

Kate Hepburn . . . and she said, 'No young new-comers ever get an Oscar in the *male* category. Young girls, yes. They have, as it were, to win their spurs—the males. The girls do it every time because all the men are suckers. It happened to me too.' I think she's probably right." Gregory Peck, at age forty-seven, with Oscar nominations in 1945, 1946,1947, and 1949, had obviously "won his spurs" and also had given a superb performance.

An analysis published in 1992 confirmed Hepburn's astute observation. Recipients of Actor Oscars are on average forty-six years of age, while Actress winners are generally eight years younger. Only George Chakiris and Timothy Hutton have won acting Oscars before their thirtieth birthday—both in the Supporting category. Richard Dreyfuss and Marlon Brando were both thirty, when they won for Actor. " 'Oscar' is a pretty hunky piece of masculinity," remarked critic Rick Sandford. "Why, then, has the Academy been so hesitant in honoring just such figures as their statue represents: young and attractive males?"

After the Best Actress Oscar was awarded to Anne Bancroft for *The Miracle Worker,* Olivia de Havilland announced the nominations for Best Picture of 1962: *Lawrence of Arabia, The Longest Day, The Music Man, Mutiny on the Bounty,* and *To Kill a Mockingbird. TIME* magazine's Academy Award coverage began: "The gait was unhurried, the paunch impressive as a Roman emperor's, the head massive as a percheron's. Producer Sam Spiegel, to the strains of the theme music from *Lawrence*

Freddie Young, in jungles of Malaya to film Seventh Dawn, *reads cable informing him of Oscar for cinematography in* Lawrence. *Looking on are director Lewis Gilbert (left) and star William Holden.*

186

Director David Lean and Producer Sam Spiegel are congratulated by Olivia de Havilland for their Best Director and Best Picture Oscar.

of Arabia, was advancing down the aisle...to accept the Academy Award for Best Picture of the Year." The for-once subdued producer accepted graciously, stating, "There is no magic formula for creating good pictures. They are made with assiduous, concerted hard work by the writers, directors, actors, and thousands of employees. On behalf of all those who sweated for months in the desert I sincerely thank you, proudly and humbly."

Lawrence of Arabia had captured seven Oscars, the second film to win exactly that number: the first was the Sam Spiegel–David Lean epic *Bridge on the River Kwai.* As of 1963, only six films had ever won in more categories: *Ben-Hur,* eleven; *Gone With the Wind* and *West Side Story,* ten; *Gigi,* nine; *From Here to Eternity* and Spiegel's *On the Waterfront,* eight.

The British Film Academy Awards followed one month later. *Lawrence* was nominated–and won–in three categories: Best Film from Any Source, Best British Screenplay (Robert Bolt), and Best British Actor (Peter O'Toole).

Other accolades were heaped upon the film: Screen Directors Guild of America, Best Directed Picture of the Year; Screen Producers Guild of Amercica, Best Picture of the Year; Film Critics of New York Foreign Language Press, Best Picture of the Year; Federation of Motion Picture Councils, "Masterpiece of Cinematic Art and Entertainment"; Michigan Catholic, Best Picture in Last Ten Years; District of Columbia Motion Picture and Television Council, Citation to Sam Spiegel for "His Creation of a Masterpiece of Cinematic Art"; and Hollywood Foreign Press Association (Golden Globe Awards): Best Production–Drama, Best Director, Best Supporting Actor and Outstanding Star of Tomorrow–Omar Sharif, and Best Cinematography–Color.

Eminent critic Judith Crist commented on the significance of the Oscar results, possibly the only critic of that era to begin to understand what David Lean's synergy of picture, sound, words, and acting had actually accomplished:

> *Lawrence of Arabia* is beyond doubt the best film of 1962...

187

To me, *Lawrence* is an extraordinary film because it accomplishes what no other medium can in presenting the story of that enigmatic twentieth-century hero. It goes beyond Lawrence's *Seven Pillars of Wisdom,* beyond Terence Rattigan's *Ross* in giving us an understanding of the *desert* and Lawrence's infatuation with it, its impact upon the many facets of his complex character, its scope in providing his experience.

And it is an extraordinary film because it is the first spectacular to use its spectacle for more than visual purpose, specifically as a probe of character, a delineation of an individual within a broad realm of experience. . .

Fred Zinnemann's postpremiere comment to Lean–"You don't know what you've done"–suggests that he also *had* understood the full significance of *Lawrence*'s triumph.

The 1960s guru and communications prophet Marshall McLuhan–labeled "Canada's Intellectual Comet"– had proclaimed "The medium is the message." *He* understood.

However, filmgoers who responded to Columbia's aggressive new campaign–and most of those who had already seen the film–did *not* experience the movie which had won all of these honors. It no longer existed. Shortly after the U.S. premiere, *Lawrence of Arabia* was subjected to the beginning of a quarter century of slashing and deterioration.

The film had become almost impossible for *anyone* to understand.

It would take nearly three decades for the world, including David Lean, to fully understand what David Lean had really done.

CHAPTER 8

THE LOST PICTURE SHOW

*"TO BE GREAT AGAIN, IT SEEMS. . .
WE NEED A MIRACLE."*

—FEISAL TO LAWRENCE, IN FEISAL'S TENT

week after *Lawrence* opened in the States, David Lean admitted, in a letter to Robert Bolt, his growing concerns about the film:

. . .Sam has been sweetness itself. Can hardly believe it! All papers have had a go about the length. They complain but they say they were never bored. It just nags them. No-one has any real suggestion to make and I have talked a lot to Sam about it. My way of thinking is that if—which we can't—we could think of some way of cutting out forty minutes I would call it very helpful, but it's no good nibbling at scenes and running the risk of ruining the impact that the film certainly has. I'm all for making cuts that would take out anything which proves to bore an audience—but we haven't yet seen it with a man-in-the-street audience to date.

I saw it here in Hollywood with the "Dine with me in Wadi Rumm!" cutting to the close up of a little girl in the feast scene. It doesn't come off very well. Quinn declaimed the line in order to lead into the eyeful long shot—so the cuts make him hammy. It also disrupts the pattern of the picture in some way and we now have one dialogue scene followed at once by another. Don't know quite what to do but somehow that long shot has got to go back.

. . .My own criticism is that the second half shows the forced pace at which you had to jump from point to point. As it nears the end, I get a bit stifled with keeping up. Know what I mean? Not your fault, of course but a lesson never to be forgotten about starting with an unfinished script.

. . .This letter has run into Christmas eve and I have just had a call from Sam in New York. Christmas Eve is *the* worst day in movie theatres of the whole year. The matinee in New York is sold right out and ditto the evening show tonight. This has never been heard of. The Boston and Philadelphia reviews have just come out and Sam says they are fantastic. The only trouble is the bloody interval [intermission] and apparently there a sort of word of mouth going round that the second half isn't as good as the first. (Poor old me. If only I had known this in Jordan!) I am sure the interval is one of the causes as is Sam. Billy Wilder said he thought an interval was death. He said to Sam it was like having an affair and Sam making a twenty-minute call from Tokyo in the middle of it—and then having to start again! He's damned right. I think that it would be better to have people rushing out to the gents and rushing back again into a still atmosphere than breaking the whole thing up now as we do. Sam wants to try and have us cut ten to fifteen minutes. He's not going mad and for once has his feet well on he ground. I am going to start thinking about this very seriously and hope you will. . . .Rest assured nothing rash is going to be done—and it can't be done in a hurry anyhow. But try and think.

It is clear that, initially at least, no great pressure to cut the film came from Sam Spiegel. The first mild criticism which Lean perceived was from "the papers"–the length "just nags them."

Alan Dent of the *Sunday Telegraph* was quite explicit.

189

In a review entitled *Lawrences of Arabia,* he observed that "the first thing to be said about *Lawrence of Arabia . . .* is that it is two big films stuck end to end. They should be shown alternately." He concluded: "The whole thing must seem over-long to all but those. . .who cannot resist two splendid pictures for the price of one."

It is also apparent that David Lean's own main criticism, reinforced by "word of mouth," was that the second half of the film showed a "forced pace" which resulted in a perceived inferiority as compared to the first half.

Lean effectively pinpoints the origins of this problem.

First, there was the challenge of having to finish the script under less than ideal conditions. Lean did not blame Bolt directly: "not your fault of course." Ironically, Bolt *had* been hired at such a late date because Lean considered his dialogue and interpretation of Lawrence's character superior to Wilson's. Nevertheless, this change of writers meant that there was a hurriedness to the whole affair. And Bolt had indeed been in jail during the break in England, and thus unable to have close communication with Lean. This situation certainly contributed to the haste with which the script for the second half was prepared.

Second, David Lean's comment "as is Sam," surely referred to the fact that Lean attributed some of the blame to Spiegel's sudden decision to get out of Jordan, which meant filming much of the second half in Spain. This obviously caused time wastage, loss of continuity and atmosphere in locations, and the subjecting of both cast and crew to great disruption. Bolt later wrote to Lean, "You were right about the importance of Jordan to *Lawrence.*"

Finally, Lean felt that the "bloody interval," which Wilder thought was "death," significantly encumbered the film.

Although Lean did not say so, it is implicit in his arguments that significant cuts might solve the problem. The film would be shorter. A shorter film could have the interval eliminated. And a film without an interval would not give rise to the faults associated with the interval: interrupting the adventure, and providing critics with two "films" to target for differing interpretations.

Secondary arguments for a shorter film were both commercial and logistical. A shorter film might be shown more than twice a day: this, however, was not to be. More important, the length of the film had caused significant problems for patrons, especially in the United Kingdom.

In that era, automobiles were relatively expensive in Britain, and their use thus somewhat restricted. The public transportation system was extensive and efficient, and people commuted into London by tube (subway) and railway from far greater distances than was the case in the United States and Canada at that time. Nonetheless, this excellent transportation system had very restrictive hours in the late evening/early morning, and this might negatively impact the film's box-office receipts.

Lean continued, reluctantly recognizing that cuts would have to be considered:

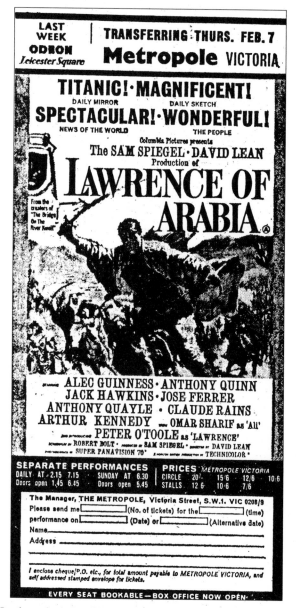

In the early sixties, films in London were scheduled to move to a smaller cinema relatively soon after opening.

190

. . .My first feelings were to resist cutting like mad. I'm not sure now. It is bloody long. I'm sure the trouble with the second half is that we're telling too much too quick – it hammers at one. Sam says that the new issue of *LIFE* says it's too long but that the scene of Ali appearing out of the mirage is worth the price of admission – which is high – in itself. Good isn't it? [Emphasis ours]

Lean then started to consider specific scenes for excision, telling Bolt "I will go through the whole film in my mind and let you know."

Robert Bolt reinforced David Lean's thoughts in his return letter:

29 December 1962
Dear David,

Very many thanks for this marvellous letter. Quite apart from anything else, it's the first news we've had from America. Sam, on the 'phone to the office, is being very grumpy and uncommunicative. The film is doing very good business here and the word-of-mouth so far as one can tell so early, is excellent.

What you say of lessons to be learnt is uncannily what I was thinking myself after last night, when we took the kids to see it with an ordinary audience.

To put it on the nail, you were right in almost all our arguments about the first and second halves. There is a sense of atmosphere and leisure in the first half which the second lacks. This is because we had to slice, pare, dovetail, more like clockmakers than filmmakers to get everything inside the time limit. And this, as you say, is because we started without a finished script. Ideally I am convinced, the film should have been three hours long. The first half should be as it is, but shorter, and we should have had much less plot.(e.g., one visit to Allenby, not two; and our point of attack could have been later in the story.) Then our climax could have flowered more gently and naturally from the atmosphere. I think we did a very fine bit of clockmaking in part two, mind you, but clockmaking is what it was.

A very intelligent friend of mine (a sculptor) said that the last half of the last part was like brilliant notes for the sequence, not the sequence itself. And under pressure of time, that is what it became. He said that he wanted leisure in which to *experience* the debacle in Damascus with Lawrence, as he had experienced the

desert and the adulation, instead of which he felt he was only able to watch him. With intense interest, but not with deep feeling, because he was on his toes simply to keep up with the story. However, all this is wisdom after the event. That we can see it now is no guarantee that we should see it next time.

I've just heard from the Office that Sam wants me to help him with prospective cuts when he returns next week. I must say he gets his money's worth from people does that one.

. . .I utterly agree about the interval. It serves no good purpose or at least no purpose commensurate with what it loses us in momentum. That is what I felt very strongly in the audience last night. I would, if I were the Producer, at any rate try it, when the cuts are made, without the interval. I think it might make a wonderful difference.

A friend of ours. . .a high pressure psychoanalyst . . . intellectual rang me up with his wife after having seen the film; they were both raving, said they had been bathed in tears, and he (a Muslim of course and very consciously so, a Prince of some kind) made a comment which I think you will like to hear: he said it was the first film he had seen in which a Muslim people were accorded absolutely equal status with the whites, being neither sentimentalized nor belittled. On the other hand you know, I don't think the Zionists could say we'd made a pro-Arab picture. The wonderful thing is that even when such inadequate talents as ours just *try* to be truthful, all these tendentious people find their guns are spiked. It's when you start truckling to this or that expectation that you give offense.

. . .We won't bandy compliments, David. You want to work with me again. Good. I want to work with you again. I admire your craft and artistry very much indeed. What's more, I find I have conceived an attachment to you and feel sad that our present connection is over.

With sincere affection,
Bob

In a 1989 London *Evening Standard* article, Robert Bolt would confirm the idea that cuts in the film were closely linked in his and Lean's minds with elimination of the intermission:

Sam got David and myself together and said he

December 28th. '62.

"Lawrence." Cutting Comments.

1. Map Room. Billiards. Murray's Office.

I am quite sure that a big cut could and should be made in this early part of the picture. The fact that no-one has remarked on the length of these particular scenes does not impress me as they occur so early in the film that length does no enter anyones head at this stage.

I find the map room a goodish scene in a goodish British film. I would, without a second thought, dispense with it but for the match incident. I am not absolutely convinced that the match incident is worth the footage involved. It would not make a non sequiter of blowing out the match in Dryden's office as I believe an audience would take it on its face value and believe that Dryden's "Funny sense of fun" referred to Lawrence's general behaviour.

Can one of us think of a way - a place - to start the map room later ? (Such as Lawrence in the middle of lighting the cigarette for Hartley and the other man coming in and saying, "Mr. Lawrence." "Yes." "Flimsey, sir.")

Whatever we do I would be happy to cut out the whole of the billiards scene and cut straight from the map room to Murray's office. I have turned more and more against this billiards scene every time I have seen it with an audience. It doesn't come off as we had hoped. Even the beer spilling falls flat. I think the audience doesn't quite know what to make of the scene. I know it introduces the Club Secretary but think we could pick up with him later when Lawrence returns with Farraj.

Murray. I think the start of the scene must be cut - under the circumstances of this length pressure. I think the scene is alright - but it is exposition - and I query if the exposition is needed. The boldest cut of all - which I throw into the arena is to cut from Murray at St. Pauls saying " . . he was on my staff in Cairo" straight to Murray's office with Hawthorne entering and saying "Lawrence, sir." and Murray replying "Show him in." I think this might work wonderfully. It would be a bold jump ahead and would, I think, make an effective time out pictorially. We would be jumping the audience forward and into the middle of a scene and I think they would soon pick up the threads. Please let us consider this. I know it sounds pretty drastic but I think it would have a good impact. I would rather be drastic in this scene than nibble at half a dozen.

2.

While on these three scenes let us remember that we could cut the map room before that scene has ended -for example, after Lawrence say's "The trick, William Potter, is not minding that it hurts" - straight to Murrays office somewhere before Lawrence enters or before the end of the billiard scene to Murray's office somewhere before Lawrence enters.

Entrance of the Desert. Now I have seen the film with several audiences I am very doubtful about cutting out the Harith country scene with the little caravan in the distance. Very doubtful.

Entry of Ali. The whole of this scene works even better than I had hoped. Please do not let us change it.

Echo scene. Sam is very anxious to make a cut here. I am not entirely against it if one of/can think of a good and smooth transition into Brighton. We can't, for instance, just dissolve from Ali's "God be with you." to Brighton yelling, "Hey !! You !!" Very clumsey from my, the director's,point of view.

We can't dissolve to the clapping unless we have some singing - and I think the singing is all or nothing. The only thing I can suggest is that we dissolve from the sky as Ali moves out of picture after his, "God be with you." to Lawrence on his camel in the long shot which is now the first shot of the singing sequence. (Thiswould mean that we cut out the extreme long shot which follows Ali at present.) And from this long shot cut straight to Brighton saying "Hi ! You !!." - thus cutting out all the singing shots.

No good pretending. I'm not very happy about this and am very sorry to give up the pan down the rock-face which introduces Brighton. This sort of cutting takes away the hand-made-article "something" that this film has. I just don't know. Perhaps we could have a bit of singing and echo what we have left. Unhappy.

Day Exodus. Alright. I know the opening long shot is too orderly, but something tells me that it's not good to go straight into Brighton looking around for planes. Before finally deciding lets look at the second camera which had a long focus lens - and I did not use - which, I believe gives a more disorderly effect and could be held shorter. Must tell you that I'm sorry to say goodbye to the womans hand in the howdah. Perhaps we could start with this shot instead of the present long shot. Think we have got to start with some sort of orientation shot after the night shot and before Brighton.

As a second thought. Suppose we started with the second camera long shot or the howdah shot - then went to Brighton looking round - and then directly to the last shot of the sequence with the lmps saying "Aurens ?" "You have no servant" etc. and as is - thus cutting out the first attempt to get a cigarette from Lawrence, the orderly and the cigarette business, plus the gooseing of the camel and the fall off.

3.

Note. I write all this in great trust. I know it's dangerous. We must be very careful not to make sequences into featherweight lantern slides which just tell the plot. This Exodus scene is a case in point. Don't let's jump. The film has a certain something which we must be careful not to destroy. Be warned.

Departure of Raiding Party. I have suggested this to Sam already. I know he doesn't approve. I still think it would work very well under the present circumstances of length trouble.

I would cut straight from Ali saying, "You are mad." to the close shot of the camels feet which now follows Feisal's "In who's name do you ride ?" I know there are one or two - what Robert calls "grace notes"-in the Feisal - Lawrence scene but I think the cut would have a real impact and jump the audience forward in an excellent way. Let us ponder this. I think 1% of the audience understand the significance of "In who's name do you ride ?". I think the question of whether Lawrence told or did not tell Brighton is unimportant. It's a preparation scene. It's quite a deal of valuable footage. I'm sure - on this occasion - that the actual cut would be most effective plus giving a feeling of speed.

The Anvil. I must start this with a warning note. I am sure that several after-the-fact"editors"will suggest some cuts in the crossing of the Nefud. Again, be warned. It is a delicate balance of near intangibles which can easily be destroyed. I am willing for one cut consisting of one shot in the actual Nefud. It works as I once had it without this particular shot. It's a 12 feet long and is the long shot which follows themirage sequence and immediately preceeds the shot of Lawrence shaving. I used an almost exactly similar shot which now follows as a dissolve from the resting during the day sequence (and please don't suggest any monkey business with that sequence.) and leads as a link to the close shot of the stones and camels feet.

The cut I am sure of is in the night crossing of the anvil. (Zinnermann - an expert - remarked on it without prompting from me.) After Ali says to Lawrence, "This is the suns anvil" I would go, as is, to the long shot of the ants going out into the anvil and dissolve to the second night sequence with the long shadows and the boy falling off his camel. This would cut out the 3-shot sequence of Lawrence looking at his watch, Ali catching him yawning, and Lawrence settling down in his saddle.

Again I have already suggested this to Sam and indeed did so originally in the actual cutting stage. His arguement was that the audience wouldn't feel that the crossing of the actual anvil

4.

wasn't long enough. I don't agree. There is a dissolve from day to night which in itself gives a passage of time. The fact that the boy falls off suggests tiredness, and in the little scene I suggest cutting nothing really worthwhile happens. It's another grace note. As Fred Zinnermann said, "Do try and get to Gasim's empty camel as soon as possible." I'm sure of this as a good cut - not so much in footage, but in eliminating a feeling of tedium in the audience. We have seen it before. It gives a feeling of leisurly pace which is surely our enemy.

Return of Lawrence, Gasim and Daud. For the above reasons (a sense of being leisurly) I would cut from the extreme long shot of Daud meeting Lawrence and Gasim to Ali hitting the ground with his stick. Thus cutting out the one shot of Farraj sitting waiting and looking down at the encampment below.

So it would go. Long shot Daud wheeling around Lawrence and Gasim. Ali hitting the ground. Long shot Lawrence and Dauds camel appearing. (The music starts here) Farraj jumping up and yelling, "Aurens !!".

Wadi Rumm. I don't like at all the new cut from, "Come dine with me in Wadi Rumm!!" to the little girls close up. It makes Quinn a ham to declaim the line which leads into an intimate close up. I was wrong and Sam was right. I would go from Quinn's line to the long shot as was but I would print it right down so as to give a near dusk effect. Then I would dissolve stright into the middle of the tracking shot inside the tent (after the child and the women) so that almost the first thing that happened was that the men were entering to carry out the feast on the tray.

Exit from Wadi Rumm. I would cut - The first shot (after "Thy mother mated with a scorpion.") of the men yelling "Auda Abu Tayi." The second shot of Auda saying, "Akaba !" and "Make God your agent." The third extreme Long shot of the column starting to move. The fourth medium shot of Auda riding towards camera saying, "God be with you." The fifth panning shot of Lawrence and Ali moving off.

I would start by dissolving from "Mother mated with a scorpion" to the present sixth shot which is a long shot of the whole procession with Auda passing by followed by Lawrence and Ali. I would cut to the first shot taken from inside the tent with the women as is. The extreme - and most spectacular Long shot - as is. The second tent shot as is. The start of the singing etc. as is - but -

After Lawrence turns around and sees the close shot of the men singing I would cut straight from the close shot of the men to the second extreme long shot of the women trilling in the foreground and the whole army spread out in the background - and then continue as is. Think this would do the trick and I have no regrets. (As far as the sound is concerned I would work backwards so we get the same result of the increasing drum noise which takes us to the moon. The first tracking shot of women trilling was - I think - a pre-mix, and it would just mean that the men singing would increase their tempo earlier.)

5.

Akaba. I like the idea of the dissolve from the end of the charge to the red sun over the sea. Inspite of the fact that I wouldn't take most critics advice as to how to shoot an insert I do know that several of them have remarked on too many sun shots. I think this shot may be the one that breaks their back.

Therefore sugges t for our consideration that we dissolve from the end of the charge to the rioting in the town which pans to Lawrence on his camel going into the sea. Again this is not done from a footage-length point of view but an attempt to eliminate criticisms of repetition. I would hate to cut any other sun shots as all the others have a real point - while this is solely mood.

Cairo. I have had two separate face-face criticisms about the scene between Allenby, Lawrence, Dryden and Brighton by the goldfish pool. The people say they cannot believe that Allenby would discuss military matters with Lawrence in front of a lot of gooping. I got in a mess with this scene, Robert, and I know I didn't put over your intention which was that Allenby was doing this on purpose.

I think two shots particularly do the damage: The first shot of the Club secretary which is a dissolve from the scene in the bar. The final shot of the first goldfish sequence with the officers peering downwards from the courtyard windows.

I therefore suggest that we dissolve from the bar to the shot of the group around the fountain, thus cutting out the Club secretary shot. (This may cause trouble as we will have to add to the front of the group shot in order to have enough dissolve footage but as there is no violent movement I don't think the loss of 2 pictures will show.) In the case of the second shot which ends with the spin to the feet I would suggest trying a direct cut from Allenby saying "Certainly !" to the tracking shot of the feet a foot before the first line. (This would cut out Lawrence's close up which ends with him looking up in addition to the spinnin shot which I know Sam loathes anyhow. Would have to try this on the cutting copy. My guess is that it will work.

Loss of Interval. Yes please. Ann will be able to time this, but my guess is that we should fade out on a 6 footer starting the fade where the fade in on the Interval title now begins. We would have, of course, to loose the music and have only footsteps.

6.

If the interval cutting idea works in whatever place Sam is going to try it out I think we may have to examine the idea of fading in a few feet later on the shot of Bentley coming up over the hill. We have got to take care here as this is the only fade out in the picture and will therefore have a punctuation all of its own. Added to this I shot it (the Bentley shot) as a curtain raiser. Don't take a lump off it but consider a 6 foot fade in so that Bentley's head can be seen on about the fourth foot. We don't want to replace a major hiatus with a minor.

Allenby - Brighton Fireside scene. As you know, Sam, Billy Wilder queried this. He didn't condemn it and said he couldn't on one running. It was just a query. I am in a real quandry about it. The footage involved tempts me very much - but only under the circumstances - for I like the scene and think it has great contrast value from a pictorial point of view, it shows Allenby's very tolerant and understanding attitude towards Lawrence (and we don't get too much of this aspect of their relationship) It shows the begining of the change in Brighton's attitude to Lawrence, and almost best of all it contains, "Not lies, poems." - which is valuable from an audiences' guidance point of view.

But if we have got to cut it could go with the audience none the wiser. The only way to do it would be to dissolve from "What do you recommend ?" to the snow blowing across the hole in the ruins.

If pure length is our sole criterion then it must come out. If it be speed or fear of boredom in the audience I think it should stay in.

Bey scene. I don't agree with the suggested cut. (This, Robert, is because it unfortunately seems that here in America at least - and I can't speak for England as I have had no opportunity to question people on this point - don't understand that anything happens to Lawrence after the beating. The buggering. The reason is that I was so "windy" that I didn't allow enough silence - it would take another 6 foot of silence on Ali's close up before the music starts I now realise.) The suggested cut is that we somehow cut directly from the beating to Lawrence being thrown out into the puddle - as if there had been no time lapse. I don't agree with this and have another idea which may even be better and more to the point than the version running at the moment.

I think the suggestion of a time lapse in which something other than the beating is taking place is very important, and believe it doesn't come over because we haven't made enough contrast but have been too smooth. Now. I would dissolve from the final shot of the Bey standing in the doorway straight to the shot of Ali and the moon. I would have no music - and this is an important part of it - but would have that track of dogs barking and only start the music when the lights came up in the windows. This would mean cutting out the shot of Ali - the long tracking shot - which starts on him listening and then walking partly from the sounds of beating down the street

7.

as the sound of feet and door bangs die away to nothing - which at present starts the music.

I think this is a first rate cut irrespective of length problems. We would go from the Bey in the doorway to Ali mooching about outside darkened windows - with no sound but barking dogs. Then the lights would go on - and I think most audiences would cotton on here if they hadn't done so before. But we must have a silence. The audience have got to wonder what's going on and music will somehow smooth it all away.

Allenby seduction scene. Yes, Sam, I'm all for going back after Dryden's "unscrupulous" line to later on in the scene. You suggested "the sixteenth." May very well be right. The more reasonably drastic the better as far as I'm concerned.

Allenby's Tent. I say this as a reserve length-trouble suggestic We could go from the Arab army streaming away from camera at the end of the Assembly sequence direct to the marching feet which starts the road to Damascus - via a dissolve please. This would cut out Allenby's tent and the "They're Turks" scenes. I like the pictorial side of the guns flashing scene, but if we are in trouble it's one of those cuts an audience wouldn't miss.

Tafas Rape scene. Length or no length I would make a cut of the first shot of the rape - after Allenby has said, "I wonder where they are now ?"- which consists of a scarf blowing up between dead bodies. I would cut directly to the shot of the hanging man with the Turks in the distance because many people have been completely misled and think the masacred people are Turks! Yes. This is because the line, "I wonder where they are now ?" implies that the people one is shown immediately after are the Turks Allenby has referred to a moment agax ago. I see this now. I know, Robert, we were trying not to be obvious. But it really does confuse so do lets cut that one shot and be quite simple about it. It isn't that bad after all. "I wonder where they are now ?", and there they are.

Hospital sequence. I have rather doubled back on my tracks about this one because of a long talk with Fred Zinnermann. He thinks I'm mad.

That's it as far as I'm concerned. As a P.S. I add that Sam Goldwyn, with whom I had a long talk, say's we should have heard the screams and the arguements when "Gone with the Wind" came out. They prophesied the length would be box-office disaster.

David.   December 30th '62

wanted to take out some scenes. We agreed, on the condition that he take out the interval as well. The sequences were taken out, but the interval stayed.

Thus, Sam Spiegel apparently had recognized the positive commercial benefits of cuts, but not the fact that Lean and Bolt had both identified a positive artistic benefit of cutting the film.

In 1963, the question was "Which scenes to cut?" Although Lean and Bolt had tentatively targeted several candidates for removal, it was Lean's "Cutting Notes"– reproduced here as a historical document–which explored in detail all of the possibilities he had been considering. The document was apparently intended for Sam Spiegel (p. 6, "As you know, Sam. . ."), Robert Bolt (p. 7, "I know, Robert, we were not trying to be obvious"), and Anne Coates.

The existence of such a substantial document, the fact that David Lean even considered cutting his masterpiece, must be considered from a historical perspective.

Opinions about the "correct" length of films change like fashions. For example, in 1992–after more than a decade of "two-hour films," partially dictated by the needs of both network television and two-hour videocassettes–we are now once again seeing a trend toward longer films.

Was cutting the film a significant concession from Lean's perspective in 1963? His peers had seen the uncut film and judged it worthy. Numerous awards had been won. David Lean, with fourteen Oscars and millions in revenue for Columbia from two blockbusters in a five-year period, *would* have financial backing for his next film. *Lawrence,* like most films of that era, could "disappear," never to be seen again except at film festivals and on commercial-ridden TV. (Perhaps A.W.'s prediction might well become fact: "the film will soon be forgotten. . .especially since it needs a wide screen.") The exceptions–like *Gone With the Wind*–were few, and it was not yet clear that *Lawrence* was an exception. Winning a Best-Picture Oscar did not, at that time, dictate preservation for posterity or guarantee periodic revivals: witness the sad fate of *Tom Jones,* which essentially vanished for almost thirty years. Videocassettes were still a dozen years into the future. Only the "second-run" audience would be burdened with a cut film.

Nonetheless, his "Cutting Comments" are of interest, and give a tremendous insight into the many interrelated factors which governed the editing of each scene and the interrelationships among different scenes. Many pages could be devoted to a discussion of these notes, to consideration of which scenes were cut from which version, and to how they relate to the final 1989 "Director's Cut." What is perhaps as interesting is the fact that Lean's apprehension about the whole idea repeatedly surfaces:

> No good pretending. I'm not very happy about this. . . .This sort of cutting takes away from the hand-made-article "something" that this film has. I just don't know. . . .We must be vary careful not to make sequences into featherweight lantern sides which just tell the plot. . . .The film has a certain something which we must careful not to destroy. Be warned. . . . [this sequence] is a delicate balance of near intangibles which can easily be destroyed.

Lean makes it clear in his "Cutting Comments" that his willingness to cut the film must include deletion of the intermission: "*Loss of Interval.* Yes please." He gave responsibility to Anne Coates for replacing the ten-minute intermission with a three second fade-out, the only one in the film. He noted that Sam Spiegel had agreed to try out the concept in a theatrical showing.

"That's it as far as I'm concerned" was indeed an appropriate remark with which to end Lean's document. His greatest consideration was always for his next film, and his letters to Robert Bolt over the next months devote substantial space to consideration of possible future projects.

For the record

'Lawrence of Arabia' banned

The film "Lawrence of Arabia" has been banned in Jordan.

Arabs in the film were presented "in a comic way and favourable Arab attitudes in modern Arab history converted into ridiculous attitudes," according to the Amman regional office of the Committee for the Boycott of Israel.

The Guardian, January 14, 1964, observed that Lawrence was banned in Jordan–citing the same arguments which were used in 1937 against Korda–portrayal of a people in a bad light.

194

Bolt had indicated that he was writing a play, *Gentle Jack*, and had an agreement with Columbia Pictures for another screenplay, *A Man for All Seasons*. Then he had a moral commitment with himself to do yet another theatrical work, which would be *The Thwarting of Baron Bolligrew*. After that, in 1964, another film with Lean would be possible. It was to be *Doctor Zhivago*.

In their letters re: *Zhivago*, concerns about *Lawrence* scenes which might have been filmed differently were raised, and the application of lessons learned from these "mistakes" to *Zhivago* was discussed. Even the Dryden–Lawrence scene, leading to the famous "blowing out of the match," was apparently not to Lean's complete satisfaction, as he explained to Robert Bolt:

June 16, 1964

I was thrown right at the beginning [of the "match scene"] because I saw the characters were having a conversation about something which had really deep meanings about the character of Lawrence, as he was to develop. A warning of things to come.

What happened to *me* was this: I had gods with suns behind them on the wall and got Claude Rains to speak the lines with warning and significance. Having got so far, I got frightened and shot the scene in uncommiting medium shot, kidding myself it would be best to have no close-ups because they would take away from the impact of the final match blowing close up at the end. Back came a scream from both you and Sam, "Retake!" I was half-prepared for it (because of my compromise) and re-shot the scene with Claude throwing away the lines—and they were

DAILY CONTINUITY REPORT			Sound	SD

Production: "LAWRENCE OF ARABIA" — Date FRIDAY 12th JAN 62 — Mute — Colour COLOUR
Director: DAVID LEAN — Cameraman F. A. YOUNG. — B. & W.
SET: INT. DRYDEN'S OFFICE. CAIRO H.Q. — Night DAY — Day

Time Started 11.55	CAMERA		SET UP	Script Number M.13 A RETAKE
Time Finished 12.18	A SC 101 B C D		75 mm 13 ft f4.5 85 fil	Slate Number 648

Take	1	2	3	4	5	6	7	8	9	10
Print						PRT				
Hold										
N/G	NG	NG CUT	NG CUT	GOOD	NG					
Film Footage	75	35	35	75	90	75 25 ⊕				
Timing										

MEDCIUM CLOSE TWO SHOT: DRYDEN behind table l.f.g.
LAWRENCE moves into position r.f.g

DRYDEN 1h trs pkt rh holding cig just above lid of box.

Lawrence (over lap) This is going to (moving in) fun...MATCH BOX in rh.

DRYDEN: (taking hand to him) LAWRENCE... ONLY TWO KINDS OF CRE*TURE GET 'FUN' IN THE DESERT.. BEDUINS... AND.... GODS. AND YOU'RE NEITHER.... TAKE IT FROM ME FOR ORDINARY MEN IT'S A BURNING FIERY FURNACE...

LAWRENCE: NO DRYDEN (strikes and lights Drdyen's cig as) IT'S GOING TO BE FUN.
Drops matchbox from 1h on to table - pulls right sleeve

DRYDEN: (looks from match to Lawrence to match) IT IS (looks up) RECOGNIZED THAT YOU HAVE A FUNNY (Lawrence raising match) SENSE OF FUN) Completes raising match - shoots left cuff..

BLOWS MATCH OUT.

Tk 1 N.G. arc flicker.
Tks 2 and 3 N.G. cut.
Tk 4 Good.
Tk 5 N.G. action.
PRT TK 6

Six takes were required to achieve the Lawrence/Dryden "two-shot" portion of the "blowing out the match" scene.

damned good—as lighthearted conversation. The scene was quite acceptable and I think most audiences would scarcely remember it.

I will now tell you what I think I *should* have done, and then guess at why you reacted as you did and asked for a retake.

I should have gone much further in the direction I started out on. I should have arranged Peter in such a position that he had a bloody great sun-god plaque right behind his close-up—so that when he stood on top of the train, the sun behind him, the audience would subconsciously connect it with the "warning" in the office. I should have had Claude speak the lines with due appreciation for his intuition that this sort of danger existed for this particular young man. Played full out for the "significance" coming straight from the characters. I think it would have been most effective and would have sounded a drum beat of things to come.

Now take *you*. I'm sure you still recoil from what I have just said, and I'll try and tell you why I think you recoil. Having written a "significant scene" (and bloody good it was) you saw you, the author, peeking

Small cinema, big film, Blackpool, England.

through over and above the actors on the screen. Your suggested remedy was to scotch any suggestions of "author's message" by having the actors throw away the lines—and hence any feeling of message. In turn, to use your favorite message, I think we threw away the baby with the bathwater and were left with an amiable enough conversation which only had a real point in the blowing out of the match. We must *stop* this throwing away of pearls! We are both guilty of it and if we can only see the reasons we can do so.

I think its funk and lack of courage on both our parts. It's something to do with this English politeness I'm always talking about. We both "want to say it" . . .but don't *quite* want to say it. Too obvious. Too vulgar. We almost take a pride in those scenes which are caught on to only by our brightest friends. . .

The most bizarre item discussed by Bolt and Lean concerns dialogue that never appeared in the film:

Michael Anderegg, in his landmark essay "Lawrence of Arabia: the Man, the Myth, the Movie," notes that censorship in 1962 "still maintained its grip on the cinema," thus limiting the freedom of expression in certain areas. "When the forbidden can only be hinted at," he maintained, "only a hint is necessary." In November 1962, Bolt had already indicated his recognition of this strategy in his exchange of letters with Liddell Hart: "We felt bound to make a reference which would be picked up by those already aware of the controversy, and will be missed by anybody who isn't." This, of course, was Bolt's allusion "to the strong homosexual colouring found in *Seven Pillars*" and "hinted at" in his script.

Bolt, however, progresses far beyond "hints" in his allusions to Lawrence's masochistic character. Lawrence's startling admission to Allenby, "I enjoyed it," referring to his responsibility for the deaths of Gasim and Daud, may be subject to interpretation. But later in the film, following the derailment of the passenger train, a wounded Turkish officer shoots Lawrence in the shoulder. His response, "Good, good, good," needs no interpretation. These words may have bewildered audiences but there was no doubt that, moments after parading himself as a "sun-god" across the rooftops of the train, Lawrence is exposed as Lean's very "flawed hero."

Bolt, however, had wanted to go even further.

Slate 1231, filmed at 11:15 A.M. on June 30, 1962, covers ten seconds of action following "Good, good, good." Freddie Young called for a wide-angle lens to film Lawrence struggling to his feet, his left hand clutching

his wounded right shoulder. "Take 1" was described on Barbara Cole's daily continuity report as "no good–slow." "Take 3" *was* selected, and in the film Lawrence very, very quietly says something indistinct: the continuity sheet records the dialogue as "OH, DEAR."

But, in "Take 2"–printed, but never used–the continuity report records that the words spoken by Peter O'Toole were "OO. . .OH, DEAR. . .DEAR. . .DEAR . . .OH, POOR NEDDY LAWRENCE. . .OO, POOR NEDDY."

Robert Bolt, in his letter to David Lean of May 25, 1963, lashed out at Sam Spiegel, with specific reference to this scene:

. . .you thought Sam, brute that he is, good for you. I know what you mean, but you're wrong. He isn't necessary. You and I, if we kept our courage high and didn't flinch from the possibility of clashing now and then, could put all the pressure on each other that either of us needs. And what, apart from pressure does Sam contribute? Not a lot, that I could see.

I'll tell you what: I miss that line "Poor Neddy. . .Poor Neddy Lawrence" like a hand. It would be the verbal equivalent of your mirage shot of Omar approaching. You do know, I imagine, that most people don't know that that shot *is* a mirage? And even those who do, don't like it for that reason but for the true reason–that it is a high-handed, masterful. . .statement by you of what you feel for Sherif Ali at that moment? It's accepted without a flicker–is that shot–even by people who simply see Omar as a flickering black flower without rational explanation. Sam would never had permitted that shot if he had not thought of it as something to advertise: "A genuine desert mirage captured for you by the magic of the Omo five-foot lens." Similarly, he utterly misunderstood the weight (or weightlessness) of that line, with his vulgar apprehensions of homosexuality. . . .Delicacy is *not* effeminacy. Beauty is *not* prettiness. Heroism is *not* brutishness. Sam would agree in principle, but in practice, never.

Kate Hepburn, who had done *African Queen* with Sam Spiegel, had advised Lean to work with Spiegel on *Kwai:* "You will learn a lot from Sam and Sam will learn a lot from you." After two distinguished, multi-award-winning films with Spiegel, David Lean did recognize both the good and bad qualities of the producer. "Sam Spiegel," Lean remarked in 1989, "was a two-edged sword: he couldn't keep his hands out of your pocket."

The two never worked together again.

David Lean's next film was Boris Pasternak's *Doctor Zhivago,* produced by Carlo Ponti. The core of Lean's creative staff was still his "dedicated maniacs": Robert Bolt, Freddie Young, Maurice Jarre, Phyllis Dalton, John Box, John Palmer, Douglas Twiddy, Roy Stevens, Pedro Vidal, Roy Rossotti, Hugh Miller, Ernie Day, Terry Marsh, Dario Simoni, Winston Ryder, Paddy Cunningham, Freddy Bennet, and Barbara Cole. Eddie Fowlie, credited as Property Master for *Lawrence,* was this time billed as Special Effects: "Nobody knows that the whole picture is a special effect—there's no snow or ice in the picture. The whole damn thing is a special effect."

Zhivago starred Geraldine Chaplin, Julie Christie, Tom Courtenay, Alec Guinness, Siobhan McKenna, Ralph Richardson, Omar Sharif, Rod Steiger, and Rita Tushingham. Released in the United States for Christmas, 1965, it received mixed reviews. Lean's *Lawrence* nemesis, the *New York Times*'s Bosley Crowther, concluded that "all these characters. . .are but characters in a sad romance that seems almost as far away from Russia as the surging revolution seems from them. They are as fustian and sentimental as the music of Maurice Jarre. . . . They are closer to Hollywood than to the steppes."

Omar Shariff recalled that *Zhivago,* initially intended for premiere in March 1966, suffered from being hastily edited. Its initial release, like *Lawrence,* was not really a "Director's Cut": "I sat with David through the cutting of *Zhivago* because he had to do it very fast, and he was bored. . . . He cut it very badly to start with . . . . It had very bad notices, and was a commercial flop—for two weeks! He had been forced to [cut] it in a month—the whole thing—because he wouldn't let anyone touch it while we were shooting. So on the opening night in New York, it was a disaster. The audience hated it, critics hated it.

"I remember sitting at four in the morning at Studio 21 in New York with David, and he was smoking out of a cigarette holder, and all of a sudden he said, 'Omar, I know! I cut it all wrong!' He was not depressed at all. We went back. He recut the whole film, and sent the copies out, cinema by cinema. It started going up and up—people started going, going, going—and it became a huge hit—it became one of the biggest hits in cinema history."

Zhivago was indeed an immense popular success. It cost $15 million to make, and soon earned $43 million:

more than half that of Fox's *The Sound of Music*—the biggest film of the decade—and twice that of *2001: A Space Odyssey,* MGM's second largest film of the 1960s. Not before 1977 would an MGM film surpass David Lean's *Doctor Zhivago* in first-run income!

Lean's 1989 biographer, Stephen Silverman, observed that *Zhivago*'s eventual gross of more than $200 million is—on an inflation-weighted basis—"outranked only slightly by *Gone With the Wind, The Sound of Music, E.T.,* and *Star Wars.*"

Kwai, which had cost Columbia $2.9 million, made $15 million initially—a staggering 5:1 ratio — and thus Lean's "most profitable" film ever. *Lawrence,* in contrast, cost $13 million and earned $16.5 million during the 1960s: it was Columbia's sixth-highest income film of the decade. Sharif claimed that Lean made little from *Lawrence,* but "he made a lot of money on *Zhivago* because he had a very strong contract—his fortune was made on *Doctor Zhivago.*"

Zhivago also was successful at the Academy Awards. Maurice Jarre, Freddie Young, and John Box (with Terry Marsh and Dario Simoni) again won Oscars, with Jarre's "Lara's Theme" literally sweeping the planet. Phyllis Dalton won a well-deserved Academy Award for Costume Design that significantly affected the fashion business: her design for Zhivago's winter greatcoat was that year's "in" look. Robert Bolt also won his first Screenplay Oscar, and would repeat the next year for *A Man for All Seasons. Zhivago*'s Lara—Julie Christie—won as Actress, but for John Schlesinger's *Darling.* Other *Zhivago* nominations were for Picture; Direction; Supporting Actor, Tom Courtenay; Sound; and Film Editing.

David Lean's next film, *Ryan's Daughter* (1970), starred Sarah Miles, Robert Mitchum, Trevor Howard, Christopher Jones, John Mills, and Leo McKern. Produced by Anthony-Havelock Allen, Lean used writer Robert Bolt—then married to Sarah Miles—together with Freddie Young, Maurice Jarre, and Eddie Fowlie. The film was made mainly in Northern Ireland, and filmed in 70mm. Lean had not been pleased with the use of 35mm—blown up to 70mm for projection—in *Zhivago.*

Omar Sharif commented: "*Ryan's Daughter* came out, and was savaged. I had seen it. David and I met in Rome, and went to dinner. He said, 'Omar, what did you think of it?' And I said, 'I'll tell you frankly, David. It's a wonderful film. It's got one big problem.'

"He said, 'What?'

"I said, 'It's too big for the story. That's all.' "

"And he thought, and he said, 'Omar, you're absolutely right.'

"And I said, 'It's all right to make a huge film about Lawrence, about Zhivago. But the little village school teacher and the little girl, it should have been a smaller film, somehow. They resented the scope, although it was wonderful – those scenes, the storms – great cinema.' "

Steven Spielberg also proffered an analysis: "David Lean suddenly made a movie which, at least in America, was a little behind the times. . . . In the early 1970s, we were very much into *Woodstock,* and *Easy Rider,* and low-budget movies were coming out, and there was a whole new wave of independent filmmaking in the States. And, suddenly, this warhorse of a classic movie comes out, which is very much like an old romantic novel, in a way almost like a Harlequin novel. "And the critics just felt it was out of step with the drummer that was beating away . . . in the States. I really don't feel that way. I think there's some very strong things in the movie, but it's not my favorite David Lean picture. "I think he was knocked unfairly."

Melvyn Bragg told Lean in 1985 that "an overall feeling of the [London] critics was that it was a small story, a modest story, that had been, using a cliché, 'pumped up' too much."

Lean replied, "That may well be true. But they don't have to *hammer* me for it. At worst, I made a mistake. And, you know, it ran at the Empire [first-run West End London cinema] for over a year. Not bad."

Bragg recalled that there was a particular savaging of *Ryan's Daughter* and Lean. The director was the invited guest of the National Society of Film Critics at a luncheon at the Algonquin Hotel in New York, just after the film came out. Lean remembered: "Oh, yes. . . . I sensed trouble from the moment I sat down. And Richard Schickel started off by saying, 'Mr. Lean, could you please explain to us how a man who directed *Brief Encounter* could come up with a piece of shit like *Ryan's Daughter?*'. . .and it carried on from there. And, you know, they're very good with their tongues, and I was there for about two hours. And . . . they just took me to bits! And in the end I remember saying, 'I don't think you ladies and gentlemen will be satisfied until I do a film in 16mm and in black-and-white.' And Pauline Kael, of *The New Yorker,* said, 'No, you can have color.'

"And that was the end of it. Horrible. It really quite had an awful effect on me. For several years. In fact, I didn't want to do a film again. . . . I thought, 'Why on earth am I making films? I don't have to.' And I didn't

for a bit. It shakes one's confidence, you know, terribly. I find it very difficult directing movies. One's awfully easily shaken, you know."

Omar Sharif offered an opinion as to why David Lean had refused to go back to directing after *Ryan's Daughter,* why he hadn't simply admitted that it wasn't "perfection," and then gone back and directed something new "to perfection": "David Lean's problem – he had a dual problem. One was to keep up [his reputation]. He was terrified of that. And it was very difficult to find a subject that he liked and that was up to his level. You know – David told me himself – that there comes a moment in every artist's life when they do what they were born to do – the one thing. And from then on, he said, it's downhill. He didn't consider that *Lawrence* was perfection – at that time."

At the Oscar ceremonies that year, cinematographer Freddie Young received his third Academy Award for a David Lean film. And John Mills won as Supporting Actor for his portrayal of Michael, the village idiot. Sarah Miles was nominated for Actress, and Gordon McCallum and John Bramall for Sound.

The year 1970 also saw the cutting and re-release of *Lawrence of Arabia.* An additional 15 minutes were ruthlessly excised, reducing the film's length to 187 minutes. And, in 1966, a production error had occurred such that almost every subsequent theatrical, video, or television print for the next twenty-three years had a 10-minute reel reversed: camels went in the wrong direction and Lawrence's watch jumped to his right hand.

On September 20, 1972, on the Canadian Broadcasting Corporation's Canada-wide network, *Lawrence of Arabia* had its North American television premiere, sponsored entirely by General Motors. Even with limited commercial breaks in a four-hour time-slot, the heavily cut version could not begin to represent the film properly: with horizontal "panning-and-scanning" combined with slight cropping of the top and bottom of the picture, only about 50 percent of the 70mm frame area was visible. The viewer literally saw only about half of the film. For example, when Ali is seen arriving at the well, both Lawrence and his dead guide have mysteriously vanished off the sides of the screen!

Also in the fall of 1972, Freddie Young was elected the second Fellow of the British Academy of Film and Television Artists, following Sir Alfred Hitchcock. David Lean would join the ranks of BAFTA fellows in 1974. Sam Spiegel received the honor in 1984.

After *Ryan's Daughter,* Lean explained, "I didn't make

a film for fifteen years. Yes. I just travelled the world, and I tried to do another film, I tried to do *Mutiny on the Bounty*. I wanted to do the true story of it, because you know, the old film—good as it was with Charlie Laughton, you know—it was completely untrue. And I wanted to do the true story, which I think is even more exciting. . . . And it's a wonderful story.

"And anyhow, that fell apart, and it was done by somebody else. And I think we—Robert Bolt—my God, I think [it was] the best script we ever wrote. [Bolt, in fact, had a near-fatal stroke early in 1979, while the script was incomplete.]

"And I gradually thought, well—and *Ryan's Daughter* was really terrible—the reaction was really terrible, and I thought, 'What the hell am I doing?' You know, I'd made quite a bit of money, and I love traveling, I love taking photographs—I had a 16mm camera—I took thousands of feet all over the world, and I thoroughly enjoyed myself."

The director's reputation was not forgotten, however. In June of 1984, David Lean was knighted by Queen Elizabeth II. The previous year, 1983, RCA Columbia had finally released *Lawrence of Arabia* for home viewing, as "panned-and-scanned" videotapes and laser videodiscs.

Lawrence of Arabia's reputation doubtlessly played a factor in the ultimate success of David Lean's difficult quest to secure funding for his "comeback" film, *A Passage to India*. However, the director was probably unaware that his film's content was also influenced by T. E. Lawrence.

Biographer P. N. Furbank recalled that, in December 1923, *Passage* author E. M. Forster borrowed a copy of the "Oxford Edition" of *Seven Pillars*. Forster "had guessed instinctively that Lawrence's book would prove important to him" and "it proved to be so beyond ex-

By the 1970 re-release, the dark head was completely gone, in favor of a more traditional war-like symbol.

pectation." The book "astonished him, and supported him in a cherished belief that sensitiveness and introspection could exist side by side with vigour, heroism, and largeness of vision. . . .The book affected him not only as a man but as a writer. He wrote the final two chapters of *A Passage to India* under its influence, completing them, and the novel, in a burst of confident energy."

Produced by John Brabourne and Richard Goodwin, 1984's *A Passage to India* again used many of the "dedicated maniacs" who worked with Lean for three decades: Maurice Jarre, John Box, Winston Ryder, and Eddie Fowlie. With Robert Bolt not available, Lean wrote the screenplay, and would edit the film. And, with Freddie Young past eighty years of age, Ernest Day—Young's camera operator for *Lawrence*, *Zhivago*, and *Ryan*—became Lean's cinematographer. *Passage* starred Judy Davis, Victor Banerjee, Peggy Ashcroft, James Fox, Nigel Havers, and—once again—Alec Guinness.

A Passage to India was celebrated by the critics, with *TIME* devoting nine pages to a David Lean–*Passage* cover story. Almost apologetically, their film critic Richard Schickel would write: "[Lean] passed some of the ensuing years [after *Ryan*] in bitterness, wounded by reviewers who so often tend to listen to movies more intently than they look at them, thus missing much of [Lean's] special grace and subtlety."

Lean told Charlie Rose on "CBS News Nightwatch" that he felt a bit of redemption about *Passage to India:* "I felt I was just rather foolish. It must seem strange to you, but if you're a—I suppose an actor or director, you—the press means a lot. Because they're the only people who you think tell you the truth. Your friends will all be nice and say, 'I loved it,' etc., etc. But the press, there they are. And another thing—the power of print. There it is in black and white: 'It's absolutely horrible.' "

At the Academy Awards in 1985, Dame Peggy Ashcroft won as Supporting Actress in *Passage to India* and Maurice Jarre received his third Oscar for a Lean film. Other nominations were for Picture; Actress, Judy Davis; Cinematography, Ernest Day; Art Direction/Set Direction, John Box and Hugh Scaife; Sound, Graham Hartstone, Nicolas Le Messurier, Michael Carter, and John Mitchell; and Costume Design, Judy Moorcroft. Lean himself was nominated for three Oscars: Direction, Editing, and Screenplay.

Although Sir David Lean's last film had now been made, his reputation was to soar even higher: *Lawrence of Arabia* was about to be rescued from oblivion.

General Motors consented to very few, but extended, commercial breaks for the North American TV premiere of Lawrence, *shown across Canada in 1972.*

CHAPTER 9

RECONSTRUCTION AND RESTORATION

"THE MIRACLE IS ACCOMPLISHED."

—ALI TO LAWRENCE, AFTER TAKING AQABA

As a youngster, Robert A. Harris wanted to be an archaeologist or a detective. In a strange way, he would realize both ambitions: he became a film archivist and restoration expert.

Harris remembers, "I started the *Lawrence of Arabia* restoration project with a gentleman named Dennis Doph, who was heading up Columbia Classics at the time. Dennis said 'It's a terrific idea. I even thought of doing it myself at one point.' He suggested I start writing letters, so I did."

Harris wrote to Arthur Goldblatt, Vice-President of Columbia Cable, in early December 1986, noting that Lawrence, in his opinion, was "the finest production of the past 25 years. . .and may well be the finest ever. Seen today, there is absolutely nothing about it which dates it as an early 60s film. It is as fine a work today as it was when first released, and quite probably, even better."

"We soon received a phone call from Doph's immediate superior who said 'Great idea. [Columbia President] David Puttnam loves it. Can you have it ready for Cannes?' Cannes was in May of '87. I said 'I really don't know. I have to look at the materials.' Dennis checked with the vaults and was told 'that the original camera negative [corresponding to *Lawrence* as seen at the 1962 Royal Premiere] has never been touched, even though there had been different versions of the film. The protection elements (including the black-and-white separation positives) were never touched. And there are complete tracks, so there shouldn't really be a problem.'

"At that time I got total co-operation. They opened the vaults to me and started shipping material from around the world. I went down to Long Island City and examined the original camera negative, and the first thing I realized was that it *had* been 'cut' (i.e., sections had been removed). But I didn't know how badly. We shipped that out to Metrocolor Labs, who eventually did all the work on the film, an absolutely incredible and herculean job. What I determined after we made a 70mm work print of the camera negative was that the negative had not only

Finding the missing "goggles scene" would be a dramatic moment in the restoration of Lawrence of Arabia.

been cut once, but twice, because there were changes in it from not only the 1963 nationwide release version, but also from the 1971 reissue!

"At that time we also requested a set of continuity sheets on the 222-minute complete version. They didn't exist. We had no guidelines.

"I wanted to get in touch with David Lean, and the studio said 'No, we're going to handle this our way,' and David Puttnam apparently sent him a letter. The other person I was trying to find who I felt could have helped—and who I was *not* forbidden to get in touch with—was Anne Coates, who edited the picture, and received the Academy Award for it. I started calling around without success."

Anne Coates had cut films like *Tunes of Glory* and *The Ladykillers* in the late 1950s. If she were still alive, Harris imagined himself coming upon some little old, retired, blue-haired lady. He called Kevin Brownlow, whom he had aided in the restoration of *Napoleon,* in England, hoping that the historian might not only know where footage was hidden, but where people were hidden, as well. However, even Brownlow drew a zero in this regard. Anne Coates seemed to have disappeared off the face of the earth.

Meanwhile, Harris went through over 5,000 pages of correspondence and notes in his search for information and a surviving *original* theatrical [positive] print of the film. He was 99 percent certain that a set of 35mm matrices existed from which Technicolor imbibition prints could have been made at Technicolor London. However, either no prints were produced or, at least, are known to have survived.

"Marty Scorsese provided me with some leads in the search. One of his suggestions was Jon Davison (producer of *Airplane*). I got Jon on the phone at Laird Studios (the old Selznick Studios) where he was working on *Robocop*. He said, 'It sounds like a really exciting project. I love the film. I don't know of a long print, but is there any other way I can help?'

"I told him I was looking for the editor of the film, and that no one could find her. He said, 'Could you hold for a second?' He comes back and asks, 'Does the name Anne Coates mean anything to you?' Turns out she was in the next room cutting *Masters of the Universe*. Richard Anderson, *Lawrence's* sound restoration editor, was also located through Davison."

Anne called Harris back in about half an hour, perky and raring to go, asking how she could help. He mentioned his desire to get in touch with Sir David. "I think

Archivist Robert A. Harris, in his Mamaroneck, New York cutting room where Lawrence *was restored.*

he's in Spain this week," she replied. "Let me phone him." Harris expressed Columbia's misgivings about his contacting Lean directly, and she responded, "Well, I can get in touch with him."

"I told her that I had the 202-minute video version, and that I'd annotated the script with what was in that version, so I knew what was in the script that wasn't in the '202,' what was in the '202' that wasn't in the script, but *not* what had and hadn't been shot of the material that wasn't in the 202-minute version.

She asked, "Well, have you found the goggles?"

"Goggles?"

"Yes. The first shot in the film that you'll be missing is Lawrence's goggles, hanging from a branch." She began giving Harris leads, then said, "You know, it's been twenty-five years. You'll have to give me the night to think about this." The next day she called back with copious notes on the film.

It was now the middle of January 1987. A truck backed up to Harris's office door in Mamaroneck, New York. Inside were almost two tons of "material." Battered 70mm cans of all sizes. Little cardboard boxes, falling apart, and little rolls of film which had fallen out of them and collected in piles at the bottom.

"My assistant, Joanne Lawson, brought all of this in and started going through it and discovered that we had been shipped the 'trims' (the pieces of a take left over after the desired portions are used in the body of the film) and 'outs' (unused, alternative takes) of the 65mm negative–about 200,000 feet of it, and some of the corresponding raw dialogue sound tracks.

"We opened every can, annotating what was inside. When we found slate numbers on the images, we marked the outside of the cans. We went to column pads and started cross-referencing scene numbers and can numbers, trying to make some sense of it.

"Then we started going through the boxes of trims. We found some trims that were black and white (B&W) and mute. And in one box there were B&W trims with sound tracks on them. I had unrolled bits and pieces of the B&W images I didn't recognize at all. The way trims are stored, wound one layer inside the next, some only five or ten frames long, you can be sitting there with five hundred different pieces of film all wrapped around one another. It can get messy. So we had everything in the cutting room coated with black velvet.

"I went back up to my place with my partner, restoration co-producer Jim Painten, who was visiting the East Coast at that time. It was eleven at night and we were sitting there, and I said, 'Wait a minute. If there are B&W trims with soundtrack on them–'slash dupe,' made off the original color workprint . . . these could be the trims from the January '63 version.' So in the middle of freezing January we got in my car, drove back down to Mamaroneck, put a few of these B&W pieces up on the flat bed, and what did we find? The goggles!

"Ninety percent of the B&W dupe footage had no sound on it. Eventually, we found about half of the twenty minutes of deleted scenes. We could have used this for restoration if we'd had to, but it was dirty, and B&W, the one thing you wouldn't want to use. But at least we had it."

Meanwhile, Anne Coates had gotten in touch with Lean, who told her, "Of course I want it to be restored, if it can be restored. You know the way they kept hacking away at it, I'm afraid the rats have gotten to it." In reference to Puttnam's letter, he responded that he hadn't been there to receive it, and was only now heading home. Harris should call him Tuesday.

Suddenly it all became a bit too real for Harris. "David Lean is kind of akin to God. Nonetheless, I called, and was informed that he'd left London and was now in Los Angeles. I stopped and thought, 'This guy's eighty years old, he's scouting locations in Spain, he stops in England for a change of clothes, and takes off for Los Angeles . . .'

"I called him in L.A. A woman answered and I gave her my name. She connected me immediately because Anne Coates had already spoken to him. I was scared to death at this point. And the next thing I heard was Sir David Lean saying 'Hello, Bob, how are you? Thank you so much for calling!' And I figured, this wasn't going to be bad.

"We were on the phone for a half hour, went over a lot of things, and he said when I was ready he would come out. He wanted to 'fine cut' the film, something he'd apparently never gotten to do. He explained that they were still doing 2nd Unit photography up through the middle of October of '62, and there was an opening set for the Queen on December 9. So in six weeks, after the final inserts and reshoots–though they'd been working on it all along–they had to do as close to a fine cut as possible, final dubs, foreign versions . . . It never really got into what he considered perfect shape. So when it opened at 222 minutes, there was a little fat on it. All through the film there were scenes that ran five or ten frames too long–not so long that the average viewer would have noticed, but–cumulatively–the pacing was affected. He had hoped to trim it after the London premiere but, as he tells it, Sam Spiegel came to him and said 'Baby, if we can take twenty minutes out this thing, we'll really have something.'"

In December of 1962, *Lawrence of Arabia,* at 222 minutes, was exactly the same length as *Gone with the Wind.* Lean felt it should have been 217 to 218 minutes, with his careful trims, but industry pressures precluded its going that route. Instead, he was forced to quickly cut out approximately twelve minutes–lopping out entire scenes rather than trimming them–because they were about to start making 35mm prints. Then Spiegel took out another eight minutes that Lean hadn't approved. All of these twenty deleted minutes should have been trimmed, rather than chopped.

Lean told Harris he was going back to New York the following week to stop in and see Kate. "As in Hepburn?" Harris asked. Lean suggested they arrange to meet after that.

Harris was anxious to show Lean a rough cut of the film. A major problem facing him was the lack of original sound track for the restoration. When he had requisitioned all of the tracks, he had found that no tracks had survived from the premiere version. The junking had occurred in 1975. Until then, all of the original mixing elements had survived, all of the original music, all of the original dialogue, and all of the original effects. Some 600,000 feet of it.

All of it was now gone.

"The other thing we couldn't find were the original color negative deletions from January '63. The goggles, etc. All of them would have fit into two little thousand-foot cans. We called back London, but the vaults had been cleared out. We had a serious problem.

"And everyday, several times a day, we were being questioned by Dennis Doph and by Loretta Savery, a most interested and helpful Columbia exec. They were anxious to get it ready.

"It was time to methodically begin the reconstruction. I pulled the 35mm B&W trims of the goggles first. I figured we'd start from the beginning and build it as we went along. We had the B&W dupe of the original footage with the track on it. I felt that for several of the scenes, such as this one, we might be able to rebuild it with trims and outs."

Joanne Lawson had gone through *every* piece of 65mm negative, compiling a master list which matched slate numbers and scene numbers with can numbers.

Harris continued:

"So I went into a can and found the slate and beginning of the shot with the goggles, and the end of the shot. All we needed was twelve feet of goggles moving around on a branch a little bit, so this was an easy one. We matched these edge numbers against the original negative. There had only been one take, but there was sixty feet of it.

"The next scene we needed was a shot of a bust of Lawrence in the crypt at St. Paul's. We had it in B&W—the camera pulls back from a close-up until you can read the legend at the bottom: 'T. E. Lawrence. 1888–1935.' We found the slate at the start of the scene, part of the close-up, and the tail of the scene, which was already fully pulled back: we could not find the scene itself. I considered starting with the close-up and doing a long, six- or eight-foot dissolve into the tail of the shot, so that it is long enough to establish what the shot originally told us.

"What we were looking for next was a shot of Anthony Quayle and another actor playing a cleric, discussing whether Lawrence really belonged in St. Paul's. We found the slate and a tail trim. Nothing usable. But we also found an alternate take, which had raw dialogue. If we could find the negative or the alternate, I figured we'd be all right.

"But that didn't necessarily follow, for when we had received the negative, we hadn't gotten all the cans. Some were missing. Some had been combined. Looking in a can where it might have been, I found more material on the goggles. Another take? I put a 65mm core on the rewinds, started winding it off and suddenly, through my white-gloved hand that I was running along the edges of the film, I felt something . . . a splice. I looked down, and it had cut from the goggles to a close-up of the bust. I rolled down a little more, and the camera's pulling back, and I hit another splice. And it's a reverse angle of Anthony Quayle and the cleric.

"Sometimes you're in a situation where your adrenalin starts pumping and the hair on the back of your neck stands up. *I realized that this was the missing negative.* Someone had put it in with the discarded trims as though it had never been in the original 'premiere version' film negative in the first place."

The restoration proceeded. Every night, Harris drove to an underground archival vault in Greenwich, Connecticut, where he would store each newly found piece of lost footage from *Lawrence of Arabia*. The vault had been specifically built to preserve magnetic computer records for some of the large corporations in the area, and it suited his needs for proper humidity, temperature, and safety.

Columbia Pictures hadn't been as careful. Harris had examined the camera negative, and it was warped, dried, and the splices were starting to open. He knew, too, that it was fading, or changing, as color film materials do. It was twenty-six years old. The negative was in Eastman color, and when Eastman color negatives deteriorate the yellow component of the negative is the first to fade.

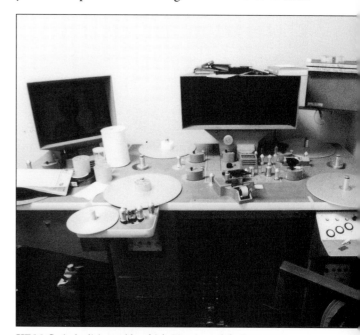

KEM flatbed editing table which Harris used for Lawrence.

This means that when the negative is printed, the black and shadows shift to blue. To correct for this, more yellow must be 'pumped' into the print, which corrects the blacks but gives the print an overall yellow cast. The first print Harris saw off the negative was extraordinarily yellow. He was now concerned about his chances of saving the film at all.

About two weeks before Harris was to go out to the West Coast for the actual restoration phase of the project, Lean visited him at his Mamaroneck office. "He was sitting at my flatbed looking at the film and saying, 'Now, watch this! That is bloody good, you know. It works.' "

Lean had not seen *Lawrence* in twenty-five years, and was unaware, until that moment, just how extensively his film had been mutilated by studio indifference and time. He committed himself fully to the project, and looked forward to finally making the Director's Cut, which the pressures of time had originally prevented him from doing. But first it had to be restored to its 1962 length.

Harris's plan had always been to restore the film at his own cost, with Columbia picking up the expenses. He would do it as a joint venture, splitting prints and advertising, and profits, fifty-fifty. "At some point, a few days before we were to go West to make a print, someone at Columbia decided that they didn't like the deal they had made. I guess they figured (and this is off the top of my head) why should they, for several hundred thousand dollars, give up 50 percent of the profits on the back end. So they had one of their people throw a killer deal point in at the last minute—basically that we would share in revenues for an extraordinarily limited period of time, even though we were putting up half the money. In late February/early March of 1987, after Lean had already visited the Mamaroneck offices and given his blessing to the project, the deal fell apart."

Over the next few weeks Harris had everything annotated, packed, and shipped back to Columbia's vaults in Long Island City. "They called back and offered to buy our services for a minimal amount, which was a joke considering the amount of labor that was going into it."

Martin Scorsese and Steven Spielberg, both avid advocates of film preservation, were not thrilled that the project was heading toward litigation, and the film toward oblivion. Columbia President Puttnam approached Lean at Cannes and asked him how he was, which was the wrong way to start a conversation at that time, since Lean was not at all happy.

Scorsese later put in a call to Puttnam, who found that some of the information that had gotten to him had been less than accurate. Puttnam agreed to move the project forward, but it wasn't long before he started running into his own problems at Columbia.

Harris speaks of it now without malice. "The project was absolutely dead in the water. They couldn't do it on their own since they didn't know anything about what the picture was supposed to be. All they had were several tons of materials: they would have had to go back to step one. My concern was that if we went through legal channels, it could be five years before anything happened, and then it would be a pyrrhic victory. The negative would be gone."

Scorsese and Spielberg interceded with Dawn Steel—Columbia's new President—on Harris's behalf, but his attorneys in L.A. wanted to continue the litigation further and further into the legal morass. "They felt we could make millions this way, but I opted to have the film put together again. I went in and negotiated the deal with Beth Berke, Columbia's attorney. It wasn't a great deal. Columbia knew how much we wanted to get it done, which was part of their power. But in the end Dawn was fair. There was minimal studio interference."

Once Harris relocated to the West Coast, in March 1988, Anne Coates came in as supervising picture editor. The running joke about her was that she had a lifetime contract with Sam Spiegel: everytime something was done with *Lawrence of Arabia* she was on call. It was rumored that, if a local TV station wanted to make a cut, they had to bring her in.

"This time around," remembers Harris, "we had to move very carefully, frame by frame. We'd get one scene done in a day, sometimes only part of a scene. Slowly but surely we got the material together. Once we had the missing picture protected and then printed, we pulled some of the alternate sound takes, had them 'dubbed' and 'coded,' and tried to fit them together. Some of the tracks just didn't work, and for some scenes alternate dialogue didn't survive. We were forced to go back to the actors to have them redub their dialogue.

"When my L.A. assistant Jude Schneider called Anthony Quinn's office and made the request, one of his assistants said, 'That's not a problem, I'm sure he'll do that for you . . .What picture was this again?' Jude said, 'Lawrence of Arabia.' She seemed startled, 'You mean the one from 1962 . . .?' Jude told her this was the case, and she replied, 'You know we get requests in here sometimes six months, even a year later for changes for television or something. But you want him to come back after twenty-six years to do dialogue?' Jude said, 'Yes.' There was a pause, then she came back on and said, 'How's 2:00 P.M. Friday?'

"Quinn was leaving for Europe in 48 hours, but was kind enough to give us an hour in a studio in New York to do his lines. We sent him the footage on video tape, and the dialogue, and twenty-six years later he was absolutely perfect. He did his dubbing for scale, as did everyone else.

"In the same scene we also needed Arthur Kennedy, but we couldn't find him. We had somebody go through Quinn's Rolodex because we knew they had worked together on a number of pictures. No luck. We went through the Screen Actors Guild and all of the other unions, and finally someone thought he was in Savannah, Georgia. Jude checked every Arthur Kennedy in that part of Georgia, and left messages on their machines. Finally, the real Arthur Kennedy returned our call. Jim Painten flew to Savanah with three-quarter-inch cassette of the footage, and Kennedy's dialogue was recorded at a TV studio."

In the forties Kennedy was known as an extremely technical actor capable of saying his lines perfectly again and again. And he was the one character in *Lawrence* whose dialogue could be lifted from one take to another with minimal fussing. Had most of the tracks not been junked, Harris wouldn't have had to find him.

The other people needed were Peter O'Toole and Alec Guinness, and Charles Gray, who was going to dub the late Jack Hawkins's lines as Allenby. "Their dubbing was done in London with David Lean overseeing the session."

O'Toole, recalling that his entire career had followed *Lawrence,* commented wryly, "Now I know how to read the lines."

Once all this material was together, Lean came to Los Angeles. The film was now 223 minutes long, a little longer than it had ever been before. For two weeks they cut and remixed parts of the picture, trimming those shots and scenes that Lean had never gotten to, rearranging shots to clear up character motivations, and so forth.

An example: In one scene, Anthony Quayle comes out of the top hatch of an armored vehicle, holding a pistol. When he goes to cock it, it doesn't work. Finally he cocks it again and it works. Lean felt that many old British films started scenes a minute and a half before they should have started and ended them a minute and a half after they were over, as if someone had simply left the camera running. It was something he used to talk to

Hitchcock about, and it was something he didn't want to occur in *Lawrence*. In the restored version, Quayle cocks the pistol, fires, and we cut to the flare in the sky.

"In doing trims like that we lost about 6 1/2 minutes. Not only is the pace tighter now, but you can actually understand the narrative better.

"When we went to reel 2A to start making trims, David pointed out that the image was flipped, left-to-right. All of the existing TV and video cassette versions were backwards before 1989 because Technicolor made an error back in 1966 when they created a 35mm master interpositive from which everything else was duplicated. The entrance into the desert—ten minutes of the film—was reversed, with no writing on screen to enable anyone to catch the mistake. Only *Lawrence* diehards realized that O'Toole's watch had jumped to his right wrist and that the camels were all marching in the wrong direction.

"Before we could print, Metrocolor technicians had to check every splice in the film and reinforce hundreds of them that were coming apart. For shots that had ripped, we had to go back to alternate takes, or have cans shipped in and have the material retimed [color corrected] and recut."

In some instances where the original camera negative had been torn, Harris went back and remade as many as two or three shots in a row from the black and white separations. The scene where Dryden and Lawrence leave Murray's office and enter Dryden's, up to the point where Lawrence rolls up his sleeve (Criterion CAV laser disc, side one, chapter 4, frames 25605-27352), was all restored from dupe material. Likewise, in the beginning of reel seventeen, there is an entire fifty-foot shot which had to be reconstructed from the separations.

"The soundtracks, no matter how good they were, were 1962 tracks. The original four-track would not run: the oxide kept flaking off and clogging the heads. So what we ended up using as our original was actually fourth-generation track elements, from which we made a new, fifth-generation dub encoded with Dolby A to suppress the noise. We also added real surround channels, where there had only been token surround information before, for sound effects such as the train.

"For the missing pieces, once we had the dialogue, we had to change the harmonics so that the actors' voices sounded as they had in 1962. In addition, we needed effects and 'foley.' So one evening, one of the dialogue editors and I went into a foley studio. He did Arthur Kennedy and I did Alec Guinness. The footsteps, the

206

rustling of the robe, the closing of the watch (which was actually two wrenches striking together). We mixed sound for a couple of weeks straight."

Finally, almost a year and a half after the project had begun, a near-complete 'work print' was to be screened for Dawn Steel at Columbia. This print was not yet color corrected, and still had both dupe and original sections with scratches. Six-channel Dolby Spectral Sound—normally on magnetic strips on the both edges of the 70mm film—was to be run on a separate, synchronized 'double-system.'

Since David Lean was unhappy about using the relatively small screen at Columbia, Steel arranged for a special showing, on Friday, May 6, 1988, at the Samuel Goldwyn Theatre of the Academy of Motion Picture Arts & Sciences. The studio closed, all employees were bussed to Beverly Hills, and a lavish buffet was held before the screening. Sir David Lean also attended, along with *Lawrence*-enthusiast Steven Spielberg.

Ironically, it was Sam Goldwyn who had once served as judge in a dispute between David O. Selznick and Louis B. Mayer over *Gone With the Wind,* which Mayer

RESTORING *LAWRENCE*

I had begun the restoration of *Lawrence of Arabia* because I wanted to see it, complete and in proper form. I had always felt that it was the finest film ever made—the pinnacle of motion picture art.

In April of 1988, over two years into the project, as we neared the conclusion of the restoration phase, a second test screening was held at Todd-AO in Hollywood to evaluate on a large screen the most recent materials added to the film and to also check sound synchronization of our 70mm work print. As David Lean readied himself for the short drive to Seward Street, my good friend Ron Haver, responsible for the restoration of George Cukor's *A Star Is Born,* arrived at our cutting room at Warner Hollywood. Although no one from Columbia had officially seen our restoration, it had not been produced in secrecy, and word was filtering out as to what it was and how it looked. After introducing him to David, Ron pulled me aside.

"I've something to tell you, that I couldn't until now," he said.

I waited for his comment.

"Several years ago, a couple of Hollywood's finest technicians decided that they'd like to attempt the restoration of *Lawrence*. They decided that it couldn't be done."

Trying for humor I answered, "It's a miracle then!"

The fact is that the restoration of *Lawrence* is very close to a cinematic "miracle". Everything was against our succeeding. But somehow the Fates were in our favor, and it all came together.

The Eastmancolor film stock was near the end of its life. The audio materials were rotting. The fragile layers of film with their microscopic bits of silver and dyes had been tucked away decades before in rusting tin cans, like so many urns of grain in an ancient tomb. The "miracle" was in the fact that those grains of silver, like millennia-old wheat thrown to the wind, could be exposed to the light once again, and Freddie Young's masterful images, painted with sunlight long ago, would be freed to rise anew to prove what the words "epic" and "cinematic masterpiece" had meant. Through the untiring work of many people on the *Lawrence* restoration, new materials would be created which would summon the like of *Los Angeles Times* critic Sheila Benson to speak of *Lawrence* as "The seventh wonder of the cinematic world."

Had I brought about a "miracle"? Certainly not. What I had been given was an honor akin to walking up to that newly-discovered tomb, and turning the elaborate key to unlock the gates through which the grains of wheat would fly and grow yet again. To me, today, the opportunity to see *Lawrence* properly projected on an epic-sized screen is worth everything that went into its restoration. To know that it is preserved for future generations gives me the greatest of pleasures. Ultimately, for anyone who truly loves film, to view *Lawrence of Arabia* is a humbling as well as an exhilarating experience.

Robert A. Harris

insisted was too long to release. Goldwyn was asked "How long should a picture be?" His reply: "As long as it's good!"

When the screening began, those not familiar with the film wondered where the picture was when Jarre's distinctive overture started. Then the spectacular 70mm Columbia logo – specially painted back in 1962, and the last piece of negative to be found – appeared and "literally leapt off the screen" to cheers from the audience.

Three hours and thirty-eight minutes later, it was evident that the film was an astounding success. Steel offered Harris congratulations, gave him complete approval and authority for him to carry out the final phases of the restoration, formerly announced that the film in fact would really be distributed, and officially approved release of *Lawrence*-related press material.

The next week, David Lean – back in London – was interviewed by NBC "Today" show's Jim Brown. The director remarked "I saw *Lawrence* the other day at the Academy – it's better than the original print. I'm very happy."

He later wrote to Steel:

May 12, 1988
Dear Dawn,

A line to thank you very much for your generous welcome and hospitality. . . . Not many directors see their twenty-five-year-old dreams brought so vividly back to life. Columbia set me off on the big time with *River Kwai*. You and Columbia have completed the circle. I hope it brings you some prestige and *money!*

David

After the screening, Harris set about making final changes and ordering new material to replace dupes or torn negative. He then put in a lab order that a 65mm 'preservation interpositive' be printed off the reassembled original negative. This 'interpositive' – a low-contrast, fine-grain, positive color print – is used to create a small number of duplicate negatives. It is these which are used to produce the positive 'prints' which are distributed to cinemas. This strategy prevents wear and tear on the original negative.

"As they began to produce the interpositive," Harris recalled with horror, "all of the splices started opening, the perforations began failing, and the negative surface started cracking up: it was starting to fall apart. We were down to the final weeks of life of the negative: it was starting to fall apart. *The negative started self-destructing*.

"There were very few rolls of negative that successfully produced an interpositive the first time through.

"One of the reasons that the original negative was in such bad shape, was that in the 60s, 70s, and even the early 80s the duping stocks were so bad that they had used the original negative to make theatrical prints. The negative had been run through a printer over 220 times."

Harris was forced to decide – in each case – whether to go to the separations, an alternate shot, or a trim piece, to replace the damaged material. What should have taken another week, took four more agonizing months.

Finally, in September 1988, the restored 'Director's Cut' of *Lawrence of Arabia* effectively existed.

Sir David Lean's lost masterpiece was ready to return to the cinema.

CHAPTER 10

PREMIERES, REVIEWS AND VIDEO: 1989

"AND SURELY THE FUTURE SHALL BE BETTER FOR THEE THAN THE PAST."

—SELIM, RECITING KORAN IN FEISAL'S TENT

In the September issue of *Premiere* Magazine, a quiet announcement informed its vast audience that *Lawrence of Arabia* had undergone a lengthy and costly restoration.

Three months earlier, on December 14, Dawn Steel, Steven Spielberg, Martin Scorsese and AFI Director Jean Firstenberg gathered in Manhattan. On behalf of Columbia Pictures and the American Film Institute, they formally announced the restoration's completion and the gala premieres in New York, Washington, and Los Angeles, which would benefit the AFI's Preservation Fund 1989 to the tune of some $500,000. Steel suggested that, following the premieres, the film would have only a limited commercial run in the three cities.

Spielberg recalled that *"Lawrence of Arabia* was the first film I saw that made me want to be a moviemaker. It was in Phoenix, I was thirteen or fourteen at the time, and it was overwhelming." He had since—he guessed—seen the film at least thirty times. Scorsese commented that seeing *Lawrence* was "one of the great cinema experiences—seeing the curtains open, hearing the overture, and then being in the presence of a masterwork."

Robert A. Harris—praised by Steel—observed that

TRIVIAL PURSUITS

F.Y.I.

LENGTH OF THE ORIGINAL "LAWRENCE OF ARABIA" (1962): 222 MINUTES

LENGTH OF THE 1971 REISSUE OF "LAWRENCE OF ARABIA": 187 MINUTES

LENGTH OF THE 1989 REISSUE OF "LAWRENCE OF ARABIA": 218 MINUTES

TIME IT TOOK TO FILM THE ORIGINAL "LAWRENCE OF ARABIA": 18 MONTHS

TIME IT TOOK TO RE-EDIT AND RESTORE THE ORIGINAL: 19 MONTHS

Premiere *magazine coyly informs readers of* Lawrence *restoration.*

Lawrence was "the most expensive, extensive, and difficult film restoration ever attempted" and described some details of the intricate processes involved.

LONDON

One week before the New York announcements, another *Lawrence of Arabia* premiered in London! In celebration of the centenary of the British hero's birth, the largest-ever exhibition of T. E. Lawrence memorabilia had opened on December 9 at the National Portrait Gallery near Trafalgar Square.

Organized by NPG curators Robin Gibson and Honor Clerk—who initially had no knowledge of the film's ongoing restoration—the exhibition included some 400 photographs, drawings, paintings, letters, manuscripts, and items of dress. Highlights included the famed Augustus John oil portraits of Lawrence; paintings of T.E.L.'s associates—Emir Feisal, Ali ibn el Hussein, General Murray, Field Marshal Lord Allenby, Shaw, Forster, Hardy, and Churchill; cameras, robes, head cloths, rings, rifles, maps, and daggers owned by Lawrence; everything from his schoolboy "knickers" to the Brough Superior SS 100 motorcycle on which he met his death. *Seven Pillars* "memorabilia" were displayed: the mapmaking pen used to write his epic; the manuscript

World premiere of restored film, New York. From left: Peter O'Toole, Omar Sharif, Freddie Young O.B.E., B.S.C., Anne V. Coates, Jim Painten, Robert A. Harris, Martin Scorsese, Steven Spielberg, Columbia President Dawn Steel, Gene F. Jankowski, Sir David Lean.

itself; one of five extant "Oxford Editions"; original illustrations for the "subscriber's edition," and the copies originally belonging to King George V and Sir Winston Churchill.

Attendance at the three-month show was nearly 30,000. The beautifully designed and illustrated 250-page exhibition catalogue, *T. E. Lawrence*, written by Jeremy Wilson, sold almost 10,000 copies. A smaller version of the exhibition then ran for one month in Japan, with a total attendance of 75,000. Eleven thousand copies of the Japanese catalogue were sold.

NEW YORK

The world premiere of the restored *Lawrence of Arabia* was at 5 P.M., February 4, 1989, at the Ziegfeld Theatre on West 54th Street. The 1,200 seats of the Art Deco-styled cinema were full. In attendance were Sir David Lean and stars Peter O'Toole and Omar Sharif. Eighty-seven-year-old cinematographer Freddie Young had flown over from the United Kingdom on the Concorde. Perpetual *Lawrence* editor Anne Coates wore a rhinestone-studded Middle Eastern caftan for the occasion. Robert Harris, with restoration coproducer Jim Painten, was joined by Scorsese, Spielberg, and Steel.

AFI director Jean Firstenberg introduced the partici-

pants as they lined up in front of the theater's gold curtains. "We are in the midst of film history tonight," she exclaimed.

Martin Scorsese noted that "this is not a film that was made in 1925. It's not a movie no one has ever heard of. This film is a legend. It won Oscars. It has stars who have household names. And there are moments from this film that people associate with these stars. That a movie like *Lawrence* could have deteriorated so quickly. That is truly alarming."

Sir David looked at the massive screen and proclaimed, "This is what the movies should be shown on." He would later elaborate: "We've almost forgotten the impact of a big screen. The big films are disappearing. . . . A film like *Lawrence* is different. Whatever you think of it as a film, it's still a visual meal. I think that's worth $7. I think it's worth $10."

Then the lights dimmed and the overture began. So did the applause, which grew thunderous when "The Sam Spiegel–David Lean Production. ." appeared. There was also applause for the stars' credits—as well as an audible gasp when the words "And introducing Peter O'Toole as T. E. Lawrence" appeared.

At the black-tie dinner dance that followed at the Pierre Hotel, reporters sought out Lean, who remarked:

210

"Well . . .you could hear a pin drop all the way through it . . .Sylvester Stallone looked at Pete and me with admiration. I almost felt like a movie fan who was just there to observe Peter O'Toole and Sylvester Stallone looking at each other."

Lean, ecstatic at the film's reception, was unusually open. He explained that his admiration for the Lawrence myth went back to his schoolboy days. "It's that way with every Englishman. Lawrence was, to young English boys, the last word in exotic heroes. We saw pictures of him in that exotic dress and headgear. We heard Lowell Thomas sing his praises over the radio. But then Lawrence is an enigma, and I've always been fond of enigmas. I like 'flawed heros.' Perfection is dull. When I was a boy, I would pick on the most eccentric person in the room and study him."

Sir David commented indirectly on the infamous 1962 Crowther review: "In the early 1960s, remember, films were more outwardly emotional. By being unsentimental, we were accused of lacking humanity. You might actually say we were ahead of our time emotionally." He also addressed the censorship constraints of the 1960s: "We knew we had to treat the subject of Lawrence's homosexuality, but we had to be careful. If the studio thought I was doing a picture about a homosexual, they would have cut it to ribbons. In those days, the business was incredibly naive and backward. Frankly, I don't

AFI President Jean Firstenburg, Sir David Lean, and Sandra Cooke (later Lady Lean).

think the censors knew what we were getting at because we didn't underline it."

The director was candid about O'Toole's performance: "Peter was wonderful . . . I didn't ever have, really, two thoughts about it."

An interviewer retorted, "But you surrounded him with some journeyman actors: Alec Guinness, Jack Hawkins, Claude Rains, Anthony Quinn . . . ."

Lean replied: "Yes, but I don't think—put them all together if you wanted to—they could support Peter. And he certainly didn't need it. He was terribly keen on the part. And it was a pleasure to work with him."

Peter O'Toole's viewpoint was different: "Making the film was like a bull fight. I felt like a toreador. I was in the ring, and every few minutes they opened the trap and out popped another bull: Hawkins . . .Rains . . . Guinness . . .Ferrer . . .Quinn . . .Kennedy . . .Quayle."

Finally, once again, the question of "length" was raised. Lean's observation suggested that three decades of ambivalence had finally been put to rest: "God knows," he admitted, "*Lawrence of Arabia* is a *long* film, but I don't apologize for it. I mean people go to the opera for five hours, don't they?" He even joked: "I said to someone the other day, the ideal for a theater owner is to have a masterpiece that's a half hour long. Twelve shows a day and make a fortune."

"Lawrence" and "Ali," 27 years later, celebrate the restoration.

Dawn Steel's comments closed the celebration: "I'm not about to compare *Lawrence of Arabia* with any of Columbia's upcoming titles. That wouldn't be fair. With this movie, you're talking about perfection—or about as close to it as you can get. You just don't get better than David Lean."

WASHINGTON

The next day, February 5, at Washington's 1,100-seat Cineplex Odeon Uptown Theater, Sir David Lean was joined by Omar Sharif, José Ferrer, Anne Coates, Freddie Young, and Bob Harris. Martin Scorsese, cochairman of The AFI's Preservation Fund 1989, represented the film institute. Lean received a standing ovation.

He later granted a two-hour interview to Charlie Rose of "CBS News Nightwatch," broadcast on February 9 and 10. CBS's "West 57th" also did an extended *Lawrence* segment on February 18.

LOS ANGELES

The restored film opened in Los Angeles at the Century Plaza 1 on February 12. By then, American newspaper coverage on *Lawrence*'s return was widespread and extensive. Reviews were invariably raves. In contrast to 1962's mixed critical reception, the film was now hailed as "the greatest epic of all time." It was the prime ex-

ample of "the way they used to make films." An era that, according to many, would never return. It was, to cinema notables, like Steven Spielberg, Martin Scorsese, Lawrence Kasdan, and countless others, quite simply, the film that changed their lives.

And it was the film that inspired some of the most literate and emotional film reviews of all time:

First love between a person and a film can be as intoxicating as first love between two people. It can mean just as much crazy behavior, just as many sleepless nights. As a young adolescent, I became so obsessed with a certain film that I saw it over and over, spent years studying the life of its hero, regarded

Above: Freddie Young—with famous "mirage lens"—and Robert Harris. Left: LA Premiere: Lean, Steel, Spielberg, Harris, Painten, Gregg Landaker (recording mixer for restoration) and Richard L. Anderson (Sound consultant for restoration).

Robert Harris with Restoration Assistant Joanne Lawson.

him as a kind of role model, and even dragged my family on to a long, dusty pilgrimage to a place where he had lived. If one measure of a film's greatness is its power to affect the lives of those who see it, then *Lawrence of Arabia* must be the best film I know.

...The sophistication with which David Lean directed...is easily eclipsed by the film's sheer excitement. The three-tiered soundtrack by Maurice Jarre (with themes for the British, the Arabs, and Lawrence himself carefully intermingled); the drollness of Robert Bolt's screenplay; the lushness of the Super Panavision cinematography: all these things contribute mightily to the film's magnetism. And at times when the material might founder in lesser hands...it is Mr. Lean's direction, adroitly weaving together music, scenery and the steely force of Lawrence's personality, that gives the film its transcendent power.

—Janet Maslin, *The New York Times,*
January 29, 1989

Lawrence of Arabia shows how ravishing films used to be. Critics revere it as cinema's greatest epic.... Lavish in visual beauty, the film also boasts economy

of style.... "The desert," says Lawrence, "is an ocean in which no oar is dipped." Lean and cinematographer Freddie Young translated that simile of the Saharan sea [sic] into screen poetry. They caught the wash of sand curling off the crest of a dune, the seaside effect of light shimmering over the parched expanse. When Lawrence finally treads in the surf of Aqaba...the sand is now water, and this miracle man can walk on both.

—Richard Corliss, *TIME,* February 6, 1989

The day before I [first] saw Lawrence [at age fifteen], I thought I wanted to be a surgeon. The day after, I knew I wanted to be a director. Whenever I want to see what great films used to be like, I watch *Lawrence. Lawrence of Arabia* twenty-five years later looks better and sounds better than any film that has been in theaters since *Lawrence of Arabia.*

—Steven Spielberg, *TIME,* February 6, 1989

This strange and great film, a colossally flamboyant mixture of pomp and neurosis, celebrates and deplores T. E. Lawrence...the tremulous classical scholar and Arabist from Oxford, translator of Homer, author of

Anne Coates celebrates the restoration in Middle Eastern caftan.

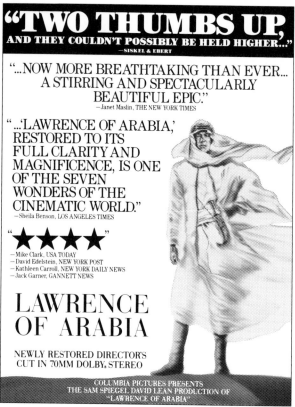

The restored "Director's Cut" of Lawrence of Arabia: *A triumph.*

the beautiful, rapturously egotistical biography *The Seven Pillars of Wisdom....* Lawrence imposed himself upon the imagination of an alien culture, turning himself into a lurid desert savior—great military hero, endurer of privations beyond measure, seeker of the Arab soul....With the restored passages...the joinings and partings that mark the stages of the journey across the desert are now clearer. Everything is clearer. Looking at the movie, you feel as if your eyesight had suddenly improved....The movie is an opening up to depths, and depths within depths....Lawrence is about conquering space; its great crossings and journeys become spiritual as much as physical feats.

—David Denby, *New York,* February 1989

There's a haunting irony in the sheer scale of the movie—all this blood, all this glory, rests on the slight, elegant shoulders of a self-invented English adventurer who ultimately recoils from the savagery he finds inside his own contradictory soul. In retrospect, it's the pivotal Hollywood epic: its stately, classical style looks back to the heroic adventure movies of the past, while its ambivalent subversive content anticipates such

future, antiheroic spectacles as *Apocalypse Now....* For almost four hours, the new *Lawrence of Arabia* reminds us of the transcendent power of the movies.

—David Ansen, *Newsweek,* Febrary 6, 1989

From the suppressed excitement in its overture to the last moments as that prophetic motorcyclist overtakes Lawrence's open car in the desert, David Lean's *Lawrence of Arabia,* restored to its full clarity and magnificence, is one of the Seven Wonders of the cinematic world. Nothing to come along since *Lawrence's* release in 1962 has diminished the power of cameraman Freddie Young's desert vistas. Stretched out in 70mm Super Panavision vastness, the movie's most pungent memory has lost nothing to time as a shimmering pinpoint in the center of the screen becomes clearer and clearer and can finally be read as a man, all in black, riding straight into the camera. It's still the greatest actor's entrance in movies, the one that launched Omar Sharif into American moviegoing consciousness.

—Sheila Benson, *Los Angeles Times,* February 15, 1989

Lawrence of Arabia is not just a great epic, but the greatest of movie epics. *Lawrence* is one of a mere handful of films that unquestionably deserve to be called great.

—William Arnold, *Seattle Post-Intelligencer*

Two thumbs up, and they couldn't possibly be held higher....I think the audience is waiting for this film. I know people who love this film in a very personal way. It may have been the first great big film that they really saw and loved. A film of ideas and greatness in size and scope. See it again. It's tremendous.

—"Siskel and Ebert," February 4, 1989

Four stars. The best film of 1989. *Lawrence* is one of the highest achievements of the filmmaker's art. It's glorious.

—Soren Anderson, *Tacoma News Tribune*

Four stars. Just go.

—Joe Leydon, *Houston Post*

The 1962 classic *Lawrence of Arabia* has been re-edited and re-released to theaters, and the majestic

Lobby cards, now a vanishing species, proliferated in the sixties. Auda and sword, Lawrence and whip, Lawrence shot, Lawrence and Bey: original German, hand-tinted, 1963 (11.5x9 inches). Lawrence and bodyguard: original French, 1963 (11.5x9 inches). Lawrence and Allenby: U.S., 1971 reissue (14x11 inches). Feisal on horse, Auda with clock, and Farraj with lemonade: recent Spanish (9.5x13.5 inches). Note "lemonade" picture is reversed.

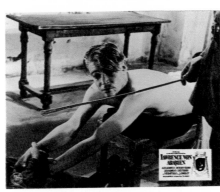

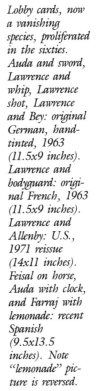

ACADEMY AWARDS

Best Picture of the Year
Sam Spiegel, Producer

Best Achievement in
Directing
David Lean

Best Achievement in
Cinematography
(Color Films)
Freddie Young

Best Music Score
(Substantially Original)
Maurice Jarre

Best Achievement in
Film Editing
Anne V. Coates

Best Achievement in
Art Direction
(Color Films)
John Box and
John Stoll

Set Decoration
(Color Films)
Dario Simoni

Best Achievement in
Sound
John Cox, Sound
Director, Shepperton
Sound Department

Right: David Lean's Oscar
for Best Director, pho-
tographed in his Thames-
side home.
Below: Sam Spiegel and the
Seven Oscars.

A new piece of artwork (right) was prepared in 1983 for the releases of the home videocassette (ad below) and the laserdisc (below right). This artwork retained the original "charging camels" motif, but updated the style of the portraits and included Sharif and Ferrer. However, Jack Hawkins (General Allenby) had mysteriously disappeared. He had somehow lost his role as a leading character in Lawrence promotional material, replaced by Donald Wolfit (General Murray). This was almost certainly a case of mistaken identity—by the artist.

Both the cassette and disc, of course, contained only an old panned-and-scanned cut version of the film. This artwork was never used again.

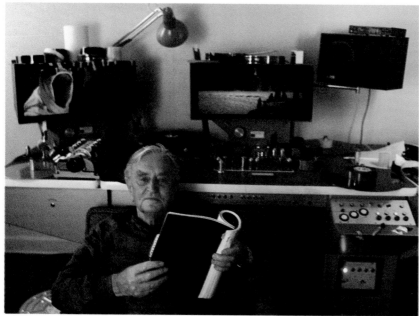

Above: In mid-1988, toward the end of his arduous two-year task, "restoration wizard" Robert A. Harris (right) received a distinguished visitor. Sir David Lean (center) spent three weeks with Harris in L.A., fine-tuning the restored film into his long-awaited "Director's Cut." "Not many films take 26 years to complete," commented Lean, I'm very, very happy."

Harris recalled: "David would always be [at the studeo] before me in the mornings. He'd be sitting on the stoop outside, and I'd drag myself up around 9:30 . . . They were worried about David being 80 years old, with this staircase up to the cutting room, but David would be up there before me. He'd look back down and say, 'What's taking you so long?' . . . David's wife Sandra was with him, and she took such good care of us. She was always grabbing the phone if it rang, so that we wouldn't have to run for it. And she'd always make sure we were fed. Great moral support."

"I remember once David said, 'Let's just cut that shot out.' And I said, 'But, it's one of the most gorgeous shots in the film. David, please!' He said, 'Too many gorgeous shots in the film. Don't worry about it.' By the way, that 'gorgeous shot' was later put back in, at the gentle urging of Richard Anderson, our sound consultant (at left, in top photo, opposite page). You know, he and Gregg Landaker, had to electronically alter our new voice tracks, so they'd sound like the actors' voices of 26 years ago.

"Another day, David said, 'I want to meet the man who's cutting my negative.' So we walked through the negative vaults into the cutting room where this poor guy is sitting there working, and David leans over his shoulder. The guy looks up, and David says, 'Quite all-right, carry on.' And you could literally see the color drain from the guy's face." – Robert Harris.

Opposite page, bottom: Lean at KEM flatbed editing table, L.A. 1988, referring to Harris's restoration notes. Left: Peter O'Toole, Sir David Lean, and "Lawrence-Editor-for-Life" Anne Coates at sound-dubbing session in London studio. At top, Peter, Anne, and Sir David look over script. At center, Lean and O'Toole watch restored scenes which require new voice tracks. At bottom, O'Toole re-dubs dialogue for the restored "Seduction" scene. Harris's L.A. assistant Jude Schneider had previously organized lip-reading experts to interpret the dialogue "spoken" on restored scenes with missing sound tracks.
Above: Sir David in Los Angeles, 1988.

Some of the restored scenes:

The entire thrilling sequence, about sixteen shots, of th[e] entry into Auda's huge camp at Wadi Rumm.

The entire fireside chat between Colonel Brighton and General Allenby, in Cairo. There, they discuss Lawrence's motivation and probable fate.

Most of the crucial "Seduction Scene," in Jersalem, wh[ere] Allenby persuades Lawrence to return to Arabia. Some [of] Allenby's lines were restored using alternate dialogue takes.

A powerful shot of slaughtered Arabs in the devastated village had been removed. Fowlie recalls dressing this set, to excess, with a disemboweled man, several blood-drenched women, and a real three-legged dog.

The shocking shot of Lawrence shooting a surrendering Turk during the "Bloodbath" sequence.

A detailed description, by Harris, of all the restored scenes can be found with the Criterion CAV laserdisc.

American poster accompanying the release of the restored version, 1989 (27x40 inches).

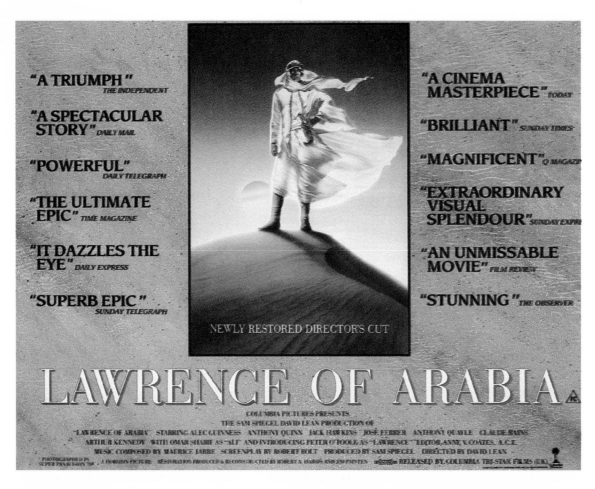

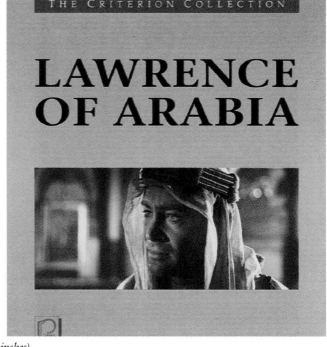

Top: British poster for restored version, 1989 (40x30 inches).
Bottom left: French poster promoting Premiere's 22-page tribute to the restoration, 1989 (16x22.5 inches).
Bottom right: Cover of Criterion CAV laserdisc set, 1989.

irony of David Lean's vision is more potent than ever. . . . Peter O'Toole as "El Aurens," Lawrence of Arabia, is one of the most indelible images of the postwar period. Lawrence appears in one scene after another, as fantasist, as great military leader, as Sun God, as driven sadomasochist, and finally, as nobody. . . . Experiencing the [old version of *Lawrence*] on video is the equivalent of lying on the floor of the Hall of Mirrors at Versailles and watching furniture slide across the marble and out the windows. . . . I can think of few complexly staged movies . . . in which the camera is so consistently ready—advancing, backing away, rising, sweeping—to reveal the essence of the action; few that keep a complicated individual and large historical forces so interestingly in focus; and perhaps none that produces as many images of frightening natural sublimity, so many scenes of landscape as spiritual alienation. Robert Bolt's screenplay—perfectly phrased and wittier than is commonly acknowledged—uses highly theatrical dialogue to suggest the self-conscious posturing of men grabbing at a chance to make history. . . . The meanings that come out of the huge and intimidating desert compositions are mostly strange and intimate. Lean, and his cinematographer Freddie Young, use the immense frame to draw us into depths, pulling us toward the distance, where something lies unrevealed, mysterious, in a state of becoming. . . . O'Toole brings to the role the kind of intellectual gaiety that Orson Welles brought to *Citizen Kane*. . . . As Lawrence seizes power, iron comes into O'Toole's voice; his gestures become larger. . . . Then, as control gives way, he shakes like a leaf. But the words are still exquisitely pronounced, with a trembling delicacy. Even as Lawrence is defeated, overwhelmed by the heart of darkness he discovers in himself, O'Toole recovers grace from savagery.

—David Denby, *Premiere*, February 1989

In addition to Denby's article, *Premiere*'s "Shot-by-Shot" feature in the same issue spotlighted a dramatic two-page center spread of a greatly enlarged 70mm film frame of Lawrence's triumphal entry into Auda's camp. Ironically, this sequence—which, as was noted by David Lean in 1962—was the first major deletion from the film.

Prior to the British premiere in May, the U.K. journals sent correspondents to view the Anglo-American masterpiece:

The tale is rich and the actors are talented. But it is the desert, astonishing in its reds and oranges and greys, its glorious rock formations and dunes shimmering like "an ocean in which no oar is dipped," that gives this epic its unparalleled hold on the imagination.

—*Economist*, February 18, 1989

Critics, who hailed Lawrence twenty-six years ago, are again falling all over themselves.

—*Daily Express*, February 23, 1989

Lawrence is my best film. . . . I love heroes and Lawrence is a hero, a flawed hero . . . therefore more interesting."

—Sir David Lean, *Daily Express*, February 23, 1989

John Hart of the *Seattle Times* observed the journalistic *Lawrence*-related frenzy and—a month after the film opened—he remarked:

The media response to the reconstructed 70mm version of David Lean's 1962 epic, *Lawrence of Arabia* is simply unprecedented for a theatrical reissue. Not even the much-ballyhooed fiftieth-anniversary re-releases of *Gone With the Wind* or Disney's *Snow White* have generated this kind of reaction.

Seeing the movie in its original 70mm glory is like going back to the days of the Cinerama and Todd-AO extravaganzas of the 1950s, before studios started cutting corners by dropping production of big-budget movies shot in crystal-clear fine-grain 70mm. . . . Commercially released 70mm films of the 1980s are simply blowups of 35mm negatives, unlike *Lawrence*, *Ben-Hur*, *Spartacus*, and *West Side Story*.

Hart quoted Robert Harris, "Most moviegoers under the ages of twenty-five or thirty have never really seen 70mm, and they're astonished at the difference."

The weekly "dollars-per-screen" at the first three venues skyrocketed, peaking at $68,000 during the premiere month. At New York's Ziegfeld Theatre, *Lawrence* almost equaled the performance of the previous year's hit, *Who Framed Roger Rabbit*. Columbia was bombarded with phone calls—including several from the authors—pleading that *Lawrence* receive wider distribution. On March 12, Columbia announced that the film would be released across the rest of the country. *Lawrence* crossed the border into Canada on St. Patrick's day.

More of the $40,000 70mm prints were struck, until sixteen cities in the United States and Canada were showing the film. One week in April 1989, *Lawrence* – in eight theaters – attracted weekly income of $35,000 per screen: five times greater than most contemporary box-office "hits" then showing nationwide. In mid-May, *Lawrence* was showing on sixteen screens. It ranked fifteenth on *Variety*'s North American poll: an amazing feat for a thirty-year old reissue.

GREAT BRITAIN

The United Kingdom Celebrity Premiere was on Sunday, 21 May 1989, at the Odeon Marble Arch, newly refitted with a special screen for the occasion. The critical reaction was overwhelming:

> Nothing is left to chance; everything is perfectly balanced. It is a fine example of what cinema should be – an interpretation of reality rather than a reflection.
> – Derek Elley, *Films and Filming,* May 1989

> *Lawrence of Arabia* was a marvel when it opened in 1962. Nowadays, because we know what it would take to make a movie like it, it seems almost a miracle.
> – Alexander Walker, *London Standard,* May 11, 1989

I cannot remember a film in which the cinematography was so crystal clear. Admittedly, the director of photography was the almost legendary Freddie Young, who couldn't put a lens wrong if he tried. The colours, the luminosity, the shimmering sands are all captured so perfectly by Young's camera that it is impossible to imagine anyone surpassing his brilliant work.
– Michael Darvell, *What's on in London,* May 24, 1989

The simplest response to this restored – 216 minute, 70mm – "Director's Cut" of *Lawrence of Arabia* would be to echo a British NCO's verdict on the capture of Aqaba: "Bloody marvelous, sir."... And what remains most surprising about the film is how...Peter O'Toole's performance manages to sustain the weight of narrative the film piles on him. Whether giggling like

a silly ass, preening himself in Bedouin robes, quivering with barely contained neurosis, or clenched with anger and self-contempt, this Lawrence is a superb amalgam of reality and legend: clown, charlatan, genius, hero. Yet O'Toole's talent serves as the focus for so many other outstanding contributions that Sir David would have every right to borrow the subtitle from *Seven Pillars,* and give his film a new name – *Lawrence of Arabia: A Triumph.*
– *Independent,* May 25, 1989

The images, shot in the lost splendours of 70mm, should make the home-video generation sit up and scream in amazement: "But we never knew cinema could be like this!" they will bleat hopelessly, as...Peter O'Toole's blazing blue eyes burn holes in our popcorn; or as the close-up of a lighted match...yields – in the most famous "cut" in cinema history – to a rouge desert sunrise as vast as time.
– David Robinson, *Financial Times,* May 25, 1989

Scrupulously reconstructed, skillfully put together, and beautiful to behold, *Lawrence of Arabia* is still the first genuine epic for adults, an intimidating film with a fascinating subject that marked the progression from the spectacular unintelligence of Cecil B. De Mille–

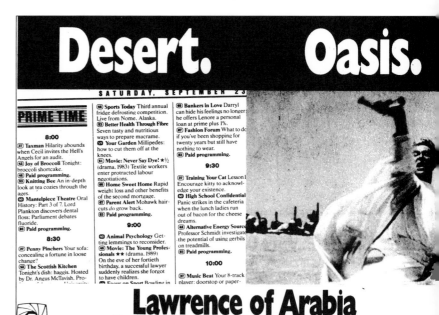

An innovative advertisement for the Canadian television premiere of the restored Lawrence of Arabia.

style extravaganzas to the intelligent spectacle of David Lean. . . .O'Toole himself is everything a leading man should be: handsome, sensitive, talented, charming. This was to be his finest four hours. . . .The film's other hero is the desert—or, at least, Freddie Young's brilliant photography of it. Typical of Young's skills is the very first sight of Sharif Ali, riding into full view out of an indistinct mirage. The audience is not merely transported to the desert—the desert is inculcated in the audience. . . .If you've never seen *Lawrence of Arabia* you're in for a treat. Even if you have, be prepared to be bowled over by the kind of experience that vindicates cinema as *the* twentieth-century art form.

—Monty Smith, *'Q' Magazine*,
June 1989

EUROPE

Raves, accolades, and an audience of 2,300 greeted the European rebirth of *Lawrence of Arabia* as it opened the Cannes Film Festival on Wednesday May 10, 1989, at the Palais des Festivals. Present—along with restoration team Robert Harris and Jim Painten—were Sir David Lean, Freddie Young, Anne Coates, Omar Sharif, Anthony Quinn, José Ferrer, and Art Director John Box.

France's print media outdid the world in their worship of the film: *Premiere France*'s Special Cannes Issue of May 1989 had a color *Lawrence* two-page foldout cover, with *"Once Upon a Time There Was Lawrence of Arabia* spanning twenty-two pages of full color. *Studio,* April 1989, in "Legends: The Most Beautiful Films in the History of Cinema," displayed twelve full-color pages on *Lawrence.*

And French fashion-consciousness yielded a unique perspective on the film:

> . . .the real subject of the film is visual: the colors of the sand and sky, the vast expanse of the desert, and the almost supernatural appearance of Peter O'Toole as Lawrence. . . .He seems to have been color co-ordinated to blend in with the desert, with his sky-blue eyes and sandy-blond hair.
>
> —Sean French, *Marie Claire,*
> June 1989

VIDEO

October 1989 saw the release of the "Director's Cut" of *Lawrence of Arabia* in "letterboxed" videotape and laserdisc versions. Letterboxing involves showing the entire 70mm frame by shrinking it until its full width fits within the TV screen. Black bands necessarily are seen, above and below the picture. *Lawrence was* the first major motion picture to be released in a videotape letterboxed version.

Sir David Lean had rejected the film-to-video transfer prepared by RCA Columbia. They then contracted with Voyager-Criterion—the deluxe letterbox laserdisc pioneers—to use their approved version. Thus three laserdisc *Lawrences* became available: RCA Columbia and Criterion CLV "popular" versions, and a Criterion "collector's" version, with the ability to access and freeze—with perfect clarity—each frame of the film. Both Criterion versions include fascinating "supplementary" material, but not to the extent that Robert Harris had initially envisioned.

In Canada, the CBS Video Club chose *Lawrence of Arabia* as their "Director's Selection" videotape for November 1989, preparing a colorful and informative booklet.

And, at Christmas, Columbia Pictures in Hollywood gifted every employee with a *Lawrence* videotape.

A high-end video journal, *The Perfect Vision,* reported in mid-1991 that *Lawrence* had then sold close to 300,000 videocassettes in North America. Other sources revealed that about 20,000 laserdiscs had been purchased. *Video Review,* an enthusiasts' magazine, would later name *Lawrence* as Best Classic Movie video release of 1989. In a 1992 poll of *The Laser Disc Newsletter* readers, *Lawrence* placed in the top three favorite discs of all time.

Thus, with a burst of worldwide publicity and acclaim, *Lawrence of Arabia* had reconquered the domain of theatrical cinema and had made a significant impact in the home video realm. T. E. Lawrence had been honored with a massive centenary exhibition and numerous publications. Jeremy Wilson's *Lawrence of Arabia* would be named by *The New York Times Book Review* as one of 1989's best books.

In 1989, Sir David Lean's reputation had skyrocketed and *Lawrence of Arabia* had once again recaptured the public's imagination.

CHAPTER 11

ACCOLADES AND CELEBRATION

"GARLANDS FOR THE CONQUEROR.
TRIBUTE FOR THE PRINCE."

—ALI TO LAWRENCE, AFTER TAKING AQABA

One of the purposes of the American Film Institute, as set forth at its founding in 1967, is that "great accomplishments of the past must be recognized, to the end that the masters of film may take their deserved place in history beside leaders in other arts." Their Life Achievement Award was established to honor "one whose talent has in a fundamental way advanced the film art; whose accomplishment has been acknowledged by scholars, critics, professional peers and the general public; and whose work has stood the test of time."

The choice of Sir David Lean as the eighteenth recipient of this award was precipitated by the reevaluation of his artistry which accompanied *Lawrence of Arabia*'s restoration and rerelease, as well as the success of 1984's *A Passage to India*.

AMERICAN FILM INSTITUTE 1990 LIFE ACHIEVEMENT AWARD.

On March 8, 1990, a glittering audience gathered in Los Angeles. To a standing ovation and the famous *Kwai* "Colonel Bogey March," Lean slowly entered the hall.

A succession of distinguished film greats came to the podium to pay tribute.

Gregory Peck noted that Lean has been called "cinema's master storyteller, cinema's poet of the far horizon" and was "a dreamer and adventurer who says to us, 'See the world through my eyes.' "

Lean's life before he became a director, and his development as a legendary editor, was visually reviewed. Single scenes from each of *Great Expectations, Oliver Twist,*

Brief Encounter, and *Summertime* were shown.

Steven Spielberg lauded Lean: "It was two of his most famous films, *Bridge on the River Kwai* and *Lawrence of Arabia,* that made me want to be a filmmaker. The scope and audacity of those films filled my dreams with unlimited possibilities. *Lawrence* gives me the same source of inspiration now, and thanks to the restoration, its inspiration can be for all of us, perpetually. There's nothing extraneous in *Lawrence*... There's nothing ever wasted. Every shot is a clue that unlocks the plot and every image is an echo of the heart. David Lean makes

---

Anthony Quinn

February 2, 1990

Dear David,

    I am sad I won't be there to see you honored.

    Besides, I'd need hours to laud your talents.

    At the moment your Auda Abu Tayi is slightly indisposed and is resting in New York.

    I send you my best -- and wish I were sitting on a horse beside you.

    Affectionately,

Tony Quinn

---

movies that are the equivalent of great novels. . . . He puts pictures on the screen that not even our imaginations can anticipate. His movies are truly the voyage of a lifetime."

One of Lean's most memorable, risky, and daring scenes—the blowing up of the bridge in *Kwai*—was shown.

Lean's good friend director Billy Wilder then asked: "I have two little questions for the AFI [re the award]: Who else? . . . And what took you so long?"

The profound impact of David Lean's work was recalled by Anjelica Huston: "I was nine years old. It was 1962. At the Odeon, Leicester Square, in London, it was the Royal World Premiere of *Lawrence of Arabia*. And I was there. I remember being excited, because that night I was going to see the Queen. But to tell the truth, I don't remember much about seeing the Queen. But the extraordinary images shown that night on the giant screen are still with me."

After a clip from what was to be Lean's last movie, *A Passage to India*, the scene shifted to a satellite feed. Peter O'Toole and Omar Sharif, live from England in the early morning hours, lightheartedly proffered words of encouragement to the eighty-two-year-old legend who—with a single film—had made instant international stars of them both. O'Toole concluded his message with the suggestion that "What would please me, and I am sure the entire cinema-going world, would be if you were simply to get off your ass and go out and make another picture."

George Stevens, Jr., founder and then cochairman of the AFI, took the podium to hand over the AFI award, and uttered the memorable words:

> The American Film Institute Life Achievement Award is given to a film-maker whose work has stood the test of time. Each of David Lean's films has stood that test. *Lawrence of Arabia* is but one stunning example. It was the best film of 1962. Twenty-seven years later, it was re-released. And, to many of us, it was the best film of 1989.

Stevens spoke of Lean as editor: "He still talks with excitement about leaving the camaraderie of his film crew on location, to return to that solitary room where he can be alone with the film. His dear friend Trevor Howard used to say that David can't wait to finish shooting so that he can begin cutting the actors out of the film."

Stevens then continued, "Now one more look at the 'far horizon' of this man, who gives meaning to the word 'picture-maker.' " Onto the screen flashed Peter O'Toole—as Lawrence—blowing out the match and transporting the audience into the Arabian desert. There followed the only extended montage of the evening: Lean directing *Lawrence,* and a number of scenes from the film itself. Reflecting on the daunting challenge of filming the huge desert vistas, Lean was heard in voice-over: "I had a thousand camels and a thousand horses all waiting. Wondering what on earth what was happening. I just couldn't get an angle on it. I finally got it, but—my goodness—they're lonely moments."

To a standing ovation and the theme from *Lawrence of Arabia,* Lean accepted the award. This elegant gentleman then gently chastised the Hollywood community. To the most powerful people in the business—the assembled agents, producers, directors, and studio heads—he lamented the fact that so few truly original films were being made. There were so many "Parts I, II, III, and IV."

"Nearly everyone here is an innovator, a pathfinder," he continued. "And all of them live on new things. O.K. Do old things: Parts I, II, and III. But don't make them a staple diet. We'll sink if we do. This business lives on creative pathfinders. . . There are some wonderful new filmmakers coming up now. They are going to be our

Cinema's poet of the "far horizon"

*At the AFI Tribute, March 8, 1990,
Lean was praised by cinema colleagues.
Top Row: Steven Spielberg, Billy Wilder,
Anjelica Huston.
Bottom Row: George Stevens, Jr., and
Martin Scorsese.*

future. Please, you chaps in the money department—remember what they are. It's a very nervous job making a film. They need help." Audaciously, Lean then quoted producer Irving Thalberg: " 'The studios have made a lot of money. They could afford to lose some.' "

"I think," Lean continued, "that the time has come where the money people can afford to lose a little money taking risks with these new filmmakers."

Jack Lemmon closed the evening: "A friend of David's recently said, 'One of the mistakes people make is thinking that a film unit is a democracy. It's not. It's a kingdom. And everyone nurtures the wishes of the king.' Well, with that in mind, let us not say 'good night.' Let us just simply say 'long live the king.' "

* * *

Eddie Fowlie remembers that, in spring 1990, David came down to Spain to inspect possible locations for *Nostromo.* Fowlie took him to Cabo de Gata, to the same dunes where Lawrence had demolished his trains twenty-eight years before. "He lay down on the sand, in the sun, thoroughly enjoying himself. And that was that. Couldn't get him to leave."

David Lean would never see the desert again.

A SERVICE OF CELEBRATION— ST. PAUL'S CATHEDRAL, OCTOBER 3, 1991

One of the truly enduring photographic images of the twentieth century is that of London ablaze in the blitz of World War II, with St. Paul's Cathedral miraculously untouched in the midst of the smoke and

229

Right: Master editor, David Lean.
Below: Sir David Lean, with AFI Life
Achievement Award: "He was thrilled beyond
any expression."

have been a field marshal, he could have been an archaeologist, a musician. He was one of those extraordinarily gifted Brits." Sir Richard Attenborough, who had filmed *Gandhi* and called it his tribute to Lean, said that "He was Britain's master filmmaker, no question about it. He had created a phenomenal narrative style which nobody else had attempted in the British cinema before. . . . World cinema will mourn him." And David Puttnam, who at the time was quietly preparing the television docudrama *A Dangerous Man: Lawrence After Arabia,* called Lean "the greatest storyteller on film." Sir Anthony Havelock-Allen, who had produced many of Lean's films, said that "All his films were beautiful. He had the most wonderful sense of location – of place. He had a wonderful visual sense, and he made you feel that you were there. . . . What he liked doing was to tell great adventure stories. . .and of this he was a master."

Lady Sandra Lean started to plan an appropriate event to celebrate her husband's memory. In Britain, there is a tradition of honoring personages of great distinction in a ceremony held in a place of great distinction. For Sir David Lean, she decided, there was really only one place: St. Paul's Cathedral. St. Paul's, the survivor. St. Paul's, where Lawrence had been mourned in 1936, where the Kennington bust of Lawrence resided in the crypt.

Thursday, October 3, 1991, started as a typical overcast London day. Crowds filed in for the 11 A.M. "Service of Celebration and Thanksgiving for the life and work of Sir David Lean, CBE." In the background, the great pipe organ played a soaring fantasy on themes from *Lawrence of Arabia.*

The dean welcomed the crowd:

fire. This image had rallied Londoners in the dark days of the war: it was an image of survival.

David Lean, too, had survived an onslaught, that of age and failing health. However, with determination he had gone forward with planning for yet another epic film, a $46 million screen version of Joseph Conrad's *Nostromo.* For two years, he had worked with Robert Bolt on the screenplay, his notorious perfectionism undiminished. The script was now complete, and preproduction was well underway. The "dedicated maniacs," including Eddie Fowlie and John Box, were once again in motion. Locations had long since been scouted and sets were being built in Spain.

But in January 1991, Lean took ill and was forced to return to England from his home in southern France. On April 16, he died quietly, of pneumonia brought on by throat cancer, in his Thames-side home in London's Docklands.

Praise flowed from around the world. Peter O'Toole noted that "David could have been anything. He could

> . . .I am sure that David Lean would have been thrilled, and possibly amused also, at seeing us all here today. But we are here to pay tribute to a most remarkable genius.
>
> At the start of the film *Lawrence of Arabia,* you will remember that one of the very early sequences takes place here in the crypt of St. Paul's where one of the clergy. . .when looking at the bust of Lawrence, says to Anthony Quayle, who plays the part of Colonel Brighton, "Do you think he really deserves all this?", referring to his place here in St. Paul's. And Colonel

Brighton replies, "He was the most extraordinary man I ever knew."

It seems to me that David Lean fits the bill here today, just in the way that Lawrence did himself—it is almost, you might say, when he wrote those words referring to this very building and Lawrence, that he could have been writing for himself. *Of course* he deserves a place here, for he was one of the most extraordinary men of our age and generation.

So, in this service, we give thanks to God for his genius, his work, and all that inspired him. . . .

Sir John Mills read from *Great Expectations*.

Then John Box recalled David Lean as "a master craftsman" who "had the ability to make one search into one's self and discover talents we did not know we had, and having found those talents, he inspired us to use them."

Box remembered a *Lawrence* reconnaissance trip into the desert with Lean:

David Lean's favorite portrait, by Cornel Lucas, London.

. . .I found myself on the heights above Wadi Rumm with him. Below us lay the deserts of Jordan and Arabia, and I found myself saying to David, "Over there to the left, is the Wadi Musa, the Valley of Moses, and beyond that is the Dead Sea and then Jerusalem, and beyond Jerusalem, Jericho, and the road to Damascus. And David, if you pan right across

Jerusalem, and beyond Jerusalem, Jericho, and the road to Damascus. And David, if you pan right across that horizon, across the basalt desert, you will come to the rivers Euphrates and Tigris, and where would have been Babylon.

It was extraordinary because the silence was there: Just David, myself, and a remarkable Bedouin—Aloosh—loaned to us by King Hussein, as our mentor and guide in the desert.

ST PAUL'S CATHEDRAL

A Service of
Celebration and Thanksgiving
for the life and work of
SIR DAVID LEAN CBE
1908 – 1991

Thursday 3rd October 1991
11.00 a.m.

ST. PAUL'S CATHEDRAL.

———

FORM OF SERVICE

USED AT

THE UNVEILING OF THE MEMORIAL

TO

THOMAS EDWARD LAWRENCE

LAWRENCE OF ARABIA

———

WEDNESDAY, 29th JANUARY, 1936

AT 5.30 P.M.

I was present.

Far Left: Cover of program for David Lean memorial service in St. Paul's Cathedral, October 1991.
Left: "Form of Service," for dedication of memorial to Lawrence, St. Paul's Cathedral, January 1936.

And I found myself saying to David, "I think we're face-to-face with eternity." And David turned, fixed me with those penetrating eyes, and said, "You are right, John. And by the grace of God, and if we keep our heads, we will make a good movie."

Later, we were down on the bed of the desert as night came. The siennas, the yellows, turned into indigos and blue. The night sky was there with many, many stars lit, and one particularly bright star shining with great intensity. And David said, "This is beginning to look like a sea stretching between these huge cliffs, and reaching out into an endless ocean."

Robert Bolt followed: "Oh dear [laughing]. David, I am here. All of what I know of the style of filmmaking, you taught me. . . . I remember a unique friend."

Sarah Miles delivered a short scene from *In Which We Serve*, with Peter O'Toole following with John Donne's sonnet "Death Be Not Proud." Tom Courtenay quoted from Pasternak's novel *Doctor Zhivago*, and Omar Sharif read a passage from T. E. Lawrence's *Seven Pillars of Wisdom*. George Correface, who was cast as Nostromo, read from the Bolt-Lean screenplay.

Melvyn Bragg, the writer and broadcaster who had filmed the documentary *David Lean: A Life in Film*, gave a brilliant and moving address, which poetically reviewed the life of Lean.

"I think that one of the fascinations of cinema," he said, "is that the lights went down, you were in the dark, it's very private, and I used to turn 'round and look at that beam going through the tobacco smoke. And it still holds a fascination for me. It's part of the magic show, I think. And that beam showed me places I thought I'd never visit. I've been terribly lucky and I have visited them. It showed me characters, and in movies, I met all sorts of people I'd never have met in an ordinary, dull suburban life."

He was meticulously inflexible. No one knew as much about the film as he did, and you deviated at your peril. "Actors," he said almost cheerfully, "hate me." All the actors here would contradict that, but several, I suspect, and many others from the crew would permit themselves a quiet little nod. They know what he meant.

But those who've spoken are but a few, and stand in for so many here today who knew him well, and were spellbound by him, infuriated by him, taxed to the limit, pushed to new heights, drawn in to participate in the adventure of his work. It was never less than an adventure. He shared many characteristics with the great Vic-

torian explorers. Dark continents are out there, to be subdued and celebrated in celluloid.

The baggage train would be assembled: Eddie Fowlie, chief scout, best friend, would. . . go and seek out the major stations; Maggie Unsworth would be lashed to the script; John Box as sort of official war artist; and then fastidious casting of crew—Freddie Young, of course—and actors would get underway, and so many here were part of that, as the safari set out and other worlds disappeared. And soon, in the jungle of the set, the shooting would begin. No prisoners were taken.

Nowadays, the words "film editor" are used. David preferred "cutter." "Cut," in fact, was his favorite word. All of you who knew him can hear him snap it out now: "Cut!" "Good!" "Jolly good!" "Right!" "Print both!"

"Cut" could be his epitaph.

On the tomb of the man who built this cathedral, Sir Christopher Wren, and on a plaque under the dome, you will find these words: "Lector, si monumentum requiris, circumspice"; "Reader, if you're looking for a monument, look around you." And *so* for David Lean. His monument is his movies. Look around and again at movies that will last as long as films are shown and seen. So today let's be thankful. For the gift he had, the gift he gave to us.

The Royal Philharmonic Orchestra, conducted by Maurice Jarre, followed with a medley of his music from

T. E. Lawrence, 1928.   *David Lean, 1961.*

Lawrence, Ryan's Daughter, Doctor Zhivago, and *A Passage to India.*

After the ninety-minute ceremony, the crowd pouring out onto the now sunlit steps eerily evoked an early scene from *Lawrence*—the crowd streaming out of "the Lawrence memorial service" at St. Paul's—life imitating art imitating life. Now, however, a full military brass band occupied the steps, playing the "Colonel Bogey March."

After the service, Peter Taylor, a member of the T. E. Lawrence Society, descended to the crypt in search of the Kennington bust. He recalled, "The crypt was empty. Somewhere amongst the Admirals of the Fleet, Field Marshals, and Viceroys, I found what I was there for. The quiet of my thoughts was interrupted by the voice of a cathedral porter. Speaking in a broad Irish brogue, he informed me that I was the third person, that morning, to have sought out 'Lawrence.' Earlier, two men had inquired of him the whereabouts of the bust and, by mistake, he misdirected them. Later, however, he found them both gazing at it. He then realized he *had* seen their faces somewhere before—Peter O'Toole and Omar Sharif."

The next day, *The Daily Telegraph's* coverage of the event at St. Paul's was headlined ECHOES FROM ARABIA AT LEAN'S FAREWELL.

Omar Sharif and Peter O'Toole in the desert epic

The two film stars at yesterday's service · Guests leave St Paul's in a scene reminiscent of Sir David Lean's Lawrence

Echoes from Arabia at Lean's farewell

Daily Telegraph, *October 4, 1991.*

Following the service, a luncheon was given at the Lean riverside home. This would be the final gathering of the "dedicated maniacs."

LADY LEAN, DAVID LEAN, ST. PAUL'S, AND THE AFI

To me, David's work was his own personal gift to the world. And to understand that work one has to understand the essence of the man.

David was a man who was constantly striving for perfection both in himself and in those with whom he worked. This was often a tortuous route. Even to the end he felt that perfection had somehow eluded him. His quest for both technical excellence and the ability to merge spirituality and humour into his storyline was one that made him give total attention to both visual details and the written word. There was a rare completeness about the seemingly simple way that he used to convey a story to his audience. One can almost imagine him there as a conductor of an orchestra, in the role of master storyteller. For he always believed that if one could not absorb one's audience totally into a story, there would be no magical transportation from the

reality of daily life into that other fantasy that one needs. His life was a perpetual journey through the mysteries and adventures of existence. And it was this that he strove so hard to give to his audience. He turned his own life from what he believed was a dull one into one of fantasy, and lived out that fantasy through the medium of celluloid. He expected high standards from others, only because he had always set himself ones that were even higher. He had the intensity and desperation of the genius that always believes that each work is his last

He was constantly tormented by self-doubts—doubts that were never allayed by either the praise or the accolades that he received consistently throughout his working life.

His work was both a demanding lover and a friend. Thus his absorption and obsession were great. If there was one aspect of his life and work

233

Continued from previous page

that emerged at the Memorial Service, from those who had known him personally or worked with him, it was this.

And it was at the Memorial Service that his friends and his colleagues lovingly shared their recollections of David's talents and spirit. The Service was ultimately a celebration of David Lean the master film maker and David Lean the man, and its construction was thus a reflection of both these roles.

It was for me, at the same time, a deeply sad and a joyous occasion. It was a service of which we were all profoundly proud, and we all strongly felt his presence among us.

It was truly fitting that David Lean's Memorial Service should be held in St. Paul's Cathedral, exactly the same place as that of T. E. Lawrence, the man in whose life David was so immersed, and the man whose legend was perpetuated by David's film.

It was in the making of *Lawrence of Arabia* that David not only discovered his love of the desert—but also began to discover himself. It was here that he found a sense of belonging—a sense of space, of inspiration, and a feeling of having finally found that elusive path for which he had always been searching. It was also here that he found, as a loner, a convergence of parallel values—a sense of kinship with Lawrence. For it was this film that forged a bond between David Lean the film maker and Lawrence the warrior. *Lawrence of Arabia* was not just a tribute to T. E. Lawrence from David, but an act of friendship.

It is, of course, only in the restored "Director's Cut" that one gets a complete sense of David's vision. It is here that one sees David Lean as the

"We all dream, and our dreams are more fantastic than anything you see on the screen."
David Lean, 1989.

master cutter, as consummate technician, as virtuoso storyteller.

To David, the film was the culmination of human strength and frailties, of intimacy and coordination—of a sense of creation unfulfilled. For there is no conclusion to creation for man. It is a way whereby one encounters many abysses and many heights.

The 1990 American Film Institute Award, an accolade about which David was totally incredulous and one of which he was thrilled beyond any expression.

He was like a child that had been given a gift far removed from any of his dreams.

This tribute was not only unexpected in terms of David's views about his own work, but also it was the first to be presented to any foreigner. To him, that was the rarest of all tributes, one that he felt, in some strange way, he must have earned. It was a tribute from his peers.

David expressed to me the feelings that he had about the AFI award in the moments leading up to the presentation ceremony: He felt both unbelieving and lost. He was as dry-mouthed and nervous as he was when first embarking on a new film. The graciousness and generosity of the AFI in bestowing this rarest of gifts upon him was something that, to the last moment, he, in his humility, could not take in.

David had a dream and a vision which he fulfilled for the rest of the world but not—totally—for himself. In genius, unfortunately, there is no boundary.

Lady Sandra Lean
Monday, June 1, 1992

CHAPTER 12

LAWRENCE OF ARABIA: AN ICON

"I BELIEVE YOUR NAME WILL BE A HOUSEHOLD WORD. . ."

—ALLENBY TO LAWRENCE, IN JERUSALEM

T. E. Lawrence, the man, and *Lawrence of Arabia,* the film, are the subject of recurring allusions in film reviews, song, literature (from comics to novels), political commentaries and cartoons, TV programs, and more. The film is the epitome of movies "as they should be," *Macleans* Newsmagazine (Canada) proclaimed. "*Dances with Wolves* does for the skies and plains of South Dakota what *Lawrence of Arabia* did for the desert." A magazine cover billed flag-carrying star Kevin Costner as "Lawrence of America." And actor Charlton Heston, referring to the dearth of newly mined epics in general, states that "They will never make a *Lawrence of Arabia* again."

All are references to the film. *Time* notes that, in Bertolucci's *The Sheltering Sky,* Debra Winger must become. . ."a Florence of Arabia ministering to [her husband's] illness." (Noël Coward had told Peter O'Toole: "If you were any prettier it would have been *Florence of Arabia*." Did *Mad* know of Coward's comment?)

Time's comment was a pun on the *man.* Yes, but without the *film's* existence, the pun almost certainly would not have been used. Without the film, who except for a group of scholars would know who T.E. Lawrence was?

Can Lawrence exist independently of the film? Not quite: all recent T.E.L. biographies make at least some reference to the film. But Lawrence obviously did exist, and as essayist Michael Anderegg (and others) have suggested, the Lean/Bolt Lawrence and Lawrence's Lawrence are two different entities.

Or are they?

The film's "Rescue of Gasim" incident, parodied in a widely syndicated "Gulf War" cartoon (Chapter 5), actually happened. But the visualization is the film's and the caption essentially Robert Bolt's dialogue. Without the film, the cartoon wouldn't work: the cartoonist has the audacity to presume that his readers are *Lawrence* fans. And, without Lawrence's description of the incident in *Seven Pillars,* the scene wouldn't have been in the film.

In Chapter 1, Lawrence's celebrity in the 20s and 30s was discussed. However, who could have anticipated that, in November 1990, the cover of *M Inc.* would feature a portrait of T.E.L., and blame him for the Gulf War? (Color section). Other journals covering the conflict spoke of President "George [Bush] of Arabia," reporter "Arthur [Kent] of Arabia," and of course, General "Norman [Schwarzkopf] of Arabia." And, in *Travel & Leisure's* 20th Anniversary Issue, *Lawrence* is one of the "20 movies that made us want to be there."

Certain of *Lawrence's* scenes have become legendary: *Entertainment Weekly,* January 10, 1992, noted among *The 20th century's 100 Greatest Entertainment Moments,* "1962: A PLACE IN THE SUN: As tiny as the blazing tip of a matchstick. As vast as the sun. David Lean could fill the screen with the minute as well as the majestic, and in *Lawrence of Arabia,* he did both, in a single stunning moment. In one breath, Peter O'Toole blows out a flame. In the next, the sun, by millimeters, creeps over the horizon, as Maurice Jarre's music builds, swells, and explodes across the Arabian desert. You can see it on video, but it's not the same: *Lawrence,* the greatest epic film ever made, fills even the biggest screen to bursting." In a film by Chuck Workman, *100 Years of Movies,* broadcast to open the 62nd Annual Academy Awards ceremonies, *Lawrence* was honored: the extinguished match closed the sequence with a fade to black, and tumultuous applause.

Since the 1989 reissue, *Lawrence* has climbed in stature: *Entertainment Weekly* named *Lawrence* in the top 30 of *60 films every cinema-literate person must have seen:* "a huge, sweeping 3 1/2 hour extravaganza at the center of which lies. . .a puzzle. An epic for the Age of Anxiety."

In *The Third Millennium: A History of the World 2000-3000 AD* (Stableford and Langford), an experimental 26th century spacecraft—the largest structure ever built—is named the *T. E. Lawrence! Foucault's Pendulum* (Eco) describes The Templars as "Lawrences of Arabia, who after a while, start dressing like sheiks." Yul Brynner's son speaks of his father: "Like Lawrence of Arabia, he had disavowed the civilized world, and would take no prisoners." And a 1991 newspaper article was headlined, "Lawrence of Croatia leads folk heroes in Yugoslavia."

The list is endless.

The man? The film? In the immortal words of screenwriter Robert Bolt, "Who knows?"

CAST AND CREDITS

Lawrence . . . . PETER O'TOOLE
Prince Feisal . . . . ALEC GUINNESS
Auda abu Tayi . . . . ANTHONY QUINN
General Allenby . . . . JACK HAWKINS
Turkish Bey . . . . JOSE FERRER
Sherif Ali ibn el Kharish . . . . OMAR SHARIF
Colonel Brighton . . . . ANTHONY QUAYLE
Mr. Dryden . . . . CLAUDE RAINS
Jackson Bentley . . . . ARTHUR KENNEDY
General Murray . . . . DONALD WOLFIT
Gasim . . . . I. S. JOHAR
Majid . . . . GAMIL RATIB
Farraj . . . . MICHEL RAY
Daud . . . . JOHN DIMECH
Tafas . . . . ZIA MOHYEDDIN
Medical Officer . . . . . . HOWARD MARION CRAWFORD
Club Secretary . . . . JACK GWILLIM
R.A.M.C. Colonel . . . . HUGH MILLER

Directed by . . . . DAVID LEAN
Produced by . . . . SAM SPIEGEL
Screenplay by . . . . ROBERT BOLT
Music Composed by . . . . MAURICE JARRE
Orchestrations by . . . . GERARD SCHURMANN
Played by . . . . THE LONDON PHILHARMONIC
ORCHESTRA
Conductor . . . . SIR ADRIAN BOULT
Photographed in SUPER-PANAVISION 70®
Director of Photography . . . . F. A. YOUNG, B.S.C.
TECHNICOLOR®
Production Designed by . . . . JOHN BOX
Art Director . . . . JOHN STOLL
Costume Designer . . . . PHYLLIS DALTON
Editor . . . . ANNE V. COATES
Sound Editor . . . . WINSTON RYDER
Second Unit Direction ANDRE SMAGGHE, NOEL HOWARD
Second Unit Photography . . . . SKEETS KELLY
NICOLAS ROEG, PETER NEWBROOK
Camera Operator . . . . ERNEST DAY
Assistant Director . . . . ROY STEVENS
Continuity . . . . BARBARA COLE
Sound Recording . . . . PADDY CUNNINGHAM
Sound Dubbing . . . . JOHN COX
Make-up . . . . CHARLES PARKER
Hairdresser . . . . A. G. SCOTT

Construction Manager . . . . PETER DUKELOW
Construction Assistant . . . . FRED BENNETT
Special Effects . . . . CLIFF RICHARDSON
RCA SOUND RECORDING
Production Manager . . . . JOHN PALMER
Location Manager . . . . DOUGLAS TWIDDY
Casting Director . . . . MAUDE SPECTOR
Set Dresser . . . . DARIO SIMONI
Wardrobe . . . . JOHN WILSON-APPERSON
Assistant Art Directors . . . . ROY ROSSOTTI
GEORGE RICHARDSON, TERRY MARSH
ANTHONY RIMMINGTON
Property Master . . . . EDDIE FOWLIE
Chief Electrician . . . . ARCHIE DANSIE

Produced by Horizon Pictures (G.B.) Ltd., London, England
Released through Columbia Pictures Corporation
Photographed on overseas locations and completed at
Shepperton Studios, Shepperton, England.
The producers gratefully acknowledge the cooperation
extended to them by the Royal Hashemite Government of Jordan
and by the Royal Government of Morocco.

THE RESTORATION
Reconstructed and Restored by . . . . . . ROBERT A. HARRIS
Restoration Produced by . . . . ROBERT A. HARRIS
and JIM PAINTEN
Editorial Consultant . . . . ANNE V. COATES, A.C.E.
Sound Consultant . . . . . RICHARD L. ANDERSON, M.P.S.E.
Spectral Recording Dolby® Stereo In Selected Theatres
Rerecorded in Dolby 6 Track SR at Goldwyn Sound Facilities
Rerecording Mixer . . . . GREG LANDAKER
65mm Negative Restoration by Metrocolor® Laboratories
70mm Prints by Metrocolor® Laboratories
35mm Prints by Deluxe®
Assistants . . . . JUDE SCHNEIDER, MAGGIE FIELD,
JOANNE LAWSON
Special Thanks to MARTIN SCORSESE, STEVEN SPIELBERG,
JON DAVISON and SIR DAVID LEAN

MPAA Rating: PG
Running Time: 216 min.
(plus overture, entr'acte and exit music)

BIBLIOGRAPHY

"... I THINK YOUR BOOK IS RIGHT."

— LAWRENCE TO FEISAL, IN FEISAL'S TENT

Books

Richard Aldington, *Lawrence of Arabia: a Biographical Enquiry*, Collins, London, 1955.*

Michael Anderegg, *David Lean*, Twayne, Boston, 1984.

Flora Armitage, *The Desert and the Stars*, Holt, 1955.*

Dirk Bogarde, *Snakes and Ladders*, Chatto & Windus, London, 1978.

Robert Bolt (uncredited), *Lawrence of Arabia*, Souvenir Program, 1962 Columbia Pictures Corp.

–––. *Lawrence of Arabia*, screenplay (unpublished), 1962.

Charles Blackmore, *In the Footsteps of Lawrence of Arabia*, Harrap, London, 1986.

Malcom Brown, and Julia Cave, *A Touch of Genius: the Life of T.E. Lawrence*, J.M. Dent & Sons Ltd, London, 1988.

Malcolm Brown (Editor), *T.E. Lawrence: the Selected Letters*, W.W. Norton & Company, New York, 1989.

Peter Brown, and Jim Pinkston, *Oscar Dearest*, Harper and Row, New York, 1986.

Louis Castelli, *David Lean: a guide to references and resources*, G.K. Hall, Boston, 1980.

Michael Darlow and Gillian Hodson, *Terence Rattigan: The Man and His Work*, Quartet Books, London, 1979.

Derek Elley (Editor) *The Chronicle of the Movies*, Hamlyn Publishing Group, London 1991.

Michael Freedland, *Peter O'Toole*, W.H Allen, London, 1983.

P.N. Furbank, *E.M. Forster: A Life (Volume Two)*, Secker and Warburg, London, 1977.

David Garnett (Ed.), *Selected Letters of T.E. Lawrence*, Cape, London, 1952.*

Robert Graves and Basil Liddell Hart, *T.E. Lawrence: Letters to his Biographers*, Cassel & Co., London, 1938.

Robert Graves, *Goodbye to All That*, Jonathan Cape, London, 1929.*

–––. *Lawrence and the Arabs*, Cape, London, 1927.*

Charles Grosvenor, *An Iconography: the Portraits of T.E. Lawrence*, The Otterden Press, Pasedena, 1988.

Ronald Hayman, *Robert Bolt*, Heineman, London, 1969.

H. Montgomery Hyde, *Solitary in the Ranks*, Constable, London, 1977.

Lawrence James, *The Golden Warrior: the Life and Legend of Lawrence of Arabia*, Weidenfeld and Nicolson, London, 1990.

John Johns & Associates (Editors), *David Lean Tribute Book (American Film Institute Life Achievment Award Souvenir Edition)*, American Film Magazine, New York, 1990.

Howard Kent, *Single Bed for Three: A Lawrence of Arabia Notebook*, Hutchison & Co., London, 1963.

Michael Korda, *Charmed Lives: A Family Romance*, Random House, New York, 1977.

P. Knightley and C. Simpson, *The Secret Lives of Lawrence of Arabia*, Nelson and Sons, London, 1969.

Karol Kulik, *Alexander Korda: the Man Who Could Work Miracles*, W.H. Allen, London 1975.

A.W. Lawrence (editor) *T.E. Lawrence: By His Friends*, Cape, London, 1937.*

––– (editor) *Letters to T.E. Lawrence*, Cape, London, 1962.*

T.E. Lawrence, *Crusader Castles*, (2 vols.) Golden Cockerell Press, 1936.*

–––. *The Diary of T.E. Lawrence*, Corvinus, 1937.*

–––. *The Essential T.E. Lawrence*, Cape, London, 1951.*

–––. *The Home Letters of T.E. Lawrence and His Brothers*, Blackwell, Oxford, 1954.

–––. *Men in Print: Essays in Literary Criticism*, Golden Cockerell Press, 1940.*

–––. *The Mint*, Doubleday, New York, 1955.*

–––. *Oriental Assembly*, Williams and Norgate Ltd., 1939.

–––. *Revolt in the Desert*, Cape, London, 1927.*

–––. *Secret Dispatches from Arabia*, Golden Cockerell Press, 1939.*

–––. *Seven Pillars of Wisdom*, Cape, London and Toronto, 1935. Also in Penguin and Anchor paperback.*

Emanuel Levy, *And the Winner Is–––: The History and Politics of the Oscar Awards*, Ungar Publishing Co., New York, 1987.

Basil Liddell Hart, *'T.E. Lawrence': In Arabia and After*, Cape, 1934.*

–––. *The Memoirs of Captain Liddell Hart*, volume I, Cassell, London, 1965.

John E. Mack, *A Prince of Our Disorder: The Life of T.E. Lawrence*, Little, Brown, Boston, Toronto, 1976.

Alistair MacLean, *Lawrence of Arabia*, Random House, New York, 1962.*

R.J. Minney, *'Puffin' Asquith*, Leslie Frewin, London 1973.

Anthony Nutting, *Lawrence of Arabia*, Hollis & Carter, London, 1961.*

Philip O'Brien, *T.E. Lawrence: A Bibliography*, G.K. Hall & Co., Boston, 1988.

Douglas Orgil, *Lawrence*, Ballantine, 1973.

Robert Payne, *Lawrence of Arabia*, Pyramid, New York, 1962.*

Gerald Pratley, *The Cinema of David Lean*, The Tantivy Press, 1974.

Terence Rattigan, *Lawrence of Arabia*, Final shooting script (unpublished), November 1957.

–––. *Ross–a Dramatic Portrait*, Hamish Hamilton, 1960.

Vyvyan Richards, *T.E. Lawrence*, Duckworth, London, 1939.

Susan Rusinko, *Terence Rattigan*, Twayne Publishers, Boston, 1983.

John Monk Saunders, *Revolt in the Desert*, screenplay (unpublished), 28 September 1935.

Omar Sharif, *The Eternal Male*, Doubleday & Co., New York, 1977.

Alain Silver, and James Ursini, *David Lean and his Films*, Frewin, London, 1974.

Stephen M. Silverman, *David Lean*, Harry N. Abrams, New York, 1989.

Andrew Sinclair, *Spiegel: the Man Behind the Pictures*, Wiedenfeld and Nicholson, London, 1987.

Desmond Stewart, *T.E. Lawrence*, Paladin, London, 1986.

Stephen E. Tabachnick (Editor), *The T.E. Lawrence Puzzle*, University of Georgia Press, Athens, 1984.

Stephen E. Tabachnick and Christopher Matheson, *Images of Lawrence*, Cape, London, 1988.

Paul Tabori, *Alexander Korda*, Living Books, New York, 1966.

Lowell Thomas, *With Lawrence in Arabia*, The Century Company, New Jersey, 1924.*

–––. *Good Evening Everybody*, William Morrow and Co., New York, 1976.

V.M. Thompson, *"Not a Suitable Hobby for an Airman"–T.E. Lawrence as Publisher*, Orchard Books, Oxford, 1986.

David Vaisey, *T.E. Lawrence: The Legend and the Man*, Bodleian Library, Oxford, 1988.

Alexander Walker, *"It's Only a Movie, Ingrid": Encounters on and off screen*, Headline Publishing PLC, London, 1988.

Jeremy Wilson, *T.E. Lawrence*, National Portrait Gallery Publications, London, 1988.

–––. *Lawrence of Arabia: the authorised biography of T.E. Lawrence*, Heineman, London, 1989.

Nicholas Wapshott, *Peter O'Toole*, New English Library, London, 1983.

Stanley Weintraub, *Private Shaw and Public Shaw*, George Braziller, New York, 1963.*

Mason Wiley, and Damien Bona, *Inside Oscar: The Unofficial History of the Academy Awards*, Ballantine Books, New York, 1986.

Herbert Wilcox, *Twenty-five Thousand Sunsets: an Autobiography*, The Bodley Head, London, 1967.

Denise Worrell, *Icons: Intimate Portraits*, Atlantic Monthly Press, 1989.

Fay Wray, *On the Other Hand*, St. Martin's, New York, 1989.

Michael Yardley, *T.E. Lawrence: A Biography*, Stein and Day, New York, 1987.

B.A. Young, *The Rattigan Version: Sir Terence Rattigan and the theatre of character*, Hamish Hamilton, London, 1986.

Freddie Young, and Paul Petzold, *The Work of the Motion Picture Cameraman*, Focal Press, London, 1972.

* These books were referenced by Robert Bolt in the 1962 Souvenir Program.

Magazine Articles and Documents

Liddell Hart Centre for Military Archives, King's College London.

Michael Anderegg, "Lawrence of Arabia: the Man, the Myth, the Movie," *Michigan Quarterly Review*, vol. 21, No. 2, Spring 1982.

Hollis Alpert, "The David Lean Recipe: A 'Whack in the Guts," *The New York Times Magazine*, May 23, 1965.

Trevor Armbrister, "O'Toole of Arabia," *Saturday Evening Post*, March 1963.

Josh Becker, "What do the Oscars Really Mean?," *Film Threat*, Issue 3, 1992.

Robert Bolt, "Clues to the Legend of Lawrence," *The New York Times Magazine*, February 25, 1962.

–––. "The Playwright in Films," *Saturday Review*, December 29, 1962.

–––. "Sam and the Shifting Sands," *Evening Standard*, May 11, 1989.

Elizabeth Bowen, "Lawrence of Arabia," *Show Magazine*, June 1961.

Richard Brooks, "Film mogul Korda was secret agent for Britain," *The Observer*, November 3, 1981.

Stephan Chodorov, "The Gentle Touch of Destruction," *The Daily Telegraph Magazine*, February 1972.

Kevin Desmond, "70 Glorious Years: A Profile of Freddie Young, OBE," *Eyepiece*, December 1988, January/February 1989, and March 1989.

James Fixx, "The Spiegel Touch," *Saturday Review*, December 29, 1962.

R. Ginna, "The return of Lawrence of Arabia," *Connoisseur*, May 1989.

Michèle Haberstat, "Il Etait Une Fois Lawrence d'Arabie," *Première (France)*, May 1989.

Maurice Jarre, "Maurice Jarre on Lawrence of Arabia," *The Cue Sheet: Journal of the Society of the Preservation of Film Music*, April 1990.

John Knowles, "All Out in the Desert," *Horizon Magazine*, July 1962.

David Lean, "Out of the Wilderness," *Films and Filming*, 1963.

Roger Manvil (Editor); Sam Spiegel, Robert Bolt, Peter O'Toole, John Box, F.A. Young, Anne V. Coates, David, Lean, "Lawrence of Arabia" (Special Issue), *The Journal of the Society of Film and Television Arts Limited*, No. 10, Winter, 1962-63.

Victoria McKee, "The Day the Words Failed," *Sunday Times Magazine*, March 18, 1990.

Jeffrey Richards and Jeffrey Hulbert, "Censorship in Action: The Case of Lawrence of Arabia," *Journal of Contemporary History*, vol. 19, no. 1, January 1984.

Steven Ross, "In Defense of David Lean," *Take One*, July-August, 1972.

Gerard Schurmann, "A Reply to Maurice Jarre about *Lawrence of Arabia*," *The Cue Sheet*, July 1990.

Thomas Sotinel, "Lawrence d'Arabie de David Lean," *Studio (France)*, April 1989.

R.S. Stewart, "Dr. Zhivago: The Making of a Movie," *The Atlantic Monthly*, August 1965.

Joanne Swadron, "Thomas Edward Lawrence: The Uncrowned Prince of Arabia," 1964, private collection, Toronto.

Gay Talese, "O'Toole on the Ould Sod," *Esquire*, August 1977.

Robert Towne, "Why I Write Movies," *Esquire*, June, 1991.

Keith Wheeler, "The Romantic Riddle of Lawrence of Arabia," *Life*, 12 January 1962.

The size and format of this book precludes giving complete references for every quote. It is the authors' intent to prepare, for scholarly purposes, a detailed list of references for all material cited.